OFF THE RECORD

OFF THE RECORD

THE PRIVATE PAPERS OF
Harry S. Truman

Edited by ROBERT H. FERRELL

HARPER & ROW, PUBLISHERS, New York
Cambridge, Hagerstown, Philadelphia, San Francisco,
1817 *London, Mexico City, Sào Paulo, Sydney*

OFF THE RECORD: THE PRIVATE PAPERS OF HARRY S. TRUMAN. Copyright © 1980 by Robert H. Ferrell. All rights reserved. Printed in the United States of America. No part of this book may be used or reproduced in any manner whatsoever without written permission except in the case of brief quotations embodied in critical articles and reviews. For information address Harper & Row, Publishers, Inc., 10 East 53rd Street, New York, N.Y. 10022. Published simultaneously in Canada by Fitzhenry & Whiteside Limited, Toronto.

FIRST EDITION

Designer: Sidney Feinberg

Library of Congress Cataloging in Publication Data

Truman, Harry S   Pres. U. S., 1884–1972.
  Off the record.

  Includes index.
  1. Truman, Harry S., Pres. U. S., 1884–1972.
2. Presidents—United States—Biography. I. Ferrell,
Robert H. II. Title.
E742.5.T6 1980   973.918'092'4 [B]   79–3390
ISBN 0–06–011281–6

80 81 82 83 84 10 9 8 7 6 5 4 3 2 1

CONTENTS

ILLUSTRATIONS

All photographs courtesy of the Harry S. Truman Library

These photographs follow page 112.

Harry S. Truman driving the cultivator on the family farm, about 1911
Clowning with cousins Mary Colgan and Nellie Noland, and James Craig
Captain Harry S. Truman in France
Harry S. Truman and Bess Wallace Truman, bride and groom, June, 1919
Truman and Jacobson Haberdashery in Kansas City, Missouri
Truman's first political platform, 1922
Senator Harry S. Truman with fellow politicians at the Democratic National Convention in Philadelphia, 1936
Truman and President Franklin Roosevelt planning campaign strategy, 1944
Bess and Margaret Truman at the Democratic National Convention in Chicago, 1944
Truman and his mother, Mrs. John A. Truman
With members of his family listening to the election returns, 1944
Ethel Noland
Nellie Noland
Rose A. Conway, Truman's personal secretary
At the piano

These photographs follow page 208.

Harry S. Truman being sworn in as President on April 12, 1945
At Potsdam with Stalin and the American and Russian delegations
Triple handshake at Potsdam: Churchill, Truman, and Stalin
Announcing the surrender of Japan on August 14, 1945

Truman awarding a Congressional Medal of Honor

With Winston Churchill on the way to Fulton, Missouri, for the "Iron Curtain" speech

With James F. Byrnes, former secretary of state and his successor, George C. Marshall

Truman displays one of his famous scambled-egg ties

At the Little White House in Key West, Florida, with Matt Connelly and Charlie Ross

President and Mrs. Truman fishing in Key West

Jimmy Roosevelt arriving in Philadelphia for the 1948 Democratic Convention

Harry S. Truman and Alben W. Barkley, the Democratic nominees, 1948

Campaigning by railroad

Discussing the problems of farmers in Dexter, Iowa

Handwritten diary entry, June 15, 1952, page 257.

These photographs follow page 304.

Harry S. Truman, President in his own right, taking the oath in 1949

Truman and the Shah of Iran at a state banquet

Blair House

President Truman riding in a heavily guarded limousine after the assassination attempt

Marching in the 35th Division reunion parade

Truman and General MacArthur meet at Wake Island

Former President Truman and family leaving Washington at the end of his term

The Truman home in Independence, Missouri

Truman walking alone in Independence

The former President addressing a high-school audience

In San Marco Square, Venice

Mr. and Mrs. Truman greet their grandchildren

With Mary Jane and J. Vivian Truman at the Truman Library

Harry S. Truman and Bess W. Truman on their fiftieth anniversary

ACKNOWLEDGMENTS

My thanks must go to the able director of the Harry S. Truman Library in Independence, Missouri, Benedict K. Zobrist; the equally helpful assistant director, George Curtis; and the wonderful members of the staff —Vicky Alexander, Dennis E. Bilger, Patty Bressman, Mildred L. Carol, Harry Clark, John Curry, Diane Farris, Niel M. Johnson, Philip D. Lagerquist, Warren Ohrvall, Doris Pesek, and Pauline Testerman. Elizabeth Safly, the librarian, produced answers to questions, and gave me books about cats to present to my daughter. And as mentioned below, in the Introduction, without the help of Erwin J. Mueller the *Private Papers* would not now be published.

Mrs. Howard Carvin most kindly opened her house at 400 North Delaware to me, as she has done for so many library researchers.

Corona Machemer, my editor at Harper & Row, compressed my tautologies, curbed my academic tendencies to relate the three sides of the coin, cut out Truman items that were repetitive or too special to be of interest to present-day readers, and called attention to gaps in the introductions, headnotes, and notes. Her help was invaluable.

My thanks, too, to Liza Pulitzer, also of Harper & Row, for much assistance, especially with the photographs.

Richard B. Morris and Henry Steele Commager have been most understanding about the publication of the *Private Papers,* which suddenly took precedence over a project for which I am responsible to them.

It is awkward to put together a book from materials in Independence when living in Bloomington, Indiana; for patience during my twenty-six trips from Indianapolis to Kansas City, I am grateful to Lila and Carolyn.

R.H.F.

Independence, Missouri
July 4, 1980

A NOTE ON THE EDITING

I have tried to keep editorial intrusions to a minimum, for in literary matters there is nothing worse than fussy editing—hemstitching, elucidation of the obvious, telling more than one needs to know. Harry S. Truman's spelling was imperfect; futhermore, these are informal papers, and when Truman wrote them he did not always have his dictionary at hand. In this collection the spelling has been corrected (unless Truman himself comments on it), without brackets or sics, with the aim of minimizing distractions to the reader. For the same reason, in the few places the President wrote so rapidly that he forgot articles or prepositions, they have been put in, without notice. Once in a while when Truman seemed to wander off the subject or described something that only he and Mamma and Mary or Nellie and Ethel Noland might have found interesting, or where there were repetitions, I have spared the reader and used ellipsis points. With these minor exceptions the prose stands as Harry S. Truman wrote it.

Strictly speaking the "S" in "Harry S. Truman" stood for nothing, and hence deserves no period. Practically, it was a family compromise between the names of Truman's paternal and maternal grandfathers, Anderson Shippe Truman and Solomon Young. The President did not much care if people put a period after the initial, but when he thought of it he was accustomed to do so himself. In editing this book, I have followed his example.

OFF THE RECORD

INTRODUCTION

Here, in the pages that follow, are the private papers of Harry S. Truman, in and out of the White House, beginning in 1945 and ending in November 1971, when only a few months of life remained and the retired President's days had become so constricted that he ran out of things to write about.

The private papers consist of three major groupings: diary entries, memoranda, and letters. Of these, the diary entries surely are the most unusual—for how many Presidents of the United States have kept diaries? Other than Truman, there come to mind only a few. John Quincy Adams was accustomed to arise at a very early hour, perhaps 4:00 A.M., read in his Bible, and then write in his diary, and the result over the years was an enormous accumulation, though not all of his diary is fascinating. James K. Polk, he of dour countenance and Methodist conscience, the President who determined to serve only one term and determined, too, that he would arrange for the enlargement of American territory either by peace or by war—Polk kept a diary which was a relentless recital of duty, its tedium relieved by harsh criticisms of his political opponents, the Whigs (who, according to Polk, were capable of undescribable infamies). Of the twentieth-century Presidents, only three, Dwight D. Eisenhower, Richard M. Nixon and Jimmy Carter, in addition to Truman, seem to have kept diaries. The Eisenhower diary is being published; but the Nixon and Carter diaries are uncertain quantities indeed (the Nixon diary apparently is on tapes and has yet even to be transcribed), and surely will not be available to would-be readers in the near future.

The Truman diary is frank, rambunctious, full of life, but no less full of a sense of duty at least equal to that of HST's nineteenth-century predecessors. It is, to put the case modestly, fascinating. Truman did not keep a diary on a day-to-day basis. It was a scrappy affair at the outset, when, during the first hectic days in the presidency, the man from Missouri found himself almost overwhelmed with work; initially all he could do was make a few notes of who came to call and what he said to them or they said to him. With a little time to take the measure of his new job, the President began to reflect upon the suddenness with which he had come into office, and made full-scale diary entries relating the event of April 12, 1945, and what happened subsequently. As the weeks began to pass, he occasionally wrote down what he was doing, usually on loose sheets of White House stationery. He also scrawled comments on his daily appointment sheets, although after several months he gave up annotating them. From 1948 to 1953, he made occasional entries in black leather-bound yearly diary books. The diarist wrote when he had time or, once in a while, when an event struck him as worth setting down. In this manner entries were made, and once the habit of recording events began, the President continued, albeit always fitfully, to the end of his residence in the White House and beyond.

For the year 1945 the President made several dozen entries in his diary. The entries for 1946, 1947, and 1949 are far fewer, but the diarist did better in the years 1948, 1950, and 1951. The latter year brought to a climax the difficulties with General Douglas MacArthur; from the outset of his presidency Truman heartily disliked "Mr. Prima Donna, Brass Hat, Five Star MacArthur," whom he considered an actor rather than a military man. Then in 1952, when it was clear that the years in Washington were coming to an end, the diarist's acute sense of history—the President was an omnivorous reader of history—drove him again to make several dozen entries, in which he recorded items pleasant and sad, important and unimportant, in an effort to set down what it was like to live in the taxpayers' house (the "Great White Prison") at Sixteenth Street and Pennsylvania Avenue and endure the barbs of the columnists and suffer the shafts of political opponents, some of them members of his own party. By that time he had spent almost thirty years in elective office, and the year 1952 appealed to him as a time for diary keeping because it marked the culmination of his political life, the height of his long career in American government.

When Truman left the nation's capital on inauguration day, 1953, having ridden to the ceremony with his successor and engaged in a snappish discussion on the way—Ike said that Secretary of the Army Kenneth Royall had tried to order him home for the 1948 inaugural but he refused because half the people cheering Truman at that time had told Ike they were for him, whereupon Truman said, "Ike I didn't ask you to come—or you'd been here"—when after this riposte, and a gasp by Senator Styles Bridges and a change of the subject by Speaker of the House Joe Martin, the retiring President left Washington, he went back to Independence on a sort of triumphal tour in reverse. Crowds gathered in front of former Secretary of State Dean Acheson's house in George-town as Truman at a luncheon bade farewell to his cabinet members, and a crowd estimated at nine or ten thousand gathered at Union Station, and several hundreds turned out at Silver Spring, and all the way back it was the same. Ten thousand people assembled at Independence to greet the Trumans at the station, and five thousand more stood in front of the old-fashioned neogothic house at 219 North Delaware Street. All this appears in diary entries. Afterward it was the little encounters with people who wanted to shake his hand, and who waved, or looked and smiled; it was a trip to Hawaii, and trips back to Washington or to Chi-cago or New York; trips to Europe in 1956 and 1958; and then the gradual restricting of life to a routine of arising early at the house and driving over to the new library building on the other side of the viaduct, where there was an office full of books and a museum of memorabilia, includ-ing a reproduction of the Oval Room in the White House, and a small auditorium, and all the papers relating to the presidency. Here the for-mer President could work in his office and also meet groups of schoolchil-dren in the auditorium and tell them about life in Washington.

A second source for the private papers is the memoranda, which were rather like diary entries, except that the President had the habit of putting down on paper his thoughts on all sorts of subjects, not necessar-ily points of daily concern or experience. He wrote little essays on what came to mind, however various. Through the years the result was several dozen memoranda, usually handwritten, many of which appear in this book.

The third source is the private letters. Some of these letters were of the "hot" variety and most of them, fortunately, were not sent to their addressees. Everyone who was an adult in the Truman era knows about the letter that was sent following the criticism in the Washington *Post* of daughter Margaret's singing at a Washington concert in 1950. What now is clear is that the letter to the *Post*'s music critic, Paul Hume, which was mailed by the President himself, was just one among dozens of such epistles, most of which never got past the eagle eyes of Truman's private secretary, Miss Rose A. Conway, and his correspondence secretary, Wil-liam D. (Bill) Hassett. A notation on one explosive letter, made by Rose Conway, says that it was found several months later in Hassett's desk drawer. And some of the letters, to be sure, were held back by the Presi-dent himself, who would write, perhaps sheepishly, on the envelope, "Not sent. HST," or some such phrase showing he had rethought his humor of the night before. In these letters the writer naturally let off steam, and felt better therefor. The letters started out properly enough, but then a note of exasperation appeared, and soon (to change the figure of speech) no holds were barred and the President reached for the jugular.[1]

Once Truman drafted a letter (unsent) to *The New Yorker* and chided its editors for their lack of sophistication in falling prey to the frauds of a would-be seventh cousin of Mark Twain, a man named Clements who took the *t* out of his name and announced himself as the International Mark Twain Society. The late Samuel Clemens, Truman told the magazine's editors, was himself something of an impostor but nonetheless beloved by Missourians. But the seventh cousin (or was it the seventeenth? wrote the President) was known to all sophisticates in Missouri.

Some of the most interesting private Truman letters were not of the annoyed, exasperated variety but simple family letters to his aged mother, Mrs. John A. Truman, who lived in Grandview, Missouri, with his sister, Mary Jane. These are the "Dear Mamma & Mary" letters, which the President dispatched faithfully until Mrs. Martha Ellen Truman passed on, in 1947, at the age of ninety-four. Thereafter the "Dear Mary" letters were just as frequent, although after some months they lost their chatty, confidential quality, their rundowns of public affairs and public figures; the President's sister took increasing interest in Eastern Star activities in the state of Missouri, and perhaps that was the reason for the change of tone.

Letters to the President's brother, Vivian, frequently had comments about the national political scene, and so did letters to cousins Ralph E. Truman and Nellie and Ethel Noland.

The President wrote to many correspondents outside his family, and to one and all he tended to say what he felt, and not always less but more: he almost thought as he wrote, and seldom hesitated to get to the point.

---

1. In an interview in 1967, Matthew J. Connelly, who was presidential appointments secretary in 1945–1953, vividly recalled the Hume letter:

> I recall it very well. I arrived in the office the next morning and the President called me in and said, "I want you to read something."
> He had this longhand letter and I read it and I said, "You're not going to send this."
> He said, "I knew you'd say that. It's already been mailed." He said, "You don't like that?"
> "Hell, no."
> He said, "Wait a minute, I'll show you something else."
> He reached in his desk drawer again. He said, "Here's the first draft."
> So, I read that. I looked at it and I said, "All right, I'll settle for the one you mailed."
> [Interviewer:] The first draft was worse, is that right?
> [Connelly:] Oh, brother!

(Oral history interview with Matthew J. Connelly by Jerry N. Hess, November 30, 1967, Truman Library, 1969, pp. 179–180.)

As his daughter, Margaret would, later put it the President was always a demon letter-writer. He would go down to the Independence post office himself to carry in the bags of his readied correspondence and bring out the received mail, almost like a farmer sowing and harvesting. The personal communion with correspondents of whatever station, whatever proximity to the seats of power, gave him access to the people's thoughts about their government, their President and their ex-President. His task was to keep in touch and to advance the purposes of the Democratic party, which were (he thought) the same as those of the American republic. For the most part, Truman dictated or penned his own letters, though Miss Conway sometimes wrote out fancy answers translated from the President's handwritten tips; occasionally he resorted to virtual forms. But many of the letters that issued from his office, in and out of the presidency, from Washington and from Independence, were his own dictation.

Some account remains to be given about the present-day location of the Truman private papers—where they now are, and how they came to be published. The private papers comprise a part, and a very small part indeed, of the massive collection of the President's papers in the Harry S. Truman Library at Independence. There in the Truman Library have the marvelous diary and memoranda and private letters been made available to researchers during the past several years (some of the diary and memos, the unsent letters and family letters, were released only in mid-October 1978, and a special collection of Noland letters was opened in December 1978).

As mentioned, the library at Independence was very much a part of the life of ex-President Truman. Before he left office, plans were made to follow the precedent set by Franklin D. Roosevelt, who arranged for his papers to be housed in a spacious building at Hyde Park. To design the library building, Truman engaged the same architect who in the 1930s redesigned the Jackson County courthouse at Independence, one of the President's favorite pieces of architecture. Somewhat to his dismay, he discovered that the architect no longer put up Georgian buildings, but designed in a style that could best be called Egyptian modern. Having made the engagement, however, Truman went ahead with the plans and even, it would seem, came to like the style of the new complex on the other side of the viaduct from North Delaware Street. It certainly was a convenient place to get to. Truman could drive out of his garage and around the corner and point his car down Delaware Street and get to the library in two or three minutes. This he was accustomed to do almost every morning, usually very early in the morning. And once he got to his office in the new building he could use his own papers, or if not use them, then watch them being arranged and stored in gray or brown archival boxes, row upon row, and labeled for the files from which they originally came.

The bulk of the Truman papers eventually found their way into archival boxes at the Truman Library, but for many years some of the best of them reposed in a considerable mass of Truman material known as the President's Secretary's Files, that is, Miss Conway's files, in a dozen four-drawer steel filing cases in the presidential wing of the library. The PSF, as this material was known, was kept back from the main body of Truman records—approximately 2,700 linear feet of files —which was opened for scholarly research beginning in the late 1950s. The former President knew there was "hot stuff" in the President's Secretary's Files (Rose Conway was wont to describe it as dynamite), and all of the PSF material was closed until after Truman's death in 1972. The ex-President used some of this material in the writing of his two-volume memoir, published in the mid-1950s, but he would be damned (as he might have put the case) if anyone else was going to riffle around in that material and perhaps make fun of him and his family and his administration and the Democratic party by publishing some silly article in a postage-subsidized magazine or in a book. In the late 1950s, a Princeton professor solicited Truman's help in the writing of a biography and his publisher sent two of his recent books. At first the President was friendly to the enterprise, but then he read the books and found them repeating some of the old accusations about him and his former associates. He became so warm on the subject that he wrote to the then archivist of the United States, Wayne C. Grover, that if Eric F. Goldman ever sought to enter the presidential wing of the library in order to look at the papers there, he, the ex-President, might attempt to throw him out.

Other than using his private papers for the memoirs, and allowing some use by his friend William Hillman for a coffee table book entitled *Mr. President* (New York: Farrar, Straus and Young, 1952), and use by his daughter, Margaret, for a biography entitled *Harry S. Truman* (New York: William Morrow, 1973)—other than for these three books, the papers remained closed. The President almost rudely denied them to *New York Times* reporter Cabell Phillips, who asked to see them for his *The Truman Presidency: The History of a Triumphant Succession* (New York: Macmillan, 1966). Nor did he permit the editors of *Foreign Relations of the United States,* the Department of State's official documentary publication, to see his private papers, despite numerous and pressing inquiries.

After the owner of the PSF material died, it was looked over by

Margaret Truman Daniel, who released the papers, and the archivists of the Truman Library gradually reviewed and opened them.

In mid-December 1978, I happened to come to the Truman Library in search of First World War letters, for use in a book about American history during that bygone era, and discovered PSF Box 333, which contains handwritten diary entries. I was thereby alerted to the extraordinary riches of the recently released files. Having written ahead to the chief archivist of the library, Philip D. Lagerquist, I found my 1917–1918 materials pulled out and ready, for Phil had one of his assistants load up a library truck with material likely to be of interest. As he told me and as was quickly evident, there was not much in the library on the former President's army service during the First World War—less than a day's worth of reading. Captain Harry S. Truman of the Thirty-fifth Division was not a well-known member of the American Expeditionary Forces, and almost no one in those days saved any of his correspondence, except his cousin Ethel, to whom he wrote a half-dozen or so letters about life with the battery near the front lines and about his detestation of regular army officers and especially West Pointers, whom he considered absurd martinets concerned only with the currying of horses.

The war letters were interesting, but in speaking about them with Phil Lagerquist's assistant, Erwin J. Mueller, I learned about Box 333.

"Would you like to take a look at all this handwritten material, just opened?" said Erwin.

"Yes indeed," said I, in hope that something important might be there but without much hope that it would be, and with a sense that Erwin was enamored of all the handwriting.

About three-thirty that Friday afternoon I opened the box, and it was at once apparent what I was looking at. The box was everything Erwin said it was, and more. I could do little except leaf through the pages, for no time was left; there was a meeting at Park College in Kansas City on Saturday, which was the principal purpose of my visit to the "K.C." area, and it was impossible to return that day to the Truman Library, though Erwin kindly offered to open the research room. But after a hurried weekend trip home to Bloomington, Indiana, I returned to Independence on Sunday evening, checking in at my accustomed place of lodging on Route 24, the Queen City Motel, a decaying hostelry grouped in a discouraging row of bowling alleys and Taco Bell and McDonald's restaurants along the four-lane highway, filled day and night with hustling trucks and pickups and cars. The next morning, skirting the open culverts and beer bottles and random collections of paper trash, I walked along the highway for a mile or so in order to reach the library, which stands on part of a cloverleaf off Route 24, and I began what proved to be months of work with Box 333, with another gray box of handwritten post-presidential memoranda and diary entries (Box 334), with the leather-bound black books containing scattered diary entries (Box 278), and with the dozen or so boxes, beginning with Box 82, that hold the daily appointment sheets, not to mention the family letters (Boxes 330–332), and the other boxes that, taken altogether, make up the approximately 113 linear feet of the President's Secretary's Files. Then there were several hundred boxes of post-presidential files, most of them never looked at since they were written. In all these boxes lay the President's private papers.

1945

President Franklin D. Roosevelt died on April 12, 1945, and soon thereafter came a rush of events marking the end of the Second World War, the greatest war in human history. The last days of the month saw the war in Europe virtually over—all, that is, but the shouting, which took place on May 8, V-E Day. The war in the Far East went on through the early summer, and ended on August 14 after the dropping of atomic bombs on Hiroshima and Nagasaki and the entrance of Soviet Russia into the war at the very last moment.

In retrospect President Roosevelt's death seems to have been almost a casual change, as compared to the deluge of events that followed. But for one man, his Vice-President, Harry S. Truman, the change held large personal meaning.

When Roosevelt, who had been in the White House since March 1933, slipped away while in a cottage in Warm Springs, Georgia, Truman was not surprised. Ever since the summer of 1944, when he had been chosen vice-presidential nominee on the ticket with Roosevelt, he had known that the President could not live out his fourth term. All the insiders at the Chicago convention of the Democratic party that summer knew that Roosevelt was a dying man. The extraordinary maneuvers by which Senator Truman of Missouri was named vice-presidential nominee, over the objections and furious strivings of FDR's "assistant president" for the home front, James F. Byrnes of South Carolina, whom the President had encouraged to seek the vice-presidency, and of Vice-President Henry A. Wallace, whom the President had also encouraged—these maneuvers showed the foreknowledge of the party's leaders. Truman did not himself lift a finger for the nomination, and told anyone who would listen that he did not want it. Mrs. Truman hated the very idea of the White House. But the party regulars disliked Wallace with a passion, and labor leaders, such as Sidney Hillman of the Congress of Industrial Organizations, did not want Byrnes, and the result was Truman. The President himself, who then was on the West

Coast, spoke to Truman and said that if he, the senator, was willing to break up the Democratic party in the middle of a war, that was his responsibility, whereupon Roosevelt banged down the receiver. Truman had no choice and therefore ran. He knew he was running for the presidency. The question was when Roosevelt's health would break, and on that score Truman was uninformed, for he saw Roosevelt only two or three times before FDR, sitting for his portrait, at Warm Springs that afternoon in April, suddenly complained of a terrific headache, collapsed into unconsciousness, and died.

 The new President found himself with a cabinet that not merely was not of his own choice but was an uncongenial group composed partly of incompetents and partly of individuals who were more loyal to themselves than to Harry S. Truman. He therefore made some changes, although he would not encounter real trouble with cabinet members until the next year, when with considerable embarrassment he had to force the resignations of two of the old Rooseveltians. Secretary of Labor Frances Perkins had been trying to resign for a long time, and Truman gave her post to former Senator Lewis B. Schwellenbach of Washington. Attorney General Francis Biddle resigned and was replaced by his assistant Tom C. Clark. Secretary of Agriculture Claude Wickard was replaced by Clinton P. Anderson. In the summer of 1945, Roosevelt's secretary of the treasury, Henry Morgenthau, Jr., said he wanted to attend the Potsdam Conference and would quit if he could not go; Truman took him at his word and appointed Fred Vinson, Byrnes's successor as director of the Office of War Mobilization and Reconversion. In September the secretary of war, Henry L. Stimson, who was seventy-eight years old, resigned, and his place was taken by his undersecretary, Robert P. Patterson.

 Naturally, Truman brought in a new group of White House aides, the principal one of which was his former high school chum Charles G. Ross, a distinguished reporter for the St. Louis Post-Dispatch *who had won the Pulitzer Prize. Charlie Ross presided over press relations until his death in December 1950. As appointments secretary, another key post, the new President chose Matthew J. Connelly, who had been one of his assistants in his senatorial office. He kept on the Roosevelt correspondence secretary, William D. (Bill) Hassett, whose job was to compose fancy letters for correspondents whose queries were not worth the President's personal attention, and also to compose proclamations for Love Your Dog Week and the other formal occasions for which the President's imprimatur or nihil obstat was solicited. As time passed, Truman gathered other helpers, such as Clark M. Clifford, a young navy veteran who for a while was naval aide and then became presidential counsel, replacing Roosevelt's counsel, Judge Samuel I. Rosenman, who had stayed on for some months. Clifford did speechwriting and gave judgments on high political matters. He was assisted by David Noyes, Charles S. Murphy, George Elsey, and David D. Lloyd. Charlie Murphy replaced Clifford as counsel in 1950 when Clifford went into private law practice in Washington.*

As his private secretary the President picked Rose A. Conway, his secretary when he was Vice-President. She remained through thick and thin, in and out of the White House, until his death in 1972.

The President retained Fleet Admiral William D. Leahy as his military chief of staff, an anomalous office created by FDR for the old admiral, whose advice always was shrewdly on the conservative side. Admiral (5 Star) Leahy, as Truman called him, accompanied the President to Potsdam, and was constantly by his side in the White House to give trenchant advice on military and, frequently, political subjects. The presidential army aide was an old artillery comrade of the First World War, Brigadier General (later Major General) Harry H. Vaughan, an ebullient, hearty man whom Truman found a constant source of humor and contentment. Vaughan tried to help everyone, and eventually involved himself in some free Deepfreezes, to the embarrassment of himself and the President, for one of these pantry behemoths had gone to 219 North Delaware Street in Independence. But no one could take Vaughan too seriously, least of all himself. It was said that whenever anything of a minor nature was askew or confused in the White House, assistants in the know would sigh and remark to each other, "Cherchez le Vaughan." Vaughan laughed with them. And perhaps with his good friends the other White House military aides, Colonels (later Brigadier Generals and Major Generals) Robert B. Landry, the air aide, and Wallace H. Graham, the presidential physician, and Captain (later Commodore) J. K. (Jake) Vardaman, Jr., and, after Jake's departure for the Federal Reserve Board, Captains (later Rear Admirals) James H. Foskett and Robert L. Dennison, naval aides.

And then there was the family—Bess and Margaret—and the relatives, who were quite a change, and by some estimates a breath of fresh air, compared to the Roosevelt family. The President's wife did her social duties with aplomb but did not enjoy them, as had Mrs. Roosevelt, and she possessed absolutely none of Eleanor Roosevelt's desire to travel and promote and espouse. Bess W. Truman was no novice to Washington society, for she had been a senator's wife for nearly a decade and had had a taste of being a Vice-President's wife; but she longed for the quiet of her house in Independence.

Margaret Truman, called by the President affectionately "my baby" (she hated the appellation) and more properly Margie, sometimes

"Skinny" because of her perennial and successful diets, was a serious student of history at George Washington University and as time went on aspired to a singing career. Intelligent, a hard worker like her father, Margaret was capable of doing anything she set her mind to. And to her father's delight she remained unspoiled, unaffected by the pomp of the White House, her head unturned.

The President's other relatives were equally attractive, beginning with his ninety-three-year-old mother. His affection for her and for his sister was boundless, as is confirmed by the innumerable letters he sent, most of them handwritten, to "Dear Mamma & Mary," and by the letters Mary wrote to him from herself and Martha Ellen Truman. The President's father had died many years before, in 1914, and Mamma and Mary were his only immediate kin, save for his brother, Vivian, who worked for the Federal Housing Administration in Kansas City. Fortunately, Vivian had a large family, four sons and a daughter, and as time went on there were grandchildren. And then, right across the street from 219 North Delaware, at 216, was the Noland family—Aunt Ella and her daughters Nellie and Ethel, with whom Truman maintained extremely close relations. He also kept in touch with his cousin Ralph, who served in the First World War and became a reserve officer and eventually a major general commanding the Thirty-fifth Division, which was taken into federal service at the outbreak of the Second World War. Ralph and Harry exchanged many letters on military and other subjects.

As for the state of the Union in early 1945, when the new President took over—it was, in a word, flourishing; the nation stood at the height of its wartime power. The country had recovered its strength from the depths of the Great Depression. All the men and women who wanted jobs had received them. The industrialists had regained their confidence after the buffetings of the Depression and performed miracles (that was the usual description, a correct one too) of production to equip the nation's twelve million soldiers, sailors, and airmen, the most impressively huge and well-equipped and experienced fighting force that ever had gone into battle. The country was almost untouched by the destruction of war; there were no ruined cities, splintered railroad networks, shellpocked farmlands, such as marked so much of Europe, not to mention the devastated Far East. By every measurement, the United States of America in April 1945 was the most powerful nation of the world. The war was almost over and it was a time of imminent triumph. But as Churchill later would put in the title of a volume of his memoirs, it was a time of imminent tragedy as well. The new President would preside over this confusing era.

TO MARTHA ELLEN AND MARY JANE TRUMAN

April 11, 1945

Dear Mamma & Mary:

I have all your letters—they come to my desk just as soon as they arrive—unopened. I think I have the best office force on the Capitol Hill and they all know my family's handwriting. So don't let Mr. Canfil's innate jealousy of anyone who talks to me or works for me get you any bad notions of how things run back here.[1] Now Miss Conway is here and writes home about all that takes place in the office, everyone at home will be surprised how well we get along.

It is hard to realize just how much I've always had to do back here. Clark[2] was never any help as a representative of the people of Missouri. He was always either tipsy or up in the clouds on some wild policy to embarrass the administration and never had time to see the ordinary customers from Missouri who had favors to ask or troubles to settle. But he was always useful and good to us in many floor fights. He'd always run guard for me when I had a controversial report to make. He also knew parliamentary law better than anyone in the Senate. But I had to see the people, answer the mail—the biggest one in the Senate after that Special Committee[3] started—and try to keep up with three other very busy Committees: Appropriations, Military Affairs, and Interstate Commerce. I used to get down here to the office at 7 o'clock and always wrote you a letter promptly in reply to yours. But now I have to take Margaret to school every morning and I don't get here until 8:30. Reathel Odum[4] is always here at that time and we wade through a stack of mail a foot high. By that time I have to see people—one at a time just as fast as they can go through the office without seeming to hurry them. Then I go over to the Capitol gold plated office[5] and see Senators and curiosity seekers for an hour and then the Senate meets and it's my job to get 'em prayed for—and goodness knows they need it—and then get the business to going by staying in the chair for an hour and then see more Senators and curi-

---

1. Fred Canfil, Truman's right arm in local Missouri politics.
2. Senator Bennett Champ Clark, son of the Senator Champ Clark who contended with Woodrow Wilson for the presidential nomination in 1912.
3. The Special Senate Committee for the Investigation of the National Defense Program, usually known as the Truman Committee, organized in 1941 by the then senator to oversee the war effort. Truman made a national reputation as head of this efficient committee.
4. An office secretary.
5. The Vice-President kept his Senate office and also used the vice-presidential suite, which he considered gold-plated.

osity people who want to see what a V.P. looks like and if he walks and has teeth.

Then I close the Senate and sign the mail and then maybe go home or to some meeting, usually some meeting, and then home and start over. When I don't get a letter about every other day I think I've missed some, which isn't true, I've had 'em all, the card from Lamar,[6] the letter from there and all the clippings and two or three letters to my one. But I have to work and I'm trying to make a job out of the Vice Presidency and it's quite a chore.

I owe all the boys in the family who are in the service a letter and have at least a hundred more to dictate. I've seen ten or fifteen people since I started this and answered the phone as often.

I wish I was there to do a little politicking in the O.E.S.[7] But you keep track of 'em and I'll pay 'em all off one of these days.

Had a letter from Olive[8] in which she told me about how they are getting along and they seem to be all right. Hope you are both well. Write when you can. Love to you both.

Harry

I'll be home one of these days and tell you all about it.

There is no evidence that Truman ever kept a diary prior to April 1945, although his pre-presidential papers are so sparse that perhaps any diary comments were later lost from sight, just thrown away. But the presidency inspired diary keeping, and the diary continued even after he left the White House. The new President seems to have composed the following entry within two or three days of the events it describes, writing it up from earlier notes, and after it was typed he revised it. Thereafter the entries were almost always contemporary, and usually handwritten.

DIARY

April 12, 1945

At 3:35 I was presiding over Senate. Senate adjourned about 5 o'clock and Sam Rayburn called me up and asked me to come over to his office —some legislative matters about which he wanted to talk. I arrived at

---

6. Locality near Independence, birthplace of Harry S. Truman.
7. Order of the Eastern Star.
8. Wife of Ralph Truman.

Rayburn's office about 5:05 and there was a call from Steve Early[1] asking me to come to the White House as quickly as possible. I told Sam Rayburn and some Congressmen, can't remember who else was there, to say nothing about it, I would probably be back in a few minutes, thinking probably I was going up to see the President because Bishop Atwood[2] was buried that day and I thought maybe the President was in town for the funeral and wanted to go over some matters with me before returning to Warm Springs.

Before going I went to my office, got my hat—Tom Harvey[3] drove me up to the White House—arrived there about 5:25 P.M., I should say, and was ushered into Mrs. Roosevelt's study on second floor.

Mrs. Roosevelt and Steve Early and Colonel and Mrs. Boettiger[4] were there—Mrs. Roosevelt put her arm around my shoulder and said, "The President is dead." That was the first inkling I had of the seriousness of the situation.

I then asked them what I could do, and she said—"What can we do for you?" Before I had a chance to answer her question, Secretary of State Stettinius came in. He evidently had received the news because he was in tears.

It was decided an immediate meeting of the Cabinet would be necessary. I called a meeting of the Cabinet to take place as quickly as possible in the regular Cabinet Room. I left Mrs. Roosevelt's study and Colonel Boettiger went to the Cabinet Room with me. Telephoned to Les Biffle, Secretary of Senate, who came up immediately. Attorney General came in at that time and they began calling other members of the Cabinet. As soon as I went to the Cabinet Room Early released the news that the President had died that afternoon. Cabinet assembled and in meantime had telephoned Chief Justice, Harlan F. Stone, to come as quickly as possible and I sent a car for my wife and daughter. Had both floor leaders of the House and the floor leader of the Senate, major and minority leader of the Senate and President pro tempore of the Senate—all called. Some of them arrived and some did not. As soon as my wife and daughter arrived, which was about 7 o'clock, an effort was made to find a bible on which to take the oath. Found bible which belonged in a White House bookcase and Chief Justice Stone administered oath, beginning at 7:08 and finished 7:09. I immediately called a meeting of the Cabinet and asked them to stay in office.

Mr. Stettinius asked me if I wanted the San Francisco Confer-

---

1. FDR's former press secretary.
2. Former Episcopal bishop of Arizona, a friend of President Roosevelt's.
3. Chauffeur.
4. Mrs. John Boettiger was the former Anna Roosevelt.

ence[5] to go on and I said the San Francisco Conference should be held as directed by the President.

Mrs. Roosevelt then asked me if it would be all right for them to take the plane to go to Warm Springs and I told her she could have anything the Government had to use in any way she saw fit. They left about a half hour after the Cabinet meeting adjourned I should say, and I went on home to my apartment at 4701 Connecticut Avenue.

I was very much shocked. I am not easily shocked but was certainly shocked when I was told of the President's death and the weight of the Government had fallen on my shoulders. I did not know what reaction the country would have to the death of a man whom they all practically worshipped. I was worried about the reaction of the Armed Forces. I did not know what effect the situation would have on the war effort, price control, war production and everything that entered into the emergency that then existed. I knew the President had a great many meetings with Churchill and Stalin. I was not familiar with any of these things and it was really something to think about but I decided the best thing to do was to go home and get as much rest as possible and face the music.

My wife and daughter and mother-in-law were at the apartment of our next door neighbor, and their daughter Mrs. Irving Wright was present. They had had a turkey dinner and they gave us something to eat. I had not had anything to eat since noon. Went to bed, went to sleep, and did not worry any more.

DIARY

April 13, 1945

Signed Proclamation for Pres. R's funeral & holiday. First official Act.... [This] morning the Secret Service came out.... They took me down the back way and I got in the car. I saw Tony Vaccaro[1] all by himself. I hailed him—had him get in the car and ride down with me. Went to the White House office and began the day. Hugh Fulton[2] came to the house that morning and he also came down with me in the car. Ed McKim[3] was not at house—he was in town.

---

5. To draw up the Charter of the United Nations.

---

1. Washington reporter for the Associated Press.
2. Former counsel for the Truman Committee.
3. Member of Truman's First World War field artillery battery, Battery D, and chief administrative assistant to the President, April–June 1945.

9:30—Merely talked to Eddie McKim, Hugh Fulton and Leonard Reinsch[4]—nothing of any importance discussed.

10:10—Saw Duke Shoop[5] and Eddie McKim again—nothing of importance discussed again.

10:15—The Secretary of State—General George C. Marshall
       Adm. Ernest J. King—Adm. Wm. D. Leahy
       The Secretary of War—The Secretary of the Navy
       General Giles[6]

Discussed the best way to get word to the troops what the new Commander in Chief expected to do. I told them I thought the first thing I would do would be to appear before the Congress and make a statement and then make statement immediately after that to the soldiers in the field and they agreed that was a good procedure.

12:00—That day at noon, Admiral Wilson Brown, Naval aide here, Colonel Richard Park and Jonathan Daniels[7] called and discussed foreign dispatches.

12:30—Went up to Capitol—had lunch and discussed with the members of the Senate and some members of the House advisability of a message on Monday—some of them opposed it. I listened to what all had to say, then said, I am coming and prepare for it. I thought it was the proper thing to do. They finally came around to my way of thinking when they found out what I had in mind—a statement of continuing the policies of the late President, outlining war effort and asking their cooperation.

The following were present at the luncheon—

The President	Senator White	Mr. Ramspeck
Senator Barkley	Mr. Rayburn	Senator Connally
Congressman McCormack	Mr. Martin	Senator Austin
Senator Hill	Senator Vandenberg	Senator La Follette
Senator Magnuson	Senator George	Senator Hatch
Senator Pepper	Senator O'Mahoney	Senator Wheeler
Mr. Biffle (host)		

2:30—James F. Byrnes called. I found out Jimmie was at Shoreham Hotel—called up and asked him to come over. We discussed everything from Tehran to Yalta, law of individual who had public office, and everything under the sun. Think message from Stalin came in—said he

---

4. Press secretary to the President, April–May 1945.
5. Reporter for the Kansas City *Star.*
6. Deputy Commander, U.S. Army Air Force.
7. FDR's press secretary.

would like to do anything he could to cooperate and I immediately sent him message back—copy of message on file in Admiral Leahy's office.

3:00—Roy Roberts[8] and Duke Shoop called just to visit.

3:30—The Secretary of State, Hon. Charles Bohlen, called. Discussed Molotov thing. Stalin wired back he was sending Molotov. Discussed matter with Stettinius before I sent wire to Stalin.[9]

DIARY

April 14, 1945

9:00—Saw John Snyder. Asked him to be Federal Loan Administrator —he did not want to do it—said he did not think he was right man for the place. Was satisfied he would be charged as Jesse Jones man and did not think that proper thing.[1] Jimmie Byrnes came in little while after that and I told him I was going to make John Snyder Federal Loan Administrator and he said that was the best pick I could make. Then I called Walter Smith, President of the Bank, told him I wanted John Snyder for Loan Administrator and he said he hated to lose him but if I wanted him I could have him. In a day or two after that I sent John Snyder's name down to Senate—called up Jesse Jones and told him the President had made the appointment and he said, did he make that appointment before he died and I said no, HE made it just now.

9:15—Secretary of Treasury wanted to discuss some financing arrangements—forget what they were. Also wanted to express his cooperation—said he would do everything in the world to cooperate.

9:45—Left for Union Station to meet the President's funeral train. Wife and daughter were not able to go down to train with me. Took Wallace and Byrnes in car with me. Went to station and as soon as train pulled in we got aboard—met all the Roosevelt family and then followed the procession—came back to office.

11:25—Mr. Andrew Higgins[2] came in to pay respects.

11:30—Harry Hopkins came in.

12:30—Had lunch at desk with Harry Hopkins and discussed the

8. Managing editor of the Kansas City *Star*.

9. Bohlen was the Russian expert of the Department of State, and the issue of the moment was whether Stalin would send his foreign minister, Molotov, to the San Francisco Conference. Truman felt that any other representative from the Soviet Union, short of Stalin himself, would demonstrate the Russians' contempt for the new world organization.

1. Jesse H. Jones was a Texas conservative, former secretary of commerce and federal loan administrator, whose relations with Roosevelt had been deteriorating; FDR described him privately as Jesus H. Jones.

2. Wartime shipbuilder from Louisiana.

whole history of the Roosevelt Administration 1933 to date—particular emphasis on the foreign visits on which the President had taken Harry Hopkins. We discussed Stalin, Churchill, de Gaulle, Cairo, Casablanca, Tehran and Yalta. That is about all.

1:00—Edward J. Flynn[3]—courtesy call. I told him to come back— wanted to discuss his visit to Rome and Moscow with him.

2:15—Admiral Leahy—talked regarding messages passing back and forth from Churchill and Stalin.

4:00—Attended funeral service in the White House. Went out to apartment after funeral. 10 o'clock that night left for Hyde Park.

DIARY

April 15, 1945

We arrived at Hyde Park about 9:30 in the morning and waited for the funeral procession to be organized. Went up to Hyde Park burial lot where the most impressive ceremony took place and the President was buried. Mrs. Roosevelt told me she would like to finish some work at the house. I told her to do anything they wanted to do and to take their time but she did not delay things. We left about 12 o'clock. I saw a great many people on train going up and coming back. That afternoon we worked on the address I proposed to make to the Congress the next day. We had outlined it going up. Mrs. Roosevelt called on me and all the Roosevelt children—that is Elliott, Jimmie and Mrs. Boettiger.[1] I saw a great many Senators and members of the House who were at the funeral. They came to the train to pay their respects. We worked all afternoon on address to Congress.

Statement my mother gave out was a jewel. If it had been prepared by best public relations it could not have been better.[2]

On visit down to Senate I saw all the Senators who were present that day. In addition to those saw Senate pages, employees on Senate side of the cabinet, all members of Senate press gallery—instructed newspaper men if they ever prayed, which I very much doubted, that they had better pray for me now.

---

3. Former chairman of the Democratic National Committee.

---

1. The other two Roosevelt sons were overseas.
2. Mrs. Truman said: "I can't really be glad he's President because I am sorry President Roosevelt is dead. If he had been voted in, I would be out waving a flag, but it doesn't seem right to be very happy or wave any flags now. Harry will get along all right. I knew Harry would be all right after I heard him give his speech this morning. I heard every word of it but Mary is going to read it to me again. Everyone who heard him talk this morning will know he's sincere and will do what's best."

Coming from funeral train—old and young were crying on the streets
—old Negro woman sitting down on curb with apron up was crying like
she had lost her son. Most of the women and half the men in tears on
Constitution Avenue when coming back from meeting funeral train.

DIARY

April 18, 1945

Session with State War, Navy on Trusteeships.[1] Authorized agreement in it for San Francisco. Authorized State, War and Navy to confer
on matters affecting political and military problems in the war areas.
(Hadn't been done before.)
Mr. Early, Mr. Hassett and Mr. Daniels, Judge Rosenman have offered to stay and help me get things organized for which I'm very grateful.

TO ELEANOR ROOSEVELT

May 10, 1945

Dear Mrs. Roosevelt:

Your note of the 8th is most highly appreciated. The whole family
were touched by your thoughtfulness.
I noticed in your good column today[1] you expressed some surprise at
the Russian attitude on the close of the European War.
I think I should explain the situation to you. On Wednesday April
25th our Minister to Sweden sent a message to me saying that Himmler
wanted to surrender to Gen. Eisenhower all their troops facing the Western Front and that the Germans would continue to fight the Russians.
Before our State Department could get the message deciphered the
Prime Minister called me from London and read the message to me. That
was the great mystery of the trip to the Pentagon Bldg.
The matter was discussed with our Staff and the offer was very
promptly refused. The Russians were notified of our joint action. Prince
Bernadotte of Sweden informed our Minister that Hitler had had a brain
blowup of some sort and would be dead in twenty-four hours—so
Himmler had informed him. The P.M. and I decided that when the Ge-

---

1. Arrangements equivalent to the former League of Nations mandates, whereby the
trustee nations submitted detailed reports to the U.N. concerning the people and territories
they supervised.

---

1. Mrs. Roosevelt wrote a syndicated newspaper column, "My Day."

stapo Butcher said a man would be dead in twenty-four hours he usually made good on the promise.

Negotiations went on for two more days—we always insisting on complete unconditional surrender on all fronts. The German idea, of course, was to split the three great powers and perhaps make things easier for themselves. Our Headquarters kept me informed all the time by almost hourly messages. We were nearly at an agreement and the famous Connally statement came out and completely upset the apple cart.[2] Himmler was displaced by Admiral Doenitz and a new start was made.

Germans delayed and delayed, trying all the time to quit only on the Western Front. They finally offered Norway, Denmark, Holland and the French Ports they still held but wanted to keep resisting the Russians. Our Commanding General finally told them that he would turn loose all we had and drive them into the Russians. They finally signed at Rheims the terms of unconditional surrender effective at 12:01 midnight of May 8–9.

In the meantime Churchill, Stalin and I had agreed on a simultaneous release at 9 A.M. Washington time, 3 P.M. London and 4 P.M. Moscow time. Then the Associated Press broke faith with Gen. Eisenhower. The Germans kept fighting the Russians and Stalin informed me that he had grave doubts of the Germans carrying out the terms. There was fighting on the Eastern Front right up to the last hour.

In the meantime Churchill was trying to force me to break faith with the Russians and release on the 7th, noon Washington time, 6 P.M. London, 7 P.M. Moscow. I wired Stalin and he said the Germans were still firing. I refused Churchill's request and informed Stalin of conditions here and in England and that unless I heard from him to the contrary I would release at 9 A.M. May 8th. I didn't hear so the release was made, but fighting was still in progress against the Russians. The Germans were finally informed that if they didn't cease firing as agreed they would not be treated as fighting men but as traitors and would be hanged as caught. They then ceased firing and Stalin made his announcement the 9th.

He had sent me a message stating the situation at 1 A.M. May 8th and asking postponement until May 9th. I did not get the message until 10 A.M. May 8—too late, of course, to do anything.

I have been trying very carefully to keep all my engagements with the Russians because they are touchy and suspicious of us. The difficul-

2. Senator Tom Connally of Texas was not the most diplomatic member of the upper house, despite his chairmanship of the Committee on Foreign Relations, and his public statement about refusing to negotiate with the Hitler government ruined the President's initiative.

ties with Churchill are very nearly as exasperating as they are with the Russians. But patience I think must be our watchword if we are to have World Peace. To have it we must have the whole-hearted support of Russia, Great Britain and the United States.

I hope this won't bore you too much—but I thought you'd like to know the facts. Please keep it confidential until it can be officially released.

Please accept my thanks again for your good message.

Most sincerely,

Harry S. Truman

Truman wrote memoranda to himself whenever the mood was right, setting down his thoughts on this or that, sometimes government or politics, sometimes anything that entered his head. On May 12, 1945, he evidently was in a mood for memos, for he wrote several, including the following.

MEMORANDUM

May 12, 1945

The Courts should be strictly judicial and not dabble in policy—except interpretation of the Constitution.

It is not at all proper for courts to try to make laws or to read law school theories into the law and policy laid down by the Congress.

We want no Gestapo or Secret Police. F.B.I. is tending in that direction. They are dabbling in sex life scandals and plain blackmail when they should be catching criminals. They also have a habit of sneering at local law enforcement officers.

This must stop. Cooperation is what we must have.

MEMORANDUM

May 12, 1945

I should like to see the Constitution amended to do away with all two-thirds rules. This means treaty ratification and Presidential Vetoes. These two matters should be accomplished by requiring a majority of both House and Senate—an *actual* majority of the membership, not a majority of those present. Every Legislator should be required to express his opinion by vote on these two most important legislative responsibilities. They should never be accomplished by unanimous consent.

Impeachment should be made simpler and an impeachment court

should be set up or the Supreme Court should conduct the trial. The result to be ratified by a majority of Senate and House—some sort of a majority as before stated.

One of Bess Truman's brothers had married the daughter of the owner of the Independence Examiner, *William Southern, Jr. The President took the time to answer a letter from Mrs. Southern.*

TO MRS. EMMY SOUTHERN

May 13, 1945

Dear Mrs. Southern:

You can't imagine how much I appreciated your good letter of May 3. All the family loved it too. . . .

It is a peculiar American complex to want to know what their President eats, how he sleeps, when he gets up, what meats he prefers etc. ad lib.[1] I told 'em I was very fond of Elk and Buffalo meat. I didn't elaborate on it by telling them I'd had some fine pork tenderloin in Buffalo, N.Y., and a tip-top steak in Elk Springs, Wyoming.

They want to know my favorite songs and when I say "Pilgrims Chorus" from Parsifal[2] or "Toreador" from Carmen or "Hinky Dinky Parlez Vous" or "Dirty Gerty from Bizerte," they are not sure whether I'm on the beam or not.

It is a very, very hard position to fall into as I did. If there ever was a man who was forced to be President, I'm that man. The week at Chicago was the most miserable I ever spent, trying to prevent my own nomination to be Vice President. I was afraid of what would happen—and it has.

But I must face the music and try to the best of my ability. You just keep on praying and hope for the best. My very best to Mr. Southern. Thank him for all the nice things he has said.

Sincerely,

Harry

Daily appointment sheets were given to the President, and he annotated them for a few months before abandoning the task. For a while they were typed up, but eventually they were left to stand with their markings in black pen or pencil.

---

1. "Etc. ad lib" was an expression Truman used often for emphasis.
2. The "Pilgrims' Chorus" is, of course, from Richard Wagner's Tannhäuser.

APPOINTMENT SHEET

May 14, 1945

9:30   [Senator George Radcliffe (Maryland)] Came in to pay respects
        and to assure me he was still the same friend he had always been
        to me and if ever he could be helpful in any way he wanted me
        to understand he was available.

9:45   [Major General William J. Donovan (head of Office of Strategic
        Services)] Came in to tell how important the Secret Service is
        and how much he could do to run the Government on an even
        basis.

                        . . . .

10:15   President Sergio Osmeña of the Philippines] Came in and signed
        the agreement to furnish the US with all the military and naval
        bases it needed.

10:30   [S. L. Altschuler] Railroad man from Kansas City—just came in to
        pay respects.

10:45   [Representatives of Gulf Ports Association] Came in to tell impor-
        tance of gulf ports—particularly Mississippi gulf port, in which I
        did not put much house [?]. I did sympathize with them, however,
        and told them I knew a great deal about the Gulf Coast. . . .

11:00   [Elmer Davis (head of Office of War Information)] Came in to
        discuss the attitude of the military government towards news in
        Germany. He has issued a statement on subject which I did not
        approve. I finally had to telephone Chief of Staff to find out if
        Eisenhower had approved order—said he had not and I had to
        correct situation.

11:15   [Herbert Rivers] From Kansas City—one of A.F. of L. pillars here
        in Washington and has always been a personal friend. Came in
        to talk labor with me.

11:30   [Rear Admiral Richard E. Byrd] Came in to tell how to settle world
        peace—in his opinion Stalin was going to ruin peace proposal or
        program and was cause of veto—when I informed him Churchill
        was cause of veto, his whole thesis collapsed.[1]

12:00   [Myron Blaylock] National committeeman from Texas, came in to
        pay respects and to say Texas was for me.

---

1. It is true that Stalin did not want to allow the General Assembly of the United Nations
to talk about anything that displeased the members of the Security Council. But the real
originators of the veto in the Council were the Americans, who feared that otherwise they
might not be able to protect the Monroe Doctrine.

12:15   [Donald Nelson (former head of the War Production Board)] Came
        in to say good-bye.

. . . .

APPOINTMENT SHEET

May 16, 1945

9:30   [Representative Augustus W. Bennet (New York)] Presented me
        with a testament—this is Congressman who beat Ham Fish, a
        very fine gentleman for that reason.[1]
9:45   [Senator W. Lee (Pappy) O'Daniel (Texas)] Came in for purpose of
        reading me a four-page letter, paragraph by paragraph, on how
        to run the Government of the United States.
10:15   [Secretary of the Treasury Morgenthau] Wanted to discuss certain
        detailed financial matters that affect the Treasury and was also
        interested in plan for the rehabilitation of Germany, to which I
        listened with interest.
10:45   [General of the Army Marshall] came in to discuss feasibility of
        having General Bradley[2] assigned Veterans Administrator for
        Veterans Bureau. Marshall later informed me that General Brad-
        ley would not be glad to take the job but if I thought the job had
        to be done, he would take it.

. . . .

11:30   [Attorney General Biddle] Came in to discuss the suit against
        Montgomery Ward and Company—whether it should be pressed
        or not.[3] Also to discuss certain judgeships which he was very
        anxious to [see] filled before he went out of office.
11:45   [Major Oliver P. Newman] Came to pay respects.
12:00   [Secretary of War Stimson] Came in to discuss with me his view-
        point on Russian situation. He has a very sound viewpoint on the
        subject.
12:30   [Solon J. Buck (archivist of the United States)] Came to pay re-
        spects.
2:00   [Judge Rosenman] Discussed food situation in Germany and Hol-
        land and necessity for a proper distribution of food for coming
        winter.

---

1. Hamilton Fish was a long-time Republican congressman from New York.
2. Army group commander in Europe, 1944–1945.
3. The president of Montgomery Ward, Sewell Avery, refused to cooperate in the government's wartime measures, and one of the best-known news pictures of the era showed Avery,
a distinguished-looking gentleman, being carried bodily out of his office when the government
took it over. The government then brought suit against the company.

2:30   [Edwin W. Pauley, Fred Schuster] Final meeting before trip to
        Russia as U.S. Representative on the Reparations Commission.[4]
3:30   [Elliott Roosevelt, Mrs. Anna Roosevelt Boettiger] Came in to dis-
        cuss with me their impressions of the Russians, British and
        French, which they received on various trips with their father.
4:00   [Sir Girja Shankar Bajpai] Came in as the Agent General for India
        to pay respects.
4:10   [W. Averell Harriman] Came in for final discussion before he left
        for Russia.

APPOINTMENT SHEET

May 17, 1945

9:30   [Representative Robert Ramspeck (Georgia)] Came in to discuss
        the Civil Service setup and advisability of accepting resignation
        of Republican member of Civil Service Commission. He told me
        that the Republican member of Civil Service was ablest member
        of the Commission and that in his opinion it would be bad policy
        to accept his resignation. The other two members fine people but
        knew nothing about the operation of Civil Service and cared less.
            I told him it was my opinion a complete survey of all Federal
        Offices should be made on efficiency basis to find out just how
        Agencies were functioning under Civil Service. I told him I knew
        where whole families were working in Departments and under
        Civil Service law there was no way to get rid of them except by
        trial and whenever a system lasted too long it was just as bad as
        a political boss in a ward in any city. Said it was my intention to
        have efficient setup—thought there should be a Manager to see
        that Department heads did a little work.
10:00   [Assistant Secretary of State William L. Clayton] Came in to dis-
        cuss lend-lease.
10:15   [Richard Burleson] Colonel in Field Artillery school in a little
        town called Montigny-sur-Aube—he had a camp in Arkansas
        from which school John Snyder and J. K. Vardaman were gradu-
        ates.... He was a great Field Artillery instructor—was known as
        "Dick by God Burleson" because he could never utter a sentence

---

4. Pauley, principal negotiator of reparations, had the task of working out with the Russians the Yalta agreement that named an approximate figure for German reparations of $20
billion, with the Soviets to obtain half. Part of his task was to ensure that the Anglo-Americans
did not pay the German food bill for their occupied zones while the Russians took reparations.
Another was to prevent the Russians from taking Germans to the Soviet Union for slave labor
(see appointment sheet for May 19).

without a string of swear words at beginning and end—nevertheless a great Field Artilleryman. He came in and asked if he could accompany Pauley to Russia in capacity of Military adviser and I sent him with Pauley.

10:30   [Martin Lewis] Former Republican State Highway Commissioner in Missouri. Very close personal friend of mine—has even gone so far as to change his politics from Republican to Democrat.

10:45   [Jonas W. Graber] Federal Housing Administration, State Director for Kansas with offices in Topeka, Kansas. Came in to discuss Federal Housing setup in Kansas and Missouri. A very good friend of my brother's, J. Vivian Truman—my brother suggested that I discuss Kansas politics with him as Graber is a good Kansas politician.

10:50   [Wayne Johnson] Came in to pay respects.

11:00   [Malcolm Ross] Discussed FEPC Bill in Congress—whole conversation is on record.[1]

11:15   [Chester Gray] Came in to pay respects.

11:30   Went to Bethesda Naval Medical Center to see Honorable Cordell Hull about San Francisco Conference and to get his viewpoint on Harry Hopkins.

2:15   [Secretary of the Navy James V. Forrestal] Held a session in projection room to outline the proposed campaign in Pacific for the Japanese war. Apparently a very detailed plan worked out with idea of invasion of Japan.

3:00   [Fred Vinson] Discussed proposed message to Congress on asking for the restoration of Presidential powers to consolidate and eliminate Bureaus—which message will be sent to the Congress tomorrow.[2]

3:30   [Acting Secretary of State Grew, General Alphonse Juin] Sent to pay respects.

APPOINTMENT SHEET

May 18, 1945

9:30   [Congressmen Alfred J. Elliott, Clarence F. Lea, Clair Engle, J. LeRoy Johnson, Bertrand W. Gearhart (all of California), Roland

---

1. One of the great civil rights issues of the 1940s was the establishment of a Fair Employment Practices Commission, the purpose of which was to benefit black American workers. President Roosevelt had made some efforts in this direction, but it was Truman who eventually took the program through to achievement.

2. Here was the genesis of the famous Hoover Commission, presided over by former President Hoover, to rationalize government administration.

Curran, Charles Kaupke] This group came to talk about Flood Control. There is a great power plant known as Shasta Dam on Sacramento River not far from Friant Dam. These two dams furnish water both in the San Joaquin and Sacramento Valley but there are a number of mountain streams which flow into Sacramento River and San Joaquin River and floods caused by winter rains and snow melting in the summer.

These people were in to try to get release of funds to build flood control dams.

9:45   [Senator Brien McMahon (Connecticut)] Came in to pay respects and discuss Connecticut politics.

10:00   [Lester Cox, Roger Kyse] [Cox] an old friend. Just came in to pay respects.

10:15   [Judge John Caskie Collet, Martin Lewis, old friends] Just came in to pay respects and to see what a Missourian looked like sitting at the President's desk.

. . . .

11:00   [The Reverend Paul McNally, S.J., vice-president of Georgetown University] He wanted me to come to graduation exercises, Georgetown University. I told him I could not come to their graduation because I have had at least 100 invitations to attend graduation exercises and have honorary degrees given me. Told him I am not very strong for honorary degrees if you have not earned them. I only have one and that was given or conferred on me by a little College out in Iowa, when I went out to make address to Graduating Class. Did not know they were going to confer a degree on me or would not have been there—it was too late when I found out about it not to let them go ahead with their plan—did not want to upset the apple cart.

11:15   [Homer Cummings] Nothing of importance.

11:20   [Acting Secretary of State Grew] Treaties proposition.

. . . .

11:45   [Jowett Shouse] Came to pay respects and said he wanted to ride the band wagon once more—wanted to support the party.

12:00   [Henry McElroy] Lives at Nashville, Tenn.—son of former City Manager of Kansas City, Missouri, who was my close personal friend—came to pay respects.

12:15   [(French) Minister of Foreign Affairs Georges Bidault, Ambassador Henri Bonnet, Undersecretary of State] Came in to discuss with me the French program. I told Mr. Bidault that I was interested in France—that every American thought highly of France and we wanted to do everything we possibly could to see France back on their feet and become a great power.

I had some difficulty with him because he was very anxious to have me commit myself on the transportation of French troops, to ——— Theater of War. I told him that would depend entirely on attitude of the General in command and our ability to transport troops and supplies—wanted him to understand I would have to have a complete agreement—if French troops were transported to ——— they would be under our command and they would have to agree to obey—they had not obeyed before and we did not like that sort of procedure and we might as well lay the cards on the table —unless France wanted to carry out their commitment we would or could not possibly furnish transportation, equipment, gun powder, planes etc. for them to fight with unless they wanted to obey orders of the general under whom they are serving.

. . . .

2:00   [Cabinet] Held Cabinet Meeting—explained to Cabinet members that in my opinion the Cabinet members were simply a Board of Directors appointed by the President, to help him carry out policies of the Government; in many instances the Cabinet could be of tremendous help to the President by offering advice whether he liked it or not but when President [gave] an order they should carry it out. I told them I expected to have a Cabinet I could depend on and take in my confidence and if this confidence was not well placed I would get a Cabinet in which I could place confidence.

I told the Cabinet members a story about President Lincoln— when he was discussing the proclamation—every member of his Cabinet opposed to him making proclamation—he put the question up to the whole Cabinet and they voted No—that is very well, the President voted Yes—that is the way I intend to run this.

2:45   [Harriman] Came to discuss Russian situation and trip of Harry Hopkins.

3:00   [Anna Roosevelt Boettiger] Ann Boettiger came back to give me further information on her father's dealings with Russia.

3:15   [Electra Waggoner Biggs, George O. Smith, E. J. Wallace, Walter Maloney, Mrs. Charley Tidd Cole, Mrs. Hammacher, Mrs. Caldwell, Edmund Tuattrocchi, Mr. Macey] These people came in about having a bronze statue of me made to put in the Capitol Building, Jefferson City, Missouri.

. . . .

4:55   [Captain Edwin H. Green] Son of a man I used to room with in 1903
        while working at National Bank of Commerce.
5:00   [James F. Byrnes] Came in to tell me I should not send Harry
        Hopkins to Russia. I told Jimmie I thought I would send him. No
        need for anyone else to get any credit but the President.

APPOINTMENT SHEET

May 19, 1945

9:45   [Robert E. Hannegan, chairman of the Democratic National Com-
        mittee] Discussed with Bob Hannegan advisability of making
        Cabinet changes and whether or not it was too soon to make them
        now—explaining to him and Steve Early, who was present most
        of the time, that I could not possibly outline a policy for my own
        administration unless I had a Cabinet who was in entire sympa-
        thy with what I wanted to do and unless I had a Cabinet with
        administrative ability.

        After we got thru our conversation I told him I wanted to get
        an Attorney General who would be satisfactory to me, that I had
        already made up my mind who was to be my Secretary of Labor
        and Secretary of Agriculture.

        I had had it in mind to appoint Clinton Anderson Secretary of
        the Interior but after some discussion of Anderson's background
        and due to fact he had made some very constructive investiga-
        tions in Food Program, I decided that Anderson would make a
        good Secretary of Agriculture.

        We decided to make those three appointments this next week
        —Attorney General, Secretary of Labor and Secretary of Agricul-
        ture.

        I had long ago decided we needed a new Food Administra-
        tor because it was my opinion Marvin Jones was tired—he told
        me that himself. Decided to put War Food Administration with
        Department of Agriculture where it belongs. The food situation
        is very serious but it is not nearly as serious as it was a month
        ago.
10:00   [Edwin Pauley] Discussed with Pauley Reparations program. He
        was appointed to have charge of Reparations with rank of an
        Ambassador and was ordered to assemble a bunch of experts, and
        he did assemble a bunch of real experts, to go to Russia and
        Germany and work out a Reparations program. Main stumbling

block is forced labor and Pauley and I have been trying to find a solution to forced labor program. Pauley made a suggestion to Foreign Relations Committee of the Senate. I suggested Pauley talk to Justice Jackson, who is to try war criminals of the U.S. After some discussion and deliberation I told Pauley to use his best judgment in the matter but under no circumstances to commit us to anything resembling slave labor.

11:00   [Harry Hopkins] Hopkins called at my suggestion—discussed proposed trip to Russia to talk to Stalin. There have been very strained relations between Russia and U.S. and between Russia and Great Britain over interpretation of certain purported agreements made at Yalta. After some discussion with Mr. Harriman, Ambassador to Russia, Harry Hopkins' name came up as a possible messenger to Stalin for me personally. I made some inquiries [with] various people who had been serving with Mr. Hopkins, including Cordell Hull, and one or two others, as to their viewpoint on Mr. Hopkins' integrity. My own judgment was that he was perfectly loyal and his integrity was beyond question.

I asked him to go to Stalin, provided his health permitted, and tell him just exactly what we intended to have in the way of carrying out the agreements, purported to have been made at Yalta—that I was anxious to have a fair understanding with the Russian Government—that we never made commitments which we did not expect to carry out to the letter—we expected him to carry his agreement out to the letter and we intended to see that he did.

I told Harry he could use diplomatic language, or he could use a baseball bat if he thought that was proper approach to Mr. Stalin.

I also told Harry to tell Stalin I would be glad to see him—facts in the case are I thought it his turn to come to the U.S. as our President had been to Russia—he would be royally entertained— only difficulty he might be nominated for President if I let him come to the States.

A night or two after that I had a conference with Joseph Davies[1] and suggested to Joe I was sending Harry Hopkins to Russia to talk to Stalin along the lines outlined above. Then I told him I was having as much difficulty with Prime Minister Church-

---

1. Former ambassador to Russia.

ill as I was having with Stalin—that it was my opinion that each of them was THE PAW OF THE CAT to pull the chestnuts out of the fire and if there were going to be any cat's paw I was going to be the paw and not the cat.

I told him it seemed to me Churchill should be informed of situation but I had no messenger I could send to him. I could not possibly send Hopkins to Churchill at same time I was sending him to see Stalin. Further said I did not want to give impression I was acting for Great Britain in any capacity, although I wanted support of Great Britain in anything we do so far as peace is concerned.

We discussed [a] number of things and Davies said he thought his health would permit him to make trip to Great Britain. Messrs. Hopkins and Davies left simultaneously and will arrive in London and Moscow about the same time—will be back in less than ten days and we will see what result is.

12:15   [The Reverends E. W. Bowman, Luther Holcomb] Dr. Bowman is pastor of the Grandview Baptist Church. Dr. Luther Holcomb, pastor of Church in Washington, invited Dr. Bowman to come to preach at his church in Washington and while here Dr. Bowman wanted to pay his respects to myself, my mother and sister—all three being members of his Church at Grandview, Missouri.

12:30   [John W. Snyder] Saw John Snyder and discussed Surplus Property situation, which is bad—we have been trying to find a solution in order to get Surplus Property in circulation and also get the Government a square deal on it. It has all the elements of a Tea Pot Dome in it and also the Forbes.[2]

John and I were of the opinion some drastic actions should be taken with Surplus Property Board—in fact Surplus Property needs an Administrative Chairman and we are going to try to get one.

2:45   [Acting Secretary of State Grew] Mr. Grew came in to talk over the situation of treaties between Alexander and Tito—I told Mr. Grew to come back later and discuss matter with Chiefs of Staff and take whatever action is necessary to put Mr. Tito in his place. That action has been taken and Tito has retired.[3]

---

2. Scandals during the Harding administration, involving lease of the Teapot Dome naval oil reserve to private interests, and large-scale graft in the Veterans Bureau under Colonel Charles R. Forbes.

3. Tito threatened to take Trieste, which was under the protection of the Allied commander in Italy, General Harold Alexander.

APPOINTMENT SHEET

May 21, 1945

9:30   [Representative Andrew J. May (Kentucky)] Talked about Universal Service Bill.[1] Also discussed the prospects for the Japanese war. He is Chairman of Military Committee of the House and is a key man in military policies of the country. I will say, it is too bad.

9:45   [Representative Frank T. Starkey (Minnesota)] I think he was talking about Federal Judge of Minnesota.

10:00   [Paul Stark] Talked about Victory Gardens. Mr. Stark is brother of Lloyd Stark, who was Governor of Missouri and who tried to unseat me from the Senate in 1940. He was not successful. His brother Paul is a fine gentleman. He is very much interested in Victory Gardens program and is anxious to see a Victory Garden started on White House lawn which I fear very much the members of White House staff will not agree to.

10:10   [Major Herbert C. Van Smith] Sergeant in "D" Battery of Independence, Missouri, which is a part of the 129th Field Artillery. When war was over he got a Reserve Commission in the Field Artillery and has been in active service of U.S. for three and one-half years and is now Major stationed at Fort Snelling—he just came in to pay his respects and to talk about first world war.

10:15   [Harriman] Here to discuss Russian situation and to get further and final instructions in connection Conversation with Stalin. Also discussed possibility of a meeting between Stalin, Churchill and myself at a later date to try to arrange to overcome the misunderstanding and difficulties which have risen since Germany folded up.

10:20   [Paul Dillon, Judge John W. Joynt] Just came in to pay respects—couple of good political friends from Saint Louis, Missouri.

---

1. Both the army's leadership and the President championed universal military service, after the experience of the Second World War. The army's leaders acutely remembered the unpreparedness of 1939–1941 and the extremely uneasy state of the war in 1942 when the Allies were losing both in the Far East and in Europe; all the while the United States did not possess a trained army. The President shared these feelings, but favored universal military service for another reason—it represented essentially the citizen army idea rather than the old regular army viewpoint; the President believed that the defense of the nation rested upon civilian preparedness. He had seen regular army officers during the First World War and detested them. Once when his unit came out of the line during the Meuse-Argonne, a regular officer bawled out the division for being all muddy and ignoring the dress code, and generally failing in military etiquette.

10:30 [Foreign Minister Bidault] Came in to see me regarding the relations between French Government and Government of U.S. I told him French Government and U.S. were traditional friends— France helped us when we needed it in the beginning and we helped France when France needed it in 1918 and in this last war —that I would like to see France a great powerful nation and it should be, but that the French had not been as cooperative as they should have been—they refused to obey orders and we did not like it. He said he would try to straighten out when he got back to France.

11:00 [Bryce Smith] Former Mayor of Kansas City—just came in to pay respects.

11:15 [Secretary of Labor Perkins] Came in to discuss her resignation. She told me ever since 1936 she had been trying to leave the Department but that President Roosevelt could not get along without her—she now felt I should have a Cabinet of my own choosing and she would like very much to quit. I reluctantly accepted her resignation.

11:45 [Michael D. Konomas] Supreme President of the Order of Aheppa.

12:00 [C. B. Baldwin, Elmer Benson] Came in to talk Minnesota politics and to discuss appointment of Federal Judge in Minnesota.

12:15 [Archbishop Athenagoras] Came in to pay respects and to have his picture taken with President of U.S.

12:30 [John R. Mott] In charge of YMCA among prisoners of war in 30 nations—came in to discuss YMCA work.

                          . . . .

1:00   [Joint session of Congress] Presented the One Hundredth Congressional Medal of Honor awarded to Infantryman, Sgt. Jake Lindsay, in the presence of Congress, Supreme Court and members of Lindsay's family. General Marshall read the citation and I placed the medal around his neck. I told the young man that it was a privilege on my part to put this medal around his neck and I would rather have that medal than to be President of the U.S.

2:00   [Harold D. Smith, director of the budget] Discussed ordinary matters of the budget.

3:00   [Chief Justice Stone] Came in to pay respects and to discuss the Supreme Court as it is presently constituted and to make suggestions as to Justices of the Supreme Court. I think he had some very excellent ideas on the subject.

DIARY

May 22, 1945

Had a long talk with Joe Davies last night on the Russian situation. Had previously discussed it with him on May 13. He suggested a cable by him to Molotov for Stalin in which he suggested a meeting of Stalin & myself in Alaska or Siberia or on a warship somewhere in that neighborhood.

He'd come over to tell me how blue he was over our deteriorating relations with Russia.

I informed him that at Harriman's suggestion and after a consultation with Hull, Byrnes and one or two others, I'd sent Harry Hopkins to see Stalin with instructions to tell Stalin what my views were and that I'd be pleased to meet him face to face.

Told Davies I'd sent Hopkins because I trusted him and because he had been Roosevelt's messenger to Russia on a previous and similar occasion, that Hopkins was noted [as] an advanced "Liberal" but not a professional one (I consider the latter the lowest form of politician), that he had horse sense and knew how to use it.

I'd previously suggested to Davies on May 13th that he go but his health would not allow it. Anyway as it worked out Hopkins is the best bet from our standpoint and from a political one. Davies suggested that if he could talk with Churchill he could make him see the light he thought. Churchill had been importuning me to urge Stalin to come to a meeting. But Churchill wanted me to meet with him first —which I do not want to do. Stalin already has an opinion we're ganging up on him.

To have a reasonably lasting peace the three great powers must be able to trust each other and they must themselves honestly want it. They must also have the confidence of the *smaller* nations. Russia hasn't the confidence of the small nations, nor has Britain. We have. I want peace and I'm willing to fight for it. It is my opinion we'll get it.

I suggested to Davies after he'd said he could talk to Churchill that he go and do it—if his physical condition would stand it. Seems a pity that our three ablest foreign relations men should now be old and physically incapacitated—Hull—Davies—Hopkins. Davies said he'd go to London.

So I've sent Hopkins to Moscow and Davies to London. We shall see what we shall see. Davies has the Order of Lenin—just conferred. He's an economic royalist—"ain't that sompin'."

APPOINTMENT SHEET

May 23, 1945

10:45   [Hilda Weinert] National Committeewoman from Texas—came in to pay respects and to hand me personal letter from Governor of Texas and congratulate me on being President of U.S.

11:00   [Secretary of the Treasury Morgenthau] Came in to talk fiscal matters and that is about all.

11:30   [The Reverend Feltham S. James] Came in to present me with picture at Walter Reed Hospital where I attended Church the first time after I was President of the U.S.—went to church out there because it was nonsectarian and wanted to call on General Pershing and pay my respects after my elevation as President as he had been my Commander-in-Chief in France and I don't believe in going to church for publicity purposes.

11:45   [Former Governor Gifford Pinchot of Pennsylvania] Discussed world conservation—pleasant conversation—exceedingly surprising to him that I knew anything about conservation.

12:00   [Roy Howard] Discussed general situation—wanted to assure me his papers wanted to get behind me and to win Japanese war and win a peace.

12:15   [Secretary of the Navy Forrestal] Came to discuss Naval appointments and promotions in the Navy.

12:30   [Senator Charles W. Tobey (New Hampshire)] Came in to see me.

12:45   [Senator Allen J. Ellender (Louisiana), Mayor Robert S. Maestri of New Orleans] Came in to pay respects.

4:00   [Press conference] Of course, I was very much disturbed about this Press Conference because it is the first one in which major changes in the political setup had to be made.

    Mr. Biddle took a very unsatisfactory attitude toward his resignation—I told him I was going to accept it. I was very sure if he got an opportunity to get the "crack pots" worked up here they would jump on me. As it was, he did not get an opportunity and they did not ask me any questions—apparently from viewpoint of unbiased spectators the Conference was a success.

APPOINTMENT SHEET

May 24, 1945

9:30   [Representative Mary T. Norton (New Jersey)] She came in to discuss FEPC Program. She explained to me the terrific fight she had been having to get out of own committee. I gave her all the encouragement I could and told her platforms of both Republican and Democratic party supported FEPC Bill and we would make every possible effort to get it thru.

11:15 [James P. McGranery, assistant to the attorney general] Discussed the appointment of Tom Clark as Attorney General. I had seen Tom Clark earlier in the day and told him I was going to appoint him Attorney General and he was very much taken aback. I told him that he had been too nice—told him Biddle had told me that Clark was no good—McGranery said it was personal prejudice on Biddle's part and as far as he thought Clark would make as good a man as we have. Also discussed Judge of Circuit Court of Appeals in Pennsylvania. Guffey and Stearn, who owns file record, have some pet they want to make the Judge of Court of Appeals in addition to one they have in that place. Guffey does not like McGranery because he was for me in Vice Presidency.

DIARY

May 27, 1945

Went out to the Burning Tree Club last night for dinner—the first time I've been away from the White House since we moved in, for a meal. Had a grand time. Listened to several very boresome speeches—made me think I was back in the Senate. The longest and most tiresome one was made by one of the oldest members paying tribute to a number of passed and gone members of the Senate & the House.

They asked me to say a few words—and I said a *few*. After the above mentioned talk by the "Old Grad," they asked me to play the piano—which I did. Paderewski's Minuet, the theme from Mozart's IX Sonata, Black Hawk Waltz and wound up by playing "Home Sweet Home" to the voices of three very able singers. They gave me a prize, as was to be expected. I was surprised and really did appreciate it—a marked deck and some loaded dice. I'd never had copies of either one so I was glad to have 'em. Will never use either, I hope.

Went upstairs and found that Steve Early, Scott Lucas and Jack Nichols had arranged a poker game.[1] They expected me to get into it. To be fair I announced that I'd leave at midnight because I didn't want to stay out after 1 A.M. and it would be that time when I "hit the hay."

For some reason I was lucky enough not to lose any money. Luck always seems to be with me in games of chance and in politics. No one

1. Scott W. Lucas was senator from Illinois, John Conover Nichols a former representative from Oklahoma.

was ever luckier than I've been since becoming the Chief Executive and Commander in Chief. Things have gone so well that I can't understand it—except to attribute it to God. He guides me, I think. My press conferences have been a grand success, I think, because I tell the truth and tell it simply. I feel that way. Politicians—professional ones, not "public servants"—are always looking for a bug under the chip and so are reporters. It is a case of the "mote and the beam."

In the picture "Mr. Smith Goes to Washington" it was perfectly all right to show Senators as either silly or as crooks but when the show put on a drunken newspaper reporter in his true character, it killed the picture.

My daughter and her two pals, Jane Lingo and Mrs. Wright—both lovely kids—are sleeping in Lincoln's bed tonight. If I were not afraid it would scare them too badly I'd have Lincoln appear. The maids and butlers swear he has appeared on several occasions. It is said that even Mrs. Coolidge saw him.

We had a picture show tonight. Jeanette MacDonald in "Springtime." Everybody including me cried a little—so they all enjoyed the show.

DIARY

May 30, 1945

Took a day off Memorial Day (May 30) and went down the Potomac on the "Potomac."[1] Coming back we met another "Potomac" going to Mt. Vernon—loaded to the guards with sightseeing soldiers and sailors, their sweeties and their mammas.

The soldiers' mammas, not the sweeties'.

Had Steve Early, George Allen, Ed McKim, John Snyder, Harry Vaughan, J. K. Vardaman, Russell Stewart of Chicago Times and Shay Minton[2] along. Don't think I ever had a more pleasant holiday. Found out Minton was in town so I had the Secret Service round him up and bring him aboard. We had a grand time discussing old Senate days and planning future good times for the country. Wish Minton were physically fit, I'd have him in the "family"—political family to help run the country.

We organized a low limit poker game and the wise cracks would

---

1. At this time the presidential yacht was the U.S.S. *Potomac;* it was soon replaced by the U.S.S. *Williamsburg.*

2. Sherman Minton, former senator from Indiana, later associate justice of the Supreme Court.

make Bob Hope laugh. My sides are sore. We make George Allen a "whipping boy" most of the time—and can he take it![3]

Think I'll organize a road show out of this gang after I'm out of the White House and I won't have to go to the Soldiers' Home to retire.

DIARY

June 1, 1945

Yesterday was "medal pinning day," with one spilling over into this morning.

Gave Steve Early a Distinguished Service Medal. He's earned one in the last 30 days—let alone the previous 12 years.

Called all the White House force into the rose garden and personally read the citation and pinned the medal on him. Said it was his mother's birthday and both of us got sort of emotional. After the pictures we took something for our nerves and to calm our feelings.

In the morning I had given Mrs. Knox a Legion of Merit badge for the dead Secretary of the Navy. It was a nice ceremony too in the executive office with Secs. of War and Navy present with their aides and assistants & wives. Mrs. Hull was present.

Gave the Regent of Iraq a merit badge this morning. He is a nice young man and not a bit upstage. His Foreign Minister is also a regular fellow.

Have been going through some very hectic days. Eyes troubling somewhat. Too much reading "fine print." Nearly every memorandum has a catch in it and it has been necessary to read at least a thousand of 'em and as many reports.

Most of it at night. I see the Secretaries at 9:15 after dictating personal mail for 45 minutes. Usually stop in the Map Room at 8:20 and spend ten minutes finding out about ship sinkings, casualties etc.[1] Gather up dispatches from Stalin, Churchill, Hurley[2] and others.

After discussing the day's prospects with Connelly, Ross, Hassett, McKim, and Early (I'll miss him) then commence to see the custom-

---

3. George E. Allen, man-about-Washington, was personal representative of the President, August 30, 1945, to January 1946. The President found him amusing. Later, to Truman's disgust, he became amusing to President Dwight D. Eisenhower. Allen was the author of *Presidents Who Have Known Me*.

---

1. "Map Room" was a euphemism for the White House's secret intelligence room. President Roosevelt had organized it after he found out that Prime Minister Churchill maintained such a room.

2. Major General Patrick J. Hurley was ambassador to China. Years earlier he had been President Hoover's secretary of war.

ers. Usually Senators, Congressmen, Cabinet members and Missourians.

Saw Herbert Hoover day before yesterday and had a pleasant and
constructive conversation on food and the general troubles of U.S. Presidents—two in particular.

We discussed our prima donnas and wondered what makes 'em.
Some of my boys who came in with me are having trouble with their
dignity and prerogatives. It's hell when a man gets in close association
with the President. Something happens to him. Study Rienzi and one or
two others.

Some Senators and Congressmen come in and pass the time of day
and then go out and help me save the world in the press.

That publicity complex is hell and few can escape it here. When a
good man comes along who hasn't the bug I try to grab him.

The family left for Missouri last evening. Went to the train with them
and rode to Silver Spring just as I did with my mother and sister a week
or so ago. Daughter was in a very unsatisfactory humor. I hope—sincerely hope—that this situation (my being President) is not going to affect
her adversely. My great predecessor had a lot of trouble with his family.
Most all of 'em sold him down the river and when they weren't selling
him they "sold" the country. But at that I sympathize with them. They
were handicapped too. I'm trying to see that they get the same just treatment that other Americans get.

I'm always so lonesome when the family leaves. I have no one to raise
a fuss over my neckties and my haircuts, my shoes and my clothes generally. I usually put on a terrible tie not even Bob Hannegan or Ed McKim
would wear, just to get a loud protest from Bess & Margie. When they are
gone I have to put on the right ones and it's no fun.

Went to church this morning and beat the publicity boys. Walked
across Jackson Park with no advance detail and slipped into a rear pew
of St. John's Church without attracting any notice whatever. Don't think
over six people recognized me. Several soldiers & sailors stood and
saluted me as I walked across the park but there were no curiosity seekers around and I enjoyed the lack of 'em.

Had dinner on the south porch all by myself. It is a beautiful outlook
across the White House lawn to the Jefferson Memorial with the Washington Monument rising just to the left of the picture. And the Sabotage
Press, represented by Mr. Waldrup, did everything possible to prevent the
building of the Jefferson Memorial. It makes a lovely picture from that
south porch.[3]

_____

3. The press got on Truman's nerves, for he believed it did not confine personal opinions
to the editorial pages and that generally the editors and owners were a conservative crew who
were trying to foist off their opinions as representative of public opinion. Throughout the

'Church was rather dull. But I had a chance to do some thinking and the time wasn't wasted. A lot of the world's troubles have been caused by the interpretation of the Gospels and the controversies between sects and creeds. It is all so silly and comes of the prima donna complex again.

The Jews claim God Almighty picked 'em out for special privilege. Well I'm sure He had better judgment. Fact is I never thought God picked any favorites. It is my studied opinion that any race, creed or color can be God's favorites if they act the part—and very few of 'em do that.

DIARY

June 4, 1945

Some day—Alabama Senators & Rep. Sparkman hear of a Board vacancy & want it for Alabama. I admire their activity.

Saw the Big Four from the Congress—McKellar, Barkley, Rayburn, McCormack.[1] Rayburn spent week end in Maryland at the fishing resort of Jim Barnes—a grand old lobbyist who charges Congressional Week Enders $10.00 for the privilege of fishing in his lake. No business is discussed—only fishing lies and Jacks or better. They took me fishing before I became V.P. and accidentally spilled me in the creek while I was changing seats in the row boat. I got wet from neck to ankles but kept my feet and head dry! Some feat. Try it sometime. I simply sat in the creek over the side of the boat, my feet stayed inside the boat and I held on to the side of the boat with my hands, keeping my head above water. But I succeeded in getting just as wet as if I'd gone all the way into the creek.

It was claimed to have been an accident—I'm not sure it wasn't. But they still discuss it and I wish I could go again and have as much fun.

---

years, he maintained, the "sabotage press" fought every legislative measure that promised to advance democracy in the United States. As a public official in Missouri, the President had had close experiences with hostile newspapers; the Kansas City *Star* of Roy Roberts and the Pulitzer-owned St. Louis *Post-Dispatch* opposed him in almost all his electoral campaigns; these powerful papers had not hesitated to smear him, drawing his purposes maliciously, making fanciful comments about his connection with the Kansas City Pendergast machine. From this Missouri experience Truman beheld a conspiracy by the alleged gentlemen of the press that was partly a family affair, for the Chicago *Tribune*, owned by Colonel Robert R. (Bertie) McCormick, was connected to the Washington *Times-Herald* and the New York *News* through family ownership. The Washington *Post* was owned by Eugene Meyer, who gave it to his son-in-law as a plaything. The third of the Washington papers, the smallest, the Scripps-Howard *News*, Truman described as "the snotty little *News*." He also detested the papers in the Hearst chain. And he animadverted often on the "gossip columnists," as he called them —news commentators such as Drew Pearson and Joseph and Stewart Alsop ("the Sop sisters").

---

1. Senator Kenneth McKellar, president pro tempore of the Senate; Senator Alben Barkley, majority leader of the Upper House; Speaker Sam Rayburn; John W. McCormack, House majority leader.

But can you imagine me taking sixteen secret service men, telephone and telegraph connections, representatives of three press associations, radio, photographers, special writers etc. ad lib on a personal excursion of that sort? It would all be off the record of course but these people would be along so if I got drowned or some nut got by the secret service and shot me or stabbed me, the news service would be intact. I'll stay in the White House back yard and let 'em stare through the back fence at the "two headed calf."

Joe Davies returned from his visit to the P.M. of G.B. Had him and Adm. Leahy to dinner and we discussed foreign affairs and Churchill in particular.

After dinner a dozen or so Senators and the White House employees and their wives, sisters, cousins and aunts came to the East Room for a show by Olson & Johnson. It was a dandy show and everyone enjoyed it. I took the show troupe over the House and told 'em what the Pres. uses the Green, Blue, Red and State Dining Rooms for. Then took 'em upstairs and showed 'em where State guests sleep; the Lincoln and Monroe rooms and my own and the family quarters. I think they got a kick out of their high powered guide—so did I.

DIARY

June 5, 1945

Another hectic day in the executive office. Saw a lot of customers. Hope they all left happy. Most of 'em did.

Took Ross, Snyder and Rosenman to the "House" for lunch. Had 'em upstairs in my so called "Study" and gave them a libation before we went to the family dining room for lunch. Told the three of them that they were most in my confidence and that I wanted frank and unadulterated statements of fact to me from them—and that when they couldn't treat me on that basis, they'd be of no use to me.

We had a nice lunch and discussed sale of war plants, surplus property board chairman, and F.E.P.C. All loaded with political dynamite. We expressed opinions of various people including Guy Gillette[1] and his successor. Guy can't make up his mind on anything. If God told him to take charge of Heaven, he'd be dead sure that Hell would be an easier place to run. I have known him to change his mind three times in as many conferences on one issue. He's very religious, very good looking and is so anxious to do what is right. But he can never make up his mind on what God wants. If he had the power of decision he'd be a great man. Too bad he hasn't.

---

1. A former senator from Iowa.

Went to a party this evening for Leslie Biffle. Max Truitt was the host. He's Barkley's son-in-law. I was a surprise guest. Arrived at the Hotel Raleigh lobby about seven o'clock. The secret service men were getting me through the lobby—pushing people right and left to make way for the President—politely of course. We came to the elevator and there were Biffle, several Congressmen and a Senator or two waiting to go up. The secret service men who take care of the Nation's Chief Executive think only of the President and his convenience. Sometimes it is very embarrassing to a modest man.

They began pushing Congressmen, Senators and other big shots out of the way at the elevator—even including the guest of honor—Mr. Biffle. Biffle is rather slight in build, weighing about 130 pounds, so I grabbed him from behind by his elbows and shoved him into the elevator ahead of me. He thought he was being too roughly treated for a regular Raleigh guest and turned on me to express his opinion. When he saw who was manhandling him, he was so surprised and happy that it made me ashamed.

The dinner was one great success. Truitt called on Biff's Senator from Arkansas, Bill Fulbright, who made some very appropriate remarks. Then he called on Judge Pine,[2] Sen. Scott Lucas, Sen. Hatch and his father-in-law Sen. Barkley. Barkley really spread himself. He not only paid a great tribute to Biffle but he went out of his way to pay a very high compliment to me.

Wish we'd had a stenographer there. It was a heartfelt endorsement of Biffle & me.

Got back to the White House at 10:30. Called the Madam and talked to her and my baby girl (she doesn't like that designation). I can't help wanting to talk to my sweetheart and my baby every night. I'm a damn fool I guess because I could never get excited or worked up about gals or women. I only had one sweetheart from the time I was six. I saw her in Sunday School at the Presbyterian Church in Independence when my mother took me there at that age and afterwards in the 5th grade at the Ott School in Independence when her Aunt Nannie was our teacher and she sat behind me. She sat behind me in the sixth, seventh and High School grades and I thought she was the most beautiful and the sweetest person on earth—and I'm still of that opinion after twenty-six years of being married to her. I'm old fashioned, I guess. But it's a happy state to labor under in this terrible job I fell heir to on Apr. 12 '45.

---

2. Judge David A. Pine, associate justice of the United States District Court for the District of Columbia.

DIARY

June 7, 1945

Looks like San Francisco [might] be a success yet. Uncle Joe agreed to accept our interpretation of the Veto. He also agreed to reconsider the Polish question. We may get a peace yet. Hopkins has done a good job in Moscow.

Davies did a good one in Britain. It was a good thought when they were sent over.

Montana went haywire and elected a Republican Congressman and Wheeler went haywire in Italy on the Russians.[1] Every time we get things going halfway right with the Soviets some smart aleck has to attack them. If it isn't Willie Hearst, Bertie McCormick or Burt Wheeler it is some other bird who wanted to appease Germany but just can't see any good in Russia. I'm not afraid of Russia. They've always been our friends and I can't see any reason why they shouldn't always be. The only trouble is the Crazy American Communist. There is only one in a million of our population but they are loyal to Stalin and not to the American President. I'd like to send them to Russia. Uncle Joe would promptly send them to Siberia or a concentration camp, I'm sure. But I can't do that and wouldn't if I could. Emma Goldman and William Z. Foster found by experience that the dictatorship of the proletariat is no different from the Czar or Hitler.[2] There's no socialism in Russia. It's the hotbed of special privilege.

A common everyday citizen has about as much to say about his government as a stock holder in the Standard Oil of New Jersey has about his Company. But I don't care what they do. They evidently like their government or they wouldn't die for it. I like ours so let's get along.

You know Americans are funny birds. They are always sticking their noses into somebody's business which isn't any of theirs.

We send missionaries and political propagandists to China, Turkey, India and everywhere to tell those people how to live. Most of 'em know as much or more than we do. Russia won't let 'em in. But when Russia

---

1. Senator Burton K. Wheeler of Montana was one of the President's closest friends, and surely his oldest friend in the Senate. When Truman was a freshman senator in 1935, Wheeler was just as nice as it was possible to be, and as chairman of the Interstate Commerce Committee he put Truman on the committee and allowed him a very considerable prominence. But Wheeler was outspoken and erratically so, and sounded off in Italy about the Russians at a time when Truman was trying to smooth relations.

2. Miss Goldman, an anarchist, was indeed disillusioned by a trip to Russia in 1920–1921, but the President was wrong about Foster, leader of the American Communist party.

puts out propaganda to help our parlor pinks—well, that's bad—so we think. There is not any difference between the two approaches except one is "my" approach and the other is "yours." Just a "mote & beam" affair.

The United States was created by the boys and girls who couldn't get along at home. So-called Puritans who weren't by any manner of means pure came to Mass. to try out their own witch burning theories. Roger Williams couldn't stand 'em any better than they could stand England under the Stuarts.

Most every colony on the East Coast was founded for about the same reason by folks who couldn't get along at home. But by amalgamation we've made a very good country and a great nation with a reasonably good government. I want to maintain it and shall do all I can in spite of the hyphenates and crackpots.

I've no more use for Polish-Americans, Irish-Americans, Swedish-Americans or any other sort of hyphenate than I have for Communist-Americans. They all have some other loyalty than the one they should have. Maybe the old melting pot will take care of it. I hope so.

DIARY

June 13, 1945

Had breakfast with Hopkins, Davies and Leahy to discuss the Russian-British-Polish situation. Seems that a good job was done by the special envoys. Anyway we are in better position for a peaceful conference than we were before. Hopkins looks better than when he left here and so does Davies. Think both of 'em were more worried than sick.

Propaganda seems to be our greatest foreign relations enemy. Russians distribute lies about us. Our papers lie about and misrepresent the motives of the Russians—and the British out lie and out propagandize us both. The best one I've heard was about a show the British gave the French on their great Paris Boulevard Champs Elysées.

They showed American lend-lease material which we'd given them and claimed credit for furnishing such stuff to the French! What a world!

APPOINTMENT SHEET

June 15, 1945

9:45   [Vice Admiral Henry K. Hewitt] To pay respects and for me to look over for a future job.

10:00   [Representative George H. Mahon (Texas)] To talk about a hospital for Vets at Big Springs.

10:15   [Senator Clark (Missouri)] To talk air policy etc.

10:30   [Judge Marvin Jones] To thank me for letting him go back to the court.

10:45   [Irving Brant, biographer of President James Madison] To tell me how to run the State Dept. & the Supreme Court.

11:00   [Lauchlin Currie, presidential assistant] To say goodbye & to tell me what to do in China & Switzerland.

11:15   [Secretary of Commerce Wallace, the undersecretary of commerce] To talk reorganization.

11:30   [Ward M. Canaday, chairman of Willys-Overland] To pay respects and to give me some cufflinks—gold jeeps. He makes jeeps for army.

11:45   [George Taylor of the National War Labor Board] Came to resign —decided to stay.

12:00   [Presentation of Medals of Honor] Did present 'em.

.   .   .   .

1:00   [Lunch] With Judge Rosenman & Charlie Ross discussed Presidential succession & possibility of constitutional amendment on treaty ratification to let House vote and change of 2/3 to majority both on treaties & vetoes. No conclusion.

2:30   [Apostolic delegate] The Pope's man wants a Catholic Peace in Russia—ain't that sompin'? Saw Patch & two other Generals.[1] Patch gave me Goering's Baton—all diamonds, gold and platinum —some bauble. $40,000 maybe.

DIARY

June 17, 1945

Went down the river today on the Potomac to discuss plans, issues, and *decisions.* Took Charlie Ross, straight thinker, honest man who tells me the truth so I understand what he means; Matt Connelly, shrewd Irishman, who raises up the chips and shows me the bugs, honest, fair, "diplomatic" with me; Judge Fred Vinson, straight shooter, knows Congress and how they think, a man to trust; Judge Rosenman, one of the ablest in Washington, keen mind, a lucid pen, a loyal Roosevelt man and an equally loyal Truman man; Steve Early, a keen observer, political and other wise, has acted as my hatchet man, absolutely loyal and trustworthy, same can be said as about Rosenman.

---

1. General Alexander M. Patch was commander of the Seventh Army in the invasion of southern France in 1944.

We discussed public relations in Germany, Italy, France, Holland, Belgium, England and Russia. Food, fuel, transportation and what to do about it. Japanese War and the relations with China, Russia, and Britain with regard to it, Supreme Commander and what to do with Mr. Prima Donna, Brass Hat, Five Star MacArthur. He's worse than the Cabots and the Lodges—they at least talked with one another before they told God what to do. Mac tells God right off. It is a very great pity we have to have stuffed Shirts like that in key positions. I don't see why in Hell Roosevelt didn't order Wainwright home and let MacArthur be a martyr.[1] Guess he was afraid of the Sabotage Press—McCormick-Patterson Axis.[2] We'd have had a real General and a fighting man if we had Wainwright and not a play actor and a bunco man such as we have now.

Don't see how a country can produce such men as Robert E. Lee, John J. Pershing, Eisenhower, & Bradley and at the same time produce Custers, Pattons, and MacArthurs.

I have to decide Japanese strategy—shall we invade Japan proper or shall we bomb and blockade? That is my hardest decision to date. But I'll make it when I have all the facts.

So you see we talk about more than "Cabbages & Kings and Sealing wax and things."

> They talked of many things
> Shoes and sealing wax and cabbages and kings.

The Potsdam Conference of July 17–August 2, 1945, met in an un-bombed suburb of the nearly destroyed city of Berlin, in a 176-room palace named the Cecilienhof, built for the last of the Hohenzollern crown princes and finished in 1917, the year when the American army appeared in France and gave promise of the downfall of Bismarck's Second Empire. There the leaders of the victorious European allies—the United States, Britain, and Russia—undertook to settle the outstanding problems of Europe and to anticipate the end of war in the Far East. President Truman left from Newport News early on the morning of Saturday the seventh, and soon was enjoying the escape from the White House routine, although he could not forget the routine and recalled it in the pages of his diary.

---

1. Instead Roosevelt had ordered MacArthur to Australia, and Lieutenant General Jonathan M. Wainwright, in command of Bataan and Corregidor, had to surrender to the Japanese and endure more than three years of prison camp.

2. Colonel Robert R. McCormick of the Chicago *Tribune* was the cousin of Eleanor (Cissy) Patterson of the Washington *Times-Herald.* Cousin Joseph Patterson owned the New York *Daily News.*

DIARY

U.S.S. Augusta
July 7, 1945

Had two rather full and interesting days. Received a committee of Congressmen and Senators who are members of the Lions Club. They presented me with an honorary membership, all framed etc. and a scroll on principles of ethics. It was stated then, by me, that business ethics would settle most trade difficulties and do away with courts of equity etc.

A couple of nice children gave me a plaque commemorating $715,-000,000.00 in bonds sales by the school children. The nice boy made me a speech. At his age I'd have surely passed out, if I'd had to make a statement, similar to his, to the town mayor let alone the President of the U.S. He didn't seem to be much bothered or impressed. These modern kids are something to write home about even if they can't spell or find a word in the dictionary or tell what 3×3 equals.

On the 7th [6th] I saw Sens. Wheeler, McFarland, Hawkes and Capehart. They'd been overseas, had seen Germany, France, Italy—and knew *all* the answers. Smart men I'd say. Since Julius Caesar such men as Charlemagne, Richelieu, Charles V, Francis I, the great King Henry IV of France, Frederick Barbarossa, to name a few, and Woodrow Wilson and Frank Roosevelt have had remedies and still couldn't solve the problem. Maybe these historical characters didn't have the brains and background of the four "able senators."

Anyway their song was that France would go Communistic, so would Germany, Italy and the Scandinavians, and there was grave doubt about England staying sane. The Pope, they said, was blue as indigo about the situation. All of 'em except McFarland assured me that the European world is at an end and that Russia is a big bad wolf. Europe has passed out so often in the last 2000 years—and has come back, better or worse than ever, whichever pleases the fancy, that I'm not impressed with cursory glances of oratorical members of the famous "Cave of the Winds" on Capitol Hill. I've been there myself and have been through crisis after crisis in each of which the country surely would disintegrate (and it never did) [so] that "Senatorial Alarm" doesn't much alarm me.

My good isolationist friend Wheeler is a natural purveyor of bad news. Capehart is a promoter gone political. Hawkes is an honest man with a good Chamber of Commerce mind and my Arizona friend is really worried but is an optimist and of all four I think most anxious to help me win a peace.

Talked to Bess last night and the night before. She wasn't happy about my going to see Mr. Russia and Mr. Great Britain—neither am I.

Had a long talk with my able and conniving Secretary of State. My but he has a keen mind! And he is an honest man. But all country politicians are alike. They are sure all other politicians are circuitous in their dealings. When they are told the straight truth, unvarnished, it is never believed—an asset *sometimes*.

Byrnes & I discussed Pauley's plans on reparations. The smart boys in the State Department, as usual, are against the best interests of the U.S. if they can circumvent a straightforward hard hitting trader for the home front. But they are stymied this time. Byrnes & I shall expect our interests to come first. Pauley is doing a job for the United States.

How I hate this trip! But I have to make it—win, lose or draw—and we must win. I'm not working for any interest but the Republic of the United States. I [am] giving nothing away except to save starving people and even then I hope we can only help them to help themselves.

DIARY

U.S.S. Augusta
July 9, 1945

Had a very pleasant Sunday. Went to church with Ship's Captain, Sec. State and aides. Then had a shower and a nap. Good lunch and a probabilities game with Ross, Vaughan and three press assn. men; ended pleasantly with my doing some satisfactory guessing on my opponents' hole cards.

Good picture show—Bob Hope in technicolor as a pirate's victim in the West Indies.

Arose at 6:15 as usual this morning, took a turn around the deck and then breakfast. Had dinner last night in the officers mess or ward room.

Maneuvers and firing at 8:30. Eight inch five inch and 40 mm. Most interesting to [me] because of field artillery experience. I'd still rather fire a battery than run a country. Had lunch with warrant officers. It was a good one. There is an excellent band of 30 pieces and an orchestra from the same thirty. They make excellent music at all meals but breakfast. They've found I like good music and they play it for me.

The Augusta *took the President to Antwerp, whence he went by air to the German capital, arriving on July 15. The conference had been scheduled to begin the next day, but Stalin had to ask for a delay until*

July 17, for he had suffered a small heart attack. Thus Truman's first diary account written at Potsdam recites the preliminaries to the conference. The President's diary entries for the Potsdam Conference itself —his experiences in the former German capital—were not discovered until 1979. Press Secretary Charles G. Ross borrowed the account, perhaps in 1945 or 1946, hoping to write a story of the conference, but never got around to it, and after his death in 1950 the diary sheets and other miscellaneous materials in Ross's White House office were given to Rose Conway, who put them away in a file labeled "Ross, Mr. and Mrs. Charles G." in the President's personal file. Miss Conway appears to have stapled the sheets hurriedly, out of sequence. The archivists of the Truman Library who organized the President's Secretary's Files did not notice them, even though the handwriting was that of the President.

DIARY

[Potsdam]
July 16, 1945

Today has been an historical one. Arrived last evening from Antwerp via the President's C-54 and was driven to the movie colony district in Potsdam. The German Will Hays apparently had what is considered the best house. It was fixed up for me as President & called the Berlin White House. It is a dirty yellow and red. A ruined French Chateau—architectural style ruined by German endeavor to cover up the French. They erected a couple of tombstone chimneys on each side of the porch facing the lake so they would cover up the beautiful chateau roof and tower. Make the place look like hell but purely German—just like the Kansas City Union Station.

We did not see but two German civilians on the several mile drive from the Airport to the yellow "White House."

The house as were all others was stripped of everything by the Russians—not even a tin spoon left. The American commander, however, being a man of energy, caught the Russian loot train and recovered enough furniture to make the place livable. Nothing matches. We have a two ton German side board in the dining room and a French or Chippendale table and chairs—maybe a mixture of both. There is a birdseye maple wardrobe and an oak chest matching the two ton side board in my bed room. It is comfortable enough all round but what a nightmare it would give an interior decorator.[1]

---

1. Only some years later, after publication of his memoirs, did Truman discover the full particulars of the Berlin White House. He had been mistaken in thinking that the house

To get down to today. Mr. Churchill called by phone last night and said he'd like to call—for me to set the hour. I did—for 11 A.M. this morning. He was on time to the dot. His daughter told Gen. Vaughan he hadn't been up so early in ten years! I'd been up for four and one half hours.

We had a most pleasant conversation. He is a most charming and a very clever person—meaning clever in the English not the Kentucky sense. He gave me a lot of hooey about how great my country is and how he loved Roosevelt and how he intended to love me etc. etc. Well. I gave him as cordial a reception as I could—being naturally (I hope) a polite and agreeable person.

I am sure we can get along if he doesn't try to give me too much soft soap. You know soft soap is made of ash hopper lye and it burns to beat

---

belonged to the German film censor (Will Hays had been postmaster general in the Harding administration, and from 1922 until September 1945 was head of the Motion Picture Producers and Distributors Association and thereby "czar," that is, censor, of American films). In February 1956 he received a pathetic letter from a member of the family that owned the house. D. Mueller-Grote remarked that his grandfather had built it in 1896, and his father lived in it, and because the family was in the book trade it had been visited by countless German and foreign scientists, artists and writers, who enjoyed its atmosphere of culture, until disaster struck in May 1945.

Our publishing house which was bombed out in the city, was . . . moved there. We even succeeded to save all archives and especially the unreplaceable library giving testimony of our 300 years old publishing house. In addition to that we moved to Neubabelsberg the very impressive collection of German writers and scientists and many drawings of well-known artists. In the beginning of May the Russians arrived. Ten weeks before you entered this house, its tenants were living in constant fright and fear. By day and by night plundering Russian soldiers went in and out, raping my sisters before their own parents and children, beating up my old parents. All furniture, wardrobes, trunks etc. were smashed with bayonets and rifle butts, their contents spilled and destroyed in an undescribable manner. The wealth of a cultivated house was destroyed within hours. Amongst others, the music of the very A-moll [flat] waltz by Chopin, which, upon Admiral Leahy's instructions, was procured from Paris for the pianist Eugene List. In the middle of May, well after the capitulation, the owners of this house as well as their tenants were put out on an hour's notice. They were permitted to take along just the barest necessities of life. Apparently this beautiful house was being set aside for a very prominent purpose. The house was completely stripped of furniture, valuable pieces of German and Italian Renaissance amongst others. The villa was refurnished from neighboring castles. The library of the publishing house, saved at great pains, and my father's large and very valuable private library, the archives, etc. were loaded on trucks with forks and served to fill up bomb craters. In this endeavor not only Russians participated, but also Germans and at a later date Americans, prepared for your arrival and adopting the Russian method of "house cleaning" by completely removing everything it contained and dumping it in the woods. Members of the US army have been seen with pictures, originating from our house. We had a collection of old Netherland and German masters as well as paintings of modern artists. When you moved into this house, its proprietor was by no means removed to Russia, as you wrote to your wife. Its proprietor lived, with his wife, no more than 500 yards away in miserable surroundings. . . . It is ironical that in surroundings where arts, science and literature were sovereign, apparently a decision should have been arrived at concerning the fatal atom bombing of Hiroshima."(Post-Presidential Files, Name File, Box 50, *Life,* corrections in memoirs.)

hell when it gets into the eyes. It's fine for chigger bites but not so good for rose complexions. But I haven't a rose complexion.

We struck a "blow for liberty" when he left in Scotch—not the right brand for the purpose as the old V.P. Jack Garner can testify.

The photo men had a field day when he left.

At 3:30 P.M. Mr. Sec. Byrnes, Adm. (5 Star) Leahy and I left in an open car for Berlin, followed by my two aides and various and sundry secret service and military guards and preceded by a two star general in a closed car with a couple of plain clothes men to fool 'em if they wanted to do any target practice of consequence on the Pres. They didn't.

We reviewed the Second Armored Division and tied a citation on the guidon of Co. E 17th Armored Engr. Bn. Gen. Collier, who seemed to know his stuff, put us in a reconnaissance car built with side seats and no top just like a hoodlum wagon minus the top or a fire truck with seats and no hose and we drove slowly down a mile and a half of good soldiers and some millions of dollars worth of equipment—which had amply paid its way to Berlin.

Then we went on to Berlin and saw absolute ruin. Hitler's folly. He overreached himself by trying to take in too much territory. He had no morals and his people backed him up. Never did I see a more sorrowful sight, nor witness retribution to the nth degree.

The most sorrowful part of the situation is the deluded Hitlerian populace. Of course the Russians have kidnaped the able bodied and I suppose have made involuntary workmen of them. They have also looted every house left standing and have sent the loot to Russia. But Hitler did the same thing to them.

It is the Golden Rule in reverse—and it is not an uplifting sight. What a pity that the human animal is not able to put his moral thinking into practice!

We saw old men, old women, young women, children from tots to teens carrying packs, pushing carts, pulling carts, evidently ejected by the conquerors and carrying what they could of their belongings to no-where in particular.

I thought of Carthage, Baalbek, Jerusalem, Rome, Atlantis, Peking, Babylon, Nineveh; Scipio, Rameses II, Titus, Herman, Sherman, Jenghis Khan, Alexander, Darius the Great. But Hitler only destroyed Stalingrad —and Berlin. I hope for some sort of peace—but I fear that machines are ahead of morals by some centuries and when morals catch up perhaps there'll be no reason for any of it.

I hope not. But we are only termites on a planet and maybe when we bore too deeply into the planet there'll [be] a reckoning—who knows?

DIARY

Just spent a couple of hours with Stalin. Joe Davies called on Maisky and made the date last night for noon today. Promptly a few minutes before twelve I looked up from the desk and there stood Stalin in the doorway. I got to my feet and advanced to meet him. He put out his hand and smiled. I did the same, we shook, I greeted Molotov and the interpreter, and we sat down. After the usual polite remarks we got down to business. I told Stalin that I am no diplomat but usually said yes & no to questions after hearing all the argument. It pleased him. I asked him if he had the agenda for the meeting. He said he had and that he had some more questions to present. I told him to fire away. He did and it is dynamite—but I have some dynamite too which I'm not exploding now. He wants to fire Franco, to which I wouldn't object, and divide up the Italian colonies and other mandates, some no doubt that the British have. Then he got on the Chinese situation, told us what agreements had been reached and what was in abeyance. Most of the big points are settled. He'll be in the Jap War on August 15th. Fini Japs when that comes about. We had lunch, talked socially, put on a real show drinking toasts to everyone, then had pictures made in the back yard. I can deal with Stalin. He is honest—but smart as hell.

DIARY

Ate breakfast with nephew Harry, a sergeant in the Field Artillery. He is a good soldier and a nice boy. They took him off *Queen Elizabeth* at Glasgow and flew him here. Sending him home Friday. Went to lunch with P.M. at 1:30. Walked around to British Hqtrs. Met at the gate by Mr. Churchill. Guard of honor drawn up. Fine body of men, Scottish Guards. Band played Star Spangled Banner. Inspected Guard and went in for lunch. P.M. & I ate alone. Discussed Manhattan (it is a success). Decided to tell Stalin about it. Stalin had told P.M. of telegram from Jap Emperor asking for peace. Stalin also read his answer to me. It was satisfactory.

Believe Japs will fold up before Russia comes in. I am sure they will when Manhattan appears over their homeland. I shall inform Stalin about it at an opportune time.[1]

Stalin's luncheon was a most satisfactory meeting. I invited him to come to the U.S. Told him I'd send the Battleship Missouri for him if he'd come. He said he wanted to cooperate with U.S. in peace as we had cooperated in War but it would be harder. Said he was grossly misunderstood in U.S. and I was misunderstood in Russia. I told him that we each could help to remedy that situation in our home countries and that I intended to try with all I had to do my part at home. He gave me a most cordial smile and said he would do as much in Russia.

We then went to the conference and it was my job to present the Ministers' proposed agenda. There were three proposals and I banged them through in short order, much to the surprise of Mr. Churchill. Stalin was very much pleased. Churchill was too, after he had recovered. I'm not going to stay around this terrible place all summer just to listen to speeches. I'll go home to the Senate for that.

DIARY

[Potsdam]
July 20, 1945

Jim Blair now Lt. Col. came in for breakfast.[1] Harry left for Paris & N.Y. Sure hated to see him go. Discussed German situation with Jim. He

1. The Manhattan Project was the wartime code name for the production of nuclear weapons. On July 16, a test device of a plutonium bomb had been exploded from a steel tower near Alamogordo, New Mexico. The plutonium bomb was to be dropped on Nagasaki on August 9; the test of the device on July 16 demonstrated that it was practical. (The bomb dropped at Hiroshima on August 6 was made of uranium, and the scientists were so confident that it would go off that they did not bother to test it; but there was only the possibility of a single uranium bomb—the gaseous diffusion plant at Oak Ridge produced bomb stuff very slowly—and hence the need to test plutonium on July 16.) The President on July 24, after the close of one of the conference sessions, sidled around to Stalin and informed the Russian dictator that the United States had just successfully tested a new weapon of great explosive power, and that he wanted the Soviets to know this fact. Stalin did not appear much impressed, and indeed gave Truman the feeling that he had not quite understood the purport of the revelation. But indeed he had, for when he got back to his quarters, Molotov was heard to say to him, "We'll have to talk it over with Kurchatov and get him to speed things up." *(Memoirs of Marshal Zhukov)* Professor Kurchatov was in charge of the Russian nuclear program, which after a lapse because of the removal of laboratories from Moscow during the war, had quickly resumed. At Potsdam, the President obviously did not know that Russian spies had already penetrated the bomb project and that Stalin would have the bomb "secret" within a few weeks of Alamogordo.

1. James T. Blair, Jr., an old friend, was later governor of Missouri.

had been in command of clean up detail which prepared the area for American occupation, especially for our conference delegation. Said it was the filthiest place imaginable. No sanitary arrangements whatever. Toilets all full and all stopped up. Basements used as outdoor toilets. Said the sewer system evidently hadn't worked for months. Same all over town. Said Germans are sore and sullen. That we would not treat them rough enough. Russians treated 'em too rough and [we] too kindly. Anyway it's a hell of a mess any way it's taken.

Saw Gen. Omar Bradley about taking over the Vets. bureau. Will take over Aug. 15th. Talked to Gen. Eisenhower about government of Germany along same lines as I'd talked to Gen. Clay.[2] Got a concrete program to present.

Raised a flag over our area in Berlin. It is the flag raised in Rome, North Africa and Paris. Flag was on the White House when Pearl Harbor happened. Will be raised over Tokyo.

Uncle Joe looked drawn and tired today and the P.M. seemed lost. I told 'em U.S. had ceased to give away its assets without returns.

DIARY

[Potsdam]
July 25, 1945

We met at 11 A.M. today. That is Stalin, Churchill and the U.S. President. But I had a most important session with Lord Mountbatten & General Marshall before that. We have discovered the most terrible bomb in the history of the world. It may be the fire destruction prophesied in the Euphrates Valley Era, after Noah and his fabulous Ark.

Anyway we "think" we have found the way to cause a disintegration of the atom. An experiment in the New Mexican desert was startling— to put it mildly. Thirteen pounds of the explosive caused the complete disintegration of a steel tower 60 feet high, created a crater 6 feet deep and 1,200 feet in diameter, knocked over a steel tower ½ mile away and knocked men down 10,000 yards away. The explosion was visible for more than 200 miles and audible for 40 miles and more.

This weapon is to be used against Japan between now and August 10th. I have told the Sec. of War, Mr. Stimson, to use it so that military objectives and soldiers and sailors are the target and not women and children. Even if the Japs are savages, ruthless, merciless and fanatic, we

2. General Lucius D. Clay was then deputy to Eisenhower, who was Commander of U.S. Military Forces in Germany; later, Clay became military governor of the American zone.

as the leader of the world for the common welfare cannot drop this terrible bomb on the old capital or the new.[1]

He & I are in accord. The target will be a purely military one and we will issue a warning statement asking the Japs to surrender and save lives. I'm sure they will not do that, but we will have given them the chance. It is certainly a good thing for the world that Hitler's crowd or Stalin's did not discover this atomic bomb. It seems to be the most terrible thing ever discovered, but it can be made the most useful.

At 10:15 I had Gen. Marshall come in and discuss with me the tactical and political situation. He is a level headed man—so is Mountbatten.

At the Conference Poland and the Bolsheviki land grab came up. Russia helped herself to a slice of Poland and gave Poland a nice slice of Germany, taking also a good slice of East Prussia for herself. Poland has moved in up to the Oder and the west Neisse, taking Stettin and Silesia as a fact accomplished. My position is that, according to commitments made at Yalta by my predecessor, Germany was to be divided into four occupation zones, one each for Britain, Russia and France and the U.S. If Russia chooses to allow Poland to occupy a part of her zone I am agreeable but title to territory cannot and will not be settled here. For the fourth time I restated my position and explained that territorial cessions had to be made by treaty and ratified by the Senate.

We discussed reparations and movement of populations from East Germany, Czechoslovakia, Austria, Italy and elsewhere. Churchill said Maisky had so defined war booty as to include the German fleet and Merchant Marine. It was a bomb shell and sort of paralyzed the Russkies, but it has a lot of merit.[2]

D I A R Y

[Potsdam]
July 26, 1945

Last night talked to Gen. Somervell on time for universal military training.[1] Regular Army wants a straight year. I am very sure it cannot be put into effect. Talked to Mr. Caffery[2] about France. He is scared stiff of Communism, the Russian variety which isn't communism at all but

---

1. Kyoto or Tokyo.
2. The former Soviet ambassador to London, Ivan Maisky, had elaborated a definition that pleased the British and the Americans—for war booty was outside the purview of reparations, and the German fleet and merchant marine largely had fallen to the Westerners.

---

1. General Brehon B. Somervell was wartime chief of army service forces.
2. The U.S. ambassador to France, Jefferson Caffery.

just police government pure and simple. A few top hands just take clubs, pistols and concentration camps and rule the people on the lower levels.

The Communist Party in Moscow is no different in its methods and actions toward the common man than were the Czar and the Russian Noblemen (so-called: they were anything but noble). Nazis and Fascists were worse. It seems that Sweden, Norway, Denmark and perhaps Switzerland have the only real people's governments on the Continent of Europe. But the rest are a bad lot, from the standpoint of the people who do not believe in tyranny.

After ten days in Potsdam, Truman was still much taken by the Russian dictator, especially by his directness and sharpness. A dozen years later, the President in retirement recalled in a letter to Dean Acheson (which he did not send) how he had been an innocent at Potsdam, believing that the Soviets desired peace; as for Stalin, he had "liked the little son-of-a-bitch." (See below, pp. 348–349.)

D I A R Y

[Potsdam]
July 30, 1945

Sent Capt. Vardaman to ship at Portsmouth, Eng., to get ready for departure to U.S. some day soon. Secretary of Navy Jas. Forrestal came to breakfast with me and we discussed universal military service after the war and navy policy on officer training etc. Gen. Eisenhower and son were also at breakfast with us. His boy is a nice fellow. Adm. Cochrane[1] and several other naval officers were present.

Conference is delayed. Stalin and Molotov were to call on me yesterday to discuss Polish question and Reparations. Molotov came but no Stalin. Said he is sick. No Big Three meeting yesterday and none today as a result of Stalin's indisposition. Send him a note expressing regret at his illness. Sent Churchill a note of consolation, telling him we regretted his failure to return and wishing him a long and happy life.[2]

If Stalin should suddenly cash in it would end the original Big Three. First Roosevelt by death, then Churchill by political failure and then

---

1. Rear Admiral Edward L. Cochrane, Chief of the Bureau of Ships.

2. Returns from soldier ballots during the British general election were slow in coming, but eventually they revealed that the Conservative party had lost its majority in Parliament, and Churchill was no longer prime minister. The wartime leader of Britain was forced to leave Potsdam in the middle of the conference, and his place was taken by the leader of the Labor party, Clement Attlee.

Stalin. I am wondering what would happen to Russia and Central Europe if Joe suddenly passed out. If some demagogue on horseback gained control of the efficient Russian military machine he could play havoc with European peace for a while. I also wonder if there is a man with the necessary strength and following to step into Stalin's place and maintain peace and solidarity at home. It isn't customary for dictators to train leaders to follow them in power. I've seen no one at this Conference in the Russian line-up who can do the job. Molotov is not able to do it. He lacks sincerity. Vishinsky[3] same thing and Maisky is short on honesty. Well, we shall see what we shall see. Uncle Joe's pretty tough mentally and physically but there is an end to every man and we can't help but speculate.

We are at an impasse on Poland and its western boundary and on Reparations. Russia and Poland have agreed on the Oder and West Neisse to the Czechoslovakian border. Just a unilateral arrangement without so much as a by your leave. I don't like it. Roosevelt let Maisky mention twenty billions as reparations—half for Russia and half for everybody else. Experts say no such figure is available.

I've made it plain that the United States of America does not intend to pay reparations this time. I want the German war industry machine completely dismantled and [as] far as U.S. is concerned the other allies can divide it up on any basis they choose. Food and other necessities we send into the restored countries and Germany must be first lien on exports before reparations. If Russians strip country and carry off population of course there'll be no reparations.[4]

I have offered a waterway program and a suggestion for free intercourse between Central European nations which will help keep future peace. Our only hope for good from the European War is restored prosperity to Europe and future trade with them. It is a sick situation at best.[5]

The Potsdam Conference did not prove decisive of anything in particular, as the conferees tended to agree to spheres of interest in Europe

---

3. Andrei Y. Vishinsky, deputy minister of foreign affairs.

4. After the First World War, American bankers lent money to Germany so the Germans could pay reparations to the Allies, who then paid their war debts to the United States—a circular exercise in which the Americans eventually lost when the Germans defaulted on reparations and the Allies refused to pay the war debts. Actually, the Americans lost twice, for the U.S. Treasury had floated bonds to lend money to the Allies.

5. The President attempted to persuade the British and the Russians that the best hope for world peace would be freedom of the world's major waterways, such as the Rhine-Danube, the Kiel, Suez, and Panama Canals, the Bosporus, etc. The proposal met with complete Russian disinterest, and not much British favor (one of the great advantages of the British Empire had been control of the world's narrow shipping lanes).

congruent with the areas their troops occupied on V-E Day. Decisions of detail were for the most part passed to future meetings of the foreign ministers of the Big Three, known thereafter as the Council of Foreign Ministers, an uneasy solution because of the inability of Foreign Minister Molotov to agree to anything without first telephoning Stalin in the Kremlin.

The Conference ended on August 2, and Truman flew the same day to England, where he boarded the Augusta *at Plymouth.*

DIARY

U.S.S. Augusta
August 5, 1945

Well we've been away from Berlin since 8 o'clock the morning of Aug. 2 and I am very sure no one wants to go back to that awful city.

Had lunch with Britain's King George VI. He is a very pleasant and surprising person. We had a short interview just before luncheon on the Renown in the King's cabin. He was very much interested in what had taken place at the Conference and in our new terrific explosion. He showed me a sword which had been presented to Sir Francis Drake by Queen Elizabeth. It was a powerful weapon, but the King said it was not properly balanced.

We had a nice and appetizing lunch—soup, fish, lamb chops, peas, potatoes and ice cream with chocolate sauce. The King, myself, Lord Halifax, a British Admiral, Adm. Leahy, Lascelles, the Secretary of State in that order around the table.[1] Talked of most everything, and nothing much. Before lunch I inspected a guard of honor and complimented the British Band on the manner in which it had played the National Anthem of U.S. There was much formality etc. in getting on and off the British Ship.

As soon as we returned to the Augusta, the King returned the call and we put on the formalities. He inspected the guard, looked over the sailors, took a snort of Haig & Haig, signed the ship's guest book, collected an autograph for each of his daughters and the Queen and, after some more formalities, went back for his ship. We've been crossing the Atlantic ever since at the rate of 645 miles every 24 hours.

On August 6, during the westward crossing, the first atomic bomb exploded over Hiroshima. Word almost immediately was sent to the

---

1. Lord Halifax was British ambassador to Washington; Sir Alan Lascelles, private secretary to the king. The British admiral is unidentified.

company aboard the U.S.S. Augusta, *and Truman enthusiastically announced the news. The ship reached port on August 9, the day of the
second atomic explosion, over Nagasaki. Next morning the President
was up early at the White House—anticipating news of the Japanese
willingness to surrender, which came later that day.*

DIARY

August 10, 1945

Up at six and ready for business. Saw Snyder, Ross, Rosenman, Connelly, Vaughan, Hassett, Vardaman, Ayers[1] at the usual 9 A.M. conference. Nothing unusual to discuss.

Snyder had met us at Norfolk on Tuesday evening when we returned
from Berlin and had discussed certain bad situations developing between War Pro. Bd. and Of. Pr. Adm. At 9:30 got Krug in and gave him
a job on reconversion, making the W.P.B. the Reconversion Board, and
then called in Bowles and made peace between them.[2]

At 10:15 had the scientists, Bush and Conant and Geo. L. Harrison,
Gen. Groves, Secs. State, War and Navy in to discuss the Atomic Bomb
and how much could be published about it. A very interesting meeting.
Ordered a press release for Sunday, covering its main features because
so many fake scientists were telling crazy tales about it.[3]

Senator Tom Connally came in to urge the appointment of his friend
as a Federal Judge for one of the Texas Districts and to give me his
opinion of Pappy O'Daniel. He considers Pappy rather small potatoes.
Tom was also interested in a hospital at Marlin to be built by the navy.
He called me later in the week to tell me I was making a mistake in
appointing Dugout Doug as Allied Commander in Chief to accept the Jap
surrender. Said Doug would run against me in 1948 if I built him up. I
told Tom I didn't want to run in '48 and that Doug didn't bother me that
way.

Barkley tells a story about Tom Heflin running for reelection to Congress in an Alabama District when he and Barkley were in the House of

1. Eben A. Ayers, assistant press secretary.
2. Julius A. Krug, head of the War Production Board, later secretary of commerce, was
engaged in internecine war with Chester Bowles, head of the Office of Price Administration,
over the speed with which price controls might be lifted after the end of hostilities. The
arrangement of the moment did not last, and Bowles eventually left the administration.
3. Vannevar Bush, science adviser to the President; James B. Conant, president of Harvard
University and adviser to the Manhattan Project; George L. Harrison, president of the New
York Life Insurance Company and deputy head of the so-called Interim Committee, appointed
by Truman in April to examine the issue of dropping a nuclear bomb on the Japanese; Major
General Leslie R. Groves, head of the Manhattan Project.

Representatives. Barkley said the House was having a night session on the last day for filing in Heflin's District and that about 11:30 old Tom began calling his secretary at Montgomery to see if a certain man in his district had filed against him. He'd call about every ten minutes and the conversation at Tom's end would go something like this: "Hello, is that you Jim? Did he file? You say he did or he didn't? Oh! he has not filed yet. Goodbye." At one minute after midnight the same conversation took place and Tom was finally assured by his secretary that the other fellow had not filed. Tom had carried on his conversation in the cloak room and a dozen members had heard each phone conversation. After the last one at 12:01 when old Tom was sure his supposed opponent had not filed and couldn't file he turned around to his audience and said "I wish the so and so had filed—I'd have beaten hell out of him!"

Sen. Dennis Chavez came in to recommend a Maj. Gen. in the Marine Corps for Gov. of Puerto Rico and to make a date for a committee of Italians to see me to talk about Italy. I succeeded in getting him to cut the number to one and I agreed to see Dennis and the one on Monday.

Cong. Mike Mansfield came in to ask for a trip to China. He was once a resident over there and seems to know a great deal about the country. I postponed decision on it. Sen. Hayden of Ariz. came in and gave me some excellent and practical ideas on the Philippines and their recovery from the war. Col. Heller & Mr. Hurley came in to resign from the Surplus Property Board and I persuaded them to stay.[4] Sen. Magnuson talked to me about a road to Alaska through British Columbia and his bill on scientific research. Had a nice visit. Sen. O'Mahoney made a recommendation of a man for District of Columbia Court of Appeals and told me how to run the country generally.

Various Ambassadors & a Minister presented credentials and then the Sec. Labor came in. We reorganized and set up a real Labor Department and that's what we intend to do. Schwellenbach is a real guy and will make me a wheel horse on the team.

Minton came to see me about an appointment to the Supreme Court.

Ate lunch at my desk and discussed the Jap offer to surrender which came in a couple of hours earlier. They wanted to make a condition precedent to the surrender. Our terms are "unconditional." They wanted to keep the Emperor. We told 'em we'd tell 'em how to keep him, but we'd make the terms.

Had a Cabinet meeting after lunch which was a very satisfactory

---

4. Edward H. Heller and Robert A. Hurley, members of the three-person board, the chairman of which was former Senator Guy M. Gillette of Iowa.

one. Getting a team together. Took them into my confidence and told them all about the Jap situation. They kept the confidence! An unprecedented thing in the immediate past.

While all this has been going on I've been trying to get ready a radio address to the nation on the Berlin Conference. Made the first draft on the ship coming back. Discussed it with Byrnes, Rosenman, Ben Cohen,[5] Leahy and Charlie Ross. Rewrote it four times and then the Japs offered to surrender and it had to be done again. As first put up it contained 4,500 words and a thousand had to be taken out. It caused me a week of headaches but finally seemed to go over all right when it was said over the radio at 10 P.M. tonight.

DIARY

August 11, 1945

Well the speech seems to have made a hit according to all the papers. Shows you never can tell. I thought it was rotten. We are all on edge waiting for the Japs to answer. Have had a hell of a day. Saw Archbishop Spellman—Cardinal Archbishop.

Japan surrendered on August 14; a formal ceremony of surrender on September 2 occurred aboard the battleship Missouri *in Tokyo Bay.*

TO MARTHA ELLEN AND MARY JANE TRUMAN

August 17, 1945

Dear Mamma & Mary:

I have been trying to write you every day for three or four days but things have been in such a dizzy whirl here I couldn't do anything but get in the center and try to stop it. Japan finally quit and then I had to issue orders so fast that several mistakes were made and then other orders had to be issued. Everybody has been going at a terrific gait but I believe we are up with the parade now. From now on however it is going to be political maneuvers that I have to watch.

Hope you all haven't been bombarded too much in the last few days. Had a press conference yesterday and Miss Gentry from the Independence Examiner was admitted. She'd never seen one before. I suppose she'll tell the home folks all about it.

---

5. Benjamin V. Cohen, counselor of the State Department.

I guess you'll have the Star meeting now, but don't let them fool you. They've never been right except for a very few.

I hope I haven't overlooked answering some question you've asked. I left your last two letters on my desk in the office. I'm writing this from the oval room in the White House.

I'm enclosing an editorial from the Baltimore Sun which is one of the nicest I've seen. It is usually very critical.

Love to you both.

Harry

I sent you a package with a luncheon set in it for mamma and a watch for Martha Ann and some handkerchiefs for Luella. I sent Gilbert the pen which I used to sign the Berlin Protocol and communique. The pen was also used by Stalin & Attlee. It is quite a pen.

Correspondence between the President and Eleanor Roosevelt was considerable, during and after the presidency, for whatever program or cause or idea Mrs. Roosevelt championed, she did not hesitate to go right to the top in search of a solution.

TO ELEANOR ROOSEVELT

September 1, 1945

Dear Mrs. Roosevelt:

I have just returned to the White House study from the executive office. The first thing I always do is look at the Scripps-Howard News and read the editorial page and your column. Today you've really "hit the jackpot"—if I may say that to the First Lady.

I am asking one of my good Senatorial friends to put it in the Congressional Record on Tuesday for the sake of history. I only turned the reports loose because I was very reliably informed that the sabotage press had paid a very large price for them in order to release them on V.J. Day. It is my opinion that they'll be a nine days cause for conversation and be forgotten in victory.

I see red every time this same press starts a ghoulish attack on the President (I never think of anyone as the President but Mr. Roosevelt).

My very best regards and greatest respect I am

Sincerely,
Harry S. Truman

APPOINTMENT SHEET

September 5, 1945

9:45 [Alabama delegation] About Hobbs for Judge D.C. Court of Appeals. I said No but sorry etc.

10:00 [Senators McKellar, Barkley, Speaker Rayburn] Congressional Policy. Pearl Harbor etc. Message and other things.

11:00 [Frank S. Land] Mostly personal and pictures.

11:15 [Herman B. Baruch, banker] Flatterer. Wants to be ambassador to France. Conniver like his Brother.[1]

11:30 [Associate Justice Jackson] Made a great contribution to International Law. One good man.

12:00 [Secretary of War Stimson] Told me he is quitting on account of physical condition. Hate to see him go.

12:15 [Harry L. Hopkins] Surprised him. Took him out in the yard to see the ceremony & pinned one on him.

12:30 [Distinguished Service Medal to Hopkins, Howard Bruce, director of matériel, army service forces] A nice ceremony.

1:00 [Lunch] With the Paul Hendersons. He's a great admirer of Calvin Coolidge.

2:30 [Nick Schenck, Basil O'Connor] Advertising for O'Connor. Mostly bunk. Gave me a blank check.[2]

3:00 [Roosevelt National Memorial Committee] Same bunch of Prima Donnas who helped drive the Boss to his grave are still riding his ghost.

In autumn 1945, Truman began to come under intense pressure from American and European Zionists, who wanted what then was known as Palestine opened wide to Jewish immigration. The issue was of course vastly complicated. After the First World War, the British government, by virtue of having expelled the Turks from Jerusalem, received a mandate for the area from the League of Nations, and thereafter, especially during the 1930s, found itself embroiled with the Zionists and the Arabs. The intense pressure on the British to allow Jewish immigration during the 1930s, because of the Hitler government's persecutions in Germany, led to a confrontation with the Arabs

---

1. Bernard M. Baruch

2. Nicholas M. Schenck, the moving picture magnate; Basil O'Connor, former law partner of Franklin D. Roosevelt, president of a foundation to combat infantile paralysis.

and the publication in 1939 of a so-called White Paper, a formal cabinet statement of policy, that established a set number for immigrants during the following years. The seething cauldron was barely prevented from boiling over during the period 1939–1945 because of the presence of large numbers of Allied troops, British and American, in the Middle East. At the end of the war the issue arose again and quickly moved toward crisis. The Arabs told the British—indeed, King Ibn Saud said this in so many words to President Roosevelt immediately after Yalta, when the king and the President met aboard the U.S.S. Quincy on the Great Bitter Lake in Egypt—that Hitler had persecuted the Jews, and the Arabs had not committed Hitler's crimes, and therefore it was up to the Germans to take care of the homeless Jews. However, many of Europe's remaining Jews, languishing in displaced persons camps, wanted to go to Palestine, the homeland from which the Romans had expelled the Jews two thousand years before. The British government, because of Arab pressure, was exceedingly wary of trying to accommodate them, and President Truman found himself in the embarrassing position of desiring to help the Jews but having to appeal to the beleaguered British government, a close ally in the recent war.

The first meeting of the United Nations was held in London, and friends with programs tried to get at Truman through his mother and sister.

TO MARTHA ELLEN AND MARY JANE TRUMAN

September 11, 1945

Dear Mamma & Mary:

Received your letter with the enclosures. Tell Mrs. Haire that there isn't a possibility of my intervening in the matter her friend wrote her about. These people are the usual European conspirators and they try to approach the President from every angle.

The London Conference is for a specific and agreed purpose and if the little country referred to is in any way involved it will have its day in court, but the call will come from the State Department and through regular channels. Don't ever let anybody talk to you about foreign affairs. It is a most touchy subject and especially in that part of the world. Wish I could accommodate every friend I have in every way they'd like—but I'm in such a position now that I can't do as I please myself. They'll have to bear with me as best I can.

We'll look into the old lady's vet. problem—but I suspect everybody now who tries to approach me by appealing to the family. I've made things easy for a front door approach especially if they are in Baltimore or Virginia.

Folks in Jackson County and Mo. friends have a right to talk to you and I'll listen of course if they have a case. But don't worry about those things, they'll get worse instead of better.

I'll be home Saturday and see you all. I'm leaving here at 1:30 P.M. Friday and stopping in Paducah, Kentucky, to unload Sen. Barkley and in Belleville, Ill., to leave Reathel to see her mother and should be home about six P.M. Will call you as soon as I arrive. Hope I can have a nice visit. Have to come back Sunday.

Love to you both.

Harry

APPOINTMENT SHEET

September 18, 1945

9:15   [Representative Clarence Cannon (Missouri)] Discussed Nurse Training and appropriations generally. Tried to convince them (there were two) that orderly approach is best.

10:00 [Senator Francis J. Myers (Pennsylvania)] Wanted something— I've forgot what—but he received it.

10:15 [Senators Guy Cordon and Wayne Morse (both of Oregon), William F. Knowland (California)] Wanted Judge Edmonds, Calif. Su. Court, on U.S. S. Court.

10:30 [Joshua B. Lee, former senator from Alabama] Talked about policy, foreign & domestic Air.

10:45 [Mrs. Harry B. Hawes, wife of former senator] Wants me to come to Stratford May 25.

11:00 [William Randolph Hearst, Jr.] Told me what papa thought. Explained, diplomatically, I didn't give a damn.

.   .   .   .

DIARY

September 20, 1945

This has been a very busy and trying week. After returning from Missouri via Paducah, Ky., where Sen. Alben Barkley and Cong. Gregory were taken aboard the Sacred Cow, much study was given pending problems.[1] There were several thousand people at the airport in Paducah, all of whom wanted to see Jumbo, the Cardiff Giant, the President of the

---

1. The *Sacred Cow* had been President Roosevelt's private plane.

United States. It is a most amazing spectacle, this worship of high office. Barkley told me on Friday, when we landed in the rain at his home town (Paducah), that I shouldn't be puffed up—the people always met him that way. But he was late at the airport on Sunday, a very beautiful sunny, cool day and there were more people than on Friday. He said that he could not understand it. Never said they always saw him off that way! He brought his dear old mother (87 yrs old) down to see me. She is a lovely old lady—just like gramma. She thinks Alben is about the zenith of everything just as mamma thinks of me—and she's right as can be.

Cong. Gregory's lovely wife and beautiful daughter were at the airport to see him off. They were invited to go aboard the Cow and see how Mr. Gregory would be placed on his way to Washington. He looks like "Mr. Smith" (Smith goes to Washington).

Katie Mize Accola, an Independence lady, whom we took back with us for an Independence week end visit, made a hit with Gregory by telling him how lovely his beautiful daughter is—and she is!

We arrived in the Capital City at 7:45 P.M., E.S.T., and Alben and I had our pictures taken, as is usual when notorious persons leave or arrive in cities.

Went to the taxpayers' house at 16th & Pennsylvania Ave. and spent a very pleasant night in sleep.

Got up Monday and spent the morning seeing various persons. Told my staff that the whole labor setup would be transferred to the Secretary of Labor and stated that a Justice of the Supreme Court, a Sec. of War, a Director of the Surplus Property Disposal Authority would be announced tomorrow (Tuesday) at 4 P.M.

Created some excitement in my immediate staff.

Every morning at 9 A.M.. I have a conference with John Snyder, head of the Office of Reconversion, Sam Rosenman, Special Counsel, Matt Connelly, Appointments Secretary, Charlie Ross, Press Secretary, Mr. Ayers, his assistant, Bill Hassett, Secretary for correspondence, Harry H. Vaughan, Brig. Gen. and military aide, and J. K. Vardaman, Commodore and Naval Aide, Judge Latta, who looks after documents for me.[2]

Well, when I told this bunch that I was transferring all Labor things to Schwellenbach, the Secretary of Labor, there was consternation—but I did it.

It is almost impossible to get action around here, even from the most loyal of the close-in helpers. It is just a natural reluctance to agree to any sort of change and a fear that something will be done to spoil the Era of Good Feeling which is now on.

---

2. Maurice J. Latta had been working at the White House since 1898 and was Truman's executive clerk from the beginning of the administration until his death on April 3, 1948.

Like every "new rich," and person who comes into power suddenly, "Labor" has gone off the beam. The job now is to bring them back. And it is going to take guts to do it. Well this terrible job was virtually crammed down my throat at Chicago and I'm going to do [it] in the interest and welfare of all the people. No pressure group need apply. I believe in this Republic and I also believe in a strong two party system. France went out with multiple pressure groups as did Italy & Germany.

There should be a real liberal party in this country and I don't mean a crackpot professional liberal one. The opposition should join together then in real opposition. Taft, Peter Geary, Walter George, the Chamber of Commerce, the Cartel boys all should be in the opposition. . . .[3]

APPOINTMENT SHEET

September 21, 1945

10:30   [Representative Albert Gore (Tennessee)] Gave me a present of old Jack Daniels.

10:45   [Senator Wheeler (Montana)] Discussed P.M. [postmaster] in Butte, Federal Trade Com. etc.

11:00   [Max Lowenthal, counsel to the Truman Committee] Worried about demobilization.

11:15   [Representative Pat Cannon (Florida)] Hurricane damage.

11:30   [Charles Harwood, governor of the Virgin Islands] Wants another job. Talked of Sec.

11:45   [David Sholtz, former governor of Florida] Promoting International Fair.

12:00   [Hubert and Mrs. Humphrey, Arthur Naftalin, E. M. Kirkpatrick] Politics. Quote me on Shipstead.[1]

12:15   [Group of women sponsoring Equal Rights Amendment] A lot of hooey about equal rights.

12:30   [Maycie K. Southall, Harriet A. Houdlette, Lelia Massey, professional educators] Gave me a great song & dance on education.

12:45   [Dorothy K. Roosevelt, Diana Roosevelt] Just came in. Don't know why.

. . . .

---

3. Taft, Geary, and George were conservative senators.

1. Humphrey was then mayor of Minneapolis, Naftalin his secretary, Kirkpatrick associate professor of political science at the University of Minnesota. Their senator, Henrik Shipstead, was one of two senators (the other was William Langer of North Dakota) to vote against the United Nations Charter.

TO MARTHA ELLEN AND MARY JANE TRUMAN

September 22, 1945

Dear Mamma & Mary:

It was nice to get your St. Louis letter. Glad you had a nice time. Sorry I didn't get to see more of you but you had to go. Hope the dress turns out all right and I'm sure it will.

We have been going through the usual Merry-go-Round here. Everybody wants something at the expense of everybody else and nobody thinks much of the other fellow. It's funny but I have almost as many prima donnas around me as Roosevelt had but they are still new at it. They don't get humored as much by me as they did by him. I fire one occasionally and it has a salutary effect.

I'm going down to Jefferson Island today to spend the week-end, and talk to a lot of Congressmen and Senators. It won't be a very pleasant time but it may be helpful.

Hope you are both well and getting along all right. I wish I could come home every week-end but I can't.

Take care of yourselves. Write when you can. Love to you both.

Harry S. T.

APPOINTMENT SHEET

September 26, 1945

11:30   [Ely Culbertson, bridge player] Has a way to save the world, but I doubt its efficacy.

11:45   [Chester Gray, a farmers' association representative] An old baloney peddler.

. . . .

TO MARTHA ELLEN AND MARY JANE TRUMAN

October 13, 1945

Dear Mamma & Mary:

Well I am up at six this morning and am hoping I may get in a long overdue letter to you. Had intended to write you before leaving for Caruthersville but failed to get it in. The pressure here is becoming so great I can hardly get my meals in, let alone do what I want to do.

Glad you sold the car. Will have the title to the coupe put in my name and then you can drive it. It may as well be in good use and it is in good condition. Keep 35 pounds of air in the tires and have it greased once in a while and have the oil changed every thousand miles.

I am enclosing a note for the good Doctor. Tell him that I am not in a position to do things like this now. I wish I could go back to the Senate again and then I could do something for my friends. As I told you I'm simply the center of things in government and there isn't any possibility of knowing what happens everywhere.

We had a nice time at the Fair if you can call it a nice time to be followed around by 30 news men and photographers everywhere and to be mobbed every time an appearance is made. When I finally managed to get into the Judge's stand on the race track I did get to look around and see a race or two. We went to the Baptist Church as usual. The preacher of that church has been my friend all the time and I have always gone there at Fair time.

We went from the Fair over to Reelfoot Lake where we were lodged in a beautiful house—but I may as well have been in the center of Chicago so far as rest was concerned. They brought in school children from every school in forty miles, the Legion, the State Police force and all the State and County officials for ten counties around to see whether a President walked and talked and ate and slept as other folks do—but it was a change of scenery anyway. They were all good people.

Went on over to Kentucky Dam some twenty miles from Paducah where I spoke again to about 3 or 4 acres of people—15 or 20 thousand I guess. At Blythesville, Arkansas, where we landed for the Fair, the streets were lined as they were in Caruthersville and Paducah. I had to ride in an open car and give 'em a chessie cat grin and almost freeze stiff but the onlookers seemed to enjoy it. If you'd been there I would probably have only had a glimpse of you.

A high-brow preacher from N.Y. has been annoying us. He's a Congressman, a smart aleck and a rabble rouser. He got nowhere.[1] Hope you are both well and happy. Can't go to any O.E.S. meetings now—will tell you why when I see you. Love to you both.

Harry

---

1. Congressman Adam Clayton Powell, Jr., had criticized Mrs. Truman for attending a D.A.R. meeting. Although he was a firm believer in equal rights (the D.A.R. refused to let blacks perform in Constitution Hall, which it owned), the President did not take kindly to criticism of his family.

APPOINTMENT SHEET

October 15, 1945

10:00   [Senator Lister Hill (Alabama)] About Unified Command in Army
        & Navy.
10:15   [Congressman Vito Marcantonio (New York)] An ax to grind for
        Italy. N.Y. Politics.
10:30   [Congressman Samuel Dickstein (New York)] An ax to grind for
        some Jews.
10:45   [Harry Carlson, U.S. consul in Stockholm] Wants to go to Quebec
        or Europe.
11:00   [Group of miscellaneous individuals] Just for picture & advertis-
        ing purposes.
11:15   [Armed services bandleaders] Had a good discussion of music &
        what I like.
11:30   [Basil Manly, economist, adviser to wartime government] To say
        goodbye.
11:45   [Alden Hatch] Writing a biography of Roosevelt.
12:00   [Secretary of Labor and members of the War Labor Board] Dis-
        cussed the advisability of a new board etc.
12:30   [Secretary of Commerce] Discussed the leak at the Cabinet meet-
        ing.

. . . .

*The Universal Military Training bill had almost no hope of passing
Congress, given the intensely antimilitary feelings of most Americans
who served in the armed forces during the war; these men were willing
to fight again if it really was necessary, but they did not want the country to adopt a permanent requirement for military service. Truman
understood their feelings, but he also saw it as his duty to push programs
he believed were good for the country, whatever the political prospects.*

TO MARTHA ELLEN AND MARY JANE TRUMAN

October 23, 1945

Dear Mamma & Mary:

   It is 10:40 and I have been listening to a rebroadcast of my address
to Congress on military training. When I listen I don't know why they
applauded—except maybe because I am the President of the United

States and they probably wanted to be respectful. But in spite of that we need the program which the President urged them to adopt. Hope you heard the address. Some said it was good and of course some didn't like it but that is always so.

I hope you have a nice party Thursday. Wish I could be there—but I can't. No more can I do what I wish or what I could do as a road overseer, as a County Judge, as a United States Senator—or even as the Vice President of the United States—although I couldn't do as much as I pleased as V.P. I also wish I could come to the meeting in St. Louis—but I can't. And now I'm going to tell you I don't believe I'll get to Kansas City on the 15th of Nov. or to Okla. on the 18th. In fact I am going to have to cancel all my dates for every place until I get things going here.

The Congress are balking, labor has gone crazy and management isn't far from insane in selfishness. My Cabinet, that is some of them, have Potomac fever.[1] There are more Prima Donnas per square foot in public life here in Washington than in all the opera companies ever to exist.

Don't say anything about these things because if you do there'd be headlines from Boston to Los Angeles. But they are all true. Also don't say I'm not coming to Missouri, for things may straighten out so I could be there for one day. As it looks now though I won't go anywhere.

Wish you all would be careful about catching cold. First thing you know you'll be down in bed. Margie and Bess are well and so am I thank goodness.

Love to you both.

                                                                    Harry

The two daughters of his Aunt Margaret Ellen (Aunt Ella) Noland, Nellie, an elementary school principal, and Ethel, a seventh grade teacher, were the President's ardent supporters and lifelong friends. During his high school years he and the then Bess Wallace studied Latin with Cousin Nellie, who was an expert Latinist. After high school he went to Kansas City to work in a bank, and upon the death of her father, Bess and her mother moved to her grandmother's house at 219 North Delaware. The Truman-Wallace courtship lapsed. Meanwhile the Nolands had moved to 216 North Delaware, an old-fashioned little Victorian house, virtually across the street from Bess. After four years in Kansas City, Harry went back to the farm near Grandview. One day he

---

1. A dread disease that, Truman said, affected the head, swelling it to abnormal proportions, in anticipation of larger personal reputation. The disease was a local malady, catchable only in the vicinity of Washington, D.C.

visited his aunt and cousins and learned that Mrs. Wallace, Bess's mother, had sent over a cake and the plate needed to be returned. According to daughter Margaret, Harry snatched up the plate with something approaching the speed of light and took it across the street. Bess answered the door, and the courtship was on again.

TO NELLIE NOLAND

November 11, 1945

Dear Nellie:

I just couldn't resist the urge to send you this. Too bad we didn't know about it some years ago![1]

Hope you and Ethel and Aunt Ella are in good health. This is one of those new "last forever" pens—not, as you thought, an indelible pencil.[2]

Mr. Attlee came yesterday and we had a brilliant—most brilliant I'd say—State dinner for him and Mackenzie King of Canada.[3] There were 52 at the table and all the pomp and circumstance you read about. It was more satisfactory than the others we've had because the President could talk to the guests of honor with some chance of being understood. On the visit of the President of Chile and De Gaulle it was a case of one sentence at a time to an interpreter and by the time I'd arrive at the thought I'd wanted to express I'd forgot what was to be said and gone off on a tangent maybe. The Regent of Iraq could speak English and was a personable young man. He and the President of Chile and De Gaulle left us considerable loot in the form of jewelry, silverware etc. I usually only get a picture in a silver frame autographed in a language I can't understand and Margie & Bess get the pretty things.

I have autographed pictures, personally presented, from George VI, Stalin, Churchill, Attlee, De Gaulle, Pres. Rios (Chile), Chiang Kai-

1. The President liked to josh Nellie and her sister, Ethel, who was the family genealogist, about all sorts of claims by would-be relatives, newly discovered after April 12, 1945.

2. The ballpoint pen, invented by an ingenious Argentinian, "came in" right after the war, and for a while it was a great curiosity. (ED. NOTE: My father bought two of them, at $18 apiece.)

3. Attlee and Mackenzie King came to Washington out of intense concern for postwar arrangements over sharing of nuclear secrets. This was an uneasy subject, for any postwar deal would have to be made in public view and probably with congressional assent. Moreover, as the Gouzenko case already had shown (and other security breaches were to show), the Russians had obtained atomic secrets through British and Canadian intermediaries; British-Canadian security left a good deal to be desired. The Washington talks in November 1945 did not accomplish much. (Over the years the repercussions of the sharing problem were very serious: the British undertook their own nuclear program at the same time that they were forced to apply for an American loan in 1946 and Marshall Plan aid in 1947, and when in 1962 they obtained an agreement to construct Polaris submarines, they infuriated the French, who went ahead with their own nuclear program and excluded the British for a decade and more from the Common Market.)

shek (presented by Mrs. Chiang), and Dr. Kung, finance minister of
China.

Didn't intend to bore you so much but I'm waiting for the British &
Canadian P.M.'s to go put a wreath on the Unknown Soldier's tomb so I
just rambled on.

Love to all of you.

Harry

*The revolutionary situation in China came into public view in late
November 1945, when Ambassador Patrick J. Hurley, home on leave,
went before the National Press Club and wound himself up and said
things he never should have said—such as that he had been undercut by
his subordinates, the career foreign service men who spoke Chinese, who
either (said Pat) were Communists or under Communist influence and
hence reported to the State Department that Chiang Kai-shek's case was
hopeless and the future belonged to the Communists under Mao Tse-
tung. Truman was no enthusiastic supporter of Chiang, but at that
moment he saw no alternative. Nor did Stalin, who had made a treaty
with the Nationalists in August 1945, confirming the allotment to the
Soviets of special rights in Manchuria as decided at the Yalta Conference. When Hurley resigned after his stirring commentary, and sent the
President a muddled several-page letter repeating his charges, there was
consternation in the White House, and a decision to ask General Marshall to go to China to mediate between the antagonists, Chiang and
Mao.*

MEMORANDUM

November 1945

Chinese set up:

We should make it plain that we are mopping up the war with Japan.
That there are more than 1,000,000 Jap soldiers in central China. That
Russia, Britain & U.S. have recognized the Central Gov't under Chiang
Kai-shek. That Stalin says the Ch. Commies are not. We are merely wind-
ing up the war.

That Chiang's gov't fought side by side with us against our common
enemy, that we have reason to believe that the so-called Commies in
China not only did not help us but on occasion helped the Japs.

We are not mixing in China's internal affairs.

On many occasions, public and private, the President testified both by word and by deed to his love match with "Miss Lizzie," as he sometimes called her—Elizabeth W. (Bess) Truman, his wife. Perhaps the ties between them were so close because both of them were strong characters and did not hesitate to let each other know how they felt about this and that. Mrs. Truman disliked the pace of Washington social life, and on more than one occasion she found an excuse to return to the spacious old house at 219 North Delaware, which her mother still owned, while her husband frantically was seeing "customers" in the executive offices of the White House and performing the social duties of his office. But the lonely life in Independence sometimes got to Bess, and when the President dashed out to Independence for Christmas 1945, staying only one night, he found his wife in not the best mood. The following letter was discovered in the President's desk after his death twenty-seven years later. Apparently he never had sent it.

TO BESS W. TRUMAN

December 28, 1945

Dear Bess:

Well I'm here in the White House, the great white sepulcher of ambitions and reputations. I feel like a last year's bird's nest which is on its second year. Not very often I admit I am not in shape. I think maybe that exasperates you too, as a lot of other things I do and pretend to do exasperate you. But it isn't intended for that purpose.

When you told me I might as well have stayed in Washington so far as you were concerned I gave up, cussed [Sen.] Vandenberg, told the Secretary of Agriculture to give all the damned cotton away for all I cared and then smiled over the phone at Henry Wallace and I'm afraid hurt Adm. Leahy's feelings by not asking him to go on the boat. At least Matt [Connelly] said I did and I called the old admiral up and asked him to go. . . .

You can never appreciate what it means to come home as I did the other evening after doing at least 100 things I didn't want to do and have the only person in the world whose approval and good opinion I value look at me like I'm something the cat dragged in and tell me I've come in at last because I couldn't find any reason to stay away. I wonder why we are made so that what we really think and feel we cover up?

This head of mine should have been bigger and better proportioned. There ought to have been more brain and a larger bump of ego or something to give me an idea that there can be a No. 1 man in the world. I didn't want to be. But, in spite of opinions to the contrary, Life & Time say I am.

If that is the case you, Margie and every one else who may have any influence on my actions must give me help and assistance; because no one ever needed help and assistance as I do now. If I can get the use of the best brains in the country and a little bit of help from those I have on a pedestal at home the job will be done. If I can't, no harm will be done because the country will know that Shoop, the Post Dispatch, Hearst, Cissy and Patterson were right.

Kiss my baby and I love you in season & out.

Harry

1946

Internationally, in relations with the Soviet Union, the year marked a downward drift, perhaps a plunge. Symptomatic of this trouble was the famous speech of Winston Churchill in Fulton, Missouri, on March 5, 1946—the famous "iron curtain" speech. On March 3, Truman and Churchill left Washington by train for Fulton, the locale of Westminster College, from which the former prime minister was to receive an honorary degree. There, in the tiny Middle Western town, Churchill delivered an address that produced a dreadful outcry from many Americans, who did not want to get into a conflict with Russia. Stalin defined it as a virtual declaration of war. The President was supportive of Churchill, to be sure. And he was not surprised by the situation—what the writer Walter Lippmann, taking a cue from a speech by Bernard M. Baruch in South Carolina, was soon to begin describing as the cold war. By this time Truman had become well acquainted with the deterioration of Soviet-American relations during the last months of the Roosevelt administration, and also had had firsthand experience with Russians at Potsdam.

Some weeks before the Churchill speech a crisis had arisen over Soviet behavior in Iran, and the President had passed the trouble to the United Nations with strong advice that the U.N. get the Russians out. The Soviets had been in Iran since early in the Second World War, when they had occupied the country together with the British to prevent German occupation, and during the war the Americans had used Iran as a supply route to the Soviet Union. At the end of the conflict the time came for the occupying powers to leave, but the Russians refused to depart, preferring to establish a puppet regime in the northernmost Iranian province, Azerbaijan. Truman felt keenly about the situation, and in addition to his public action in the U.N. seems to have pushed hard in a private way—years later he claimed to have told Stalin in one-syllable words to get out. On April 3 the Soviets announced that their troops would withdraw from Iran on May 6, and the troops duly departed.

The major domestic problems during the year were economic. During the war the economy had been under tight rationing, and inflation thus had been controlled. With the end of hostilities the lid came off public expectations; it proved impossible to keep the controls until the economy could shift into peacetime production and crank out the goods that people wanted to buy with the dollars they hitherto could not spend. The President tried in vain to hold the line, and was reduced to delaying actions, all the while trying to instill public spirit into labor leaders and industrialists to prevent them from raising wages and prices unduly. He lost his usual good humor, and became quite bitter, though he managed to hide his wrath from public view.

The cabinet continued to be a source of dissension, and there were three more changes. Chief Justice Harlan Stone died in April 1946, and Truman replaced him with Fred Vinson, a sage politico unlikely to engage in obiter dicta from the supreme bench. Vinson had been secretary of the treasury, and to this key spot Truman moved his old friend John W. Snyder, whom he had known as a fellow army reservist since the First World War. But the largest cabinet problems in 1946 occurred over the resignations, both of them forced, of Secretary of the Interior Ickes, replaced by Julius A. (Cap) Krug, and of Secretary of Commerce Wallace, whose place was taken by the wartime ambassador to Russia, by now ambassador to Britain, Averell Harriman.

Not a resignation, but surely trouble, was a misunderstanding between the President and his secretary of state, which came to the fore, albeit in a private way, late in December 1945 when Byrnes returned from a Council of Foreign Ministers meeting in Moscow. Truman had him down immediately to the Williamsburg, *moored south of Washington along the Potomac, and gave him a tongue-lashing, so the President said years later in his memoirs. Early in January the secretary was summoned to the White House, where, so Truman also asserted, the President read him a letter that he had written out in longhand. The full truth about the letter may never be known. It was first published in William Hillman's* Mr. President *in 1952 and Byrnes immediately denied that Truman ever had read it to him, and said he would have resigned if such a confrontation had occurred. (By this time, 1952, the former secretary of state had broken politically with the President.) There is considerable evidence that Truman did bawl out Byrnes aboard the* Williamsburg. *As for reading him the letter, it is a case of one man's memory against the other's.*

TO JAMES F. BYRNES (UNSENT)

January 5, 1946

My dear Jim:

I have been considering some of our difficulties. As you know I would like to pursue a policy of delegating authority to the members of the cabinet in their various fields and then back them up in the results. But in doing that and in carrying out that policy I do not intend to turn over the complete authority of the President nor to forgo the President's prerogative to make the final decision.

Therefore it is absolutely necessary that the President should be kept fully informed on what is taking place. This is vitally necessary when negotiations are taking place in a foreign capital, or even in another city than Washington. This procedure is necessary in domestic affairs and it is vital in foreign affairs.

At San Francisco no agreements or compromises were ever agreed to without my approval. At London you were in constant touch with me and communication was established daily if necessary.

That procedure did not take place at this last conference. I only saw you for a possible thirty minutes the night before you left after your interview with the Senate Committee.

I received no communication from you directly while you were in Moscow. The only message I had from you came as a reply to one which I had Under Secretary Acheson send to you about my interview with the Senate Committee on Atomic Energy.

The protocol was not submitted to me, nor was the communiqué. I was completely in the dark on the whole conference until I requested you to come to the Williamsburg and inform me. The communiqué was released before I even saw it.

Now I have the utmost confidence in you and in your ability but there should be a complete understanding between us on procedure. Hence this memorandum.

For the first time I read the Ethridge letter this morning. It is full of information on Rumania & Bulgaria and confirms our previous information on those two police states. I am not going to agree to the recognition of those governments unless they are radically changed.[1]

I think we ought to protest with all the vigor of which we are capable

---

1. In October 1945, Secretary Byrnes had dispatched the publisher of the Louisville *Courier-Journal,* Mark Ethridge, to Eastern Europe to check on the accuracy of state department reports regarding Russian activities in Rumania and Bulgaria. Ethridge had submitted a report to Byrnes on December 7.

[against] the Russian program in Iran. There is no justification for it. It is a parallel to the program of Russia in Latvia, Estonia and Lithuania. It is also in line with the high handed and arbitrary manner in which Russia acted in Poland.

At Potsdam we were faced with an accomplished fact and were, by circumstances, almost forced to agree to Russian occupation of Eastern Poland and the occupation of that part of Germany east of the Oder River by Poland. It was a high handed outrage.

At the time we were anxious for Russian entry into the Japanese War. Of course we found later that we didn't need Russia there and the Russians have been a head ache to us ever since.

When you went to Moscow you were faced with another accomplished fact in Iran. Another outrage if ever I saw one.

Iran was our ally in the war. Iran was Russia's ally in the war. Iran agreed to the free passage of arms, ammunition and other supplies running into millions of tons across her territory from the Persian Gulf to the Caspian Sea. Without these supplies, furnished by the United States, Russia would have been ignominiously defeated. Yet now Russia stirs up rebellion and keeps troops on the soil of her friend and ally, Iran.

There isn't a doubt in my mind that Russia intends an invasion of Turkey and the seizure of the Black Sea Straits to the Mediterranean. Unless Russia is faced with an iron fist and strong language another war is in the making. Only one language do they understand—"How many divisions have you?"

I do not think we should play compromise any longer. We should refuse to recognize Rumania and Bulgaria until they comply with our requirements; we should let our position on Iran be known in no uncertain terms and we should continue to insist on the internationalization of the Kiel Canal, the Rhine-Danube waterway and the Black Sea Straits and we should maintain complete control of Japan and the Pacific. We should rehabilitate China and create a strong central government there. We should do the same for Korea.

Then we should insist on the return of our ships from Russia and force a settlement of the Lend-Lease Debt of Russia.

I'm tired babying the Soviets.

General Dwight D. Eisenhower succeeded Marshall, who had retired from the army, as chief of staff in November 1945 and faced an appalling military task—presiding over the disintegration of the victorious U.S. Army. By a ruinous point system, the army fell apart; the men with the most combat experience were released first. Demobilization was not fast

enough for many servicemen, and there were near riots as they clamored
for release. Matters reached a point where Eisenhower had to intervene,
and in a speech to Congress he promised that any soldier with a good
case for immediate release could write his office and that he, personally,
would consider the case. In subsequent weeks the army's chief of staff
made it his business to consider these cases each morning, as his first
order of business. What to do, then, about the army—how to revive its
effectiveness? Truman was concerned about its leadership.

TO DWIGHT D. EISENHOWER

January 16, 1946

Dear General Eisenhower:

I have been thinking about the situation about which you addressed the Congress.

In the 1st World War it was my duty to command a battery of field artillery in a National Guard Division and after the war to take part in the training of National Guard and Reserve Officers.

As a result of my limited experience I came to the conclusion that if the top command, that is Supreme and Army commanders, are able and efficient and company and battalion commanders have the confidence of the men whom they command, the in-between officer material is not of much consequence so far as discipline and control are concerned.

I wonder if the Lieutenants, Captains and Majors of our present home and overseas forces haven't gotten too far away from their commands.

As you know, a real leader who is a unit commander at the company level knows exactly what his men are thinking. He knows how to keep them busy in a constructive way—even if there is apparently nothing to do. He feeds them, sleeps them, and his whole life should be in their welfare.

He stands between the next higher commander and his men. He makes his non-coms responsible and if he is real makes the morale of the army. I know what you've been up against in this demobilization. I know you've lost your best and that the untrained and the inefficient are what we have left now.

But can't we start over—from the squad up, rebuild that pride and morale which are the backbone of any organization? What can I do to help?

Sincerely,
Harry S. Truman

The Trumans, including genealogist Ethel Noland, had believed for years that they were related to President John Tyler, whom Truman ranked about equal to Buchanan in ineptitude, so it was with an air of relief that the President convinced himself that his forebear was another John Tyler.

TO ETHEL NOLAND

January 21, 1946

Dear Ethel:

I took time out the other day to look up John Tyler, the President. I have come to the conclusion that he is not our great uncle. He was born in Virginia and never left there so far as any life of him I've read shows.

The John Tyler who was the brother of our great grandmother seems to have been a different person entirely, although the President's features in all the pictures of him and in the fine painting in the White House look like our family. He may have been a close relative of our John Tyler but I don't think he was as close as we've been led to think.

Not that I give a hoot but I don't ever like misrepresentation. Old John didn't amount to a great deal and his purported great nephew probably won't either.

When you have time look it up. Hope Nellie and Aunt Ella are well. My best to all of you.

Harry

The pent-up purchasing power at the end of the war proved impossible to contain, and when price controls went off and too much money chased too few goods, not merely was the result inflationary, as classical economics predicted, but (as the classical economists would have been horror-struck to imagine) the strong industrial unions moved quickly to preserve their wage positions and, if possible in the demand-churned marketplace, improve them. Businessmen who during the war performed miracles of management had regained the courage they lost during the Great Depression, and resisted. The result was a series of long strikes against the railroads and the steel, coal, and automobile industries.

TO MARTHA ELLEN AND MARY JANE TRUMAN

January 23, 1946

Dear Mamma & Mary:

I was glad to get your letter and the almanac with all the quotations and sayings of Jefferson and Franklin. It is a most interesting one. I have been reading it. It will stay on my desk and I hope I can keep track of my dates in it.

Things seem to be going the wrong way here in labor matters, but I am hopeful of an ultimate settlement. The steel strike is the worst. We can handle most of the others. People are somewhat befuddled and want to take time out to get a nerve rest. Some want a life guarantee of rest at government expense and some I'm sorry to say just want to raise hell and hamper the return to peacetime production, hoping to obtain some political advantage.

The steel people and General Motors I am sure would like to break the unions and the unions would like to break them so they probably will fight a while and then settle so both will lose and in the long run only the man in the street will pay the bill.

Big money has too much power and so have big unions—both are riding to a fall because I like neither. Hope you are both well and stay that way. Margie is having exams and Bess is having luncheons and teas and I'm having the customary hell. Love to you both.

Harry

Secretary of the Interior Harold Ickes was an old progressive whose bluff honesty had made an impression on President Roosevelt; by 1946 he had been at Interior a long time and almost took his residence for granted. Ickes was not the greatest administrator but he was a good man and Truman hated to lose him. And yet what could the President do when Ickes, summoned before a Senate committee to testify concerning the qualities of a Truman appointee, behaved in an outrageous manner? Truman had nominated his friend Edwin Pauley, admittedly an oilman, to be undersecretary of the navy. Pauley had been treasurer of the Democratic party in 1944 and a leading conspirator in the intrigue to displace Henry Wallace from the vice-presidency and nominate Harry Truman. In the first weeks of the presidency, Truman appointed Pauley to represent the United States in negotiations over reparations in Moscow, and Pauley was just the intelligent, tough sort to excel in such a discussion. But Ickes, testifying before the Senate, implied that Truman had asked him to whitewash Pauley, and implied also that Pauley's oil connections would lead the administration into another Teapot Dome scandal. Truman was sensitive to this comparison, for people early in 1946 were saying that the Truman administration was like that of Harding. There was talk of a Missouri compromise, and jokes were making the rounds, such as "To err is Truman." Truman's temper flared. The following memorandum was written over, and parts crossed out. The President planned to issue it, but the staff advised against such a course.

*In the event, Ickes threatened to resign and the President instantly ac-
cepted the resignation. Some weeks later, Ickes, crestfallen, seemed to
have recognized that he had behaved badly, and friendly relations
resumed between him and Truman.*

MEMORANDUM

February 14, 1946

Just a statement of fact in regard to the Ickes-Pauley controversy. Mr.
Ickes has a peculiar complex about himself when he speaks of any epi-
sode in which he takes a part. In his own mind he is always a hero and
he usually manages to twist the facts so as to suit his own dramatic
approach to the hero-complex in his own mind.

Time after time I've had him relate incidents to me about his contacts with the late President, with Harry Hopkins and with various other
public figures.

A short time after I succeeded to the Presidency Mr. Ickes sent for Mr.
Pauley and asked him what my attitude toward the Secretary of the
Interior was at that time.

Pauley told him he knew I was friendly. I saw Mr. Ickes frequently
both before and after I became President. In the latter part of July or the
first part of August he told me he was going to quit. The gossip columnists
were giving him some unpleasant moments.

I asked him to stay and assured him that I had no one in mind for
the place he held.

The conversation got around to Pauley and Mr. Ickes expressed high
admiration for him and said that Mr. Pauley had been very helpful to
him as petroleum administrator. Mr. Ickes seemed very much relieved
that I was not considering Pauley for Sec. of the Interior.

At that time Pauley was handling reparations for the government
and was doing an outstanding piece of work.

Mr. Ickes seemed very happy and very cooperative in the Cabinet.

A few weeks ago he was talking to me about other matters and again
he expressed a high regard for Mr. Pauley.

Mr. Forrestal, the Sec. of the Navy, came to me one day about six or
eight weeks ago and said that he would like very much to have Mr.
Pauley as Undersecretary of the Navy, that Mr. Roosevelt had intended
to appoint Mr. Pauley to that place when the gentleman then handling
that position quit, as he intended to do soon.

I sent Mr. Pauley's name to the Senate over his protest. He only took
the appointment because Sec. Forrestal and I urged him to do it.

By the way, Mr. Pauley has never discussed oil or land titles or campaign contributions with me and has never asked me to appoint or favor anybody for anything.

Two weeks ago Mr. Ickes at a Cabinet meeting told me he had been summoned to appear and testify on Mr. Pauley's nomination. I told him to tell the truth but be as kind as possible to Mr. Pauley. In his statement at his press conference he made it appear that I had asked him to perjure himself. Quite the contrary, I told him to tell the truth . . . he left out my admonition to him to tell the truth.

I regret the necessity of having to make this statement—but I want the record straight. Mr. Ickes has tried to ruin an able public servant in Mr. Pauley and I have had to dispense with the service of another. . . .

APPOINTMENT SHEET

February 14, 1946

10:15 [Congressman Compton I. White (Idaho)] Mines, timber woods etc.

10:30 [Congressman Sol Bloom (New York)] Wanted me to know he'd be with me.

10:45 [Senator Wheeler] Wanted Worth Clark for Interior and didn't want me to use Paul Porter.

11:00 [Senator Hatch (New Mexico)] Was for O'Mahoney for Interior, but wanted me to know he was for me always.

11:30 [Senator O'Mahoney] Wanted a western man for Interior, himself preferably.

11:45 [Lieutenant Colonel and Mrs. O'Keefe] A nice girl and an army man. Her father was my friend.

12:00 [Jim Blair] Wants to run for Congress. Gave him some good advice.

12:15 [Senators Thomas and Abe Murdock (both of Utah)] Wanted Hinkley for Interior.

. . . .

The following letter to the President's uncle-in-law didn't do any good. The road running east and west outside the Truman house in Independence was duly renamed Truman Road, to Mr. Truman's everlasting annoyance.

TO WILLIAM SOUTHERN, JR.

February 25, 1946

Dear Mr. Southern:

Bess called my attention to an article in the Independence Examiner Saturday, February sixteenth edition, in which a proposal is made to change the name of Van Horn Road to Truman Road.

If you will remember when I was Presiding Judge of the County Court, people wanted to name every road in the County for me and I wouldn't allow it. The only place my name appears is on the new Court House in Kansas City and the remodeled one in Independence, along with other members of the Court and the Architects, in very inconspicuous places. I have no desire to have roads, bridges or buildings named after me.

Old man Van Horn was a good old Republican who helped the "red legs" rob Jackson County and served two or three terms in Congress. I certainly don't think they ought to take his name off the road where he built that fine house. It doesn't hurt us to honor an old newspaper man with one road name.

I hope Mrs. Southern is well and that I'll have an opportunity sometime in the not too far distant future to pay another visit to my home town. I hope this time without too much pomp and circumstance.

Sincerely yours,

Harry S. Truman

Foreign aid was not popular in certain quarters. A propos, the President's brother, Vivian, sent a mimeographed sheet evidently given out by the manager of the Larabee Mills in Kansas City, depicting a flour sack labeled: "80% Truman's Best New Deal Patent/Looks like Eleanor/ Smells like Wallace/Byrnes Yer Guts Out/100 lbs."

TO VIVIAN TRUMAN

February 26, 1946

Dear Vivian:

... That Larabee Mill sheet is a rather dirty procedure when you take into consideration the objective is to keep about ten million people from starving to death. It is too bad the Manager of the Larabee Mills couldn't be taken to Poland and be allowed to spend the rest of the winter and spring in a Polish village on the rations they have to eat. Maybe he would be willing to get a little more flour out of the wheat in order that he could have a slice of bread, which would look exceedingly good to him. . . .

Harry

APPOINTMENT SHEET

March 16, 1946

10:00   [Secretary of the Interior Krug] Brought his father in to see me. A grand man—raised six boys and gave all of them a college education. He is a good Democrat from Wisconsin. Cap asked me to make Chapman under secretary before I could tell him I wanted to do just that.[1] He agreed to work out the differences between Interior and Agriculture and to implement the proper development of Alaska for the support of 1,000,000 people at the air crossroads of the Northwest. Had a good talk with Lister Hill on the spineless so called "liberals" in the Senate. Expressed my opinion to him of Byrd, Peter Geary, Publicity crazy Pepper, Joe Guffey, Tom Stewart, old man hypocrite Crump and some others— Wheeler, Walsh et al.[2] Mr. Dulles[3] came in to report on U.N.O. and to tell me I'd made a "pretty good" speech at Columbus to the Federal Council of Churches. He's a stuffed shirt.

        . . . .

        Had a long interview with Byrnes. Asked old man [Bernard] Baruch to act as U.S. representative on U.N.O. Atomic Committee. He wants to run the world, the moon and maybe Jupiter—but we'll see.

6:45   [Dinner at the Mayflower, for the Friendly Sons of St. Patrick] Had a good time at this function. John L. Sullivan, Asst. Sec. Navy for Air, made a good speech. Paid my respects to the Ancient Order of Hibernians upstairs in the Grand Ball Room (we were down in the Jefferson Room). The Sons gave me a gold medal—"me & George Washington are the only ones to date." Ain't that sompin'.

James M. (Jim) Pendergast, whom Truman had met during the First World War when both men were officers in the Thirty-fifth Division, had

---

    1. Oscar Chapman was then assistant secretary of the interior.

    2. Truman did not think highly of Senators Claude D. Pepper of Florida, Guffey of Pennsylvania, Stewart of Tennessee, David I. Walsh of Massachusetts, and Boss Edward H. Crump of Memphis. Despite the comment here, he indeed did like Wheeler of Montana.

    3. John Foster Dulles, then a member of the United States delegation to the U.N. General Assembly.

helped the President get a start in Kansas City politics by introducing
him to his father, Michael J. (Mike) Pendergast, and later his uncle,
"Boss" Thomas J. (Tom) Pendergast. Jim Pendergast had given his sup-
port to Congressman Roger C. Slaughter, a Democrat from the Presi-
dent's own county, who had once made a promise to Truman and to
Speaker Rayburn, on the basis of which he was put on the House Rules
Committee, and then turned against his benefactors. To Truman, who
was a tried-and-true politico, loyalty was the number-one necessity for
any sort of political organization. Jim Pendergast, supporting Slaughter,
was wandering off the political reservation.

TO JAMES M. PENDERGAST

May 21, 1946

My dear Jim:

I had hoped to see you Sunday afternoon or evening. A great many
friends and acquaintances dropped in.

I wanted to talk with you about Slaughter. He has become insuffer-
able to the Administration, because of his actions as a member of the
powerful Rules Committee of the House. He owes his position on that
Committee to me. After giving Speaker Rayburn and myself unqualified
assurance that he would go along without question on Administration
measures Rayburn appointed him to the Committee. That happened
while I was in the Senate.

After I came to the White House, Slaughter again assured me that he
would cooperate. The meanest partisan Republican has been no more
anti-Truman than has Slaughter.

Now if the home country organization with which I have been affiliated slaps the President of the United States in the face by supporting
a renegade Congressman it will not be happy for the President nor for the
political organization.

Now you have told several people that had you been in Slaughter's
place you would have slapped me in the face worse than he did. That
rather surprised me as I hadn't understood you felt that way toward me.

Of course I don't intend to rehash history with which you and everyone in the United States is familiar. Nor did I suppose that it would ever
be necessary for me to ask a Pendergast to make a choice between an
upstart little Rabbit[1] and the President of the United States.

---

1. A term used in Jackson County politics a generation earlier, when anti-Pendergast
Democrats allied themselves to a county leader named Joseph B. Shannon. In the melee that
followed, the Shannonites were known as Rabbits and the Pendergast loyalists as Goats.

It seems that that is what confronts me—much to my regret. Slaughter is obnoxious to me and you must make your choice.

Hope your family are well.

Sincerely,

Harry S. Truman

Senator Charles W. Tobey was a poser and hardly endeared himself to Truman for that reason alone. The President's chance came when the New Hampshire Republican sent a telegram to the White House announcing the dire shortage of grain for chicken feed and asking Truman to lift the price ceiling on grain. He began the long telegram with the announcement, "This is a Macedonian cry."

TO CHARLES W. TOBEY

May 29, 1946

Dear Senator Tobey:

Replying to your telegram of May twenty-third, in which you say you are making a "Macedonian cry," it seems to me that you have been making Macedonian cries or yells ever since I have been in the White House. For what reason I never could understand.

Your unwarranted attacks on Mr. Pauley almost ruined a good public servant. Between you and Mr. Ickes you have made it exceedingly difficult for me to get good men to fill the necessary places in the Government. You are still continuing your Macedonian cries and I hope you will get a lot of pleasure out of them.

As far as your food situation is concerned, the Secretary of Agriculture has been instructed to meet the situation as well as he possibly can both in New England and the far Northwest, where the situation is exactly the same. It is a matter of chickens or people and, if it comes to the decision as to which should be kept from starving, naturally, if I make the decision, it will be the people. I don't know whether that will please you or not, but I hope it will.

Sometime when you have reached a cooling-off period, I'd be glad to talk with you about the whole situation.

Sincerely yours,

Harry

[P.S. in longhand] Come and see me.

Richard M. Duncan, judge of the U.S. district court, St. Joseph, Missouri, an old friend, congratulated the President on the appointment of Fred Vinson as Chief Justice.

TO RICHARD M. DUNCAN

June 11, 1946

Dear Dick:

I certainly appreciated your letter of the seventh and I am going to look forward to a visit with you when you get to Washington. I am in the White House all by myself and it is a big lonely barn of a place under those conditions.

It looks as if the Supreme Court has really made a mess of itself. You and I know, of course, that you can't run an organization if everybody dissents. It seems to be the ambition of every member of this Court to be a Holmes or a Brandeis. They seem to forget that under our system somebody must be in agreement and it is much more important to be in agreement than to be in dissent.

The Press and the news gatherers have made so much of the dissenters that there seems to be no cooperation any more. That is true in Congress and it is true in the Cabinet of the President. It really takes a lot of maneuvering to get two people to agree to go down the same road. When we get a whole hundred and thirty million dissenters it is going to be a lovely country to operate. I think you and I can do it though.

Sincerely yours,

Harry

TO ETHEL NOLAND

June 13, 1946

Dear Ethel:

I am enclosing a letter from a lady in England who is interested in the family connections.

I received some interesting information the other day. One of our friends in London sent me an oilcloth facsimile of a sign on the back of a London streetcar. It said—

"If Its Truman's Its Best"

This sign referred to Truman's beer, which has been famous in England, so I am told, since 1666, when the brewery was founded by Benjamin Truman, about the same time the Johnnie Walker distillery was founded.

If you will remember, our records indicated that a certain Ben Truman came to this country about 1666—I wonder if this Ben Truman might not have been a son of the famous British brewer—maybe that is the reason that I don't like beer.

I am enclosing another letter from a gentleman who signs himself as Editor of The World Almanac. Now I don't think there is anything to all that fancy name spelling that he has in there. It is my opinion that our people came from the English "Beer Baron."

Sincerely yours,
Harry S. Truman

The White House was set up for privacy, what with the battery of assistants and especially Appointments Secretary Matt Connelly, who if necessary could wall off the President from would be interlopers. Yet it was helpful to have a change of scene, and in the summer of 1946, Truman tried to arrange a cruise in the Williamsburg *along the Maine coast. But too many people wanted to see him, and everything became too complicated. The alternative proved to be a trip to Bermuda.*

TO MARTHA ELLEN AND MARY JANE TRUMAN

Bermuda
August 22, 1946

Dear Mamma & Mary:

Just received two letters from you and they were both highly appreciated. The Shoop clipping is right in character of course. I am glad the cousins from Texas enjoyed the visit.[1] I suppose it was just as well you didn't go see them off but our Cousin Olive has her nose in a lot of things that are no concern of hers. That good for nothing woman she had down at the plane the day I left had no business there. She is a plain unadulterated promoter of herself and she was trying her level best to get herself into a picture with some of the family. I hope she didn't succeed.

My Maine coast cruise ended in a blow up. Everybody and his brother whom I didn't want to see tried by every hook or crook to rope me into letting him come aboard or having me be seen with him. So I just cancelled the trip and came down here unannounced until I pulled in. The weather is fine, the swimming good, and no politicians or social hangers on are here. All I have to do is to call on the Gov. General and then do as I please.

Will be here for a week and then go back to the White House and *stay*

---

1. The Texas cousins—there were six of them—were the children of Truman's father's brother, William T. Truman, by a second marriage (General Ralph Truman was a child of the first marriage).

there from now until the end of the term. It is the only place I should be. Took me a long time to find it out. But it is the fact.

This little island is a beautiful place. Right out in the Atlantic, it is only 22 miles long and not quite an average of one mile wide. There are twenty square miles in the area. It is a coral formation and no wells or fresh water on it except rain water. They catch the rains in big cisterns for the water supply and it rains nearly every day. But the sun shines all the time too. The rains are local showers at this time of year but they have a rainy season when it pours down. Will be back in Washington on the 2nd of Sept. But they forward your letters by plane.

Love to you both.

Harry

[*The President had to give up the idea of Bermuda as a vacation spot. For one thing, the communications setup was inadequate. For another, the Atlantic was too choppy for a small yacht. The trip back to Hampton Roads was far from delightful—rain squalls and a rough sea. The President lost a little weight and did not mind; his seasick assistants were fit to be tied.*]

The international president of the United Farm Equipment and Metal Workers of America, part of the C.I.O., sent a telegram expressing the opinion of its board that Secretary of State Byrnes had sabotaged the peace, uniting with America's World War II enemies instead of its friends—this because of the secretary's speech at Stuttgart in which he invited the Germans to organize politically for the sake of freedom. Byrnes, the telegram said, also was "unalterably prejudiced" against minority peoples; he was anti-labor, pro-poll tax, allied with the least democratic elements in the United States.

TO GRANT W. OAKES (UNSENT)

September 12, 1946

Dear Mr. Oakes:

I read your telegram of the tenth with a great deal of interest and outside of the fact there isn't a true statement in it, it is an interesting document.

As far as the Secretary of State is concerned, the President appoints a Secretary of State in whom he has confidence and that will continue to be the policy of this Administration. Mr. Byrnes will stay.

The relations between Secretary of Commerce Henry A. Wallace and the President necessarily were awkward because of the way the party's regulars had forced the selection of Truman as the party's vice-presidential nominee in place of Wallace at the Democratic convention in 1944. Wallace had not taken the substitution lying down, and had marshaled his supporters at the convention to fight what seemed an uncertain or a reluctant presidential choice—all that the national chairman of the party, Robert Hannegan, had to show to prove Roosevelt wanted Truman was a short note in which the President said he would be happy to run with Truman or Justice William O. Douglas of the Supreme Court. (There may have been a second note—Truman some years later thought there was—which contained only Truman's name, but no trace of it has ever been found.) The byzantine FDR, meanwhile, had given a Wallace supporter another note, saying that if he, the President, were a delegate to the convention he would vote for Wallace. After a near donnybrook in Chicago, during which the Wallaceites packed the convention galleries and even the floor, when things got to the point that the convention organist was playing the Wallace song, "Iowa, Iowa, That's Where the Tall Corn Grows," and it was necessary to threaten to cut the instrument's cable with an ax—after all this, and the postponing of the vote for nomination of the vice-presidential candidate, Truman received the convention's support. Wallace could hardly forget his near miss at the presidency, and he was not grateful when FDR early in 1945 nominated him as secretary of commerce, and Truman with difficulty managed to push the nomination through the Senate. Sooner or later something was going to happen between him and Truman. The onset of the cold war bothered Wallace and he was not about to keep his mouth shut when foreign affairs were moving toward a crisis between the United States and the Soviet Union. What he did was to mousetrap Truman into an impossible situation. In a speech before the political action committee of the CIO at Madison Square Garden, he virtually proposed a new foreign policy for the United States. He said that the Western powers had failed to recognize and accommodate themselves to Russia's innate suspicions of the capitalist world, that the United States and Britain should avoid pressing the Soviets about affairs in Eastern Europe, that they should avoid, unilaterally if necessary, building up postwar armaments, and especially atomic armaments. The British, Wallace said, couldn't be trusted. "To make Britain the key to our foreign policy would, in my judgment, be the height of folly. Make no mistake about it: the British imperialist policy in the Near East alone, combined with Russian retaliation, would lead the United States straight to war." And he told his

*auditors that President Truman had approved his speech. It was, of
course, quite the opposite of the policy that Byrnes, negotiating treaties
of peace with the former Nazi satellite nations in Paris, was enunciat-
ing.*

DIARY

September 17, 1946

Henry Wallace, at my request, wrote me a memo in the form of a
letter on July 23 '46, at my request (repeat), on the foreign situation. We'd
had a cabinet meeting before Byrnes was to go back to Paris. Everyone
had expressed his opinion, including Henry. I asked all of them to send
me memos on the subject.

All of them approved the decision and instructions to Byrnes except
Henry—so none sent real memorandums. When Henry's came on July 23
I told my morning conference that I'd received a great political document
from Mr. Wallace. I sent it over to the State Dept. to Mr. Byrnes to read.
Or I gave it to him at one of our 12:30 Conferences. The latter I think is
correct. He brought it back the next day—in either case. I did not acknowledge it for a few days because I only considered it as a memorandum for my use. But I did acknowledge it after it occurred to me that *"my
friend"* Henry was making a record *"for himself."* This letter was twelve
single-space typewritten pages. It covered everything from Genesis to
Revelation.

Now I know it was a political document and not intended for my
information.

On Thursday Sept. 12, Mr. Wallace asked me for an appointment. He
received it, of course. He had only fifteen minutes. We talked of his trip
to Mexico, my vacation to Bermuda, the desirability of a special representative to the Mexican inauguration, politics etc. Then Henry pulled
out a speech he proposed to make at Madison Square Garden, N.Y., that
night. He asked me to read it. Twelve minutes of his fifteen were gone
and there were important people to see. I tried to skim through the
speech—supposing always that Henry was cooperating in all the phases
of the administration—including foreign policy. One paragraph caught
my eye. It said that we held no special friendship for Russia, Britain or
any other country, that we wanted to see all the world at peace on an
equal basis. I said that that is, of course, what we want.

Henry made his Madison Square Garden speech—and did I catch
hell. At a press conference I had approved the speech on the basis of the
one paragraph that really appealed to me—trusting Henry to play square
with me.

Two days afterwards I had to admit my error and back up Byrnes. Henry called me up and said he was pleased with what I'd said and that he knew I'd have to say that I backed up Byrnes and the policy we'd discussed and agreed to in the cabinet meeting.

Then he gives out a statement saying he would reiterate his Madison Square Speech! I thought he was mistaken.

A news man told Ross my press secretary that [Drew] Pearson had a copy of Wallace's statement to me of July 23 and that he intended to make a "column" out of it. Ross called Henry and Henry expressed alarm and wondered what to do.

At a luncheon given by the Postmaster General—Mr. Hannegan—for Congressional candidates who had shaken hands with me earlier in the day, Ross, Wallace, Clifford[1] and Hannegan discussed the situation and decided that maybe the letter should be given to the regular news men if I approved.

Ross, Clayton, Clifford & I discussed the matter and I decided that the memo-letter should not be released. Ross had called Wallace at the start of the conference and told him not to release the paper until he had my decision. Wallace said "O.K." After listening to all sides I decided that the memo-letter was a confidential document and should not be released. That if Pearson published it in his column there would be doubt on its authenticity because the former President Mr. Roosevelt had branded him a liar, I had, so had all the Senate and House leaders. Therefore it would not be looked upon as an authentic document.

I told Mr. Ross to call Henry and say that I disapproved the release. Henry said that *P.M.*[2] had a copy. Then he said that another copy had gotten away. All this after he'd told Charlie that it wouldn't be turned loose without my approval.

Well, I'm sure it was an arranged proceeding. N.Y. speech, based on memo to me, rushing me to read speech, release of memo and misstatement to Ross that it would be held.

So, we'll see what results.

TO MARTHA ELLEN AND MARY JANE TRUMAN

September 18, 1946

Dear Mamma & Mary:

Received your good letter and I am glad you went for the ride. I'm sure it did both of you a lot of good. I hope you'll take a lot more of them and take someone with you too. Watch those good tires and keep them at

---

1. Clifford had replaced Judge Rosenman as counsel to the president on July 1, 1946.
2. A New York City newspaper.

about 35 pounds and you'll have no trouble. They should go another year.

I am sorry to hear about the sunflower crop but there's no use saying anything about it because it would just stir up a useless row and the sunflowers would still be there when you finished up. It takes pride to run a farm same as anything else. Maybe the boys will get it later. They must have something in them because they are making money.

Now don't be in too big a hurry about selling all your land. You've done right well by holding on so far. It seems to me you might get an excellent price for the station and the railroad lot one of these days and then the other property would sell easily. Then we'll look around for some good investment that will keep you in clover the rest of your life. Don't worry about the house. You can have it as long as you want anyway. But if and when you feel you have to buy it you can have it too.

I'm still having Henry Wallace trouble and it grows worse as we go along. I think he'll quit today and I won't shed any tears. Never was there such a mess and it is partly my making. But when I make a mistake it is a good one.

Love to you both.

Harry

TO MARTHA ELLEN AND MARY JANE TRUMAN

September 20, 1946

Dear Mary & Mamma:

Well I had to fire Henry today and of course I hated to do it. Henry Wallace is the best Secretary of Agriculture this country ever had unless Clint Anderson turns out as I think he will. If Henry had stayed Sec. of Agri. in 1940 as he should have there'd never have been all this controversy—and I would not be here—and wouldn't that be nice? Charlie Ross said I'd shown I'd rather be right than President and I told him I'd rather be anything than President. My good counselor, Clark Clifford, who took Sam Rosenman's place, said *"Please* don't say that." Of course Clark, Charlie and all the rest of my good friends are thinking in terms of 1948 —and I'm not.

Henry is the most peculiar fellow I ever came in contact with. I spent two hours and a half with him Wednesday afternoon arguing with him to make no speeches on foreign policy—or to agree to the policy for which I am responsible—but he wouldn't. So I asked him to make no more speeches until Byrnes came home. He agreed to that and he and Charlie Ross and I came to what we thought was a firm commitment that he'd say nothing beyond the one sentence statement we agreed he should make. Well he answered questions and told his gang over at Commerce all that had taken place in our interview. It was all in the afternoon Washington News yesterday and I never was so exasperated since Chicago.[1] So—this morning I called Henry and told him he'd better get out and he was so nice about it I almost backed out!

Well now he's out and the crackpots are having conniption fits. I'm glad they are. It convinces me I'm right.

Hope you and Mamma feel better now. Appreciated your letter and I knew all the time you were taking good care of the car. But I couldn't help talking about the tires. They always have been an obsession of mine. Glad the flat happened in the garage instead of on the road.

I've never heard from Vivian yet as to whether he arrived home safely or not and as to whether Fred came out safely.[2] If I hadn't known him for sixty years I'd have been uneasy and mad as hell. Maybe he was sure you would tell me. Glad the land deal is progressing. I'm sure it will turn out all right.

Hope you'll both continue to feel in good health. Hope also you have a nice time in Milwaukee. But don't, for goodness sake, let that bunch of trash entice you into the Grand O.E.S. again. They'll simply mistreat you again for malicious political purposes against your brother.[3]

Lots of love to you both.

Harry

According to the diary of Charles Ross for September 27, 1946, "The President showed me today a little piece he wrote yesterday, September 26, the anniversary of the beginning of the Argonne Offensive of 1918. It was a very simple and vivid piece of writing. The point is that we are now going through the same experiences that followed the last war. I told the President this afternoon that if he wanted to capitalize on his office, I would guarantee to sell this piece of writing for $5,000. He said, of course, as I knew he would, that he was not doing any writing for profit." (President's Secretary's Files, Box 322, Ross, Mr. and Mrs. Charles G.)

---

1. When the vice-presidential nomination was literally forced on him; Truman had gone to Chicago prepared to nominate James Byrnes.

2. Apparently Vivian and his son Fred had been in a car accident.

3. Mary Jane aspired to become Grand Matron of the Stars of Missouri, and the President believed that his political enemies were working against her candidacy. Mary became Grand Matron in 1950. Her brother was an ardent Mason. A member since 1909, he had founded the lodge at Grandview. In those early years, when he was on the farm nearby, he memorized the rituals, he later said, by teaching them to the horses as he walked the fields. Truman had become Grand Master in 1940.

DIARY

September 26, 1946

Sept. 26, 1918, a few minutes before 4 A.M. a service man of my acquaintance was standing behind a battery of French 75's at a little town called Neuville to the right of the Argonne Forest. A barrage was to be fired by all the guns on the Allied front from Belgium to the Swiss border.

At 4 A.M. that barrage started, at 5 A.M. the infantry in front of my acquaintance's battery went over. At 8 A.M. the artillery including the 75 battery referred to moved forward. That forward movement did not stop until Nov. 11, 1918.

My acquaintance came home, was banqueted and treated as returned soldiers are usually treated by the home people immediately after the tension of war is relieved.

The home people forgot the war. Two years later, turned out the Administration which had successfully conducted our part of the war and turned the clock back.

They began to talk of disarmament. They did disarm themselves, to the point of helplessness. They became fat and rich, special privilege ran the country—ran it to a fall. In 1932 a great leader came forward and rescued the country from chaos and restored the confidence of the people in their government and their institutions.

Then another European war came along. We tried as before to keep out of it. We refused to believe that we could get into it. The great leader warned the country of the possibility. He was vilified, smeared, misrepresented, but kept his courage. As was inevitable we were forced into the war. The country awoke—late, but it awoke and created the greatest war production program in history under the great leader.

The country furnished Russia, Britain, China, Australia and all the allies, guns, tanks, planes, food in unheard of quantities, built, manned and fought the greatest navy in history, created the most powerful and efficient air force ever heard of, and equipped an army of 8½ million men and fought them on two fronts 12,000 miles apart and from 3,000 to 7,000 miles from the home base, created the greatest merchant marine in history in order to maintain those two battle fronts.

The collapse of the enemies of liberty came almost simultaneously in May for the eastern front and in August for the western front.

Unfortunately the great leader who had taken the nation through the peace time and war time emergencies passed to his great reward just one month before the German surrender. What a pity for this to happen after twelve long years of the hardest kind of work, three and a half of them in the most terrible of all wars.

My acquaintance who commanded the 75 battery on Sept. 26, 1918, took over.

The same elation filled the home people as filled them after the first world war.

They were happy to have the fighting stop and to quit worrying about their sons and daughters in the armed forces.

Then the reaction set in. Selfishness, greed, jealousy raised their ugly heads. No wartime incentive to keep them down. Labor began to grab all it could get by fair means or foul, farmers began blackmarketing food, industry hoarded inventories and the same old pacifists began to talk disarmament.

But my acquaintance tried to meet every situation and has met them up to now. Can he continue to outface the demagogues, the chiselers, the jealousies?

Time only will tell. The human animal and his emotions change not much from age to age. He must change now or he faces absolute and complete destruction and maybe the insect age or an atmosphereless planet will succeed him.

TO NELLIE NOLAND

October 23, 1946

Dear Nellie:

I appreciated your letter of the sixteenth very much and I have been so covered up that I haven't had a chance to sit down and write you as I usually do.

That good for nothing Cyril Clemens is worse than a "goose bite"— he spends most of his time promoting himself on his seventh cousin's reputation. I wouldn't pay too much attention to him—I never answer his letters. His letterhead is a big joke in our office—all he lacks having on it is Jesus Christ and General Jackson. He is a nut.

If Mrs. Townsend got to Washington I didn't hear about it. I would have been glad to let her see the White House. If you send me Mr. Townsend's Scottish Rite certificate I'll sign it.

I hope Ethel and Aunt Ella are all well—we will be seeing you next week, I hope.

Sincerely yours,

Harry

Mr. Clemens has published a book about me that's about half false and that's the reason I'm put out with him.

It was a cranberry receipt I sent you, not pudding. But you didn't need it—you know how now!

My best to everybody in the family.

The President occasionally wrote out drafts of speeches he would never be able to give and the drafts constituted memoranda of what was on his mind. At the end of June 1946, virtually all price controls came to an end. Prices shot up, with veal cutlets going from fifty to ninety cents a pound, milk up from sixteen to twenty cents a quart. Truman did his best to stem the tide, but the Republicans would have the votes after the coming congressional elections, they said, and at the end of October, just before the election, with the cattlemen striking, the President dropped all price controls on beef. About this time he drafted the following speech and then filed it, but it got a few things off the presidential chest.

DRAFT SPEECH (UNDELIVERED)

October 1946

It has been my duty, as the successor of that great humanitarian and world leader in the greatest crisis through which the world ever came, Franklin D. Roosevelt, to wind up two wars, continue the outline for peace, reconvert the greatest industrial plant in the history of the world from an all out war basis to one of production for peace. These almost insuperable duties were assumed by me with humility and a prayer to Almighty God for guidance.

These duties were assumed with promises, voluntarily given, from the Congress, from labor, from management, from farmers, from the everyday man in the street, from bankers, from men and women in all walks of life—even from the economically controlled press, promises of help, cooperation and support.

On Sept. 6, 1945, just four days after the official signing of the Japanese surrender, I sent a message to the Congress outlining the necessary steps for the procedure down the road to peace. In July 1945 I had attended a meeting of the Prime Ministers of Great Britain and Russia at Berlin.

A meeting at which certain plans and principles were agreed to and at which a declaration of the terms of surrender for Japan were agreed to between China, Great Britain and ourselves. Russia afterwards agreed to these terms and Japan accepted them.

After the end of the two wars, the objective was a demobilization of our armed forces—an orderly one and a release of the restrictions of war time on the economy of the country, also an orderly one.

The message to the Congress on Sept. 6, 1945, set out in detail the program. That program was restated in the Budget and State of the Union message of the President in January 1946.

Instead of action the Congress chose to debate and the Republicans began to think of the selfish idea of control of the next Congress.

The public welfare was sacrificed to this one selfish interest. Dilatory tactics on the part of the minority prolonged the price control law's renewal for seven weeks beyond its expiration date and then a bill impossible of administration became the law.

A statement on the beef situation.

It has been my privilege as President to bestow the Congressional Medal of Honor upon more than a hundred men who have won it.

I placed it around the neck of General Wainwright in the Rose Garden of the White House. The General shed tears and told me that he expected to come home a disgraced man because he'd had to surrender to a vastly superior force on Bataan. I was happy to assure him that the American people considered him a man, a leader and a hero.

I placed the medal around the neck of a good looking young man in a wheeled chair—with both legs torn off in action. I myself felt like shedding tears when I fastened the medal. I told him that the country was grateful to him for his sacrifice. He replied, "Mr. President, my life is my country's and my country may still have it."

I placed this same greatest of medals—one I'd rather earn than be President—around the neck of a young sailor—a conscientious objector—who had served in the naval hospital corps and who had carried a number of men who were previously wounded to safety under fire and who was himself finally wounded. That young conscientious objector was one of the bravest of men—and he was honest. He told me that he loved his country and would serve it anywhere—but he would not kill a fellow man.

Why do I tell you these things? Because you have forgotten them. You have forgotten the ideals for which we fought under Franklin Roosevelt. Your vision is dimmed by greed, by selfishness, by a thirst for power. You would sacrifice the greatest government that was ever conceived in the mind of man for a mess of pottage—for a piece of beef, for a slice of bacon.

Wainwright wanted to sacrifice his life for his country—and he was starved, was beaten, and almost died in a prison of a ruthless enemy for his country.

My young infantryman gave his legs and would still give his life for this glorious country of ours. My young conscientious objector was and is willing to do the same thing.

Selfish men, greedy men who wanted to exploit your country in the war—men who profited and profited safely far from the line where good old Vinegar Joe Stilwell was willing and anxious to give his life, far from Bataan, far from St. Lô and Anzio, far from the Solomons and Midway —these greedy industrialists and labor leaders who are now crying beef and bacon made no sacrifice, gave up nothing to win the war. These men received time and a half and assured profits and now they have convinced you, the people who are the government, that they should get the profits which we kept them from getting for the blood and sacrifice of the brave men who bared their breasts to the bullets; now [they] have your attention.

You've deserted your President for a mess of pottage, a piece of beef —a side of bacon. My fellow citizens, *you* are the government. This is a government of, by and for the people. If you the people insist on following Mammon instead of Almighty God—your President can't stop you all by himself. He can only lead you to peace and happiness with your consent and your willing cooperation.

You've decided that the Office of Price Administration should be a goat and a whipping boy. You've decided not to support price control although price control has saved your bonds, your insurance policies, your rent—in fact has kept our economic structure sound and solvent.

I can no longer enforce a law you won't support, botched and bungled by an unwilling Congress. You've gone over to the powers of selfishness and greed.

Therefore I'm releasing the controls on meat and will proceed to release all other controls in an orderly manner as soon as I can.

Tell 'em what will happen and quit.

The president of the United Mine Workers, John L. Lewis, did not hesitate to take advantage of what seemed to be the weakness of the presidency in the autumn of 1946, and called another strike.

DIARY

December 11, 1946

Lewis called a coal strike in the spring of 1946. For no good reason. He called it after agreeing to carry on negotiations without calling it. At least he told John Steelman[1] to tell me there would be no strike. He called one on the old gag that the miners do not work when they have no contract.

After prolonged negotiation I decided to exercise the powers under the second war power act and take over the mines. After they were taken over a contract was negotiated between the Secretary of the Interior, Mr. Krug, and John L. Lewis.

The contract was signed in my office on the 5th of May and Mr. Lewis stated for the movies that it was his best contract and would not be broken during the time of Government control of the mines.

Along in September and October 1946 there arose some minor disputes between the Solid Fuels Administrator and Mr. Lewis. Nothing of vital importance—purely details of interpretation of the contract with regard to coal weights on which the new welfare fund is based and some other small details that could have been settled easily by a half hour discussion.

But Mr. Lewis wanted to be sure that the President would be in the most embarrassing position possible for the Congressional elections on Nov. 6. So he served a notice on the first day of November that he would consider his contract at an end on a certain date. Which was, in effect, calling a strike on that date. He called his strike by a subterfuge in order to avoid prosecution under the Smith-Connally Act. But he'll be prosecuted never the less. [This last sentence was written in later.]

The strike took place as planned by Mr. Lewis. It lasted seventeen days and then Mr. Lewis decided for the first time in his life that he had "over-reached himself." He is a Hitler at heart, a demagogue in action and a traitor in fact. In 1942 he should have been hanged for treason. In Germany under Hitler, his ideal, in Italy under the great castor oil giver, or in Russia now he would have been "eliminated." Only in the greatest country on earth could he operate and have the support of such harmless wonders as Murray and Green, Whitney and Johnson.[2]

---

1. Special assistant to the President for labor matters.

2. Philip Murray, president of the Congress of Industrial Organizations; William Green, president of the American Federation of Labor; Alexander F. Whitney, head of the Brotherhood of Railroad Trainmen; Alvanley Johnston, head of the Brotherhood of Locomotive Engineers.

There was only one thing for me to do when he called his strike by indirection and that was to take him to a cleaning.

I discussed the situation with the secretaries in the White House at the morning meeting after the fake strike call and warned them that it was a fight to the finish. At the Cabinet meeting on Friday before the election the Attorney General was instructed to take such legal steps as would protect the Government. Discussions were held with all the Cabinet and special meetings were called at which the Solid Fuels Administrator, Mr. Krug, the Secretary of Labor, Mr. Schwellenbach, the Attorney General, Mr. Clark, the Special Counselor to the President, Mr. Clifford, and the Special Assistant to the President, Dr. John Steelman, were present.

The instructions were a fight to the finish, by every legal means available, and in the end to open the mines by force if that became necessary.

Mr. Lewis was hauled in to Federal Court, fined no mean sum for contempt. Action was started to enforce the contract and I had prepared an address to the country to be delivered on Sunday evening Dec. 8, [to commemorate the] anniversary of Pearl Harbor.

Mr. Lewis folded up on Saturday afternoon Dec. 7 at 3 P.M. He is, as all bullies are, as yellow as a dog pound pup. He cannot face the music when the tune is not to his liking. On the front under shell fire he'd crack up. But he can direct the murder, assault and battery goon squads as long as he doesn't have to face them.

He tried to get into communication with me while I was taking a sun treatment at Key West for a cold. He tried to talk to Dr. Steelman; he tried to approach the Secretary of the Navy, Mr. Forrestal; he tried to get in touch with the Secretary of Labor on the night before the fold up. For [the] first time he found no pipe line to the White House. I had a fully loyal team and that team whipped a damned traitor.

1947

One observer, writing in the early 1950s, called 1947 the Year of Divergence, the time when the nation at last put away the precepts of George Washington and Thomas Jefferson and decided that it was necessary to take part in the ordinary combinations and collisions of Europe. On March 12, 1947, the President went before Congress and asked for $400 million for military and economic aid to Greece and Turkey, and broadly promised assistance to nations threatened by world communism. The two countries bordering on the Eastern Mediterranean were, of course, in trouble. The Soviets were putting almost unbearable pressure on Turkey to yield special privileges for transit rights through the Bosporus and also for return of border territories lost at the end of the First World War. The Greeks were in far worse condition than the Turks, for Greece was embroiled in a virtual civil war, with Communist guerrillas infiltrating from Yugoslavia, Albania, and Bulgaria. The occupation of Greece by German troops during the Second World War had been heavyhanded, and after their departure the country's economy and politics were in shambles. The British government had intervened to try and preserve order, but because of Britain's economic woes it was now impossible for them to continue to aid the Athens government. The same went for the Turks.

Since the regimes in Athens and Ankara were authoritarian and corrupt, aid to them was not unlikely to be something of an embarrassment to the government of the United States, and there was a good deal of public criticism of the President's proposals. Some argued that the United Nations should handle the problem, rather than the United States. Others conceding the dire nature of the situation in Greece, thought it was not necessary to take on Turkey as well. One indigent, dictatorial regime was bad enough. Why was the Truman administration trying to slip in a second? And yet it was im-

possible to allow either of these two small countries to pass into the
hands of the Soviet Union.

    The Truman Doctrine, as it quickly was called, was followed on
June 5 by the notable speech of Secretary of State George C. Marshall
(who replaced Byrnes in January) before the Harvard faculty, stu-
dents, and friends, after he had received an honorary degree at com-
mencement. Marshall's speech, carefully prepared, proposed that the
nations of Europe get together and draw up a list of their require-
ments for economic recovery and present it to the United States. The
European Recovery Program, or ERP, became known as the Marshall
Plan, after sixteen nations met at Paris and drew up a proposal. The
Russians sent a large delegation to Paris, but then raised objections
and withdrew, and ordered their satellites, Poland and Czecho-
slovakia, to avoid taking part. The division of Europe between East
and West, already evident in the politics of the satellites, became
crystal clear.

    In some sense reflecting the new division of the Continent and the
increasingly awkward relations with the Soviet Union, but reflecting
even more the far smaller budgetary slices available to the army, navy,
and air force in peacetime, the American military establishment took
the first step toward unification in 1947 with creation of a new cabinet
office, that of secretary of defense, and reduction of the service secretar-
ies to secondary importance, with loss of the right to attend cabinet
meetings. Along with the new secretaryship and what at the outset was
a skeletal Department of Defense went the organization of the Central
Intelligence Agency and the National Security Council.

DIARY

January 1, 1947

    Spent New Year's Eve on the yacht Williamsburg with the White
House Staff and ex staff—eighteen of them. Gave each of them a gold seal
White House card wishing a "very happy new year," signed. We had a
very happy evening together.

    Went to bed at 1:30 after the ship's Chief Pharmacist's Mate gave me
a good pounding with alcohol. Had breakfast with my naval aide R. Adm.
Foskett and Capt. Freeman, the commander of the yacht.

    Came back to the White House at 8:45 A.M. New Year's Day.

    Read the morning papers as usual. Some gave me hell and some did
not. It makes no difference what the papers say if you are right.

    Called the "boss" (Mrs. T.) at 10 A.M. and had a talk with her and the daughter. Never was so lonesome in my life. So I decided to call the Cabinet and ex Cabinet officers.

Talked to Byrnes, Snyder, Clark, Patterson, Forrestal, Krug, Harriman, Schwellenbach, Anderson and left word for Hannegan, who was out on a fishing trip.

Then Gen. Fleming, Gen. Eisenhower, former Sec. of War Stimson and Miss Perkins were called. Apparently they were all pleased by the calls—and so was I.

Called Sen. Vandenberg.[1] Had a very pleasant conversation with him. He expressed the opinion in answer to a question on the subject that it would be better for me to see the Republican leaders after my State of the Union Message, on Monday, Jan. 6, 1947, rather than before the delivery of the message.

Called Joe Martin.[2] He assured me that cooperation was at the top of his consideration. And that he wanted very much to help run the country for the general welfare. He told me that he would be most happy to talk to me at any time on any subject. I am inclined to believe that he meant what he said.

Talked to Sec. Byrnes in White House study at 12:45 on the subject of the President of the World Bank. [John J.] McCloy, former asst. sec. of War, had been called in. He was hesitant about taking the job, although John D. Rockefeller Jr. and Winthrop Aldrich, Pres. of the Chase Natl. Bank, had told him he should.

Byrnes and I discussed the Roosevelt agreement with Churchill and Mackenzie King on the Atomic Energy program. It is a mess. No one seems to have thought the thing would work out as it has. So I am the heir to a hell of a mess. But I'm not blaming anyone. Suppose that two billion six hundred million dollars had been spent in vain! What a terrible mess that would have been! So let's be thankful for what we have.[3]

Sec. Snyder came in at 2:15, stayed until 3:30 P.M. discussing McCloy, Byrnes, Morgenthau, labor legislation, message etc. etc. etc.

TO MARTHA ELLEN AND MARY JANE TRUMAN

February 9, 1947

Dear Mamma & Mary:

Just received your letter of yesterday. It is unusual to have a dust storm in February but I guess anything can happen these days. I hope you

1. Arthur H. Vandenberg of Michigan was the new majority leader of the Senate and chairman of the Foreign Relations Committee.

2. Joseph W. Martin, Jr., of Massachusetts, the new speaker of the House.

3. The atomic bomb project cost about two billion dollars.

both stay well and that Mamma's cold gets entirely well. I have been fighting one for two weeks, but seem to have the best of it now. For four or five years I had no colds but have had two bad ones this winter. Took some cold shots along in December. I suspect that they gave me the cold. Also all this handshaking with the sneezing public does not tend to keep colds away. The paper says today that Bess and I have shaken hands with 7000 people this season. That may be a thousand too many but even that number is not to be "sneezed" at as handshaking goes.

I can't find out what Bess and Margaret want for their birthdays. They say they don't want anything but you know they'd be mad as hell if they got nothing. Some time that's what they'll get when they tell me that. I should think that something Margie could use on her singing travels would be all right for her and I can't think of a thing Miss Lizzie needs. You can give her some trifle she can use or carry around and she'll be as grateful as if it were a silver service. It is cold here—about ten above—but the wind is south and the sun is shining. Would be a good day to fly south, but John Snyder has my plane. He went to Max Gardner's funeral[1] and then was going to Denver to the famous miner's dinner known as the "Sow Belly Dinner." I was there and spoke in 1943 or 1942, I forget which year. It is quite an affair, held in the Brown Palace Hotel, and everyone who is anyone in eleven states is there. It will be a good antidote for a funeral. We all hated to lose Max. He was a grand man. I am having a hard time replacing him. Stay well and write when you can.

Love to you both.

Harry

APPOINTMENT SHEET

February 18, 1947

10:30 [Senator James E. Murray (Montana) and friends] Wanted an air line from Chicago to Seattle. Told him CAA has charge.

10:45 [Senator Ernest W. McFarland (Arizona)] Wants water in Arizona. Well it would be nice.

11:00 [Representative Robert Crosser (Ohio), William J. Kennedy, chairman of railroad retirement brotherhood] Wants the total R.R. income allocated to labor with no rate increase.

11:15 [Representative Hale Boggs (Louisiana)] A nice young man. Wants me to stop at N. Orleans on way to Mex.

---

1. O. Max Gardner was a White House assistant, formerly a governor of North Carolina.

11:30 [Former Senator Radcliffe] Wants chosen instrument for foreign air line. Brewster has him.[1]

12:00 [Emir Saud, crown prince of Saudi Arabia, and party] Gave him a medal.

12:30 [Secretary of State Marshall] The more I see and talk to him the more certain I am he's the great one of the age. I am surely lucky to have his friendship and support.

. . . .

9:00   [Congressional reception] It was a nice party.

TO MARTHA ELLEN AND MARY JANE TRUMAN

February 19, 1947

Dear Mamma & Mary:

I was glad to get your note of Monday. It was written on Margie's birthday. She's one nice girl and I'm so glad she hasn't turned out like Alice Roosevelt and a couple of the Wilson daughters. We went to Constitution Hall to hear the Baltimore Civic Opera Company sing H.M.S. Pinafore. John Charles Thomas was Porter the 1st Lord. He dressed up so he looked exactly like Churchill, and he was as funny as De Wolf Hopper and that's giving him real credit. In addition he has a most pleasing voice. He came out between acts and sang a half dozen songs —one dedicated to Margie. After he sang it he said "Now just to clear the air I'll sing my wife's favorite." At the end of the show the whole chorus sang Happy Birthday to Margaret. We went around and thanked Mr. Thomas.

Last night was our last reception thank goodness. It was the Congressional. There were 760 paws to shake, which was fewer than usual. Most of the Senators and Congressmen I was glad to see, but there were half [a] dozen I'd rather have punched in the nose. I told Bess if she'd trip Bricker up so he'd sprawl on the floor in front of us I'd give her the big diamond out of the scimitar the Crown Prince of Arabia gave me. It is about 5 carats. But she didn't have the nerve to do it. If she had he'd been out sure enough.[1] Then there was Taft and old Taber of N.Y.

---

1. Radcliffe, apparently, in the President's opinion, at the behest of Senator Owen Brewster of Maine, was urging that foreign routes be granted to certain American airline.

---

1. Senator John W. Bricker of Ohio, a staunch conservative, was Republican candidate for the vice-presidency on the ticket with Thomas E. Dewey in 1944, and failed to congratulate the then Senator Truman upon the latter's electoral victory, a slight (or was it an oversight?) that Truman never forgot.

The scimitar was eventually put on display in a glass case in the Truman Library in Independence. At 6:30 A.M. on March 24, 1978, thieves hacked the scimitar and two other

Now Mary don't you work too hard. If you need help, get it.

Dr. Graham has gone to Boston today to carve up Bob Hannegan. They are taking out a piece of his nerve next to his backbone. Well he always had too much anyway. But he used it for me so I didn't kick.

Take care of yourselves and love to you both.

Harry

TO ETHEL NOLAND

March 27, 1947

Dear Ethel:

Here is one for the book. This lady addresses me as "Cousin Harry." I never heard of her or any of her connections. Maybe you can find out whether she is real or not.

You'd be surprised at the relatives I meet these days.

Sincerely yours,
Harry

Hope Aunt Ella is getting along all right. Give my best to Nellie.

TO MARY JANE TRUMAN

March 28, 1947

Dear Mary:

I was more than glad to get your letters. I have been uneasy about you, because I know you've had too much to do. I am more than glad you are back on your feet and that you have decided to let Lilly come and help you.

I am having the usual amount of trouble and bickering. When the Congress gets all snarled up it is necessary for them to find someone to blame—so they always pick on me. But they aren't fooling anyone. The People, I'm sure, are not to be fooled by a lot of hooey put out by ignorant demagogues. Woodrow Wilson said that most members of Congress just had a knot on their shoulders to keep their bodies from unraveling. I don't go that far, but I sometimes think that if Congressmen talked less and worked more for the public interest they would come out much better and so would the country. That's the plan I followed in the Senate. It led me into a lot of trouble but I'm sure I did more for the taxpayers and the war effort than the present aggregation is doing for taxpayers or country.

---

ornamented swords and two daggers out of their case in the foyer and made off with a fortune in jewels, estimated at between $700,000 and $1,000,000.

Hope the pictures show Mamma's leg knitting and that the wheeled chair idea works out.[1]

It's time for a conference and I'll have to quit.

Love to you both.

Harry

For years David E. Lilienthal had been head of the Tennessee Valley Authority. His appointment as chairman of the new Atomic Energy Commission raised all kinds of emotion in Congress and Truman found himself with a fight on his hands. For one thing, it rubbed the anti–New Dealers the wrong way, for they saw the T.V.A. as a threat to private enterprise and now expected the A.E.C. to behave in the same manner. For another, it looked to a liberal management of nuclear affairs that might include a sharing of nuclear secrets with the government of Great Britain, not to mention the Soviet Union. For a third, it provided an easy issue for the anti-Trumanites in Congress, of whom there were increasing numbers; they could raise any point they pleased about Lilienthal's supposed incapacity, and thus flout the authority of the President. After a bitter fight, Lilienthal was confirmed. But, as he wrote in The Journals of David E. Lilienthal, II, *The Atomic Energy Years: 1945–1950 (New York, 1964), the abuse heaped on him by senators was almost overwhelming. It could not help but make his years as chairman of the A.E.C. difficult and may have caused him to act in a more conservative manner than he otherwise would have.*

In the fight for Lilienthal's confirmation, the President resorted to all the stratagems he could think of, and came within an ace of releasing the following inflammatory statement.

DRAFT STATEMENT (NOT RELEASED)

March 1947

I would like to discuss with you the fiasco now taking place before the Joint Atomic Energy Committee in regard to Mr. Lilienthal. Mr. Lilienthal has twice or three times been confirmed by the Senate as a director and manager of the Tennessee Valley Authority. Twice I was in the Senate as the Junior Senator from Missouri when Mr. L. came up for confirmation.

On the last occasion before the present one I sent his name to the Senate for confirmation as manager of T.V.A. On that occasion I asked

---

1. The President's mother fell on February 14, 1947, and broke her hip, for the second time.

Senators McKellar and Tom Stewart to come in and discuss the appointment with me. They came and we went over the appointment and while
they were not happy over it no organized fight was made by either of
them.

When the Atomic Bill became a law, it was my duty to appoint a
commission of five members to take over the Manhattan project. It was
necessary to get a chairman. I asked Mr. Conant of Harvard to take the
job. He'd just recently signed up a new contract with Harvard and was
of the opinion he should stay with that school and help take it through
the reconversion period. I talked with three or four other prominent men
with administrative and public relations experience and each one had
commitments which would prevent him from taking the job.

Finally I called in Mr. L. and told him my difficulties and explained
to him that I thought it would be necessary for him to take the Chairmanship of the Atomic Commission. He did not want it. He told me he was
very happily situated, that T.V.A. is a successful and going concern and
that he would like to stay with it.

Mr. L. had worked with a committee of military and scientific men
who had compiled the Smyth Report, and I knew he was as familiar with
the problem as anyone in the country.[1] I asked him to talk to Mr. Baruch,
Mr. Byrnes and Mr. Acheson as well as Gen. Groves and Sec. Patterson.
I also told him that the Chairmanship of the Atomic Commission would
be a challenging position and one which could do the country and the
world a great service.

After he had talked to Mr. Baruch, Mr. Byrnes and Mr. Acheson and
the other prospective members of the Commission, I had another conversation with him on the subject and virtually drafted him. He finally
consented to serve.

I called in all the present appointees of the Commission and gave
them my views on their duties and discussed the appointment of the
scientific advisors of the Commission. No inquiry was even made by me
as to the political or Congressional connections of a single member of the
Commission.

I was trying to get men to do the greatest job facing the country and
the world. I think I persuaded an excellent body of men to assume a
terrible responsibility. It was not expected that a political job-seeking
state organization would begin to drag a red herring into the most important program facing the republic.

I did not anticipate that a Congress, whether in opposition to me or

---

1. The report, named for the professor of physics at Princeton who put it together, made
public as much information about the atomic bomb project as was deemed safe at the time.

HST driving the cultivator on the family farm near Grandview, Missouri, about 1911.

Clowning with cousins Mary Colgan and Nellie Noland. *At left:* James Craig. About 1911.

Captain Harry S. Truman in France, 1918.

Bridegroom and bride,
Independence, Missouri,
June 28, 1919.

The Truman and Jacobson haberdashery at the northwest corner of Twelfth and
Baltimore Streets, Kansas City, Missouri, about 1921. *(Kansas City Star)*

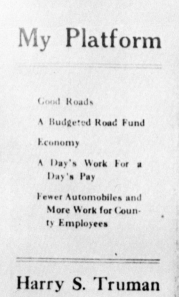

My Platform

Good Roads

A Budgeted Road Fund

Economy

A Day's Work For a
Day's Pay

Fewer Automobiles and
More Work for Coun-
ty Employees

Harry S. Truman

New Road and Precinct Map Showing

WHERE TO **VOTE FOR**

Harry S. Truman
Democratic Candidate For
JUDGE, EASTERN DISTRICT
Jackson County

Harry S. Truman's platform
for this first campaign, when
he ran for judge (county
commissioner) in Jackson
County, Missouri, in 1922.

Left to right: Senator Harry S. Truman, Thomas J. Pendergast, James T. Aylward, David A. Fitzgerald, James A. Farley, and N. G. Robertson, at the Democratic National Convention in Philadelphia, 1936. *(UPI Photo)*

HST and FDR planning campaign strategy in Washington after the Chicago convention, at lunch on the White House lawn, August 18, 1944.

...nan wins the vice-presi-...ial nomination at the ...ocratic National Conven-...in Chicago, 1944. Bess ...Margaret Truman.

Truman and his mother during the 1944 campaign. (*Wide World Photos*)

HST listening to the election returns with his family, 1944. *Left to right:* Private Fred Truman, nephew; Mary Jane; Truman; Bess; Vivian; Margaret; and Martha Ann Truman, niece.

Ethel Noland.

Nellie Noland.

Rose A. Conway, private secretary.
Photo taken in 1949. *(Leon Perskie)*

Truman at the piano.

not, would take a low party viewpoint on a matter of such vital importance.

If Mr. L. is a Communist so am I. No member of Congress should let the Communist red herring fool him. If Joe Starnes and his Committee could find no taint of Communism there is none.[2]

I shall carry this fight all the way to the end. It is a matter of principle and we cannot let the peanut politicians ruin a good man for their personal satisfaction and the detriment of the country and the world.

Truman's detestation of Congressman Slaughter led him into an imbroglio involving the Pendergast machine, or what was left of it under the leadership of Jim Pendergast, and also a libelous charge by the syndicated newspaper columnist Westbrook Pegler. As a result of the President's letter of May 21, 1946, Pendergast had supported a young navy veteran named Enos Axtell in the democratic primary of 1946, and Axtell had defeated Slaughter by 2,771 votes. In four strong Pendergast wards in Kansas City, Axtell received 12,000 votes to Slaughter's 2,000. (Axtell then lost in the fall election to a Republican.) Early in 1947, a grand jury sifted some of the primary ballots and indicted 71 persons. Then on May 27, burglars broke into the election commissioner's safe in Kansas City and stole the impounded ballots. In a letter dated July 3, 1947, Vivian Truman sent his brother a clipping from the Indianapolis Star of June 15 offering the columnist Pegler's interpretation of the affair of the stolen ballots: "There is no fool in the United States fool enough to believe that Truman could not find out right now the names of the yeggs who blew the Courthouse vault and stole the evidence proving that his old friends had stolen the primary and where they could be picked up."

TO VIVIAN TRUMAN

July 9, 1947

Dear Vivian:

I appreciated very much your note of July third in regard to Pegler's article.

The Legal Departments here have been looking into the advisability of smashing him but they always cite the case of Theodore Roosevelt who sued a rat like Pegler for libel and who received damages of one cent.

---

2. Congressman Joe Starnes of Alabama was a member of the special committee for investigating un-American and subversive activities in the Seventy-sixth Congress.

Although they won the case he made himself ridiculous and that is about what would happen in a case of this kind.

The best thing that could happen to him would be for somebody to put his face around on the back of his head but you can't do that either very well without creating a situation such as they have in Russia and that, of course, we don't want to do.

                                        Sincerely yours,
                                                Harry

The President was always worth a line in the newspapers, whatever he was doing, and if he wasn't doing anything it was always possible to make up a story.

TO THE RICHMOND *TIMES-DISPATCH* (UNSENT)

                                                July 9, 1947
Gentlemen:

In your issue of yesterday, you go out of your way to inform your readers that the President of the United States exceeded the safety speed limit in the drive from Monticello to Washington. That is not a true statement. I certainly did not expect a great Virginia Daily to misrepresent the President of the United States, willfully, when he was a guest of that great State.

Here are the facts if you are interested in the *facts*.

Arrangements were made to leave Colle, the home of Hon. Stanley Woodward, where I stayed for my Virginia visit, which is just south of Monticello, at 8:15 A.M. so as to avoid the heavy Sunday traffic. We left Colle exactly on time. I was driving because I like to drive and very seldom get a chance to drive. The Chief of Staff to the President, Adm. Leahy, the Sec. of the Treasury, Mr. Snyder, and Gen. Graham, the White House physician, were passengers in the car.

The pace was set by a capable, efficient State Policeman, in a State Police Car. His instructions were to obey every regulation—and he did just that. I could not have exceeded the Virginia speed law if I had desired to do so—which I did not.

A true story—the only one I saw in all the press—appeared in the New York Times. Yet the Times wrote almost as misleading an editorial as did your paper. I'm sorry in both instances.

The only reason I write you is that for more than twenty-five years I've been working for road safety. I've driven a car more than a million miles—and have never been charged with a traffic violation. I am doing all I can to stop what amounts to murder on the road.

Yet to put a kick in an editorial you use a wrong premise, to put it mildly.

I thought, perhaps, you might be interested in the facts.

TO MARY JANE TRUMAN

July 25, 1947

Dear Mary:

Was glad to talk to you yesterday morning. Dr. Graham was in New York yesterday but is leaving for Kansas City today. He said that medicine he sent is for Frank and Margaret and he said Margaret would know hers.[1] He sent nothing for Mamma. It is certainly too bad after all the effort and work you've put forth for her that Mamma can't get up. But it has been a great fight and we almost won it. Anyway we know that everything possible was done.

I'm glad you have Mrs. DeWitt and Mrs. Lester there. Evidently it was curtain washing time all around. Bess wrote me the same day you did that she and Vietta[2] were washing all the curtains at the old house in Independence.

The Congress, the Post Dispatch and the Star seem to be having spasms over the K.C. vote situation. I am reliably informed that as many Republicans as Democrats are expected to end up in the jug before it's all over. All I hope is that they get that fat no good can of lard named Roberts of the Star. They may do it too.

I am informed that the only reason I was at home when Mamma was so sick was not to see her but to dabble in vote frauds! Well the Star will sink to any level, even to hell, to discredit the present occupant of the White House. I'm expecting to sink them to hell and put the lid on before I'm done.

Don't work too hard. I hope I can get home next week.

Lots of love,

Harry

[Martha Ellen Truman died on July 26, when the President's plane was over Cincinnati en route to her bedside.]

1. Frank Wallace, Margaret Truman.
2. Vietta Garr, long-time helper at the Truman house in Independence.

TO MARY JANE TRUMAN

August 6, 1947

Dear Mary:

It looks as if I may get a letter off to you today. Things have been in a turmoil ever since I returned—bills to sign, bills not to sign, Congressmen and Senators with special things to talk to me about—so they can go home and say the President would or wouldn't do the right thing depending on which side they may be.

But now it looks as if the end is in sight and of course other difficulties appear. The Sec. of the Army, feeling his oats in his new job, has been talking too much and of course has embarrassed me and the Sec. of State.[1] It hasn't happened since Wallace & Ickes left. Anything to make life a little more strenuous for the Chief Exec. is fair it seems.

Bess arrived on time Monday morning. I met her at Silver Spring. She said her mother came to Indp. from Colorado the day before on a plane and had announced that she is now air minded.

Bess & I probably will go up to Shangri La[2] for the weekend on Friday and come back down here on Sunday or Monday A.M.

I may have to go to Brazil[3] about the end of the month in which case I won't be back in Washington before Sept. 15th.

Tell Mary & Myra hello.[4] I'm glad Mary is coming back with you. Have a nice time and get a good rest. It must be a fine place.

Love to you.

Harry

In conference in Brazil twenty-one Western Hemisphere countries produced a mutual assistance pact, the Rio Treaty, the first of four such regional pacts (NATO, SEATO, and the Baghdad Pact—known as the Central Treaty Organization or CENTO—were the others). The signatories agreed that aggression against an American nation, whether by an outside power or by signatories, required joint action against the aggressor. The pact was full of loopholes, for among other things, the form of action was not specified, but it constituted an act of solidarity.

1. Secretary of the Army Kenneth C. Royall had talked too much during a trip to Berlin.
2. The presidential retreat in the hills of Maryland, later named Camp David by President Eisenhower, in honor of his grandson.
3. For the inter-American conference then in session there.
4. Mary and Myra Colgan were daughters of Rochester Campbell Colgan and Emily Ricks Truman Colgan (sister of HST's father).

TO MARY JANE TRUMAN

Rio de Janeiro
September 7, 1947

Your good letter came in the pouch and I was most happy to get it. The note from the lady in Los Angeles was very nice and kind. Who is she? I don't think I know her.

I was glad to hear of the bills being paid. I suppose Vivian intends to have a settlement of rents and such matters when I see him. He had some money in a special account that belongs to me. I sure hope you can get those grave markers set up. It ought to have been done long ago. Have a nice time in St. Louis. . . .

We have had one go-around here, but it has been very pleasant. I addressed the legislature or Congress on Friday at 4:00 P.M. and had a most enthusiastic reception. We went to the Presidential Palace (and palace it is) to a state dinner that night after which some beautiful dances were put on. We sat at one end of a beautiful pool of water lighted all the way around by candles and on which four swans swam, and at the other end was a stage. The pool was flanked by royal palms at least a hundred and fifty feet high.

After the concert and dance we walked around and met people. That good for nothing King Carol of Rumania came and sat by me. I turned my back on him and he got up and left me alone. The President of Brazil said he had crashed the party.

Last night we had our State dinner for the President at the embassy. It was a nice affair. Today we review the parade, go aboard the Mo[1] and start home and will I be glad!

Love to you.

Harry

TO MARY JANE TRUMAN

October 21, 1947

Dear Mary:

I received your letter of Saturday and I know you must have felt very badly when you cleaned out Mamma's closet. It must have been very hard on you. Wish I could have been there and helped.

Margaret seems to have pleased the audience immensely but not the critics in Pittsburgh. One critic I read very carefully and there may be

---

1. Battleship *Missouri.*

something in what he says. He was very constructive and kindly. I am going to tell Margaret to weigh carefully what he said. The others were just simply mean. Most of them suffer from stomach ulcers and most of them can do nothing well themselves and hate to see anyone else do it.

Hope it has rained out home by now. I have a most hectic week ahead of me. Have to make a radio speech Friday after an all day session on Thursday with the Cabinet and the Congressional leaders. Spend the balance of the time getting ready.

Glad you liked the ring. I thought the set was very pretty.

I gave General Marshall a gold medal yesterday—one I had asked the Congress to vote. He was very well pleased with it. The Congress as usual ran in a couple of ringers on me by voting one to Pershing and one to King. I told Marshall I had only asked for one and that one his.

Hope you have a good time in St. Louis and I am sure you will. Don't let them fool you. . . .[1]

Take good care of yourself. We ought to have a nice time at Christmas if everything works out and I believe it will.

Lots of love.

Harry

TO MARY JANE TRUMAN

November 14, 1947

Dear Mary:

I've been trying to write you all week but have been covered up with work and am so tired when night comes, I just fall into bed and go to sleep. Went to bed at 8:30 last night and I'm still tired after sleeping at least eight hours.

Have been trying to get the message ready for the special session and it is a job.[1] The Republicans and the Republicats, their helpers in the Democratic Party, are of course doing what they can to put me in a hole.

But I've got to face the situation from a national and an international standpoint and not from a partisan political one. It is more important to save the world from totalitarianism than to be President an-

1. Mary was heading for the Order of the Eastern Star state convention in St. Louis.

1. After the announcement of the Marshall Plan, the President called Congress into special session to arrange for short-term aid while the long-term program was being organized.

other four years. Anyway a man in his right mind would never want to be President if he knew what it entails. Aside from the impossible administrative burden, he has to take all sorts of abuse from liars and demagogues like Hearsts, Pattersons, McCormicks, Tafts, Mrs. Tafts, and such incompetent Congressional committees as Brewster's, Bender's and Thomas's.[2]

The people can never understand why the President does not use his supposedly great power to make 'em behave. Well all the President is, is a glorified public relations man who spends his time flattering, kissing and kicking people to get them to do what they are supposed to do anyway.

Then the family have to suffer too. No one of the name dares do what he'd ordinarily be at liberty to do because of the gossips. They say I'm my daughter's greatest handicap! Isn't that something?

Oh well take care of yourself and some day the nightmare will be over and maybe we can all go back to normal living.

Love to you.

Harry

TO VIVIAN TRUMAN

November 17, 1947

Dear Vivian:

. . . .

I am attaching a letter from some fellow named Morris, whom I never heard of. You can tell him, if you like, that if all the things he suggests could be done by the President they would have been done long ago, but the President has very little to say about the things to which he refers. He is like everybody else, he believes all the President has to do is snap the finger and things happen. I spend most of my time trying to get people to do what they ought to do.

Sincerely,

Harry

For the first Christmas after Martha Ellen Truman's death, the President invited the whole family to the White House.

---

2. Senator Brewster (Maine), Special Committee to Investigate the National Defense Program; Congressmen George H. Bender (Ohio), Expenditures in the Executive Departments; Congressman J. Parnell Thomas (New Jersey), Un-American Activities.

DIARY

December 25, 1947

We have a most happy and pleasant Christmas, with all the brothers of Bess present, Frank, George and Fred, with their wives, Natalie, May and Christine, with two children of Fred—David and Marian, a couple of very disrespectful young people.

My sister, Mary Jane, came on the 22nd, and I am sure spent an enjoyable time. My brother could not come—in fact, I didn't ask him because he'd told me he intended to have all his family at the farm. He has four boys, all married but one, and a lovely daughter. I called him, and he said 22 sat down to dinner at his house. I am sure they had a grand dinner—a much happier one than a formal, butler-served one, although ours was nice enough.

But a family dinner, cooked by the family mother, daughters, grand-daughters and served by them, is not equaled by White House, Delmonico's, Antoine's or any other formal one.

1948

In foreign affairs in 1948, the loss of Czechoslovakia in February could be regretted but hardly prevented or alleviated. It did have the effect of nudging the initial appropriation for the Marshall Plan past Congress. Then came increasing Russian restrictions on traffic into and out of Berlin, far inside the Russian zone of occupation in Germany, and on June 24 the Berlin blockade, which inspired the President to a terrible feeling that World War III was at hand. Fortunately, the scratch creation of an airlift, a marvelous piece of American ingenuity, led to an increasingly effective demonstration of the solidarity of the Americans, British, and French with the beleaguered Berliners, and toward the end of the summer, the situation simmered down.

Civil rights was the major domestic issue, and Truman submitted to Congress the most ambitious program ever proposed by a President. Based on the report of a committee of distinguished Americans, it called on city, state, and federal authorities to close the gap "between our ideals and some of our practices." The President asked for a commission on civil rights, a joint congressional committee on civil rights, and a civil rights division in the justice department. He asked for a Fair Employment Practices Commission, protection of the right to vote, a federal anti-lynch law. In a press conference a reporter asked him for background comment. "The Constitution, containing the Bill of Rights, was the only document considered in the writing of that message," Truman responded.

All the while, the President's mind was moving toward the perplexing problems of an electoral campaign in which his own party was going to be divided three ways. The followers of former Secretary of Commerce Wallace long ago had gone off into their own corner to establish the Progressive party. The Dixiecrats, or the Republicats, as Truman called them contemptuously, moved into another corner to support their own version of civil rights, known as Southern rights, and act as spoilers in the election of 1948. They expected to be able later to reassemble the *pieces of the old Democratic party, which was an alliance of the city bosses of the North and the solid South, into a new party that would drop the civil rights enthusiasts such as Mayor Humphrey of Minneapolis.*

As for the Republicans, they had a few small problems, such as the sotto voce candidacy of General MacArthur, but it was clear that Governor Dewey of New York once again was a shoo-in for the nomination.

The campaign then followed in which Truman fought for his political life and won against all odds in a series of whistle-stop speeches that would have worn out a leather-lunged elephant, and a series of huge evangelistic sessions in hangars and cow barns and auditoriums. The President would carefully begin a set speech, a voice from the rear would yell out, "Give 'em hell, Harry!" a rousing roar would go up from the crowd, and when it began to subside, the President would shout back, "That's just what I'm about to do!" whereupon pandemonium would break loose. When those storms of applause came thundering toward him, nearly splitting his eardrums, the President knew he was going to win.

Symbolic of the mixture of personal triumph with the continuing crisis of relations with Russia, the pluses and minuses of the time, was the sudden collapse of the flooring in the White House in the weeks just before the election. After the election and a vacation in Key West, the President and his family moved across the street to Blair House while the White House was gutted to its walls and rebuilt from the cellar up.

DIARY

January 6, 1948

Congress meets—Too bad too.

They'll do nothing but wrangle, pull phony investigations and generally upset the affairs of the Nation.

I'm to address them soon. They won't like the address either.

DIARY

February 2, 1948

I sent the Congress a Civil Rights message. They no doubt will receive it as coldly as they did my State of the Union message. But it needs to be said.

John Gates, editor of the Communist paper, The Daily Worker, *sent the President a long telegram on February 2, 1948, about the proposed civil rights legislation, making some proposals of his own and prefacing them with the remark, "HERE IS WHAT YOU CAN DO TO PROVE IN DEEDS THAT YOU ARE NOT ENGAGING IN CHEAP ELECTION ORATORY." Truman was touched by this impertinence, and his attempted response, eventually unsent, went through three drafts.*

TO JOHN GATES (UNSENT)

February 6, 1948

My dear Mr. Gates:

I read your telegram of the second with considerable interest.

You are making suggestions that could only be carried out in a country where legislative opposition can be hanged without trial; where the ordinary opponents of the Government are sent to concentration camps and their families are punished for their beliefs; where patriots, who serve in emergency, are shot as the opposition when the emergency no longer exists; where opposition leaders are assassinated by paid assassins; where free thought and free expression mean prison and slavery.

This great free country is not confused by lies and propaganda and, therefore, your suggestions are all beside the point.

In a Soviet State you would be in a concentration camp and your propaganda sheet suppressed. For that reason I'm happy that you live in a country which respects the rights of the individual and the right of free expression.

Yours for a World Bill of Rights,

DIARY

February 8, 1948

I go for a walk and go to church. The preacher always treats me as a church member and not as the head of a circus. That's the reason I go to the 1st Baptist Church.[1]

One time I went to the Foundry Methodist Church, next door to the 1st Baptist, because Rev. Harris was Chaplain for the Senate when I was V.P. He made a real show of the occasion. I'll never go back. I don't go to church for show. I hate headline hunters and showmen as a class and individually. It's too bad I'm not a showman. My predecessor was, and I suppose profited politically by it. Fate put me here, and fate can keep me here or put me out—and out would suit me better.

---

1. The minister of the First Baptist Church was Russell H. Pruden. Truman was of course a Baptist, a member of the church in Grandview.

DIARY

February 12, 1948

I go to Lincoln's monument for a ceremony. Have three aides now and a Chief of Staff. Bess and I stand on a carpet at the foot of the steps leading up to the statue with Adm. Leahy, C.S. to C in C, on my right, and Gen. Vaughan, Chief Aide, on his right. Capt. Dennison, Naval Aide, and Col. Landry, Aide for Air, on Mrs. T's left. Presidential Honors are sounded, the master of ceremonies calls for the Presidential wreath—the Capt. and the Colonel walk up the steps with it after taking it from a high-ranking sergeant and lay it against a pillar of the memorial, not at the foot of the statue where it should be. The picture men were where the flowers should have been!

The Capt. and the Col. face me and salute; the Marine Band plays the Star Spangled Banner; the two Aides come down stairs in a stately manner, salute me, line up on Mrs. T's left; Presidential Honors are sounded; we shake hands with U. S. Grant No. 3, get in the car and go to the W.H. All done in ten minutes.

Isn't it too bad for a great man to have a Junior? It's hell to have a III.

DIARY

February 14, 1948

St. Valentine's Day. Fog, rain and 49 degrees.

My "baby" and her best friend give me valentines as does Bess, and I couldn't get out to get them one.

In times past I was the giver; now things are reversed, and I'm the *givee*. It's hell to be the Chief of State!

DIARY

March 6, 1948

Attend White House Correspondents dinner at which Tony Vaccaro is made President. Have to give an award to a guy who got it by writing a pack of lies! Freedom of the press. Ain't it grand!!!

On March 13, 1948, Eleanor Roosevelt wrote Secretary Marshall about the marked deterioration of Russian-American relations, and sent

a copy to the President. "I do not think I have been an alarmist before,"
she informed Truman in an accompanying letter, "but I have become
very worried and since we always have to sit down together when war
comes to an end, I think before we have a third World War, we should
sit down together."

TO ELEANOR ROOSEVELT

March 16, 1948

Dear Mrs. Roosevelt:

I appreciated most highly your letter of the thirteenth enclosing copy of the one which you had written to the Secretary of State. I think all of us are in practically the same frame of mind and I, of course, am glad to have your ideas and viewpoint.

I think if you will go over the history of the relationship between Russia and us you will find that every effort was made by President Roosevelt and by me to get along with them. Certain agreements were entered into at Tehran and Yalta and so far as our part of those agreements is concerned we carried them out to the letter.

When I arrived at Potsdam for that conference I found that the Poles at the suggestion of Russia had moved into eastern Germany and that Russia had taken over a section of eastern Poland. The agreement at Yalta provided for free and untrammeled elections in Rumania, Bulgaria, Yugoslavia and Poland. I found a totalitarian Soviet Government set up in Poland, in Rumania, in Yugoslavia and in Bulgaria. Members of our Commissions in Bulgaria and Rumania were treated as if they were stableboys by the Russians in control in those two countries. Russia has not kept faith with us.

I myself discussed the Polish situation with the Polish Government in Potsdam and got no satisfaction whatever from them—yet we made certain agreements in regard to the government of Germany which we have religiously tried to carry out. We have been blocked at every point by the Russians and to some extent by the French. The Russians have not carried out the agreements entered into at Potsdam.

The Russians are of the opinion that Henry Wallace and a depression are facing this country—they honestly believe that Wallace is going to be the next President. Of course, we all know that is absurd—we are much more likely to have the worst reactionary in the country for President than we are to have Wallace.

I shall go to the Congress tomorrow and state the facts. Beginning with my Message to the Congress on September sixth, 1945, I have constantly informed the Congress and the country of our needs in order to make the United Nations work and to arrive at a peace for the welfare and benefit of every country in the World.

The first decision I had to make after being sworn in at 7:09 P.M. April 12, 1945, was whether to have the United Nations Conference at San Francisco on April 25, 1945. The Charter of the United Nations is a document under which we could work and have peace if we could get Russian cooperation. Twenty-two vetoes have been exercised in the last two and one-half years by the Russian Government. As you know, I had to send Harry Hopkins to see Stalin in order to get Molotov to agree to the fundamental principles of the United Nations Charter.

I am still hopeful and still working with everything I have to make the United Nations work.

Our European Recovery Program and the proper strengthening of our Military setup is the only hope we now have for peace in the World. That I am asking from the Congress.

If the people who know the facts and who understand the situation are willing to say that we've done wrong in this matter I don't see how we can expect to come out at all in its solution. It is the most serious situation we have faced since 1939. I shall face it with everything I have.

Of course, I am always glad to hear from you and I appreciate your frankness in writing me as you did.

Sincerely yours,
Harry S. Truman

In 1947, the British government had dumped the Palestine issue in the lap of the United Nations. The result was a U.N. investigation and then a vote in the General Assembly in November in favor of a virtual partition between Arabs and Jews.

President Truman became much annoyed with the pressure tactics used by some American Jews to obtain passage of the U.N. resolution and for several months refused to see almost anyone on the Palestine issue. When the possibility arose that the American government would send troops somehow or, more likely, find a diplomatic solution to the Palestine issue less satisfactory to the Zionists, Truman's old haberdashery partner, Edward Jacobson, succeeded in obtaining an interview for the head of the Jewish Agency, Chaim Weizmann, then in New York City. Truman privately assured Weizmann, who entered the White House by the side entrance, that he would go ahead with the U.N. solution for Palestine. Then, most unfortunately, the day after the Weizmann interview, March 19, the American representative on the Security Council, Senator Warren Austin, announced a new proposition for Palestine, a temporary tripartite trusteeship by Great Britain, France, and the

United States. The proposal was the State Department's fail-safe policy in case the U.N. resolution did not promise to work. The department advanced it without advising the President, who probably had agreed generally to such a proposal but then forgotten it and in any event expected to be informed in case of a change. The trusteeship proposal gave the appearance that the President had broken faith with Weizmann.

DIARY

March 20, 1948

This morning I find that the State Dept. has reversed my Palestine policy. The first I know about it is what I see in the papers! Isn't that hell? I'm now in the position of a liar and a double crosser. I've never felt so in my life.

There are people on the 3rd and 4th levels of the State Dept. who have always wanted to cut my throat. They've succeeded in doing it. Marshall's in California and Lovett's in Florida.[1]

DIARY

March 21, 1948

I spend the day trying to right what has happened. No luck. Marshall makes a statement. Doesn't help me a mite.

TO VIVIAN TRUMAN

March 22, 1948

Dear Vivian:

I was glad to hear from you about your visit to the Kansas City Club.[1]

.... The things go up and down—one day you do things you think are for the welfare of the country and the next you are up against a complete reversal of feeling because something else that is right doesn't please.

I think the proper thing to do, and the thing I have been doing, is to do what I think is right and let them all go to hell.

Sincerely,

Harry

---

1. Undersecretary of State Robert A. Lovett succeeded Acheson in the summer of 1947.

---

1. Vivian had lunched at the club, whose members were mostly Republican, and related that his brother's political stock was rising.

TO MARY JANE TRUMAN

March 30, 1948

Dear Mary:

I have had two letters since I wrote you. Your last Wednesday letter and your Saturday one which enclosed a poem from some old woman in California. That is, it was purported to be a poem.

California crackpots are the most incongruous people. They come from Iowa, Nebraska, Kansas and, I'm sorry to say, our own good State of Missouri. They join such outfits as the one headed by Aimee Semple McPherson, Yoga, and any other nut set-up a good salesman starts.

When I was in Los Angeles in 1944 on the Presidential campaign, we drove by Aimee's Temple and a sacrilegious Californian told me that the "handwriting on the wall" had been changed from "Mene, Mene, Tekel Upharson" to "Aimee, Aimee, Semple McPherson." It is probably a fact so far as Aimee's followers are concerned.

I went to a press party at 6:30 last night, came home and had dinner with Bess, Mrs. Wallace, Mary Bostian (Salisbury) and Roslyn Allen—Pete's daughter. She's Agnes Salisbury's child. She now teaches school at the Benjamin Harrison School in K.C.

Agnes as you know is now married to the Gibson man. They are horse enthusiasts. Roslyn rode a prize horse at the last American Royal. She's a nice young woman—not the least like Spencer and old man Salisbury. Mary Bostian isn't either. Kenneth called Mary last night while we were at dinner and I talked to him. He seemed to be struck by the fact that he talked to "the President" over the telephone.

After dinner we turned the television machine on and saw a vaudeville act and a half dozen prize fights. I had to leave for a Greek meeting at 9:50. And was it a meeting. There were over 1,000 there including 271 members of Congress. I had to speak after being introduced by Dean Alfange, head of the Liberal Party in New York. They really gave me an ovation, and then some. It was very gratifying—especially when Curlie Brooks, Bertie McCormick's Senator from Illinois,[1] Brewster from Maine and a dozen other dirty lying Republicans had to look on and take it. Hope your poison ivy is well.

Lots of love.

Harry

---

1. Senator C. Wayland Brooks.

On April 3, Truman signed the initial $5.85 billion appropriation for the European Recovery Program, the Marshall Plan, which between April 3, 1948, and June 30, 1952, was to cost over $13.3 billion.

DIARY

April 3, 1948

Arrive at White House at 10:20 and dive into unfinished business. Have secretaries' conference. Talk to Dean Acheson about his running E.R.P. He reluctantly accepts on condition the Senate is in the right mood. Talked to Vandenberg about Acheson. He turned thumbs down. Said the Senate wanted no one connected with State Dept. Silly idea. Want some industrialist without experience.

Signed E.R.P. bill with Senators, Congressmen and Cabinet officers present. Talked to Carl Hayden of Arizona about Sec. of Agriculture. Attended Women's Press Club dinner.

DIARY

April 4, 1948

Took a walk at 10 A.M. Went to the Mellon Gallery and succeeded in getting the watchman on duty to let me in. Looked at the old Masters found in salt mine in Germany. Some very well-known paintings by Holbein, Franz Hals, Rubens, Rembrandt and others. It is a pleasure to look at perfection and then think of the lazy, nutty moderns. It is like comparing Christ with Lenin. May there be another awakening. We need an Isaiah, John the Baptist, Martin Luther—may he come soon.

TO VIVIAN TRUMAN

April 8, 1948

Dear Vivian:

I am enclosing you a letter from a "bird" down at Montrose, Missouri. I don't think I ever heard of him and I am sure if I ever met him it was by accident and not intentional.

You might try to worm out of him what is on his mind. I think he is trying to get a trip to Washington paid for by me.

Sincerely,

Harry

TO MARY JANE TRUMAN

April 8, 1948

Dear Mary:

I've had two letters from you since I sent you the last one. I've had the usual hectic week. I guess I'll never have any other sort from now on.

Tuesday I went to the funeral of the White House chief clerk, Judge Latta. He'd been in the White House as an employee since July 1, 1898, and had been on a temporary assignment for forty years of that time!

After attending his funeral at a Presbyterian Church at 18th & Kalorama Road I reviewed the Army Day Parade from a stand on Constitution Ave. south of the White House. Then came back to the House, put on my go-to-hell pants and received the Prince Regent of Belgium, a blue-eyed, red-haired young man about 35 who was very nervous. Gave him a state dinner Tuesday night, put him in the rose room where you and Mamma stayed, and bade him goodbye Wednesday morning in the office. Had a citation and a Belgian cross for the Unknown Soldier of World War II presented to me by the Prince when he was moving out of the White House. I don't know what to do with it because the Unknown Soldier of World War II is still unknown. Will go to the Belgian Embassy tonight to a state dinner in my honor given by the Prince. Hope they don't have fresh paint on the chairs, as was the case at the Mexican Embassy when Aleman, the President of Mexico, was here. I was lucky on that occasion. I sat in a "plush" chair—so did the Mexican President.

Margie and I went to see a new picture last night called "The State of the Union." It is a scream. If you get a chance go and see it. It gives the Republicans hell and, believe it or not, is favorable to your brother.

MacArthur and Dewey are in a mess as the result of the Wisconsin primary. A lot of good stories are going the rounds about the Almighty going back on his boy Mac. Another one about a meeting between Nimitz and Mac. Nimitz said he couldn't swim but he didn't want it known. Mac said he couldn't walk on water but the Admiral should keep it a secret. Hearst, the old beast, gave a party in Los Angeles for Luella Parsons. There were about 700 guests and Bob Hope presided. Hearst couldn't be present. Bob was explaining why. Said Hearst was not feeling well, that he was devoting all his time to building up a candidate for President (MacArthur) and that it was rumored that Hearst's candidate would fly home soon to campaign. Bob leaned over and very confidentially told the audience that the flight rumor was not true—the candidate intended to walk home!

Glad you're well again. Take good care of yourself. Write when you can.

Love to you.

Harry

Concerned about foreign affairs, the President drafted the following speech, undelivered of course.

DRAFT SPEECH (UNDELIVERED)

April 17 (?), 1948

You are naturally interested in foreign affairs. I will discuss foreign affairs with you for a few minutes and try to show you a foreign policy in the making.

In 1920 we refused to assume our proper place in world affairs because we thought we were the original 13 colonies and that we could follow advice given the country based on the situation in 1796.

In the early 1920's we decided to disarm so we made a treaty with Britain and Japan based on a 5-5-3 basis.[1] Then we proceeded to sink our half finished then modern ships and cut our land army to the bone.

We did an excellent job of it, too. Some people would do the same thing today.

The first decision I had to make when I took the oath of office as President was whether the United Nations Conference should proceed in San Francisco on Apr. 25, 1945. That conference met. Molotov represented Russia. On his way to San Francisco he stopped here, stayed at the Lee House over here on Pa. Ave. I was staying at the Blair House next door.

Molotov called on me at the Executive Office and began to tell me how I could cooperate with Russia by doing what Russia wanted. I explained to him in words of one syllable and in language he could understand that cooperation required agreement and concessions on both sides and that cooperation is not a one way street. He remarked that he had not been so bluntly addressed since he'd been foreign minister.

At San Francisco he held up the Conference at every turn. I finally

---

1. At the Washington Naval Conference of 1921–1922, the three major naval powers made a treaty limiting the tonnage of battleships and aircraft carriers, with the battleship limitation in hundreds of thousands of tons roughly on a basis of 5-5-3—5 for the U.S., 5 for Britain, and 3 for Japan. The Japanese came to resent the inferiority of their position.

sent Harry Hopkins to Moscow, and Stalin ordered Molly to quit stalling and sign up. He did.

Germany folded up on May 8, just 26 days after I became President. All the smart prophets had said six months or a year from May 1 would be Germany's end.

Then came Potsdam. I went to Potsdam with a plan and an agenda. It was presented. Some of it [was] adopted. I had the kindliest feeling for Russia and the Russian people and I liked Stalin.

But I found after a very patient year that Russian agreements are made to be broken.

We had demobilized completely—in fact too completely—but mamma and papa and every Congressman wanted every boy discharged at once after Japan folded up.

In November 1945 I asked for universal training and I kept asking for it at intervals up to March 17, 1948. In the early part of 1947 I appointed a commission to get the facts and report to me on U.M.T.

That committee had two leading college presidents on it, two able men of the cloth, two big business men and an able lawyer and a fine woman. They were not for U.M.T. when they started. They assembled the facts and on May 29, 1947, made one of the ablest reports I've ever seen. They were unanimous in their conclusions & recommendations. You should read it if you haven't. No action to date.

The Russians began in 1946 to make trouble in UN and in Germany and Korea. In March 1947 I went to Congress on Greece and Turkey. On May 8, 1947, Dean Acheson, Undersecretary of State, made a speech to the Delta Conference in Miss. on Greece, Turkey and Europe generally and in June 1947 General Marshall made his famous Harvard speech. The European countries called a conference of sixteen nations and the first step of the European recovery program was taken.

Russia was not barred. Everyone was invited to the Paris conference. Czechoslovakia wanted to come but was prevented.

I have always been willing to talk to Russia on any subject. At Potsdam I invited Stalin to come to Washington—he said God willing he'd come.

I sent him word after Churchill's speech I'd be glad to give him an opportunity to come and talk to the American people.[2]

There are people who keep yelling for big three conferences—for

---

2. After Churchill's Iron Curtain speech, the President had written to Stalin, offering to send the *Missouri* to bring him to the United States, promising to escort him to the University of Missouri at Columbia "for exactly the same kind of reception, the same opportunity to speak your mind." The answer was no.

what purpose I wonder. Our position has not changed. All we want is peace in the world.

That is all we've ever wanted—what [we] have tried to get and what we are trying to get.

In all the history of the world we are the first great nation to feed and support the conquered. We are the first great nation to create independent republics from conquered territory, Cuba and the Philippines. Our neighbors are not afraid of us. Their borders have no forts, no soldiers, no tanks, no big guns lined up.

We are a peaceful nation. But we must be prepared for trouble if it comes. Twice in a generation brave allies have kept the barbarian from our borders. It can't happen that way again.

I have asked for a balanced preparedness program. Preparedness for enforcement of peace through the United Nations.

When I took office our military budget was on the basis of 100 billions a year. It has come down to eleven billions. I had hoped to get it to six or seven. Had U.M.T. been authorized when I asked for it we might have succeeded.

Now I'm asking for a balanced program—an immediate one and a long range one.

The immediate one calls for return of selective service and certain increases in Army, Navy & Air.

The long range one calls for U.M.T., intensive research programs and a balanced force.

All this controversy over the number of [air] groups is beside the question. If the Congress succeeds in running from U.M.T. with a slight air force increase then our defense budget can *never* come down. Never is a long time too.

Now let me explain this situation. Do it.

Our friends the Russkies understand only one language—how many divisions have you—actual or potential. . . .

As the spring wore on into summer, the President still found himself incessantly busy, and there was no letup in the international crises; but the summer meant the assembling of the Democratic convention, and because Truman was the incumbent President, his nomination. Looking forward to a very tough campaign, Truman worried about his ability to make a convincing speech. He possessed a Missouri twang, his voice was monotonous, and he feared that almost any sort of orator on the Republican side could outdo him. Just in time for the whistle-stop campaign

that autumn he discovered the possibilities latent in a speech done on
an impromptu basis, off the cuff, without a manuscript.

DIARY

May 6, 1948

I appeared before a family life conference at 12:30 and spoke over all four networks without a manuscript. The audience gave me a most cordial reception. I hope the radio and television audiences were half as well pleased. I may have to become an "orator." I heard a definition of an orator once—"He is an honest man who can communicate his views and make others believe he is right." Wish I could do that. Because I think I've been right in the approach to all questions 90% of the time since I took over. I was handicapped by lack of knowledge of both foreign and domestic affairs—due principally to Mr. Roosevelt's inability to pass on responsibility. He was always careful to see that no credit went to anyone else for accomplishment. The Palace Guard was the cause. I am troubled in the same way.

The objective and its accomplishment is my philosophy, and I am willing and want to pass the credit around. The objective is the thing, not personal aggrandizement. All Roosevelts want the personal aggrandizement. Too bad. Byrnes and Baruch also have that complex.

DIARY

May 7, 1948

Returns from the radio on the family life speech are very satisfactory. Looks as if I'm stuck for "off the cuff" radio speeches. It means a lot of hard work, and the head at 64 doesn't work as well as it did at 24.

Had a most important conference with Marshall, Forrestal, Snyder, Jim Webb of budget and Forrestal's budget man. We are faced with a defense problem. I have wanted a universal training program, a balanced regular setup, Ground, Air, Water and a reserve to back up the regular skeleton training force. The Congress can't bring itself to do the right thing—because of votes. The air boys are for glamour, and the Navy as always is the greatest propaganda machine. I want a balanced sensible defense for which the country can pay. If the glamour boys win, we'll have another 1920 and another 1941. God keep us from that! And it is so sensible and easy to keep from it. But—. Marshall is a tower of strength and common sense. So are Snyder and Webb. Forrestal can't take it. He wants to compromise with the opposition!

The President never forgot his political defeat of 1924, when he ran
for eastern judge (county commissioner) of Jackson County. Nor could
he forget the primary fight of 1940, when he sought renomination as
senator. By 1940 the district attorney, Maurice Milligan, had put Boss
Tom Pendergast in jail for income tax evasion, and while Truman's
relations with the boss were by no means dependent (see below, pages
228–232), he had cooperated with him, as any Democrat in Jackson
County who hoped for public office had to do. In the early spring of 1940,
Governor Lloyd Stark, of Stark apple fame, promised Senator Truman
he would not run against him, and then changed about and ran. Presi-
dent Roosevelt did not endorse Stark, but neither did he endorse Tru-
man, and he offered the senator a job on the Interstate Commerce Com-
mission, a sure sign that the boss in Washington expected Truman to
lose. Roy Roberts of the Star *felt the same way and plumped for Stark*
—until Truman, by going into more than half of Missouri's 114 counties
and carrying his campaign to the people, won the primary.

TO NELLIE NOLAND

May 9, 1948

Dear Nellie:

Thanks a lot for the beautiful handkerchief. I've never seen or possessed a finer one.

I hope all of you are well. We sent Aunt Ella some White House
flowers. Hope they arrived in time.

Tell Ethel that Dr. Harcourt Morgan came in to see me a day or two
ago and told me his mother's name was Truman and that she was a
Canadian descended from the same old English family from whom our
first Truman ancestor is supposed to have come. He is 80 years old and
looks very much like Uncle Will Truman.

It is remarkable, these days, how anxious people are to be, even
distantly, related to me. That wasn't the case in 1924 when I was defeated
for Eastern Judge—nor in 1940 when F.D.R. and nearly everybody else
was of the opinion that Stark was an angel and I was the representative
of the devil in the person of Tom Pendergast. And I'll make a bet that Roy
Roberts, Maurice Milligan and [the] rest of that ilk will be asking Old
Tom for water from the depths of hell while he smiles at 'em from on
high and petitions that they be allowed mercy.

This is a hell of a thankyou note.

But I do thank you.

Love to all of you.

Harry

TO MARY JANE TRUMAN

May 12, 1948

Dear Mary:

I hope you had a nice time on your various visits around the state. I wrote you just before you went to St. Louis last week and enclosed your check. I just want to be sure that letter was delivered to you. I am sure it was.

I've been having the usual difficulties. They, no doubt, will continue, no matter who is President. I've been reading a couple of books—one about "The Presidents and the Press" and another one called "This Was Normalcy." It seems that every man in the White House was tortured and bedeviled by the so-called free press. They were lied about, misrepresented and actually libeled and they had to take it and do nothing.

The old S.O.B. who owned and edited the St. Louis Post Dispatch and the New York World was in my opinion the meanest character assassin in the whole history of liars who have controlled newspapers—and that includes old man Hearst and Bertie McCormick!

Some day, I hope a mucker will come along and dig up the facts on the distorters of news and facts.

I had thought that pictures and the radio would cure the news liars —but they—the liars—have taken over both.

Pearson, Winchell and local scavengers paid by such stations as WGN and WDAF make it impossible for the listeners to get the facts.

When I am finished here maybe I'll do it myself. I'll make a bet however that hell has become almost untenable for the devil since old Pulitzer, Horace Greeley, Chas. Dana, the old copperhead Bill Nelson[1] and William Allen White arrived.

Hope you've been well and things are all right with you.

Write when you can.

Sincerely,

Harry

TO MARY JANE TRUMAN

May 19, 1948

Dear Mary:

I was glad to get your letter yesterday. You really have a trip ahead of you. I hope the weather will behave. It is very cold here

---

1. William Rockwell Nelson was Roy Roberts's predecessor at the Kansas City *Star* and founder of the Nelson Gallery of Fine Art.

this morning. The wind is from the north and blowing a gale.

Bess is expecting to have a garden party at noon for the Senate women. I fear they'll have to wear fur coats. Every day there's something. I had to receive about 800 folks here on a Citizenship Conference yesterday and Bess shook hands with 600 Psychiatrists (Nut Doctors). Today I have dentists on hand. Saturday Lou Holland was in with the School Safety Boys and Girls. All this in addition to the regular round of business and callers.

Tomorrow I go to Philadelphia to make a speech to the kids at Girard College on the 100th anniversary of the College. And so it goes and goes but maybe it will end some day.

Take care of yourself.

Love to you.

Harry

Margaret goes to N.Y. Friday to do some Boy Scout stunt. She has some meeting or some stunt nearly every day too. Don't know why in hell anybody would fight for this awful job—but they do.

Among Mrs. Roosevelt's many causes was the problem of conscientious objectors. The President found her inquiries on the subject awkward, the one of May 1948 not least, for his initial draft of a reply was dated May 17, the second, dated May 22, was not sent either, and a final version—dated May 25 and sent—merely acknowledged the letter and enclosed a memo from the attorney general ("it covers the situation completely," sighed the President).

TO ELEANOR ROOSEVELT (UNSENT)

May 22, 1948

Dear Mrs. Roosevelt:

I read very carefully the memorandum re pardon for conscientious objectors which you forwarded with your letter of May thirteenth. Since the Department of Justice has all of the records I asked the Attorney General to prepare a memorandum covering the subject. It is enclosed herewith.

Both this office and the Attorney General have been in correspondence on this question with the Federal Council of Churches of Christ in America.

I admit that I have strong views on the question of dishonest and insincere "conscientious objectors." While your four sons and my three nephews were risking their lives to save our government and the things for which we stand, those who are now asking for mercy were virtually stabbing our boys in the back.

I ran across one conscientious objector that I really believe is all man —he was a young Naval Pharmacist Mate who served on Okinawa carrying wounded sailors and marines from the battlefield. I decorated him with a Congressional Medal of Honor. I asked him how it came about that he as a conscientious objector was willing to go into the thick of the battlefield and he said to me that he could serve the Lord and save lives as well there as anywhere else in the world. He didn't weigh over one hundred and forty pounds and he was about five feet six inches tall. I shall never forget him.

My experience in the first world war with conscientious objectors was not a happy one—the majority of those with whom I came in contact were just plain cowards and shirkers—that is the reason I asked Justice Roberts to make a complete survey of the situation and to release all those that he felt were honestly conscientious objectors and that has been done. My sympathies with the rest of them are not very strong, as you can see. While I am determined that no honest man shall suffer unjustly, I am equally determined that no impostor shall escape retributive justice.

I am glad that you and I and Secretary Marshall were all in accord on the wisdom of immediate recognition of the State of Israel. I was glad to have your letter of May eleventh. I am more convinced than ever that we followed the right course.

With his ever present instinct to promote his home state, Truman arranged for the president of Venezuela and his wife to visit Bolivar, Missouri.

DIARY

June 27, 1948

Margie goes back to Missouri today. I wish she would stay until next Sunday and go back to Bolivar with the Venezuelan President. I'm very much afraid she's seen too many dignitaries and that they haven't made the proper impression. Dignitaries are much more ideal in print than face to face. Old Judge Battle McCardle told me, when I was elected to the Senate in 1934, not to go to the Senate with an inferiority complex; that for six months I'd sit in that august body and wonder how I'd attained a seat in it, and after that I'd wonder how in hell the rest of them ever arrived in the Senate! How very true that turned out to be—especially after April 12, 1945.

Robert B. (Bobby) Stewart, twenty-seven years old, a naval officer during the war, one of Margaret Truman's favorite dates, was attending Harvard when he was killed on June 17, 1948, in the crash of a United Air Lines DC–6 in Pennsylvania. The Trumans went to the funeral and burial in Arlington. It was a tragic death, and the President wrote the bereaved parents.

TO GEORGE EARLE AND LOUISE STEWART

June 27, 1948

Dear Earle and Louise:

I am taking the liberty of making a suggestion to you. I hope you won't think I am, in any way, trying to interfere in your private affairs.

I was very fond of Bobby. I think he had a great future. It is my hope that you will make Bobby's spirit realize that future. I believe you can do it.

You know of various great foundations. Rockefeller, Carnegie, Guggenheim and others. I am of the opinion that Girard and Father Flanagan are the best of all of them. Girard and the good father were not salving a conscience as the others were.

I am suggesting that Earle and Louise Stewart, in the name of Bobby, pick out a boy and a girl in Anderson, Ind., and Columbia, Mo., and see them through High School, and do it every year.

In a four year course that would mean you would be supporting sixteen young men and young women for a fundamental education—much more important to the young people than college. You would only take those who could not afford the cost of going to high school. If that is too great [a] burden you could take a boy and a girl turn about in Anderson and Columbia. That would be a total of eight over a four year period.

It would on the smaller basis cost about $200 per month or $2000.00 per year. Probably for four years one half the cost of one tour of Europe such as you are accustomed to take.

And you'd make Bobby immortal! You'd have the greatest life interest in the world looking after these young people—and I'm sure God Almighty would be pleased.

I hope you'll think about this suggestion anyway.

Sincerely,

Harry S. Truman

DIARY

June 28, 1948

Bess and I are eating supper on the south porch of the White House at 7 P.M. I am facing the Jefferson Memorial across the White House lawn. There is a fountain in the center of the lawn surrounded by petunias— we had dwarf cannas last year, and the Jap beetles ate them into rags and tatters.

A ball game or two goes on in the park south of the lawn. Evidently a lot of competition, from the cheers and calls of the coaches. A robin hops around looking for worms, finds one and pulls with all his might to unearth him. A mocking bird imitates robins, jays, red birds, crows, hawks—but has no individual note of his own. A lot of people like that. Planes take off and land at the National Air Port south of the Jefferson Memorial. It is a lovely evening. I can see the old Chesapeake and Potomac Canal going across the Washington Monument grounds, barges anchoring west of the Monument. I can see old J. Q. Adams going swimming in it and getting his clothes stolen by an angry woman who wanted a job. The old guy did not have my guards or it wouldn't have happened. Then I wake up, go upstairs and go to work and contemplate the prison life of a President. What the hell!

DIARY

July 5, 1948

Arrive at Springfield, Mo., at 7:15 Central Time. Leave at 8:15. The Venezuelan President is looking for two old ladies who were kind to him and the Senora in 1937 when they stopped in Springfield after a trip from Los Angeles by car. They had a wreck at Williams, Ariz., in which the Senora was badly hurt. At Springfield, Mo., they stopped at a tourist place run by these lovely old ladies. They obtained a doctor for the future Venezuelan President and did other services for him and the Senora— and would not take pay. The President has been trying to find them. He wanted them to come to Venezuela for his inauguration. He wanted to decorate them on this trip. They can't be found. Too bad.

Arrive in Bolivar at 9:45 on time, met by Gov. Donnelly of Mo., the Mayor of Bolivar. Drive to the Court House, review a grand parade and go to the park to dedicate the statue of Simon Bolivar presented by the Gov't of Venezuela to the people of the U.S. Sat in the sun at 104 in the shade for two hours. It is a grand ceremony but hotter than hell. The Gov.

of Mo. collapses at the end. We go back to Springfield. The President of V. and party leave us at Springfield airport and go to N.Y. in the Independence.[1]

To complicate the President's political troubles, a boomlet developed for the nomination of General Eisenhower on the Democratic ticket. Ike never had voted, and until 1952 did not know whether he was a Republican or a Democrat.

DIARY

July 6, 1948

A pleasant trip across the country. Thousands of people out at every town. Wave at them from the back platform and say nothing. Arrive at White House at 10:30 E.D.S.T. and meet with Democratic Convention strategy board. Everything in order. Jim Roosevelt, Jake Arvey, A.D.A.[1] and Frank Hague are for Eisenhower. Doublecrossers all. But they'll get nowhere—a doubledealer never does.

The thorough political professionalism of the President is apparent in his diary, for in the summer of 1948 he watched the maneuvers to obtain the nomination for someone else and for the most part was quite unmoved. Even the arrangement, if such it was, by which the President of the United States, seeking nomination by his own party, was forced to wait in the convention hall in Philadelphia until 2:00 A.M., well after the radio networks' prime time, to make his acceptance speech did not especially bother him, for he took it as a portion of political life.

DIARY

July 12, 1948

Douglas says he can't quit the Supreme Court. Says the family are of the opinion that his lack of political experience would cause trouble in the campaign. Says no to my request that he take second place on the ticket with me. I'm inclined to give some credence to Tommy Corcoran's crack to Burt Wheeler that Douglas had said he could be a number two

1. The presidential plane, a DC-6, successor to the *Sacred Cow.*

1. Colonel Jacob Arvey, Democratic leader of Chicago; Americans for Democratic Action.

man to a number two man. Call old man Barkley and smooth his feathers so he'll go ahead and make the keynote speech. McGrath[1] calls me and suggests I call Barkley again and say I am not against him. I don't do it. Barkley makes a real keynote speech. Ends up at midnight. I can't get him by phone. My "good" friend, Leslie Biffle, spends all his time as sergeant-at-arms of the Convention running Barkley for President. I watch the demonstration on television. Having been in on numerous demonstrations I'm not fooled. I can see everything taking place on the platform. The "actors" forget that. Barkley in his good speech mentions me only casually by name.

DIARY

July 13, 1948

I call Barkley and smooth him down again. Tried to call him last night after his good speech but can't get him. Call McGrath and tell him I'm coming up tomorrow on the train and accept. He is not very happy over it. Talk to Hannegan, Ed Flynn and Frank Walker.[1] All disgruntled as has-beens always are with a new chairman. It means not one thing. The result is what counts. Platform fight this afternoon, postponed until tomorrow. But they have a good fight on credentials. A Negro alternate from St. Louis makes a minority report suggesting the unseating of Mississippi delegation. Vaughn is his name. He's overruled. Then Congressman Dawson of Chicago, another Negro, makes an excellent talk on civil rights. These two colored men are the only speakers to date who seem to be for me wholeheartedly. Snyder calls and says Jimmy R., Leon Henderson and Wilson Wyatt[2] are running Barkley for President. Maybe so, but Barkley is an honorable man. He won't give me the double cross, I'm sure.

Some months before the Democratic convention, the leaders of the ADA had begun a campaign to introduce a strong civil rights plank in the party's platform, and their efforts produced a real confrontation in Philadelphia. Truman was in a quandary over this agitation, for he needed to avoid a southern bolt if at all possible. His personal sympathies certainly were with the ADA. At the convention his floor managers tried to quiet the ADA's leaders, Mayor Humphrey of Minneapolis and ex-Congressman Andrew J. Biemiller, but the ADA refused to give

---

1. J. Howard McGrath, chairman of the Democratic National Committee.

---

1. All were former chairmen of the Democratic National Committee.
2. Henderson was prominent in the ADA; Wyatt was the former mayor of Louisville.

in to statesmanship and took the issue to the floor. At first it appeared as if Sam Rayburn, the chairman, might not merely cut off the floor microphones, to deaden the noise of tumult in the hall, but decide the issue by voice vote, which would give the conservatives a chance; but when both sides approached him privately and asked for a roll call, he agreed.

DIARY

July 14, 1948

Platform fight in dead earnest. Crackpot Biemiller from Wisconsin offers a minority report on civil rights. Moody from Texas offers states rights amendment. Some old gal from Mass. offers an amendment to consolidate and free Ireland! and old man Curley, Mayor of Boston, makes a demagogue speech on it!

The Convention votes down States Rights and votes for the crackpot amendment to the Civil Rights Plank. The crackpots hope the South will bolt. Rayburn adjourns the convention after adoption of Platform. Alabama tried for recognition. I'm sure they want to bolt.

Take the train for Philadelphia at 7 P.M. Eastern Daylight Time. Arrive in the rain at 9:15. Television sets at both ends of trip. No privacy sure enough now. Hear Alabama and Mississippi walk out of the Convention. Hear Gov. Donnelly nominate me. Both on the train radio. Hard to hear. My daughter and my staff try to keep me from listening. Think maybe I'll be upset. I won't be. Arrive at Convention Hall, see a horde of politicians, masculine and feminine. Have a pleasant time visiting with Barkley out on a balcony of the hall back of the stage. It was an interesting and instructive evening. I make my acceptance speech at 2 A.M.

[After Truman's nomination the convention nominated Barkley for vice president.]

In his acceptance speech, Truman called a special session of Congress, trying to force the Republicans to keep their campaign promises —he knew they wouldn't, knew they'd be furious at having to give up their summer vacations.

DIARY

July 15, 1948

Arrived in Washington at the White House at 5:30 A.M., my usual getting up time. But I go to bed at 6:00 and listen to the news. Sleep until 9:15, order breakfast and go to the office at 10:00. I called a special session of the Congress. My, how the opposition screams. I'm going to attempt to make them meet their platform promises before the election. That is, according to the "kept" press and the opposition leadership, "cheap politics." I wonder what "expensive politics" will be like! We'll see.

DIARY

July 16, 1948

Editorials, columns and cartoons are gasping and wondering. None of the smart folks thought I would call the Congress. I called 'em for July 26, turnip day at home.[1] Dewey synthetically milks cows and pitches hay for the cameras just as that other fakir, Teddy Roosevelt, did—but he'd never heard of "turnip day." I don't believe the USA wants any more fakirs—Teddy and Franklin are enough. So I'm going to make a common sense, intellectually honest campaign. It will be a novelty—and it will win.

DIARY

July 18, 1948

Pay my respects to Gen. Pershing.[1] I go to the Capitol in my role as a Field Artillery Captain in World War I. Have no police escort, only the aides in the car—Leahy, Vaughan, Graham, Dennison, Landry. We get a stop order on the way back to the White House by a cop on a motorcycle who wants to get Gen. Marshall through. It's funny as can be. Marshall won't go through and the cop has a bad half minute. I feel sorry for him

---

1. "In Missouri in days gone by when farmers worked with mules and horses and walked behind the plow and the cultivator and planted gardens by hand as soon as spring came, everyone knew about blackberry winter, that potatoes should be planted in the dark of the moon in March, with the eyes up, oats should be sown in the light of the moon in February and turnips should be sown on the 26th of July wet or dry." (Undated letter to Carol Taylor, PPF, General File, Box 286 [handwritten].)

---

1. General John J. Pershing died on July 15, 1948, at the age of eighty-seven. His body lay in state under the dome of the Capitol.

and wish I'd put the flags on my car. But I don't like pomp and circumstance when it can be avoided. Nobody's feelings hurt but the poor policeman, and I'm sorry for that.

Barkley and I have a confab at the White House at 4:00 P.M. Very satisfactory.

DIARY

July 19, 1948

Have quite a day. See some politicos. A meeting with General Marshall and Jim Forrestal on Berlin and the Russian situation. Marshall states the facts and the condition with which we are faced. I'd made the decision ten days ago to *stay in Berlin.* Jim wants to hedge—he always does. He's constantly sending me alibi memos which I return with directions and the facts. We'll stay in Berlin—come what may. Royall, Draper[1] and Jim Forrestal come in later. I have to listen to a rehash of what I know already and reiterate my "Stay in Berlin" decision. I don't pass the buck, nor do I alibi out of any decision I make.

Went to Pershing's funeral in the marble amphitheater in Arlington. The hottest damn place this side of hell and Bolivar, Mo. An impressive ceremony. This is the 5th time I've prepared to attend the General's funeral. It came off this time.

Bess and Margaret went to Mo. at 7:30 E.D.T. 6:30, God's time. I sure hated to see them go. Came back to the great white jail and read the papers, some history and then wrote this. It is hot and humid and lonely. Why in hell does anybody want to be a head of a state? Damned if I know.

DIARY

Independence, Mo.
July 31, 1948

Up at 5:30 as usual. Get my shave, bath and clothes changed in about forty minutes. Had another "round table" on N.Y. appearance. Think it worked out O.K. Landed at 10 A.M. Went to White House. Had Prettyman[1] pack grips for N.Y. and Mo. trip to vote in primary.

Great reception in N.Y. O'Dwyer, Mayor of N.Y., met me for the *first time!* He's either been sick, out of town, or too busy before. It's a good sign because he's a bandwagon boy. Reviewed parade of the air. A grand

1. William H. Draper, Jr., investment banker, undersecretary of the army.

1. Arthur S. Prettyman, valet.

success. Flew back to Washington, unloaded the brass and took on some Mo. voters and arrived K.C. 7:50.

DIARY

August 3, 1948

Voted at 6:30. Pictures ad lib and smart aleck questions galore.

Took off at 8:00 A.M. Central Standard Time. Arrived in Washington at 1:20 E.D.T., just three hours and twenty minutes flying time. Think of that! Takes 27 hours by train and two days and a half by automobile. My old plane, the "Sacred Cow," took 4½ hours. We haven't adjusted ourselves to this speed.

Went to the "Great White Jail"—White House—had lunch, a short nap, then went to the executive office and worked until 6:30.

Found the White House falling down. My daughter's sitting room floor had broken down over the family dining room. How very lucky we are that the thing didn't break when Margie and Annette Wright were playing two-piano duets where the floor broke.

The White House Architect and Engineer have moved me into the Southeast or Lincoln Room—for safety—imagine that!

With all his political troubles in the year 1948, the President remained firm on the issue of civil rights. An old friend, a one-time corporal in "C" Battery, 129th Field Artillery, now associated with the Faultless Starch Company of Kansas City, advised the President to go easy on the civil rights issue, appealing to him as a Southerner.

TO ERNEST W. ROBERTS

August 18, 1948

Dear Ernie:

I appreciated very much your letter of last Saturday night from Hotel Temple Square in the Mormon Capital.

I am going to send you a copy of the report of my Commission on Civil Rights and then if you still have that antebellum proslavery outlook, I'll be thoroughly disappointed in you.

The main difficulty with the South is that they are living eighty years behind the times and the sooner they come out of it the better it will be for the country and themselves. I am not asking for social equality, because no such thing exists, but I am asking for equality of opportunity for all human beings and, as long as I stay here, I am going to continue that fight. When the mob gangs can take four people out and shoot them in the back, and everybody in the country is acquainted with who did the shooting and nothing is done about it, that country is in a pretty bad fix from a law enforcement standpoint.

When a Mayor and a City Marshal can take a negro Sergeant off a bus in South Carolina, beat him up and put out one of his eyes, and nothing is done about it by the State Authorities, something is radically wrong with the system.

On the Louisiana and Arkansas Railway when coal burning locomotives were used, the negro firemen were the thing because it was a back-breaking job and a dirty one. As soon as they turned to oil as a fuel it became customary for people to take shots at the negro firemen and a number were murdered because it was thought that this was now a white-collar job and should go to a white man. I can't approve of such goings on and I shall never approve it, as long as I am here, as I told you before. I am going to try to remedy it and if that ends up in my failure to be reelected, that failure will be in a good cause.

I know you haven't thought this thing through and that you do not know the facts. I am happy, however, that you wrote me because it gives me a chance to tell you what the facts are.

Sincerely yours,

Harry S. Truman

[Note in longhand:] This is a personal & confidential communication and I hope you'll regard it that way—at least until I've made a public statement on the subject—as I expect to do *in the South.*

HST

[In the campaigning that autumn the President was as good as his word. He spoke to an integrated audience in Rebel Stadium in Dallas; in Waco he shook hands with a black woman and the crowd booed. He boldly told the southerners that black citizens had the same rights as white Americans.]

TO BESS W. TRUMAN

U.S.S. Williamsburg
September 11, 1948

Dear Bess:

I accompanied Margie to the train yesterday at noon. We arrived at the station just about two minutes ahead of leaving time for the train. They drove us into the east entrance but we walked from the fence to the train. Margie thought that was showing discrimination.

We made it to the car and she plastered my left cheek with lipstick as she went aboard and very carefully wiped it off with her glove! Had a wire from her about 5 P.M. signed "Skinny." I'd been stewing around about not hearing from her and Capt. Dennison started to call Mrs. Stewart, and they told him at the White House that this telegram signed "Skinny" was there. He very timidly asked me if that by any chance could be Margie. Went back to the White House and saw a lot of customers and finally arrived aboard here at 1:30 when I was due at 12:30. It rained and rained but I won a bet that the sun would shine all day today, and it has and is. I'm out on the "back porch" of my deck in a swimming suit taking more burning. We've had a very satisfactory conference on the western speeches.

Farm speech at Des Moines on Sept. 18, conservation at Denver on the 20th, reclamation at Salt Lake City on the 21st—in the great Mormon Tabernacle, believe it or not—only Presidents of U.S. and high Mormons can do that. Then San Francisco, L.A., San Diego, Arizona, Texas, Oklahoma, Ky., West Va. and Washington, D.C. Seems like a nice little trip— what?

Charlie Ross is flying up to D.C. to attend the wedding of his niece, Virginia's daughter. I'm sending letter up on the plane that brings him back. We are anchored at the mouth of the Potomac at Blakiston Island where Lord Baltimore landed in 1734. There is a monument on it which says that's so. I went and looked at it—that's how I can tell you. This is a most restful day—and how I needed it. Six speeches on Monday was rather strenuous. I told the press boys on Thursday that Labor Day was only a sample of what they'd get on the western trip.

We had pictures on Wednesday and Thursday night. Had Irve, Annette and Mrs. Davis Wednesday & Jane, Drucie and Irve & Annette on Thursday.

My finance meeting Thursday was a grand success. Margie "stole the show." We're off to win I think.

Lots of love.

Harry

DIARY

September 13, 1948

Have a terrific day. Forrestal, Bradley, Vandenberg (the Gen., not the Senator!), Symington[1] brief me on bases, bombs, Moscow, Leningrad, etc.

---

1. General Hoyt S. Vandenberg, nephew of the senator, chief of staff of the air force; Stuart Symington, secretary of the air force.

I have a terrible feeling afterward that we are very close to war. I hope not.

See Marshall at lunch and feel better although Berlin is a mess.

Have usual Monday Cabinet luncheon. These luncheons are great. They have kept the Cabinet a team.

My staff is in a turmoil. Clifford has gone prima donna on me. So has Howard McGrath. It's hell but a part of the game. Have had to force McGrath to behave and Clifford too. But I get a headache over it. But a good night's sleep will cure it.

Spoke to the scientists and knocked them for a goal.[2]

DIARY

September 14, 1948

Another hell of a day. I'm sitting for an old Polish painter, and I don't like to pose—but it's also a part of the trial of being President. He's painted a nice stuffed shirt picture. This is about No. 7 or No. 8. Hope it's the last.

Had the gang in at 6:00 P.M. and worked on farm speech for Des Moines.

Papers gave science speech good coverage. Hope it does some good.

TO MARY JANE TRUMAN

October 5, 1948

Dear Mary:

I am three letters behind but it is a wonder I ever catch up. The trip just ended was a most strenuous one. I started out with a sore throat and the dust at Dexter, Iowa, just west of Des Moines, didn't help it any. Dr. Graham just sprayed, mopped and caused me to gargle bad tasting liquids until the throat gave up and got well. When we arrived in D.C. it was back to normal and good as new. We made about a hundred and forty stops and I spoke over 147 times, shook hands with at least 30,000 and am in good condition to start out again tomorrow for Wilmington, Philadelphia, Jersey City, Newark, Albany and Buffalo. Be back in Washington Saturday night and start again

---

2. The President spoke to the American Association for the Advancement of Science and called for the honest and uncompromising commonsense of science, a method of thought characterized by openmindedness, honesty, perserverence, and above all unflinching passion for knowledge and truth. "When more of the peoples of the world have learned the ways of thought of the scientist, we shall have better reason to expect lasting peace and a fuller life for all."

the following Monday, finally winding up in K.C. Sunday morning Oct. 31.

It will be the greatest campaign any President ever made. Win, lose, or draw, people will know where I stand and a record will be made for future action by the Democratic Party.

We had tremendous crowds everywhere. From 6:30 in the morning until midnight the turnout was phenomenal. The news jerks didn't know what to make of it—so they just lied about it!

I hope you have had a successful trip in Wisconsin and Illinois and that you arrive home safely.

Vivian called me on the last day of the trip and told me Aunt Ella was dead. The funeral was Saturday and I couldn't get there except by canceling appointments with the Cabinet and the Chief Justice and flying out and back. I was so tired I just couldn't do it.

Margaret and Bess were nearly worn out so we didn't go to the funeral. I suppose the Nolands will be madder than ever at you and me. But we can't help it.

Margaret has gone to St. Louis with John Snyder and family to appear at the Veiled Prophet's Ball. Bess & I will have to make out without her on this trip.

Take care of yourself and let me hear from you when you can. Lots of love.

Harry

The triumphant return to the White House after the election—whatever shape the old mansion was in—was, well, just wonderful, with crowds all the way, and with the great homemade banner emblazoned across the building of the Washington Post *reading:* MR. PRESIDENT, WE ARE READY TO EAT CROW WHENEVER YOU ARE READY TO SERVE IT.

TO MARY JANE TRUMAN

November 7, 1948

Dear Mary:

I am up at an early hour [3:00 A.M.] because I have to see that Bess takes her medicine at 3:30. She has a very bad cold, sore throat and she can't talk. But you shouldn't say anything about it. For some reason Bess doesn't like being in bed and she resents sympathy even from her own mother. I'm somewhat the same way.

The reception here was the greatest in the history of this old capital. When the train backed into the station the police band played the ruffles and Hail to the Chief and then people began piling on the train. Barkley and I must have shaken hands with at least five or six hundred—some of them Johnnie come lately boys. I finally put a stop to the handshaking. Barkley, Bess, Margaret and Barkley's daughter, Mrs. Max Truitt, stepped into the big, open seven-passenger car which belongs to the White House fleet. Mr. McGrath tucked himself between Barkley & me. The seat's rather narrow for three—especially three with Barkley. So Barkley and I sat up on the back of the back seat.

There were about 800,000 people on the street between the station and the White House. Said to be the biggest crowd ever out in Washington. Barkley & I made speeches from the front steps of the great white jail and then went to a Cabinet meeting to decide on the first message to the Congress.

I found the White House in one terrible shape. There are scaffolds in the East Room, props in the study, my bedroom, Bess' sitting room, and the Rose Room where you and Mamma stayed. We've had to call off all functions and will move out as soon as I come back from Key West.[1]

It will require at least ten months to tear the old second floor out and put it back. In the meantime I guess we'll live at the Blair House across the street. It is a nice place but only half as large—so we have no place to put guests.

I hope you looked at that envelope I gave you at Independence. It contained your check!

Lots of love.

Harry

Unlike her brother, Mary Jane Truman was thin-skinned, and her aspirations to the post of worthy grand matron of the O.E.S. for the state of Missouri sometimes led to agonizing second thoughts.

TO MARY JANE TRUMAN

Key West
November 14, 1948

Dear Mary:

I have received all your letters. They come promptly. I always answer them just as soon as I can. I sent you two from Washington and two from here. This is No. 2 from here.

---

1. Two years before, in 1946, after a considerable search for a vacation spot, Truman found one that suited—the submarine base at Key West. Key West had a fine climate, was suitably protected by the navy, and easily provided for twenty or thirty reporters, a staff of sixteen, and another fifteen or sixteen secret service men. Indeed, Truman's visits to Key West became so frequent in the next years that reporters began to speak of his modest quarters there as the Little White House.

I have been signing and dictating as fast as I can here. Just finished signing a folder full of public documents and I must now sign some three or four hundred letters. It is no vacation—only a change of scenery.

You must not get touchy about things in your Chapter O.E.S. or anywhere else. Don't read Doris Fleeson and those fool columnists. No one pays any attention to them at all.

Now if you go around all the time expecting someone to do you a bad turn you can always find them doing it. That K.C. introduction was my fault and I didn't do it on purpose. It won't happen again. Now we've got 'em licked let's be generous and make 'em like it.

I didn't mean to give you a lecture but your letter sounded rather sorry for yourself. You don't have to be that as long as I live.

Hope you have a nice time at all your meetings now and keep going. Pay no attention to supposed slights and think only of the nice treatment.

Where would we have been if I'd paid attention to the smart alecks. Take care of yourself.

Lots of love.

, Harry

TO MARY JANE TRUMAN

December 13, 1948

Dear Mary:

. . . The Gridiron Dinner was quite a trial to me because I couldn't say what I wanted to say. If I'd been beaten it would have been much easier to speak. They ribbed Dewey unmercifully. Had a lunatic engineer act that was a scream. They took Jake Arvey, Hague, Flynn of N.Y. and old Crump for a long hard ride. But they were exceedingly nice to me.

Dewey made a speech in which he tried hard to be funny. It was funny in the beginning but he became very sneering & sarcastic in the last half. Of course when I came to speak—the last thing on the program —I couldn't be the least bit elated, triumphant or overbearing. I told them I'd not seen most of them for three months, supposed they'd been on a vacation from the White House. Told them they'd ridden in the wrong boat and then made a very solemn and serious speech on the grave responsibility we are facing and told them that the country is theirs not mine but they'd have to help me run it. Complimented Dewey on being a good sport and sat down.

You never saw such an ovation. Had to get up three times. Some of those old hard boiled Republican news men openly cried. So I guess it went over.

Marg & Bess will be in Indp. on Thursday Dec. 16. I hope I can get in on the 22nd or 23rd. I must come back on the 29th.

Take care of yourself. Lots of love.

Harry

1949

After the preceding years, 1949 seemed a breather, a time when more things were settled than broke loose. Surely the year started off well with the inauguration, a seven-mile-long celebration that ended with a steam calliope playing "I'm Just Wild About Harry." The Republicans in Congress had anticipated the inauguration of President Dewey and appropriated a generous sum for the ceremonies, a fact that Truman noted with relish.

Foreign affairs were under new management effective in January, when General Marshall retired—he had been in the hospital—and his place was taken by Dean Acheson, who was to remain for the next four years. In April the North Atlantic Treaty was signed in Washington, and the next month the Russians ended the blockade of Berlin.

A disquieting note was the suicide in May of former Secretary of Defense Forrestal, who had resigned in March. He was replaced by Truman's treasurer of the Democratic National Committee during the campaign of 1948, Louis A. Johnson, who had performed prodigies for the campaign and seemed capable of other prodigies in managing the three branches of the armed services. Johnson's task was not merely to make peace among the army, navy, and air force but to push the three subdepartments into the strait jacket of a total military budget of less than $15 billion. The budget was unrealistic in view of the imminent Korean war, but Johnson and his chief, Truman, could not see that far ahead.

The other disquieting development in 1949 was the explosion of a Soviet nuclear device late in August. It came considerably sooner than American officials expected, and at once the question arose as to whether the United States should go ahead with a hydrogen bomb. The decision was taken in January 1950. Domestically the Soviet bomb lent substance to Republican accusations of communist infiltration of the Truman *administration. Not long afterward, in February 1950, Senator Joseph R. McCarthy of Wisconsin loosed the first salvo in his anticommunist attack on the administration.*

On the domestic scene, the President was pleased to see his new secretary of agriculture, Charles E. Brannan, obtain recognition from the pundits of the press as the author of the Brannan Bill, frequently called the Brannan Plan, for farm relief. Secretary Anderson's successor proposed that instead of government support of high consumer prices for agricultural products, farm prices should find their own levels; the thirty million farmers of America would be paid a government subsidy equal to the difference between market prices and what farm products brought in the best of times (that is, so-called parity prices). The Brannan Plan had the advantage of directness; it was easy to understand. But the Congress was Republican, and turned it down.

For Truman personally, the year went well. Former White House assistant Jonathan Daniels, an expert newspaperman, undertook a new book about the President, a volume that would rest on testimony of Truman's friends, relatives, and neighbors in Independence and Kansas City rather than on erroneous surmise, as had previous biographical efforts. The President wrote his relatives that they should talk to Jonathan and give him the truth, and this big-D Democratic truth was published the next year under the title The Man of Independence.

In 1948, Congress, again in anticipation of President Dewey, had raised the President's salary from $50,000 to $100,000 and given him a $50,000 tax-free expense fund. But the expenses of his office were large and Truman hardly was getting rich, and when the columnist Frank Kent protested the largesse (because, so Kent afterward wrote, the tax-free allowance was to be unaccounted for, which he considered a bad precedent), the President set him straight on the subject.

TO FRANK KENT

February 12, 1949

My dear Mr. Kent:

Today I read your piece in the Washington Star of this date on the salary and expense account of the President of the United States. That piece is a most interesting and astonishing document, to say the least that can be said about it.

Your President is responsible for the administration and management of the greatest, most complicated and most *expensive* organization in the history of the world.

When, on April 12, 1945, *your* President was inducted into that greatest office in the world, by a simple ceremony in the Cabinet Room at the White House at 7:09 P.M., he inherited *two* wars. As Chairman of a Senate Committee, he had furnished co-operative help to President Roosevelt which, according to reliable authority, had saved for the taxpayers some fifteen billions of dollars and which service prevented scandal and corruption in sales to and contracts with the Government.

Your President was forced into becoming a candidate for Vice President by President Roosevelt, who made a personal and national and also a Party appeal to the then Senator in charge of the Special Committee referred to, to become the candidate.

Your President knew what he faced. Just eight days short of three months after he became Vice President, the blow fell.

He found himself in the top position of responsibility in all the world. Two wars going at top pace. Both ended within five months—a year and a half ahead of the best guess of the "experts." A budget of 103 billions of dollars had been voted for the fiscal year 1945–46. Sixty-five billions of that authorization were cut off—by the President. Expenditures that year were about 45 billions. The next year's expenditures ('46–'47) were 33 billions. Twenty-five billions of dollars were paid on the national debt of 277 billions.

Attempts were made for efficiency and economy by sending reorganization plans to the Congress. All rejected but one of minor importance.

An attempt made to utilize wartime experience to reorganize the military establishment. Same result as the reorganization plans—it was bungled by *your* 80th Congress.

For working eighteen hours a day *every* day in the year and for assuming the responsibility, greater than any other dozen men in the *world, your* President received *net* pay of $4,200.00 per year! A most liberal and munificent salary! Probably what you receive for one month's blurbs! From that most liberal salary your President must cloth [himself], and meet regular family expenses—he can't put his wife on the payroll as his secretary as he did in the Senate to meet the "rent" payments.

So the Congress votes certain pay and allowances, to meet this extraordinary situation—and you, of all people, have a spasm about it. I'm really surprised because I've always thought you intellectually honest. From Dave Lawrence, Pegler, Pearson, Winchell, I'd expect just such statements as you made—but we know that they are all liars, and intellectually dishonest.

I'm sorry you joined them.

Sincerely,
Harry S. Truman

TO NEAL D. BISHOP

May 5, 1949

Dear Senator:

I appreciated very much your letter of April twenty-ninth, suggesting John L. Lewis as Ambassador to Russia.

I've already appointed a good man to that post and for your information I wouldn't appoint John L. Lewis dogcatcher and, I think, you understand that is the case. I appreciate the good humor in your letter.

Sincerely yours,

Harry S. Truman

[Bishop, at the time a Democratic state senator from Denver, Colorado, later released the President's letter to the newspapers, and it was published on October 4, 1950. The next day Lewis wrote to Bishop: "Naturally, the first duty of the bureau of the dog, if staffed by the undersigned, would be to collect and impound the sad dogs, the intellectual poodle dogs, and the pusillanimous pups which now infest the State department—the President could ill afford to have more brains in the dog department than in the department of State."]

TO ETHEL NOLAND

June 22, 1949

Dear Ethel:

It sure was nice to hear from you. I'm glad the Leedys were pleased with their reception at the executive office. I was glad to see the Judge and his boy. He has always been my friend in politics when I needed one. I'm thinking of 1934 & 1940.

Tell Mr. Barry to call the White House when he comes to Washington, ask for Mr. Matt. Connelly, my appointment secretary, and tell Connelly that I told him to call and he'll get in without any trouble. I'll inform Connelly that Mr. Barry will call.

Hope you've seen Miss Lizzie by this time. This being the lady house keeper at the White House isn't all it's cracked up to be. She and I lived in Independence off and on about sixty years apiece and [now] it takes police and secret service combined to get us into the Gates' front door![1] You and Nellie were not aware of what a mess you were getting into

---

1. The Truman house at 219 North Delaware was built by Bess's grandfather, George P. Gates.

when we were at your house trying to find out what "Omnia Gallia est divisa in partes tres," "O tempora, O mores" and "Et tu Brute" meant in everyday conversation.

But you never can tell what the three old ladies and the dice will do to you. Suppose Miss Lizzie had gone off with Mr. Young, Julian Harvey or Harris. What would have been the result? For Harry I mean. He probably would have been either a prominent? farmer in Jackson County or a Major General in the regular army and not have been half so much trouble and worry to his "sisters and his cousins and his aunts."

Hope you are both well and that all goes right with you.

My best to Nellie.

Sincerely,

Harry

TO BESS W. TRUMAN

June 29, 1949

Dear Bess:

Well, the first day has gone by thirty years ago! I need no commiseration, only congratulations.

Thirty years ago I hoped to make you a happy wife and a happy mother. Did I? I don't know. All I can say [is] I've tried. There is no one in the world anyway who can look down on you or your daughter. That means much to me, but I've never cared for social position or rank for myself except to see that those dear to me were not made to suffer for my shortcomings.

I've told Ethel on many occasions that ancestors, as such, do not appeal to me except for good physique and an honorable name. We can never tell what is in store for us. I'm very sure that if you'd been able to see into the future on May 8, 1919, when we had our final argument, you'd have very definitely turned your back on what was coming.

Business failure, with extra responsibility coming, political defeat at the same time. Almost starvation in Washington those first ten years and then hell and repeat from 1944 to date. But I wouldn't change it, and I hope you wouldn't.

Margie is one in ten million, there's none to compare with her mother. I had a good mother and so have you and a good sister. My brother is himself but in the end "right." Yours are the same sort, so— what have we had but the best of luck and a most happy thirty years. Hope we can have thirty more equally as happy without so much responsibility.

Wish you were here for the river trip Saturday, Sunday and Monday. But we can't have everything. We never have.

Remember the Blackstone, the first visit, not the last, Port Huron, Detroit Statler and the trip home? Maybe in 1953 we will be able to take that trip over again.

Hope you have a good weekend—I'm going to try as best I can to have one—it would be so much better if you were here. Lots & lots of love to you. Glad you liked the "doodads."

Harry

As publisher of the Independence Examiner, *William M. Southern, Jr., sometimes seemed unenthusiastic about the town's best known citizen.*

TO WILLIAM M. SOUTHERN, JR. (UNSENT)

July 8, 1949

Dear Mr. Southern:

Most days I read "Solomon Wise" in my home town paper. I'm always disappointed when "Solomon" has hay fever or is otherwise incapacitated and his "column" doesn't appear.[1]

Of course there are days in a row when I do not receive the "home town" paper, through no fault of anyone, but due to the fact that some 23,000 letters and as many circulars, advertising sheets and papers come to the White House *every day.*

I have a very efficient staff to look after the mail but some times it is too much for the most efficient. Eighteen years ago one man could take care of the White House mail. He assigned it to a half dozen people to answer. Now we have twenty-five to mark and assign it besides a half dozen secretaries and executive assistants and four hundred helpers to answer it all. I myself sign my name six hundred times a day to documents, orders, and private mail.

When I was on the County Court I signed my name six hundred times a day to orders, warrants and letters—so it is natural to me.

What I started out to say was that I see Less Byam, an indicted County Judge, mentioned in your ten and twenty year ago columns. I see Mel Pallette. I see numerous and sundry people most of whom I know—*some* favorably—but I never see any mention editorially, ten year, twenty year or thirty five-year ago, about a former resident of Independence, who was

---

1. Colonel Southern was the author of "Solomon Wise."

Eastern Judge for two years, Presiding Judge for eight years in Jackson County and ten years United States Senator from Missouri; also Vice President for *almost* three months and then President for and elected to be President for a full term.

This no good fellow who fooled you on the road fund expenditure, who fooled you on his first campaign for US Senator, who fooled you for his second campaign for Senator and who really put you in the hole on his campaign for President of the United States—is and will be President for three and a half more years—come hell or high water—and maybe longer if he wants to be.

This is all true—yet his home town editor—a grand old man I'd say —can't possibly admit that his home town has a number one world citizen who *may?* be a credit to his home town. I wonder why!

It makes no difference to me. I won both senatorial elections with all the press against me and a presidential election with ninety percent of them against me, all the pollsters, all the "ivory tower" columnists, the gamblers and everybody but the people against me.

And I'll do it again if it becomes necessary.

What I wonder about is why my friend, my original backer and my home town editor acts like that old character assassin Joe Pulitzer or Bertie McCormick or William Randolph Hearst. Is it circulation, advertising or what? I thinks it's a what.

An economic royalist, Stanley Marcus of Neiman-Marcus, complained about excise taxes.

TO STANLEY MARCUS (UNSENT)

July 12, 1949

My dear Mr. Marcus:

I read your letter of June twenty-eighth in regard to excise taxes with a great deal of interest. As you know, most of the expenditures recommended in the Federal budget are due to the fact that we had a war and those war expenditures are still the principal burden on the tax payers, but they must be paid.

The 80th Congress made a very serious mistake in passing the rich man's tax bill over the veto. I hope you will read my veto message and you will find we are faced with the condition which I was very careful to warn the Congress we would be faced with. Means must be found to meet the war-incurred expenses in the budget and to decrease the national debt and that can't be done if all the revenue-producing taxes are repealed. Nobody likes to pay taxes—a man will cry his head off over paying $100 taxes on his income, but he will go out and throw away $500 or $1000 on a poker game and say nothing about it. I guess that is the way the human animal is made. It is my business, however, to see that the country remains solvent and that is what I intend to do to the best of my ability—but the people and the congress must help me.

TO ETHEL NOLAND

August 13, 1949

Dear Ethel:

I appreciated your good letter of Aug. 2. It was a pleasure to see and talk with Mr. & Mrs. Barry. I think he told me he'd been in the K.C. Schools for over 42 years. That's a long time.

Don't worry about what Life, Time or any other Luce (loose) publications may say about you. Of course I'd be glad to have both of you cast a critical eye over my speeches if you were situated more closely to the capital city. A President, I've found from tough experience, can't have too much advice from real friends.

It seems to be the objective of such publications as the ones referred to, along with Look, Newsweek, Colliers, Sat. Evening Post and most of the big city newspapers to misrepresent and belittle the present occupant of the—I was going to say White House—but that old wreck is vacant now —so I guess I can't say that. Anyway they want me to appear in a false light. They are worse now than ever because of the drubbing they received last Nov. 2. They found by those returns that the so called influence of the "press" is nil when the people can be reached by the truth. So pay no attention to what they say. It is a terrible handicap these days to be a close relative of the President of the United States. I feel sorry for Margy, Vivian's children, sister Mary and my cousins. People are always watching for something mean to say because they think it will hurt me. It only hurts because I don't want anyone close to me hurt. Personally it runs off me like water off a duck's back.

Yesterday was Mary Jane's birthday. She is sixty years old. Seems impossible. I always remember her as a little girl I had to rock to sleep every afternoon, and who always wanted to follow me everywhere I went. She was surely good to Mamma and she still thinks pretty well of her older brother.

Hope you and Nellie have enjoyed the hot summer. It has been baking here. Margy came home yesterday to spend the week end. She & Bess are going to N.Y. Monday and then to Independence Wed. the 18th.

They want to be remembered to you and Nellie.
Always glad to hear from you. My best to Nellie.

Sincerely,
Harry

Ralph wants to know if the Truman bandits[1] have a coat of arms. Have they?

The executive director of the Democratic National Committee inquired about a good name for the Dixiecrats, and suggested "Demicans."

TO INDIA EDWARDS

August 20, 1949

Dear Mrs. Edwards:

Mrs. Truman handed me your good letter of August fifteenth about a name for the Dixiecrats. I am in agreement with you that Dixiecrat is too good a name for them and your suggestion of "Demicans" is all right but it sounds as if it might be a high sounding grade appellation for some scientific program which, of course, the Dixiecrats are not.

It has been suggested Republicrats might do. You might leave the "r" out and make it "Republicats" but I don't think there is anything that will very well describe them except that good old fashioned word "bolter" and that is the classification they will stay in in my book. Just between you and me and the gatepost I don't care what you call them—you can make it as unprintable as you choose.

Sincerely yours,
Harry S. Truman

TO ETHEL NOLAND

September 1, 1949

Dear Ethel:

I can have no greater respect and affection for you & Nellie than I have for my first cousins. Besides I suspect that this Indiana Congressman added a "d" to his name very recently. I am sure of it since he misquoted the "President of the United States." No public official, when he sees the President, as such, is supposed to quote any conversations with him.

---

1. The Truman ancestors.

I rarely ever give any of them things they can quote. Sometimes the quotes are made of whole cloth, sometimes only garbled a little as this one was. Congressman Noland is a charming person and a good Democrat—anyway he votes for my programs—and I told him, very proudly, that I had *cousins* in Independence who spelled Noland as he did and there might be some family connection. I told him if he would get in touch with Miss Ethel he could find out. Instead of following that suggestion he apparently managed some publicity for himself. Oh well that happens every day.

I asked some senators & congressmen to come to the White House and talk with the Sec. of Agriculture and me about a farm program. It was to be behind closed doors and not publicly advertised. But the old senator from Oklahoma who is chairman of the Agri. Committee in the Senate and whose name is Elmer[1] immediately called in reporters and told them that he had a date with me to tell me what my farm policy should be. Of course all the other gentlemen were as mad as D.A.R. committee women when the chairwoman gets her picture in the paper without them and my conference started off in ice cold atmosphere (not air conditioned). But by a few "well turned phrases" and some conversation about Democrats getting elected next year—and they all with one exception come up in 1950—my conference was a success. But you can see what can happen when the President is quoted by unauthorized persons—even Senators.

I haven't seen Ralph but I'll tell him about the coat of arms. I think I'll tell him it is three hands each holding a bottle of the famous Truman Ale which started about 1666. You reckon he'd like that?

Hope you are both well and I hope I'll see you next week.

Sincerely,

Harry

TO NELLIE AND ETHEL NOLAND

September 8, 1949

Dear Nellie & Ethel:

It was a very great pleasure to spend a few minutes with you on the 6th. I wish there had been more time to spend. Being what I am—President of 149 millions of people and the representative to the world of the most powerful nation of all time—I find that I can't do what I'd like to do. Never in my wildest dreams did I ever think or wish for such a position. When I became the junior United States Senator, representing the great

---

1. Elmer Thomas.

State of Missouri, I was sure I'd reached the pinnacle of political success. I was in the line of Benton, Cockrell, (I'm sorry to say)—Jim Reed. You see the Senate is a continuing body. One third of it is elected every two years. So there are three classes in the Senate. I happened to be in the Benton succession.

But having read a lot of inconsequential stories about people in U.S. history and world history, I'd run across the "Committee on the Conduct of the War"—a committee of Civil War days which was a thorn in the side of Mr. Lincoln (which mamma would have applauded enthusiastically) and which Gen. Robt. E. Lee said was as good as two divisions to him. An old Senator named Chandler from Michigan was Chairman, Ben Wade, a mean old S.O.B. from Ohio, was a member, as was an old Congressman named Gooch from Mass. Well they raised all kinds of hell, caused the appointment of Burnside who lost the battle of Fredericksburg, Hooker who lost the battle of Chancellorsville and old Pope who lost the 2nd Bull Run. Pope should come first because he lost the first "Committee battle." He said that his headquarters were in the saddle. Old Horace Greeley in his N.Y. Tribune said after the 2nd Manassas that Pope's Hqtrs were undoubtedly in the saddle and that he sat on his brains!

Well, I wouldn't let my notorious Committee make the Chandler-Wade-Gooch mistakes. Vandenberg, Brewster et al. tried hard to force me to make them. I tried to help Roosevelt win the war—and I headed off scandals, inefficiency and saved the taxpayers $15,000,000,000.00—and then succeeded in getting myself into more trouble than Pandora ever let loose in the world.

I've made all my family, including my sister, my cousins, and my "aunts," as much trouble as if I'd robbed the biggest bank in town, pulled a Ponzi,[1] or taken the savings of all the widows and orphans in Missouri. But I'm still having a good time.

I'll tell you a secret which you must not under any circumstances repeat. Coming from Des Moines Tuesday, No. 4 engine on my fine plane conked out! You should have seen the scurrying and running to & fro. I sat still and watched 'em. Then we straightened out and came in on 3 engines. We were only up 6000 feet so there was no jump out and anyway I wouldn't jump until everybody else had—and it couldn't have been done at 6000. What a headline that would have made! I ordered no report—and there wasn't any. But I was not as sad as I appeared when Bess had to stay back with her mother! Politics is Government so they say, and I guess it is. That's the why of my Pittsburgh and Des Moines

1. Charles Ponzi was a notorious swindler of years before—indeed he was caught in Boston in 1920—and a particular kind of scam is named after him, whereby earlier investors are paid dividends taken from the monies put up by later investors.

speeches. It was my intention to put the Republicans and Republicats on the defensive. They are and we'll keep them so until the first Tuesday in Nov. next year.

Be sure and give Jonathan Daniels the right view point. His book will be the historical basis for a lot of future statements both true and false.

Take care of yourselves and see about that "three bottle" coat of arms! We'll have to join the Sons of King John yet.

Sincerely,

Harry

Dr. Sam E. Roberts of Kansas City had spent a summer in England and been warned by friends "Not to let THIS happen in the United States." Fearful of national health insurance, he wrote the President of the danger of welfare states, especially because "where they guarantee everything from birth to the grave, incentive is destroyed."

TO DR. SAM E. ROBERTS

September 8, 1949

Dear Sam:

I read your letter of September first with a lot of interest. You evidently got an immense amount of political information in the two and one-half months you were in Britain and it is most interesting. I have many reports on the situation in Great Britain and I have come to the conclusion that the British have always handled their internal affairs to their own satisfaction and I propose to let them continue to do it. We have never been in complete agreement with them on anything. That disagreement started in 1776. If you remember fundamentally, however, our basic ideas are not far apart—they gave us our fundamental and basic law and have been our allies in nearly every war we have fought since 1860. You must remember, they have been through two of the most terrible experiences in the history of the world—experiences which cost them the young men of two generations. Had our losses been in proportion we would have lost between twelve and fifteen million of our young men. Try to contemplate what that would mean to this country.

I note carefully what you say about Mercy Hospital and the General Hospital. I am not worried about that end of the population nor am I worried about those who make $25,000 a year and over. The health of the people between those two extremes is what is most important to the country and when we find 34% of our young men and women unfit for military service because of physical and mental defects, there is something wrong with the health of the country and I am trying to find a remedy for it. When it comes to the point where a man getting $2,400.00 a year has to pay $500.00 for prenatal care and then an additional hospital bill on top of that there is something wrong with the system. Before I get out of this office I am going to find out what is wrong and I am going to try and remedy it. I'd suggest you Doctors had better be hunting for a remedy yourselves unless you want a drastic one.

Sincerely yours,
Harry S. Truman

TO HAROLD E. MOORE

September 27, 1949

Dear Mr. Moore:

My cousin, Miss Nellie Noland, forwarded your letter of the twenty-third to me and I read it with a great deal of interest.

The bulwark of our free institutions, of course, is based on a public school system where every person, no matter what his station, may have access to education. Our public school system has been a shining success in the history of the Nation and I know it will continue to be just that.

One of the difficulties with all our institutions is the fact that we've emphasized the reward instead of the service. I can remember school teachers, both men and women, who received a stipend for their services but whose ideals consisted of teaching the rising generation that service is much more important than the reward for service. I fear very much that we haven't emphasized that fact enough, although our increasing population, increasing cost of living, and our insane idea of keeping up with the Joneses have probably had their effect also on the public schools.

I've been trying to work out a Federal system of help to education, particularly along material lines—that is improved buildings and increased salaries for teachers—but I think the fundamental purpose of our educational system is to instill a moral code in the rising generation and create a citizenship which will be responsible for the welfare of the Nation.

I do appreciate very much receiving your letter.

Sincerely yours,
Harry S. Truman

TO NELLIE NOLAND

October 29, 1949

Dear Nellie:

I appreciated your good letter of the 24th very much. I am glad you agree with me in what I had written to Dr. Moore. I think we need to spend more time and money to make *good* teachers, both men and women. No one has more influence on the young mind except his mother.

My first, second and fourth grade teachers made more impression on me than all the rest put together. I skipped the third grade. They were good women who taught moral integrity as well as a.b.c.'s and readin', writin', & 'rithmetic. It makes not much difference what sort of a building you're in when you are after knowledge, but it does count entirely on who teaches you. Of course I believe in an adequate plant too. But we've been thinking too much about the plant and not enough about what the plant is for.

I am glad to hear that we are making some progress with the fence.[1] It is quite a reflection on the American public when the President of the U.S.A. has to fence 'em out to keep them from carrying off the house bit by bit.

You know I've lived in Jackson Co. and Independence off and on for nigh on to 65 years and the last time I was at home it took two secret service men and four policemen to get me to my own front door. Then I lost a couple of buttons and a handkerchief! Have I become so much of a curiosity by becoming the President—under protest?

Margie has had a grand reception. The press has been kind and so have the critics. She sent me a paper from Winston-Salem, N.C., and wrote on the front of it—"Dear Daddy: I hope you'll notice my picture on page one—you'll find yours on page 18." Can you beat that?

Bess is in St. Louis to hear her there. Otherwise all's well here.

My best to Ethel.

Most sincerely,
Harry

---

1. Truman was having a cast-iron fence constructed around the house in Independence to keep tourists from peeking in the windows, ringing the doorbell, and generally camping on his doorstep.

DIARY

October 29, 1949

Margaret sings in St. Louis tonight. Wish I could be present. It would spoil the performance were I to go. Bess is there and the V.P. with his lady. They have decided to make a go of it. I surely wish them well.

[Later.] Talked to Bess & Margie in St. Louis. The concert was a wow —"Hangin' from the rafters," says Margie. She says the terrible Post Dispatch (which hates me) and the old dyed in the wool conservative Globe-Democrat have been kind to her. Just read an old editorial from the Globe-Democrat today which came from Roosevelt's files of 1940. They'd decided that Missouri had gone to hell because I'd beaten the double crosser Lloyd Stark for the nomination for the Senate! Stark had sent the piece to Roosevelt. It's hell how fate works. Stark wanted to be President—I didn't. Stark's buried politically because he is intellectually dishonest. I'm forced on the Democratic ticket as V.P. by the man who thought Stark was tops—and I'm the President and in my own right.

It's hell on Margie but she's a good trouper!

DIARY

November 1, 1949

I have another hell of a day. Look at my appointment list. It is only a sample of the whole year. Trying to make the 81st Congress perform is and has been worse than cussing the 80th. A President never loses prestige fighting Congress. And I can't fight my own Congress. There are some terrible Chairmen in the 81st. But so far things have come out *fairly* well. I've kissed and petted more consarned S.O.B. so-called Democrats and left wing Republicans than all the Presidents put together. I have very few people fighting my battles in Congress as I fought F.D.R.'s.

Had dinner by myself tonight. Worked in the Lee House office until dinner time. A butler came in very formally and said "Mr. President, dinner is served." I walk into the dining room in the Blair House. Barnett in tails and white tie pulls out my chair, pushes me up to the table. John in tails and white tie brings me a fruit cup. Barnett takes away the empty cup. John brings me a plate, Barnett brings me a tenderloin, John brings me asparagus, Barnett brings me carrots and beets. I have to eat alone and in silence in candle lit room. I ring—Barnett takes the plate and butter plates. John comes in with a napkin and silver crumb tray—there are no crumbs but John has to brush them off the table anyway. Barnett brings me a plate with a finger bowl and doily on it—I remove finger bowl and doily and John puts a glass saucer and a little bowl on the plate. Barnett brings me some chocolate custard. John brings me a demitasse (at home a little cup of coffee—about two good gulps) and my dinner is over. I take a hand bath in the finger bowl and go back to work.

What a life!

1950

The Korean War broke out in June 1950, and it marked a watershed in American foreign and domestic politics. The war meant that the Soviet government was not going to leave the 1945 settlement alone, that it would try to change it if maneuvering (by egging on its North Korean puppet) could do so. It meant also, when the Chinese Communists intervened late in November, that Asia was no longer for Europeans, that to the already complicated equations of world politics was to be added the People's Republic of China. And with the onset of the war the old post-1945 ceilings on military expenditure were no longer acceptable and the country entered a new period greatly affected by what a later President, Eisenhower, described as the military-industrial complex. The Korean War inspired a burst of inflation. It also inspired a burst of Republican partisanship, led by the senator from Wisconsin, but joined by such party stalwarts as Taft of Ohio. The Republicans attached their sympathies, real and pretended, to such tattered causes as Nationalist China, and to a new cause, the man whom the President described as the Far Eastern General, Douglas MacArthur.

The day-to-day movements of foreign relations and domestic politics corresponded to the ups and downs of the military campaign in the faraway peninsula of Asia. In late June, when the North Koreans struck across the 38th parallel, South Korean forces virtually disintegrated and it was all that MacArthur and his Eighth Army commander, General Walton H. Walker, could do to establish a defense perimeter around the southern port of Pusan. Meanwhile, the members of the United Nations established a U.N. command in the Far East, with MacArthur as commander and Walker as field commander; but this move was more symbol than substance, for the bulk of the U.N. forces was U.S. army. At last, in September, when the U.N. forces attacked Inchon, to the west, they closed a pincer on the overextended North Koreans and drove the enemy back across the parallel, and then pursued them to the Yalu, a fateful move, for it brought in the Communist Chinese. U.N. forces were driven back *toward Pusan, and disaster faced the U.N. command, with MacArthur losing his nerve, though not his voice. At the end of the year, General Matthew B. Ridgway took over from Walker, who had been killed in a jeep accident, and the military picture was dark.*

DIARY

January 4, 1950

Mahmoud.

For Ed Flynn.

Ed came in and reiterated his claim that he'd never asked for anything, which is, of course, not in agreement with history. He asked me and insisted that I be Mr. Roosevelt's running mate in 1944, he has asked for the appointment of numerous judges, etc. This time he wanted to breed a mare to Sonny Whitney's stallion Mahmoud! Wanted to ask.

DIARY

· *January 15, 1950*

Bess and I go to a "brunch," whatever that is, at the Smiths' place out in Va. They have a lovely place out on the road to Leesburg, about a mile south of the road and seven or eight miles west of Falls Church.

The party was for the daughter of the Sec. of the Treasury, one of my oldest and very best friends. I remember—as all men over sixty do —when Drucie was born. She has grown up along with Margie and Jane Lingo, and now she is getting married to a nice boy, John Horton of Kansas City.

When I came into the Blair House from the party above mentioned, a call from my Air Aide, Gen. Landry, was awaiting me. He told me that Gen. H. H. (Happy) Arnold had died. The first of the Big Five to go. A grand man, a great commander and one of the original U.S. Air Force. He was a good friend of mine—a great loss.

They come, they get married, they pass. It is life—but sometimes hard to bear.

Senator McCarthy sent Truman a telegram stating his case against the State Department—the department, as he had said publicly in Wheeling, West Virginia, a short time earlier, was a nest of Communists and

Communist sympathizers, and he had in his possession the names of
fifty-seven Communists in the State Department, etc., etc.

TO JOSEPH R. McCARTHY (UNSENT)

February 11 [?], 1950

My dear Senator:

I read your telegram of February eleventh from Reno, Nevada, with
a great deal of interest and this is the first time in my experience, and
I was ten years in the Senate, that I ever heard of a Senator trying to
discredit his own Government before the world. You know that isn't done
by honest public officials. Your telegram is not only not true and an
insolent approach to a situation that should have been worked out between man and man but it shows conclusively that you are not even fit
to have a hand in the operation of the Government of the United States.

I am very sure that the people of Wisconsin are extremely sorry that
they are represented by a person who has as little sense of responsibility
as you have.

By early 1950, the President was unhappy with Missouri politics; he
felt the two senators from his home state were about the worst in the
Senate and the governor was working against him. That year Missouri-
ans would choose a senator. The President resolved to get a good one, and
had arranged with Governor Forrest Smith to keep the state attorney
general, J. E. (Buck) Taylor, from running in the Democratic primary,
in favor of State Senator Emery W. Allison. But Governor Smith's wishy-
washy behavior brought in Thomas C. Hennings, Jr. In the event, Hen-
nings won over Allison by some four thousand votes, then defeated the
Republican senator, Forrest Donnell, an arch opponent of Truman's
congressional program.

TO FORREST SMITH

February 25, 1950

Dear Governor:

I know that you have been associated with the Democratic faction in
Missouri that does not give much weight to promises when they are
made. I belong to the other school. When I make a statement to a private
citizen, or to the Governor of the State of Missouri, that I intend to do
something, I immediately proceed to do just exactly what I have stated
I will do.

I am very certain that if you had told Tom Hennings exactly what I told Buck Taylor, we would not be bothered with him now, as a filed candidate for the Senate. Buck came to see me after our conversation, and I told him that it was not his turn to run for the Senate at this time, that he would do me a favor if he would stay out of the race. I am very sure that if you had made that same statement to Tom Hennings in your hour's interview with him when he called on you, he would not have filed.

I think it is up to you to get him out, if you expect to keep the agreement that you and I made in the Muehlebach Hotel, at your suggestion.

It was you who suggested that we call Emery Allison, and it was you who told Emery that we were both for him. And I confirmed it. We made an arrangement whereby you would see Emery on Friday, have him file, and announce that you were for him—and that on the following Thursday when I had my press conference, I would make the same announcement.

I made the announcement as agreed upon. But to this day I haven't heard a word from you as to your support of Emery.

I have heard reports that you have informed Hennings and Reagan[1] that you are for both of them, as well as having told Emery that you are for him.

Now, Forrest, that is not my way of doing business, and I am very frank to tell you that I am not pleased with the way the situation has worked out.

I sincerely hope that you will find a way to get Hennings out of this race, so that the Governor of Missouri and the President of the United States can get behind a man who will support the policies of the Democratic Party in the Senate.

Such maneuvers as have taken place since our interview contribute to the possibility of the election of the poorest representative that Missouri has had in the Senate since 1850. And that's saying a good deal.

It is disgraceful to have two such men in the Senate as Missouri now has. My only hope is to send a couple of men to the Senate to take their places who understand the welfare of the Nation and the magnitude of our position in the world. You can make a great contribution toward accomplishing that, if you feel inclined to do it.

I am writing you very frankly, because I think you and I ought to understand each other completely and thoroughly, if we expect to get along.

Sincerely yours,
Harry S. Truman

---

1. Franklin E. Reagan, St. Louis lawyer and former Assistant State Attorney General.

TO JONATHAN DANIELS (UNSENT)

February 26, 1950

Dear Jonathan:

I wonder if you have thought to go into the background and ability of each member of the cabinet and those who sat with the cabinet which I inherited on April 12, 1945. It should make an interesting chapter in your book. Maybe I shouldn't bring the subject to your attention, but as I look back on that situation it makes me shudder. I am sure that God Almighty had me by the hand. He must have had a personal interest in the welfare of this great Republic.

There was Stettinius, Sec. of State—a fine man, good looking, amiable, cooperative, but never an idea new or old; Morgenthau, block head, nut—I wonder why F.D.R. kept him around. Maybe you know. He fired himself from my cabinet by threatening what he'd do to me under certain circumstances. Then there was Stimson, a real man—honest, straightforward and a statesman sure enough. Francis Biddle, attorney general—you make your own analysis. Frank Walker, P.M.G.—my kind of man, honest, decent, loyal—but no new ideas. Miss Perkins, Sec. of Labor, a grand lady —but no politician. F.D.R. had removed every bureau and power she had. Then Henry Wallace, Sec. of Commerce, who had no reason to love me or to be loyal to me. Of course he wasn't loyal. "Honest" Harold Ickes who was never for anyone but Harold, would have cut F.D.R.'s throat—or mine for his "high minded" ideas of a headline—and did. Agriculture's Wickard, a nice man, who never learned how his department was set up. Then there was Leo Crowley, whose sense of honor was minus and Chester Bowles, price control man, whose idea of administration was conversation with crazy columnists. Thank God Fred Vinson was there as O.W.M.R. and Bill Davis as Chairman of the Labor Board.

But, Jonathan, there was not a man in the list who would talk frankly at a Cabinet meeting! The honest ones were afraid to and the others wanted to fool me anyhow.

Am I wrong? Take a look and see how and in what manner they left me. Poor Forrestal, you'll have to evaluate yourself. He never could make a decision. Harold Smith, A 1 conniver.

TO FRANK KENT (UNSENT)

March 5, 1950

My dear Mr. Kent:

I've been reading the Sunday Washington Star. Your revival of the Republican Party is most interesting. Nothing in the world would please me more than a real revival of the G.O.P. It won't happen though unless the people are concerned that the leadership of the Republican Party have a program.

You know, of course, that the G.O.P., to start with, was a sectional party. Until it ceases to be a sectional party it can't win.

What I was trying to prove and did prove in 1948 was that the Democratic Party is a national party. We won without New York, Pennsylvania, New Jersey and the industrial east. We won without the "solid south." We won as the party of the people as a whole—farmers, laborers, small business men—and even some big business men. Now why?

You say 25% did not vote. Therefore we won on a minority. If the 25% had voted it would have been a landslide. You and your columnist friends, along with the pollsters, had convinced some six or seven million people that there was no reason to go to the polls! Remarkable! Isn't it? or Wasn't it?

People no longer in this great country can be fooled by people who write for money. Nor can they be misled by such busy editors and managers as Hearst, McCormick, Roy Howard, Roy Roberts and old man Gannett.[1]

I fear very much that the band wagon has long ago passed you and Mark Sullivan by. In my youth both of you were flaming liberals. Now you are in the Grover Cleveland, John Garner class. You are living in 1888. Too bad. We need your brain power to meet 1950 situations. I wish Ponce de Leon had been successful—we'd still have you and Mark as liberal democrats.

TO NELLIE NOLAND

March 11, 1950

Dear Nellie:

Glad to get your letter of March 3. Have been trying to answer it ever since. But I've had a hectic ten days—let's say a hectic *five years.* Whenever a report gets around that I may leave Washington, every Senator and every member of the House who has an ax to grind in the form of some special privilege bill or who may be hunting for an alibi to prevent the passage of some program measure in which the executive department is interested, must see me personally come hell or highwater. More's the pity, I have to see all of them I can. So I couldn't comply with your request. I would much rather have seen your school superintendent than many I did see. One old Congressman who rides in a wheeled chair and

---

1. Frank E. Gannett, editor and publisher of a chain of papers.

who is a chairman of a key committee talked to me for forty long, nerve wracking minutes about his favorite candidate for postmaster in a town of a million people where there are two other Congressmen with a favorite. Seven people stood on first one foot and then another outside my door. That's one example. A Mayor of a city with a million people and lots of smoke and soot, and a Senator almost talked me into nervous prostration over the appointment of a Federal Judge—whom I had no intention of appointing. There are two examples of dozens and I have to grin and bear it and make them like it. Then get ready to see the real Congressional leaders, the Cabinet, Ambassadors etc. and make real decisions that may mean peace or war, prosperity or depression.

Nobody but a damn fool would have the job in the first place. But I've got it damn fool or no and I have to do it as best I can. Hope you and Ethel are in good health. Glad you saw Vivian. Maybe that Hunkie could write a more objective article than some of our so-called friends.

Sincerely,

Harry

TO NELLIE NOLAND

Key West
March 31, 1950

Dear Nellie:

It was a pleasure to receive your good letter. Tell Dan to go ahead with his arrangements on the basis that I won't be in town. Then if it happens that I am there we can get together and see what we can do. I can never tell from one week to the next what I can do.

It is contemplated that I will receive an honorary degree at the University of Missouri on June 6th or 9th, I don't know which, and then go to St. Louis for the 35th Division Reunion on the following day. Independence is not on the list of stops on that trip. When I try to make firm commitments for dates there is always an upset. You'd think that a President of the U.S. could at least have dinner with friends and relatives on his birthday. Tom Clark, the former Atty. General and now Justice of the Supreme Court, asked me to have dinner with him on May 8 as I have done for the last five years, and Ralph had contemplated a dinner for us both at the Statler. You see Ralph will be seventy on May 10th and I'll be 66 on May 8th. How "time do fly"!

But I had to cancel out on both because of the international political situation. A pathological liar, now in the U.S. Senate from Wisconsin, and a block headed undertaker in the same "great body" from Nebraska are going along with the Kremlin to break up our bipartisan foreign policy.[1] So I have to start out on May 7 for a cross country trip to Washington State to dedicate a big dam and incidentally damn the two above named gentlemen? at the same time, all due to the fact that the Republicans and the Republicats (Dixiecrats) can't find an issue. They've been whipped on "Statism," "Welfare State," "Socialism" and the budget. So they are trying to dig up a very dead and a very malodorous hoss called "Isolationism." I must throw some more dirt on his grave or let Russia conquer the world. So my personal affairs just have to go to grass.

Hope you have a grand time in Old Kentuck—but watch would-be relatives. Some of them are dynamite. There's a gal in Atlanta, Ga., who is a promoter par excellence and there is a Roland Truman in Los Angeles who is a real "crack pot."

My immediate and recognized family have been tops in the trying five years just passed and I appreciate it. All the Presidents have had trouble with eager beaver relatives—particularly the Franklin Roosevelts. Thank God I haven't. My best to Ethel. May you have a grand vacation.

Harry

DIARY

April 16, 1950

I am not a candidate for nomination by the Democratic Convention.

My first election to public office took place in November 1922. I served two years in the armed forces in World War I, ten years in the Senate, two months and 20 days as Vice President and President of the Senate. I have been in public service well over thirty years, having been President of the United States almost two complete terms.

Washington, Jefferson, Monroe, Madison, Andrew Jackson and Woodrow Wilson as well as Calvin Coolidge stood by the precedent of two terms. Only Grant, Theodore Roosevelt and F.D.R. made the attempt to break that precedent. F.D.R. succeeded.

In my opinion eight years as President is enough and sometimes too much for any man to serve in that capacity.

There is a lure in power. It can get into a man's blood just as gambling and lust for money have been known to do.

This is a Republic. The greatest in the history of the world. I want this country to continue as a Republic. Cincinnatus and Washington

---

1. The "block headed undertaker" was Kenneth S. Wherry.

pointed the way. When Rome forgot Cincinnatus its downfall began. When we forget the examples of such men as Washington, Jefferson and Andrew Jackson, all of whom could have had a continuation in the office, then will we start down the road to dictatorship and ruin. I know I could be elected again and continue to break the old precedent as it was broken by F.D.R. It should not be done. That precedent should continue—not by a Constitutional amendment but by custom based on the honor of the man in the office.

Therefore to reestablish that custom, although by a quibble I could say I've only had one term, I am not a candidate and will not accept the nomination for another term.

TO BESS W. TRUMAN

June 7, 1950

Dear Bess:

I was surely glad to get your letter yesterday. You are right about the Un. of Mo. being late in every particular. They have always taken their cue from old Joe Pulitzer and Bill Nelson's successors. Both made their money and their reputations on character assassination just as did Hearst and the McCormicks.

But I have other fish to fry. One of them is Donnell, and this trip is to kindle the fire. I had always said that I'd never accept a degree from my home State U. because of their attitude, but for various and sundry reasons I'm doing it.

Charlie [Ross] urged it, and the president and half the faculty came and *begged* me to do it, and since it is timed right to help Allison I accepted.

Looks like we won a victory in Iowa. This morning's paper said that Dr. Graham in N.C. would have a run-off. They blame the Supreme Court decision on segregation for it. There always has to be a reason of some sort.

That was a nice note from the Mayor. Hope he is doing a good job. If he is, it shows that no man is indispensable. I'm sure that is true. Old man Baruch received a degree from Washington U. in St. Louis and, of all things, made a McCarthy speech. He had been to see every member of the Cabinet trying to get a front door entrance to the White House. He'll never get it. He and old Jones[1] may stand in the snow as far as I'm concerned from now on. I had the pleasure of tell-

---

1. Jesse Jones.

ing off a lot of "fat cats" last night. Matt said it was a superb job. I hope so.

I'm hoping to see you before too long.

Lots of love.

Harry

Two weeks before the Korean War broke out, the President made a trip to Missouri and gave several speeches, two of which—at the commencement in Columbia of the University of Missouri, and at the dedication of the Jefferson memorial in St. Louis—set out what Truman and his principal assistants, notably Secretary Acheson, considered the foreign policy of the United States. What is striking about these speeches, especially the major ones, is that the President foresaw a period of continuing economic development and clearly did not suspect that American policy and that of other democratic nations was going to have to include military measures. The President called upon young people of the country to enter what he beheld as a world of economic opportunity, and stressed economic measures for peace, including his program for helping the underdeveloped nations—the fourth point in his inaugural of 1949, known as Point Four.

TO BESS W. TRUMAN

June 11, 1950

Dear Bess:

Here it is Sunday and the most beautiful day I've seen here this year. I didn't get up until seven! Been working on the pile of papers that had accumulated while I was away and reading all the New York, Baltimore and Washington newspapers since Friday.

For a wonder, there's not a mean remark in them—even the Sops, Pearson and old Mark Sullivan are friendly. Then the Post Dispatch and the Globe-Democrat had friendly editorials. I am sure I'm slipping.

The St. Louis meeting was a most successful one. The Battery breakfast was short, dignified and to the point. There were seventy-five of them there.

We marched from 17th and Olive to the old court house—about a mile and a half. It was hot but no one fell out. The Governor, the Mayor, Louis Johnson and all my fat and thin aides had to march also. I reviewed the parade for an hour and then looked over the River Front Park plans, went over the speech and then went to the platform about two blocks away. The Mayor, Stuart Symington[1] and the French Ambassador made excellent speeches, and then I came on.

I've never had such profuse statements and congratulations. Four of our Congressmen were on the platform, Sullivan, Karst, Karsten and Carnahan, the Archbishop of St. Louis, Dr. Reader, Past G.M. of Mo. and present Secretary of the Grand Lodge and a Baptist preacher, the Governor, Forrest Donnell and 35th Div. big wigs.

When high Catholics, low Baptists and cross purpose politicians of both parties seem to be in accord—it must be right. I hope it is. The speech at Columbia and the one in St. Louis make a complete résumé of the foreign policy of the United States. No one can misunderstand it or garble it. Acheson will make six speeches in the next month, and I am sure there will be no misunderstanding our position. It has taken five years to get to this point. I am hoping two more will wind it up.

Think—Byrnes, Baruch, Marshall, Molotov, Vishinsky, Attlee, Bevin, Mackenzie King, Churchill—and now Dean Acheson, Schuman, St. Laurent and Stalin.

Byrnes, Molotov, Vishinsky and Bevin have been anything but constructive.

The others have brought us to this point. I hope all of us who are left may take us to the right conclusion. It's an awful responsibility. That's what I was thinking when I looked down on those 2,000 young people in the rain on Friday.

Lots of love. I miss you—but you *must* take care of your mother.

Harry

TO ROY ROBERTS (UNSENT)

June 12, 1950

Dear Roy:

I have been going through your centennial edition. It is most interesting. I wish you'd had someone talk to me about some of the events mentioned and some of the pictures displayed. At the top of the funnies you show the junction, 9th, Main and Delaware. Ninth Street was double track, Main, north bound and Delaware, south bound. Independence Ave. cars were green, you have that right. 9th St. cars were red, and made connection with the "Dummy Line" which went to Independence. The crossing watchman to whom you refer in this picture once pulled my

---

1. Former Secretary of the Air Force, at the moment chairman of the National Security Resources Board.

mother back from the curb in front of the C. & A. office and when she turned on him to tell him off he said "only saving your life madam, only saving your life." He was too, for he pulled her back in time to miss a westbound car. We, of course, wanted to go east.

I also casually notice an article about John Wornall. My father was named for him because he was a great Baptist. My father was also named for his Uncle John Truman who, also, was a great Baptist.

I noted your article about 3rd & Campbell Sts. My Aunt Laura lived at 3rd and Campbell. She was voted the most beautiful girl in Jackson County and awarded the prize, but as is usual in such cases there was a protest. She gave the prize back to the judges and she was again given it unanimously. Her married name was Mrs. W. B. Eberhart. Two of her daughters are still living, and will confirm what I'm saying.

Again, at 9th & Main and Delaware just north of the C. & A. office was the Soda Fountain and Candy Shop of Jesse James, Jr. I was a pupil at Spalding's Commercial College in the New York Life Bldg. in 1901 and early 1902, studying debit and credit and Pitman Shorthand. Carfare and a quarter for lunch was all I received when I left home. I also took a music lesson from Mrs. E. C. White on these trips.

Well on one occasion I stopped in Jesse's place and had an Ice cream Soda—5 cents. When I'd finished it I found I had no nickel, only a car ticket home. Jesse said, "Oh that's all right, pay when you come in again." I paid the nickel the next day! My father stood for honesty.

My Grandmother Young saw the flood of 1844 and we took her to see the flood of 1903. Her comment was, "This flood is no greater, but more property is destroyed." She was a grand old Kentuckian, and she had the most beautiful red hair.

In reading of the growth of the city I can't help but remember the part the owner of the Star had in placing a cemetery at Washington Park and stopping the city's eastward growth. Placing the Union Station where it is cut the city in half and almost ruined the central business district.

Karl Klemm shot himself because Bill Nelson, Bill Kemper and Henry Ford prevented Kansas City from becoming the Air Capital of the country. You were in the Capitol City at that time.

If the Star is at all mentioned in history it will be because the President of the U.S. worked there for a few weeks in 1901. One theater will also be mentioned because he was an usher at the Grand, 7th & Walnut, when he worked at the National Bank of Commerce in 1903.

Kansas City has the most efficient and from a public standpoint most convenient Court House. In front of it is an equestrian statue by the greatest sculptor of our time.[1]

A plan for Kansas City and adjoining counties in both Kansas and Missouri was worked out by this same President of the United States.

No mention of any of these things is made in your great issue. You also seem to be afraid to give credit to your great friend Hon. Henry F. McElroy and to T. J. Pendergast for the real improvements and forward looking plans which made Kansas City what it is today.

Your airport, your city hall, your auditorium, your traffic way system, your city-county plan—all are the result of McElroy-Truman-Pendergast vision. Why don't you admit it? You can't of course and be a modern present day publisher. No one expects it. But I'm sure history will take care of that. In fact I'll see to it that it does.

Best of luck to you Roy.

TO ETHEL NOLAND

June 16, 1950

Dear Ethel:

I certainly did appreciate your letter of the 13th in reply to mine about Paddy, the Welshman. You know I do a lot of kidding about ancestry but I'm always as happy as you are when our progenitors turn out to be honorable men and women. And so far as we know to date, our ancestors have all been good people.

Just to show you how things can be garbled by "good intentioned people"—and you know hell is paved with "good intentions," just the other day Dr. John Steelman brought me a letter from a friend of his who had stopped at the Old Stone Inn eight miles south of Shelbyville, Ky. And do you know what he came up with? That he'd learned that Jesse Holmes married *Margaret Taylor* and that their daughter Margaret was my grandmother! That's how things get all mixed up. I am depending on you to keep the record straight.[1]

There are two things I'd like to have, maybe it'll be three or four. I'd like to know the names first and married of all the brothers and sisters of our grandparents and of the Young grandparents. Reckon you could get them for me? It's a large order.

Hope you and Nellie are well and happy and that all goes well with

---

1. The sculptor Charles L. Keck's life-sized equestrian statue of General Andrew Jackson. A smaller replica is at the west end of the Independence court house.

---

1. According to the record, Jesse Homes married Nancy Drusilla Tyler, and their daughter Mary Jane Holmes Truman was Truman's grandmother.

you. This letter was started at 9:15 this morning and I've been adding to it in sections. I've had a cabinet meeting—an important one, seen a thousand people in groups, made four speeches and have had a dozen individual appointments with Congressmen & Cabinet members—and oh yes, I've vetoed a controversial bill, signed forty others, made a dozen criminals honest men by signing full pardons for them and now I only have to read a dozen or so documents and start about that many orders to various people on their way, get this letter off to you, one to Mary Jane and one to "Lizzie." How would you like to be President?

I understand that our Grandmother Mary Jane Holmes had a half dozen brothers and sisters and that Anderson Shippe Truman had a half dozen of each. Grandma Young had exactly twelve brothers and sisters —she was no. 13, and that Solomon Young had a lot of brothers and sisters. One of his sisters married old man Goodnight, a Texas rancher. I've heard mamma mention Uncle Harrison Young, Michael, William and John who was a doctor. So you see?

Harry

John D. Rockefeller, Sr., in his latter years, was accustomed to tip his golf caddies with dimes that he squeezed carefully as he presented them. His penurious habits reminded the President of "Pittsburgh Plus," the equally tidy though somewhat different arrangement by which the nation's steelmakers long absorbed the freight costs of their products and quoted uniform prices across the country, thereby lessening competition. These presidential thoughts came into focus when Congress passed the Basing Point Bill, which would have legalized certain practices in the basing point pricing system, and which the President vetoed on June 16, 1950, remarking that its language was unclear and that it would have lessened competition by reviving Pittsburgh Plus. Small businessmen rejoiced in the veto, and large businessmen announced the end of the capitalist system. The columnist David Lawrence sided with the "malefactors of great wealth."

TO DAVID LAWRENCE

June 20, 1950

My dear Mr. Lawrence:

Your article on the veto of the Basing Point Bill, S. 1008, is not based on the facts. I've an idea that there is no one who has gone into the details of basing point legislation as they have been examined by me. From the ancient John D. and his dimes to "Pittsburgh Plus" I know the record.

The bill was carefully studied by me personally. I read every speech made in Congress on it. Did you?

I had memos from the Treasury, Commerce, the Budget Bureau. *I* sat with my experts and analyzed S. 1008 sentence by sentence.

You should carefully read the record on Pittsburgh Plus; you should read the cement case, which I'm sure you haven't.[1] Don't let the N.A.M. write *all* your columns.

No one passes on my messages but the President.

Stanley Woodward, formerly chief of protocol for the State Department, had been appointed ambassador to Canada.

TO STANLEY WOODWARD

June 24, 1950

Dear Stanley:

Being a good Episcopalian you know, of course, that this is St. John's Day. I know it because of my long Masonic connections. But whether it's the Baptist's or the Divine's I can't answer.

I am leaving for Baltimore shortly to dedicate an airport—why I don't know. I guess because the Governor of Maryland, the two Senators from that great state, all the Congressmen and the Mayor of Baltimore high pressured me into doing it.

What I started out to do was to tell, ask, invite or order you to Key West this coming winter. I've been looking over the report of our last visit. Don't get the idea that just because you are now Mr. Ambassador that the guy in the White House can't still harass you.

Seriously, Stanley, if we go south again I hope you will be able to come for a visit.

My best to Mrs. Ambassador.

Harry S. Truman

I'm going home from Baltimore to see Bess, Margie and my brother and sister, oversee some fence building—not political—order a new roof on the farmhouse and tell some politicians to go to hell. A grand visit—I hope?

---

1. In the Cement Institute Case of 1948 the Supreme Court outlawed the multiple basing point system, which had replaced Pittsburgh Plus, and held that the practice of freight absorption was illegal.

The Korean War broke out and Truman was called back to Washington.

DIARY

June 30, 1950

Frank Pace[1] called at 5 A.M. E.D.T. I was already up and shaved. Said MacArthur wanted two divisions of ground troups. Authorized a regiment to be used in addition to the authorizations of yesterday, to be used at Mac's discretion.

Was briefed by Col. Acoff at seven o'clock. Called Pace and Louis Johnson and told them to consider giving MacArthur the two divisions he asked for and also to consider the advisability of accepting the two divisions offered by the Chinese Nationalist Government. That gov't is still recognized as the 5th permanent member of the Security Council U.N. Since Britain, Australia, Canada and the Netherlands have come in with ships and planes we probably should use the Chinese ground forces.

What will that do to Mao Tse-tung we don't know. Must be careful not to cause a general Asiatic war. Russia is figuring on an attack in the Black Sea and toward the Persian Gulf. Both prizes Moscow has wanted since Ivan the Terrible who is now their hero with Stalin & Lenin.

TO ETHEL NOLAND

July 7, 1950

Dear Ethel:

You're right when you say we knew not what was coming when we were having such a fine time "relatively" speaking. I get a kick out of the folks who are so anxious to be akin to us now, don't you? Martha Ann told me of an experience of hers in Kentucky. She was at Shelbyville or Bardstown or some other town where the Trumans, Campbells and Greggs were thick. She said that they were very cool to her. Now they are writing to find out the connection! Mr. Shakespeare said in Midsummer Night's Dream "Oh what fools these mortals be!" But life wouldn't be any fun if mortals were not what they are.

The most interesting thing is to watch the effects of Potomac fever —a peculiar disease that those mortals Puck spoke of who come to Washington to become "important" people in Government get. Woodrow Wilson said some people come here and grow up with responsibility. Some come and just swell up.

---

1. Pace had replaced Royall as secretary of the army.

I've been here permanently almost since Jan. 1, 1935, and I can diagnose that awful disease at once. It skips no office. Congressmen, Senators,
clerks, Cabinet officers, Presidential Secretaries and their "sisters and
their cousins and their aunts." But life here would be unbearable if it did
not happen. Although when a member of the Cabinet has to be fired or
a pin slipped into a Senator's balloon it is sometimes a painful proceeding—that is to the one who uses the pin or the firing machinery. Your
cousin has had to do it time and again.

One thing I'm proud of, my cousins, those I *recognize,* nephews,
niece, in-laws, brother and sister have never caused me one minute's
embarrassment. That makes me proud. Hope you can find all those
grandaunts and uncles for me. I don't like a liar or a cheat and we can
unmask quite a few.

Hope you and Nellie are having a good vacation. Everyone seems to
have gotten "porch fever." You built one, so did Lizzie and Mary Jane is
at it now.

Sincerely,

Harry

*Sometimes Truman enjoyed instructing newspapermen in the de-
tails of history, European and Near Eastern as well as American, and got
into a discussion with Ed Harris of the St. Louis* Post-Dispatch *about
whether great military leaders were also great statesmen. He sent Harris
a note about Hunyadi, the Hungarian hero, and misspelled the name,
causing Harris some confusion in research. The schooling continued,
and perhaps with tongue in cheek Harris informed the President that as
a novice historian he was getting in deeper and deeper: after poring over
books long into the night, he had found that Truman had not mentioned
Tabarnash and Shuppiluliumash, of Hittite days.*

TO EDWARD HARRIS

July 19, 1950

Ed:

I think you are going too far back for your purpose. The wars between
the Hittites and the Egyptians and between Assyria and the Hittites,
between Egypt and Babylon are in the same pattern as today.

But we can't very well evaluate the leaders beyond Cyrus the Great
because we know so few facts about them. The Hittite King to whom you
refer has no less than four names and it may have been four Kings
instead of one.

Egypt had some great Pharaohs—Thothmes III, Ramses III, Seti I— but we don't know for sure exactly what they did.

The times of Cyrus, Darius I, the great, Alexander, Hannibal, Caesar and some of his Roman successors it seems to me is far enough into the past to go. You don't even have to go that far to learn that real history consists of the life and actions of great men who occupied the stage at the time. Historians' editorializing is in the same class as the modern irresponsible columnist.

Hillaire Belloc tried to smear Gustavus Adolphus because Gustavus was the great Protestant he was! So study men, not historians. Even Gibbon, Green and Guizot were as prejudiced as old man Beard!

H.S.T.

TO NELLIE NOLAND

July 26, 1950

Dear Nellie:

"Twenty sixth of July, Sow turnips, wet or dry." If I'm not too far off the beam this should be your birthday—and I'm not saying for how many years either!

Not long from now you, Ethel and Lizzie and I will be posing and giving interviews as "the oldest inhabitant." Look at old man Bernard Shaw, Rees Alexander[1] and countless others!

Any way I hope you had a most happy birthday and that you'll have as many or more than your mother and old man Shaw. I am hoping to count as many as my mamma had and still be compos mentis with no non in front of it. Some of my political enemies say the non is already there! They may be right too. If some old moron like Beard writes the history of these times he may be able to prove that the non belongs there!

I've had a hectic time since June 24th when Bess & I paid you a call. At 12:30 Sunday the Secretary of State called me and said that the U.N. had passed a resolution that needed my attention. I told the Chief of the Secret Service to tell my plane pilot I'd leave the airport at K.C. at 2:00 P.M. C.S.T. When I arrived at the port my air aide was missing, so was my military aide. The pilot fooled around trying to wait for them but I ordered him off the ground. We left at 2:11 P.M. and made the trip in three hours and eleven minutes, a record.

After we'd been up thirty minutes my air aide reported that he was

---

1. "Uncle" Rees Alexander lived on Van Horn Road, near 219 and 216 North Delaware, and was about ninety years old.

in a C-47 fifteen minutes behind me. I ordered him back to K.C. with instructions to bring Harry Vaughan, my military aide, and others left behind to D.C. the next day. Gen. Vaughan was at his mother's bedside in Glasgow. Gen. Landry had gone to play golf with my permission, but did not say where. So nobody was at fault and the generals didn't get an army bawling out—as I would have gotten under the same conditions from my colonel in World War I.

Well you know what happened on Sunday night. I had some terrible decisions to make. I made 'em and here we are.

I made a "turnip day" speech in one of my transcontinental tours. I hope I can make many more.

Good luck to you both. How's the porch coming? Mary Jane can't get hers finished.

Sincerely,
Harry

DIARY

August 15, 1950

A prayer said over & over all my life from eighteen years old and younger.

Oh! Almighty and Everlasting God, Creator of Heaven, Earth and the Universe:

Help me to be, to think, to act what is right, because it is right; make me truthful, honest and honorable in all things; make me intellectually honest for the sake of right and honor and without thought of reward to me. Give me the ability to be charitable, forgiving and patient with my fellowmen—help me to understand their motives and their shortcomings —even as Thou understandest mine!

Amen, Amen, Amen.

The prayer on the other side of this page has been said by me—by Harry S. Truman—from high school days: as window washer, bottle duster, floor scrubber in an Independence, Mo., drug store, as a time-keeper on a railroad contract gang, as an employee of an untruthful and character assassinating newspaper, as a bank clerk, as a farmer riding a gang plow behind four horses and mules, as a fraternity official learn-ing to say nothing at all if good could not be said of a man, as a public official judging the weaknesses and shortcomings of constituents, and as President of the U.S.A.

Secretary of Defense Johnson, a Wheeling, West Virginia, lawyer, assistant secretary of war in the late 1930s under President Roosevelt, had at first seemed a good appointment, but then he caught Potomac fever and soon was communicating to newspapermen on all sorts of subjects not his business. Truman did not know it, but Johnson also intrigued in scandalous fashion against Secretary of State Acheson, undercutting Acheson's China policy by allowing Assistant Secretary of Defense Paul Griffith to pass administration secrets to the Nationalist ambassador, Wellington Koo. When the Korean War broke out, it was clear to the President that he no longer could put up with Johnson, although the secretary of defense's removal was a delicate problem, not least because Johnson seems to have had no inkling of presidential displeasure or of his own ineptitude.

TO BESS W. TRUMAN

September 7, 1950

Dear Bess:

You are one up on me for letters. That is not customary. I'm glad it happened. The editorial from Roy Roberts' Star was very good. I had not seen it and had no other copies. I don't know what's happening—Life, dated Sept. 11, has a most favorable editorial on the same subject. Maybe I'm on the wrong track.

Tomorrow I have to break the bad news to Louis Johnson. I think I have a way to do it that will not be too hard on him. General Marshall came to see me yesterday. I told him what I had in mind. He said, "Mr. President, you have only to tell me what you want, and I'll do it. But I want you to think about the fact that my appointment may reflect upon you and your administration. They are still charging me with the downfall of Chiang's government in China. I want to help, not to hurt you." Can you think of anyone else saying that? I can't, and he's of the *great*.

Harriman went to Leesburg and had lunch with him today, and they talked it out. Wonder of Wonders, Mrs. Marshall is for it! He could not possibly hurt me.

I'm hoping that I can get Louis Johnson to say publicly that he thinks because of the attacks on him I should ask Gen. Marshall to take over. He can make himself a hero if he'll do that. If he doesn't, I shall simply fire him as I did Wallace and Morgenthau.

As usual I'm having hell and high water every day. But I seem to thrive on it, and Dr. Graham can't find a thing wrong except my propensity to gain pounds when I eat what I want. We were to have a complete checkup beginning Friday afternoon, but because of the Saturday night speech we put it off until Sunday. It requires some strenuous preparations—purgative, enema, etc., ad lib. So the postponement. . . .

Had Mrs. Roosevelt and a U.N. promotion committee in today. She was ecstatic over my world broadcast.[1] Sen. Austin also came in. He was highly pleased over a phone call I'd made complimenting him on his set-to with Malik.[2] I have a most interesting cable from Adm. Kirk[3] on his meeting with Vishinsky, who wanted to hand the ambassador a note protesting the shooting down of the Russian plane west of Korea. We advised the Adm. to tell Vishinsky to take it up with the U.N. He protested vehemently—but we did not accept the note. The Russian Embassy here sent a copy to the Sec. of State who sent it back.

Mon Wallgren came in at this point to talk to me about gas for New England. It is a complicated proposition. Tobin, McCormack and the Mass. Gov. on one side; the Rhode Island Senators, McMahon, Benton et al. on the other. I told Mon to get all the facts, as we did on our Committee, make the decision, and I'd back him.

Send me another *note,* and I'll return a longer and more complicated communication.

Lots & lots of love from

Harry

TO ETHEL NOLAND

September 13, 1950

Dear Ethel:

You wrote me a one page note about my Saturday night talk and I appreciate it very much—but two pages would have been more highly appreciated! Not about the speech but family gossip. Ralph had something resembling a stroke last week and is now in the Army & Navy hospital at Hot Springs. Vivian passed out a few days ago and I have

---

1. On September 1, the President spoke to the American people, over radio and television, on the situation in Korea, and invited all the nations of the world, without exception, to join in the fight.

2. Relations with the Soviets in the U.N. had resumed when Ambassador Jacob Malik, the Russian representative on the Security Council, returned to his seat, but this meant acrimony in the Council, suitably orchestrated by Malik's superiors in Moscow. The problem of the moment was the shooting down of a Russian two-engine bomber over Korean waters, with the death of at least one Russian lieutenant, whose body was recovered. The American representative on the Council, Ambassador Austin, merely stated what had happened. Malik was awaiting instructions, apparently, and said only that the downing of the plane was just one more United States provocation.

3. Admiral Alan G. Kirk had succeeded General Bedell Smith as ambassador to Russia. Smith had replaced Harriman in 1946.

urged him to take a vacation. Bess told me last night that Mrs. Wallace is in a bad way. No one seems to be able to take all the blows but your cousin HST. I've spent my life trying to have all the family get along and love each other. Having the same trouble with the Cabinet. Fired the Sec. of Defense last night but gave him a patriotic reason for quitting. I've had a great experience with cabinet officers. First I had to replace Stettinius with Byrnes. Then Wallace had to be kicked out and old man Ickes tried to browbeat me and received a brow beating. Before I went to Potsdam Morgenthau came in and told me what I could do or he'd quit. He quit! Then Byrnes became obsessed with a "bad heart" and quit me at a crucial moment. But he's never been missed. When he made his Biloxi speech I sent him a missive in which I told him that while I was not a Caesar and never expected to be—I knew how Julius felt when he said "Et tu Brute." Byrnes would have had a stroke when he received that communique if he'd been fat enough—but he's a Cassius. See "Julius Caesar" by Wm. Shakespeare, Act I Sc. II. . . .[1]

Sincerely,

Harry

D I A R Y

September 14, 1950

On General Pershing's birthday, Sept. 12, 1950, I had to insist that the Secretary of Defense sign his letter of resignation—*and I had* to insist. When I saw Jim Forrestal was cracking up under the pressures of the

---

1. The break between Truman and Byrnes surely had its beginnings in the offhand manner in which Senator Byrnes treated the junior senator from Missouri in the 1930s—Byrnes paid little attention. The awkwardness of the Chicago convention in 1944 was embarrassing; and after Byrnes became secretary of state Truman felt that he didn't keep the President informed. Truman also felt that in December 1945 Byrnes had gotten soft on Russia. Still, when Byrnes resigned in January 1947 on the advice of a physician, sensing that his heart might not take the continued strain of public office, there was no real break, and this did not come even when Byrnes in 1948 made a speech in Biloxi and opposed Truman's domestic policies. At the end of a friendly letter to Byrnes, Truman, apparently having just read the Biloxi speech, scrawled that he now knew how Caesar felt when he said, "Et tu Brute." Byrnes responded primly that he, Byrnes, was no Brutus and Truman was no Caesar. The split finally did occur when Frank Walker early in January 1950 told Truman that at the Chicago convention in 1944 Byrnes knew President Roosevelt no longer favored the then "assistant president" and had sought to take advantage of Truman by getting the Missouri senator to nominate him for the vice presidency. [*Ed. note:* On this latter point there is disagreement, for Byrnes' close friend Walter Brown recently related that Byrnes did not know of Roosevelt's move against him when he asked Truman to nominate him. The Walker papers at the University of Notre Dame, carefully studied by Douglas Small and Robert Messer, show considerable contact between Walker and Byrnes, about the time Walker was deputized, but there is no record of what they talked about.]

reorganization of the defense department, I looked around for a successor. Louis Johnson had been known to me since 1918. He had been Woodring's assistant secretary in the old War Department. He had worked on an industrial mobilization plan. He had helped me to win the election of 1948. I consulted the West Virginia Senators, talked to Mr. Stimson, Mr. Woodring and numerous others.

I came to the conclusion that he could relieve Forrestal and do the unification job that needed to be done. He was appointed and did good work with Mr. Forrestal.

Then something happened. I am of the opinion that Potomac fever and a pathological condition are to blame for the fiasco at the end.

Louis began to show an inordinate egotistical desire to run the whole government. He offended every member of the cabinet. We never had a cabinet meeting that he did not show plainly that he knew more about the problems of the Treasury, Commerce, Labor, Agriculture than did the Secretaries of those departments. He played no favorites; all of them were included. He disliked Cap Krug—a kindly person who finally left under pressure; he disliked Chapman, Krug's successor. He never missed an opportunity to say mean things about my personal staff.

Then he tried to use the White House press men for blowing himself up and everyone else down, particularly the Secretary of State. He had conferences with enemy Senators of mine—Wherry, McCarthy, Brewster, Taft, Hickenlooper—and made terrible statements to them. After doing a good job on implementing the unification plan which I'd drawn up after World War II, on the advice of every field commander, army, navy and air, he almost wrecked the whole thing. He misrepresented the facts to every committee before which he appeared. All this was carefully reported to me factually by men who were present—I have no spy system!

Finally along in June 1950 I made up my mind he'd have to go. I made a trip to Leesburg with my daughter and talked to Gen. Marshall—about China, Formosa, Japan, MacArthur, Chiang Kai-shek and finally about the defense department. A most interesting morning.

Finally things came to a head. Gen. Marshall was on his first real vacation in Michigan. I called him and asked him to come to see me when he returned. About ten days after the call and perhaps two weeks before Sept. 11 the General came to see me. I told him I had to get rid of Johnson. I asked him if he'd act through the crisis as Sec. of Defense if I could get Congressional approval. He said, "You know, Mr. President, I'll do whatever you think is necessary." But he told me he'd be haunted by Hearst and Scripps Howard, McCormick and all the rest of the traitorous and sabotage press—but he'd take it if I wanted him to. I told him I wanted him to do it although I felt as if I was letting him down, because I'd promised him a happy retirement as President of the Red Cross. He agreed to take the job if Congress would approve.

I had made up my mind to tell Johnson what was necessary. That was Friday Sept. 1, 1950. I had to talk to the nation that night and I postponed the terrible chore until Monday—and then another week.

In the meantime in the usual Washington manner a leak appeared in the form of an article by Tony Vacarro saying Johnson was to be fired. Where it came from no one can find out.

Johnson called me Monday morning about Vacarro's article and I told him to come in at 4 P.M. I told him by phone in the morning to come at 4:00 P.M. and I'd talk with him. This was Sept. 11. Well he came and I opened the conversation by telling him he'd have to quit. He was unable to talk. I've never felt quite so uncomfortable. But he finally said he'd like a couple of days to think about it. I said all right. He came in Tuesday morning with Finletter.[1] There was no chance to talk to him. Then I called in Matt & Charlie Ross and told them what was happening. After the Tuesday interview with Johnson and Finletter I called Steve Early and told him that Johnson should bring me a letter of resignation, saying he had felt the pressure on me and that he thought he should quit and that he should recommend Gen. Marshall to take his place. Then I called Mr. Ross and told him to press Steve to get it done. Johnson came to the 4 o'clock Cabinet meeting Tuesday. He looked like he'd been beaten. He followed me into my office after the Cabinet adjourned and begged me not to fire him. Then he handed me the [to-be-] published letter—unsigned. I said "Louis you haven't signed this—sign it." He wept and said he didn't think I'd make him do it.

Then I called in Charlie Ross who had been in touch with Steve Early, working on a reply to Johnson's letter of resignation. We finally made the release after I'd phoned to Gen. Marshall informing him of what had happened.

I tried to make it as easy on Johnson as circumstances would permit —but I had to force him to work in his own interest. He is the most ego maniac I've ever come in contact with—and I've seen a lot.

On Pershing's birthday 1918 Sept. 12—I pulled into the Foret de Haye to support the St. Mihiel drive. Never fired a shot. It wasn't necessary. Gen. George C. Marshall was one of Pershing's staff officers. I was a Capt. of F.A. On Sept. 12, 1950, Gen. Pershing's birthday—Gen. Marshall and I with positions reversed are still working to save the country and our way of life.

---

1. Thomas K. Finletter, secretary of the air force.

TO ETHEL NOLAND

September 24, 1950

Dear Ethel:

Your good letter of the 19th was highly appreciated. The "peace makers" have a hell of a time "relatively" speaking especially with Stalin in the picture.

Vivian has agreed to take a vacation. I hope he does. Ralph is in the Army & Navy Hospital at Hot Springs. I sent my Brig. Gen. Doctor down to see him and had Louis go along.[1] Both came back highly pleased with his condition and his treatment. I'm surely sorry to hear of the condition of Truman's wife.[2] I hope she won't be paralyzed—that would be terrible —although paralyzed people have made a mark in the world. Franklin D. for instance.

Ralph wrote me a real sentimental letter about the visit of Louis and the Doctor. You know all of us have a very deep sentimental streak in us, but most of the time we are too timid or too contrary to show it. Don't you think?

I've been reading Jonathan's book and I think the facts are all right but he's not very respectful to my father & mother. But as you say it is on a much higher plane than most pieces about me. I've become ironclad in that respect, because everything mean that can be said has been said about me—so there's nothing new in that line. So when something good is said about me it's brand new but not "news."

Lies and mud make "news"—the truth and flowers do not. But when I read what the lousy press of the days of Washington, Jefferson, Jackson, Lincoln, Grover Cleveland and Woodrow Wilson had to say about those great men, I'm comforted for I've had it easy by comparison.

Margie came down Friday and spent the week end with me. I just took her to the train at 7:30. She came down to get a couple of fur coats, as well as to see me, and went off without them! You should have heard her moan when she found they weren't on the train. You see what happens when you get too much waiting on. The maids around here treat her like she's lavender and old lace—and she doesn't look after things herself. I didn't sympathize with her at all and that made her madder than ever. The poor maid forgot to put them with the baggage so they didn't go. I told Margie she should have looked after them before she left the house and not at the train. I'll send 'em to her tomorrow.

---

1. Ralph Truman's son Louis was in the army. He eventually became a lieutenant general.

2. The wife of Robert Truman Ragland, a nephew of Nellie and Ethel, was paralyzed as a result of a riding accident in Colorado on August 1.

You know I have a valet, four ushers, five butlers, seven or eight secretaries, a dozen or so executive assistants, an assistant president—three of 'em in fact—and I can't open a door, get my hat, pull out my chair at the table, hang up my coat or do anything else for myself—even take a bath! I won't be worth a damn when I come out of here—if I ever do.

Write when you can to your nutty old cousin.

Sincerely,
Harry

My best to Nellie.

When he wrote the following, the President was on his way by plane to confer with General MacArthur on Wake Island. He had never met the general, who had not visited the United States since 1937. At the end of July 1950, MacArthur went to Formosa and conferred with Chiang Kai-shek, giving the impression that the United States strongly supported the Nationalists. This was hardly the case; the administration long since had lost confidence in Chiang's ability to gain support among the new nations of Asia, not to mention the Nationalist leader's inability to help the military situation in Korea (his troops were aging, they lacked equipment). A few weeks later, the general sent a statement to the national encampment of the Veterans of Foreign Wars, to be read on August 28. Truman learned of it two days earlier, after a newsmagazine jumped the gun and published it. In the statement MacArthur said: "Nothing could be more fallacious than the threadbare argument by those who advocate appeasement and defeatism in the Pacific that if we defend Formosa we alienate continental Asia," and he added: "Those who speak thus do not understand the Orient." Truman forced the general to withdraw the statement. The situation called for a meeting and hence the decision to go to Wake.

TO NELLIE NOLAND

The Flying White House
October 13, 1950

I appreciated your letter of the 9th very much. Glad you had a chance to see "Lizzie" before she left. They had a nice trip and arrived in good condition. I arrived back at old man Blair's house Saturday afternoon and met them Sunday morning. Then I went to St. Louis on Wednesday and took part in Mary's installation as Grand Matron of the Eastern Star.

Vivian, Luella and Martha Ann were present too. Bess couldn't leave because of her mother and my singing daughter had a contract engagement. Vivian, Martha Ann and I took part in the ceremony before some 14,000 spectators and I guess it went off well. As you know a relative of mine has a hell of a time doing anything on his own. But Mary did a very good job of it. She shut out the reporters and the picture takers and no one could get in except on an O.E.S. dues card or a pass signed by her! I bet there are a thousand mad politicos and sycophants in St. Louis and I'm glad of it!

I left St. Louis at 2:30 central time and flew over the Rockies at 20,000 feet. They looked just like high hills. When we went over Kansas City I could see Independence, Grandview, Leavenworth, Atchison, St. Joseph and Topeka. We made the trip from K.C. to Salt Lake City in three hours, taking in Denver on the way. It took Grandpa Young three months to make that trip one way.[1] We landed at Fairfield Airport at 7:15—six hours and forty-five minutes out of St. Louis—1715 miles. Talk about seven league boots I've got 'em. Left there after seeing a lot of wounded boys from Korea, at 12:30 A.M., Friday the 13th! We took off and I arose by San Francisco time at 5 o'clock and it was two hours earlier where I am. Ain't that sompin'? It is now 10:30 A.M. Washington time, 7:30 San Francisco time and 5:30 Hawaii time, which we'll reach in two hours and a half.

Hope you and Ethel are all right. I've a whale of a job before me. Have to talk to God's righthand man tomorrow, make a policy speech in San Francisco Tuesday night at 8:30, 10:30 your time and then tell the UN where to head in on the 24th. Too much for a farm boy. My best to you both.

Harry

TO ETHEL NOLAND

October 21, 1950

Dear Ethel:

While I was in San Francisco and studying on my speech a nice young man came in to see me. His name is Eugene Noland Cahill. He said his grandfather was a brother of your father's father and by that route claimed to be your second cousin once removed and therefore mine likewise. If you can figure it out you are better than I am on relations and I'm *good!*

---

1. The President's grandfather Solomon Young drove wagon trains from Jackson County to Colorado, Utah, and California from 1846 to 1860.

He is a nice young man. I autographed his Bible for him and marked some passages for him to read. Then I asked him what Church he belonged to. He said "I'm a Christian Science reader." Period, paragraph. He gave me his blessing and his prayers. So everything turned out all right—in spite of the passages I marked. 149th Psalm, Isaiah 40, Ecclesiastes 12, Matthew 5, 6, 7 and Luke 6, v. 26. Hope he doesn't look at Ecc. 12.

Hope you and Nellie are well. Tell me about Fred's wedding—and his wife.[1]

Sincerely,
Harry

DIARY

October 25, 1950

I had a conversation with Mr. Andrei Y. Vishinsky on October twenty-fourth, in which we exchanged compliments. I inquired of him as to the health of Marshal Stalin and Mr. Molotov. I told him I wished very sincerely that our differences would be ironed out and he expressed the same wish and also made the statement that he was sure that eventually they would be ironed out. That was about the extent of the conversation when we were interrupted. I also sat near him at the Lie[1] dinner and he reiterated his statement that he hoped our differences would be ironed out.

On November 1, two young Puerto Rican nationalists attempted to assassinate the President. They approached Blair House along the sidewalk, from different directions, and sought to bound up the steps. The guards and the Puerto Ricans exchanged fire. One of the nationalists was shot dead and the other, Oscar Collazo, was wounded and captured. Two of the Blair House guards were wounded and Officer Leslie Coffelt was killed. Collazo was imprisoned for life. (On September 10, 1979, he and three Puerto Rican nationalists imprisoned after shooting up the House of Representatives in 1954 were released, their sentences commuted by President Jimmy Carter. On September 17, Premier Fidel Castro of Cuba freed four Americans who had been imprisoned in the 1960s.)

1. Fred Truman, one of Vivian's sons, married Audrey Bradshaw of Humansville, Missouri.

1. Trygve Lie, secretary general of the U.N.

DIARY

New Jefferson Hotel, St. Louis
November 5, 1950

Arrived at Belleville Air Port at 3:55 Central Standard Time. The C.O. turned out the guard and I inspected it. Found several men with many ribbons and stars for engagements. One negro man had four stars and a citation. He must have been with Gen. Eichelberger.[1] Anyway he was in the Pacific. He was naturally embarrassed when the President stopped to talk with him. For some reason, which I could understand if conditions were reversed—they all are! After inspecting the guard and inquiring about their stars and ribbons, we started for St. Louis in a closed car. It was cold and the wind was northwest. People all along the way wanted to see the President—not me! Some of them saw me and the usual "There he is!" "Hello, Harry" was the result. Most all the people in the USA are kindly happy people and they show it by smiling, waving and shouting as above.

Because two crackpots or crazy men tried to shoot me a few days ago my good and efficient guards are nervous. So I'm trying to be as helpful as I can. Would like very much to take a walk this morning but the S.S. say that there are more crackpots around and the "Boss" and Margie are worried about me—so I won't take my usual walk.

It's hell to be President of the Greatest Most Powerful Nation on Earth—I'd rather be "first in the Iberian Village."

TO ETHEL NOLAND

November 17, 1950

Dear Ethel:

Appreciated your good letter of the 13th very much. I'll write Heinie and thank him for his appreciation of my safety. I've signed some 2000 letters like that in the last ten days. But I felt that if people were interested enough in my personal safety to write or wire me about it, the least I could do would be to thank them for their interest.

I was sorry I didn't get to talk to you and Nellie at the dinner or after it. But I'm really a prisoner now. I'm like the "600" and the cannon—only mine are guards and they are trying to keep me out of the "mouth of hell." Everybody is much more worried and jittery than I am. I've always

---

1. General Robert L. Eichelberger, commander of the Eighth Army in the Pacific during the Second World War.

thought that if I could get my hands on a would-be assassin he'd never try it again. But I guess that's impossible. The grand guards who were hurt in the attempt on me didn't have a fair chance. The one who was killed was just cold bloodedly murdered before he could do anything. But his assassin did not live but a couple of minutes—one of the S.S. men put a bullet in one ear and it came out the other. I stuck my head out the upstairs window to see what was going on. One of the guards yelled "Get back." I did, then dressed and went down stairs. I was the only calm one in the house. You see I've been shot at by experts and unless your name's on the bullet you needn't be afraid—and that of course you can't find out, so why worry.

The S.S. chief said to me "Mr. President, don't you know that when there's an Air Raid Alarm you don't run out and look up, you go for cover." I saw the point but it was over then!

Hope it won't happen again. They won't let me go walking or even cross the street on foot. I say "they" won't, but it causes them so much anguish that I conform—a hard thing for a Truman to do as you know, particularly when he could force them to do as he wants. But I want no more guards killed.

So much for that. Tell Nellie I'll write her soon as I get another minute and tell you all about the "Right Hand Man of God," Wake Island, Honolulu, 14,404 miles in practically nothing flat etc. ad lib.

Hope you both are well.

Sincerely,
Harry

A Chicago Tribune *reporter named Holmes allegedly was in Kansas City mousing around. Truman heard about it from his friend Joe McGee, an insurance executive in Kansas City.*

TO JOSEPH J. McGEE

November 22, 1950

Dear Joe:

Matt handed me the longhand note which you wrote him. There isn't a word of truth in that Chicago Tribune venture. You might tell the gentleman named Holmes that if he comes out with a pack of lies about Mrs. Truman or any of my family his hide won't hold shucks when I get through with him.

Sincerely yours,
Harry S. Truman

When Truman and MacArthur conferred on October 15 everything seemed all right, but United States troops had crossed the 38th parallel into North Korea on September 30, and this fateful move brought intervention by the Chinese. Soon information arrived that the Chinese were sending masses of troops south across the Yalu into North Korea. MacArthur imperturbably went ahead with the strategy of occupying all of Korea, north as well as south. He spoke of ending the war by Christmas, and split his forces for what he called a giant UN pincer, with the Eighth Army and the independently commanded X Corps moving northward, separated by a massive mountain barrier that made liaison impossible. It was a situation fraught with disaster, and the President recalled the general's words at Wake.

MEMORANDUM

November 25, 1950

Wake Island

We arrived at dawn. Gen. MacArthur was at the Airport with his shirt unbuttoned, wearing a greasy ham and eggs cap that evidently had been in use for twenty years.

He greeted the President cordially and after the photographers had finished their usual picture orgy the President and the General boarded a two door sedan and drove to the quarters of the Airline manager on the Island.

For more than an hour they discussed the Japanese and Korean situation.

The General assured the President that the victory was won in Korea, that Japan was ready for a peace treaty and that the Chinese Communists would not attack.

A general discussion was carried on about Formosa. The General brought up his statement to the Veterans of Foreign Wars, which had been ordered withdrawn by the President. The General said that he was sorry for any embarrassment he'd caused, that he was not in politics at the time and that the politicians had made a "chump" (his word) of him in 1948 and that it would not happen again. He assured the President that he had no political ambitions.

He again said the Chinese Commies would not attack, that we had won the war and that we could send a Division to Europe from Korea in January 1951.

DIARY

November 30, 1950

A most trying and hectic week. The last session of the 81st Congress has been in session for a few days and it looks as if there are more morons than patriots in it. My "friend" Harry Byrd says he has the professional southerners lined up against Yugoslav Aid. Wonder if he'd like being branded Stalin's No. 2 helper in the Senate. McCarthy of Wisconsin is No. 1. Ellender, a leftover of the Hughie Long regime in Louisiana, and Jim Eastland, a Dixiecrat from Mississippi, have decided against Statehood for Alaska and Hawaii—color and power!

Fulbright from Arkansas, an Oxford man, wants the R.F.C. handicapped and Gene Cox of Georgia wants to restore the power of the Rules Committee in the House to throttle legislation. I suppose that Presidents in the past have had hostile Congresses—but they were frankly of the opposition. This one—the 81st—happens to be of my own party on the surface. But the majority is made up of Republicans and recalcitrant Southern "Democrats"—who are not Democrats. So I get the responsibility and the blame.

There are liars, trimmers and pussyfooters on both sides of the aisle in the Senate and the House. I'm sorry. I wish I had straight out opposition and loyal support. I guess it is too much to ask for!

DIARY

December 2, 1950

Decided to go to Philadelphia to the annual contest between the West Point and Annapolis football teams. Army had won nearly all its games. Navy had lost nearly all. Army, rated No. 2 in the nation, Navy No. 64 or 65. There was a contest on 64 or 65!

All the odds were on Army. Some of my party were giving from 12 to 21 points and betting even money on the Army team.

I was the guest of the Navy and I'm always for the underdog. In spite of my Army background I bet on the Navy, and, as in 1948, against all the dope, the sport experts etc.—Navy Won 21 to 14.

When I arrived at Blair House I had a call from Sec. of State Acheson. He, General Marshall and General Bradley came to see me. General MacArthur is in serious trouble. He's made some very undiplomatic statements. One I had to force him to withdraw. He made a bad one just before the election and another just after.[1]

Now he's in very serious trouble. We must get him out of it, if we can. The conference was the most solemn one I've had since the Atomic Bomb conference in Berlin. We continue it in the morning. *It looks very bad.*

In what the President thought was a good press conference on November 30 he had said that he was considering all means to stop the Chinese, including the atomic bomb. Prime Minister Attlee panicked and asked to come to Washington. He arrived on December 4.

DIARY

December 5, 1950

A most busy and hectic day. Charlie Ross and I went to the National Guard Armory at the east end of Capitol Street where I addressed the White House Conference on Youth and Children. Had a very cordial reception. (See speech.) Went back to the office, signed mail and documents as usual. Talked to Charlie Ross on the way back about releases of Attlee conference. Saw some customers, the Budget, HH,[1] and General Marshall. Harriman, Gen. Marshall, Charlie Ross and I went to the Williamsburg for lunch with the British Prime Minister and his aides.

It was a very satisfactory gathering. The Speaker, Sam Rayburn, Sen. Connally, Sen. Wiley, Cong. Eaton, Richards, Gen. Bradley, Field Marshal Slim,[2] and others had lunch.

After lunch the Senators and Congressmen left the ship and State,

---

1. Before the congressional elections MacArthur had spoken of the Chinese privileged sanctuary, the air bases in Manchuria from which Chinese pilots dashed across the Yalu, bombed U.N. forces, and fled back to base. With good reason the President had refused to allow the general to bomb Manchuria. After the election MacArthur spoke of his forces' "massive compression envelopment," the pincers. On November 28, after 260,000 Chinese troops had crossed the Yalu River, he announced that "We face an entirely new war" and that "this command . . . is now faced with conditions beyond its control and strength."

---

1. Herbert Hoover. When Truman came into the White House in 1945 he was anxious to enlist the talents of former President Hoover, who had been ostracized by President Roosevelt; Hoover had not been in the White House since March 4, 1933. Within a short time Truman welcomed Hoover to the Oval Office, and the former President responded in an almost emotional way, vastly appreciating Truman's kindness. Thereafter the two men kept closely in touch, and Truman used Hoover first to survey the food situation abroad and then to help reorganize the federal bureaucracy.

2. Slim was with Attlee's party.

Defense, Treasury and their aides discussed the Asiatic situation. The British still seem to think that all should be given up in the Far East to save Europe. I said No!

We talk some more tomorrow. The position of the British on Asia is, to say the least, fantastic. We cannot agree to their suggestions. Yet they say they will support us whatever we do!

Congressman F. Edward Hebert of Louisiana wrote the President on December 5 about the possibility of setting aside a special Sunday, ideally before Christmas, "to appeal to Almighty God for guidance and wisdom in what I believe to be the Gethsemane of our existence," namely, the fight against a godless ideology.

TO F. EDWARD HEBERT

December 7, 1950

My dear Congressman Hebert:

I appreciated very much your letter of the fifth, and am enclosing you a copy of my Thanksgiving Proclamation, inviting your attention to the wind-up of that Proclamation beginning, "NOW, THEREFORE." I think that effectively answers your suggestion.

I am extremely sorry that the sentiments expressed in your letter were not thought of before November seventh, when the campaign in your State, Utah, North Carolina, Illinois and Indiana was carried on in a manner that was as low as I've ever seen and I've been in this game since 1906.

Sincerely,
Harry S. Truman

[Hebert wrote back the next day that he was stunned, and regretted "that you failed to grasp the real purpose and intent of my suggestion, but it is even more regrettable that you saw fit to gratuitously inject political distemper in your reply."]

Truman's much talked about letter, dated December 6, to the music critic of the Washington Post, *Paul Hume, lambasting him for a "lousy review" of Margaret's Constitution Hall concert on December 5, was written hurriedly. The President mailed it himself and afterward could do little save listen to the tongues wag about how he lost his temper. Actually, he had too much on his mind—the Chinese intervention in Korea, the press conference of November 30 and the Attlee visit. And there was another development. On the afternoon of December 5, just before Margaret's concert, the President's press secretary and high school chum of half a century before, Charlie Ross, was sitting at his White House desk preparing to speak into a microphone. His secretary, Myrtle Bergheim, kidded him: "Don't mumble," she said. "You know I always speak very distinctly," Charlie replied. Suddenly the cigarette he had just lit fell from his lips and he slumped back in his chair, dead of a heart attack.*

DIARY

December 9, 1950

Margie held a concert here in D.C. on Dec. 5th. It was a good one. She was well accompanied by a young pianist name of Allison, whose father is a Baptist preacher in Augusta, Georgia. Young Allison played two pieces after the intermission, one of which was the great A flat Chopin Waltz Opus 42. He did it as well as it could be done and I've heard Paderewski, Moritz Rosenthal and Joseph Lhevinne play it.

A frustrated critic on the Washington Post wrote a lousy review. The only thing, General Marshall said, he didn't criticize was the varnish on the piano. He put my "baby" as low as he could and he made the young accompanist look like a dub.

It upset me, and I wrote him what I thought of him. I told him he is lower than Pegler and that was intended to be an insult worse than a reflection on his ancestry. I would never reflect on a man's mother because mothers are not to be attacked although mine has [been]!

Well I've had a grand time this day. I've been accused of putting my "baby" who is the "apple of my eye" in a bad position. I don't think that is so. She doesn't either—thank the Almighty.

In addition to personal matters I've had conference after conference on the jittery situation facing the country. Attlee, Formosa, Communist China, Chiang Kai-shek, Japan, Germany, France, India etc. I've worked for peace for five years and six months and it looks like World War III is here.

I hope not—but we must meet whatever comes—and we will.

TO BARBARA HEGGIE

December 20, 1950

My dear Miss Heggie:

I have just read your story in the Woman's Home Companion— "What Makes Margaret Sing?"

It is lovely. Thank you from my heart. The vast majority of our people can never understand what a terrible handicap it is to a lovely girl to have her father the President of the United States.

Stuffed shirt critics and vicious political opponents of mine sometimes try to take it out on Margie. It's her dad they are after and Margie understands. You have come more nearly stating the situation in its true light than anyone who has made the attempt.

I hope sometime you'll make a study of the families of the Presidents. It is most interesting. Martha Washington and her children and what happened to them. Abigail Adams, Dolly Madison, the wife of Andrew Jackson and how she was hounded to her grave. Mrs. Lincoln the most mistreated of all the White House First Ladies except Mrs. Cleveland, the first Mrs. Woodrow Wilson and the Wilson daughters, Alice Roosevelt Longworth, Mrs. Coolidge and Herbert Hoover's sons. Of course we are too close to Franklin Roosevelt and his daughter and sons properly to evaluate what the White House did to them.

You've made a contribution to history that will help some Ph.D. in the future to evaluate all these families I've mentioned.

Hope you'll regard this communication as one from a fond father and keep it confidential. Only my "mad" letters are published!

Sincerely,

Harry S. Truman

DIARY

Independence
December 22, 1950

Frank Land had a dinner for the Red Cross of Constantine. He asked Roy Roberts to speak. Made an ass of himself, and I gave him a kick where it would do the most good to anybody else—but his anatomy is so surrounded with lard that he didn't feel the kick!

DIARY

Independence
December 24, 1950

Took a nice walk. Not many followers.

Dedicated the Grandview Baptist Church. Made many contributions to its construction, hoping the church would be a monument to the worship of God. I hope it will be—but it looks like a funeral home and not a church. Anyway it was dedicated with my small help. I am hoping to buy the site of the old church and build a good looking structure for Grandview Lodge 618 A.F. & A.M. No "modern nut" architect will have anything to do with that.

Had to hurry away from the church dedication to press a button at Independence to light the National Christmas Tree on the White House lawn.

Stopped by Vivian's and saw all his family on the way to Grandview. Went by and had a visit with Mary. Took her to the dedication. Vivian, Luella and Fred, his wife and J.C. were present at the dedication.

DIARY

December 27, 1950

Dean Acheson called, and I had to go back to Washington. Never been home in the last five years that something didn't happen.

1951

The year 1950 had been an annus terribilis, *but matters began to improve early in 1951. General Ridgway turned the Korean War around, slowly but surely, reorganizing the U.N. forces by grouping the Eighth Army with the body of troops that had landed at Inchon, the X Corps, rather than having two separate commands, each reporting to Tokyo. After carefully managing a slow retreat toward Pusan, he halted his forces and then turned on the Chinese, chopping up their troops with massive artillery fire, moving the front northward again until it stabilized at approximately the 38th parallel.*

Perhaps it was Ridgway's command success, or maybe it was memory of the despair expressed to Washington when the Chinese attacked at the end of November, but General MacArthur could not stomach the new tactics of his largely independent field commander, and began to belittle them by commenting to visitors to his headquarters and in teletypes to Washington that the only way to "win" the war was to take the fighting into China, maybe with nuclear weapons. The minority leader of the House of Representatives, Congressman Joe Martin, wrote MacArthur for advice on the military situation and received plenty of it. The "Far Eastern General" answered: "It seems strangely difficult for some to realize that here in Asia is where the Communist conspirators have elected to make their play for global conquest, and that we have joined the issue thus raised on the battlefield; that here we fight Europe's war with arms while the diplomats there still fight it with words; that if we lose the war to Communism in Asia the fall of Europe is inevitable, win it and Europe most probably would avoid war and yet preserve freedom. As you point out, we must win. There is no substitute for victory." Martin at first did not know what to do with the MacArthur letter. He had asked the general to write "either on a confidential basis or otherwise," and MacArthur had not labeled the response as confidential. Then Senator Connally, chairman of the Foreign Relations Committee, declared his belief that there would be no world war that year, 1951. On the same day, the speaker of the House, Sam Rayburn, warned, "I think that we stand in the face of terrible danger and maybe the beginning of World War III." Martin found this Democratic confusion "intolerable" and released the MacArthur letter, reading it to the House.

At that, Truman fired MacArthur, the general was invited back to address a joint session of the House and Senate and did so on April 19, and the Senate's foreign relations and armed services committees jointly began hearings that went on for weeks. Eventually all the talk wore out the participants and the American public, and reason began to dominate the forums, as epitomized by the testimony of General Bradley that a war against China would be the wrong war in the wrong place at the wrong time. After public appearances in major American cities, the "Far Eastern General" established himself in the Waldorf Towers in New York and disappeared from view.

Early in September, Secretary Acheson in San Francisco signed the Japanese peace treaty in the presence of a group of delegates from the nations against whom Japan had warred a decade earlier. Just before the conference, the President in Washington signed a treaty of mutual assistance with the president of the Philippines, Carlos Romulo, and there was another treaty, known as ANZUS, with Australia and New Zealand. An alliance with Japan was signed the same day as the peace treaty, and subsequent alliances were formed with Nationalist China and with South Korea.

At the end of the year, Truman found a developing scandal in the Bureau of Internal Revenue and fired an assistant attorney general, T. Lamar Caudle, and the general counsel of the bureau, Charles Oliphant. An outside investigator was called for, but a fiasco resulted when, early the next year, Truman chose a New Yorker, Newbold Morris. Morris acted with such lack of finesse that the attorney general, J. Howard McGrath, fired him, whereupon Truman fired McGrath.

DIARY

January 10, 1951

It has been a very strenuous ten days. Left Kansas City Dec. 26 at a few minutes after ten A.M., arrived in Washington a short time after two P.M. Had quite a reception—State, Defense, Treasury and several other cabinet and prominent people to meet me.

General Eisenhower came to see me Sat. Jan. 6 and spent an hour talking over his duties in Europe.[1] He called me when he left his hotel

---

1. Eisenhower had been recalled from his duties as president of Columbia University to command N.A.T.O. troops in Europe.

Harry S. Truman being sworn in at 7:09 P.M., on April 12, 1945, in the cabinet
room of the executive offices. *Left to right:* Philip B. Fleming, public works
administrator; John B. Blandford, Jr., housing administrator; Leo Crowley,
foreign economic administrator; Frances Perkins, secretary of labor; Henry L.
Stimson, secretary of war; Henry A. Wallace, secretary of commerce; Julius A.
Krug, war production board administrator; James V. Forrestal, secretary of the
navy; Claude Wickard, secretary of agriculture; Francis Biddle, attorney
general; Edward R. Stettinius, Jr., secretary of state; Harry S. Truman; Mrs.
Truman; Harold R. Ickes, secretary of the interior; Margaret Truman; Harlan
Fiske Stone, chief justice; Sam Rayburn, speaker of the House; Fred M. Vinson,
director, Office of War Mobilization and Reconversion; Joseph W. Martin, Jr.,
minority leader, House of Representatives; Representative Robert Ramspeck,
Democratic whip; John W. McCormack, House majority leader. *(Harry Goodwin,
Washington Post)*

At the Big Three meeting in Potsdam. *Left to right:* General Vaughan, Stalin, Charles Bohlen, HST, Commodore Vardaman, Andrei Gromyko, James F. Byrnes, Molotov. *(U.S. Army)*

Triple handshake, Churchill, Truman, and Stalin. *(U.S. Army)*

Announcing the surrender of Japan, August 14, 1945. On the couch *(left to right):* unidentified, Bess Truman, Samuel I. Rosenman, John W. Snyder, James F. Byrnes. Above Byrnes, Tom C. Clark. *(Abbie Rowe, National Park Service)*

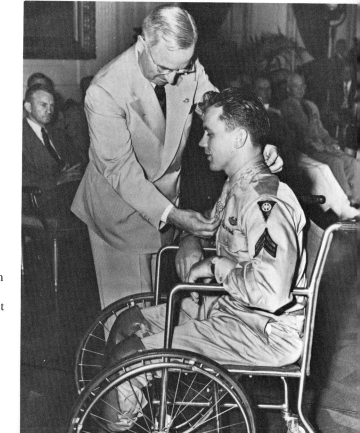

sident Truman handed out more igressional Medals of Honor than the Presidents before him put ether. Here he decorates Sergeant ph G. Neppel, twenty-one, of lden, Iowa. Neppel, a farm ·ker, lost both legs in action near gel, Germany. James A. Forrestal background, left. *(UPI Photo)*

With Winston Churchill on the way to Fulton, Missouri, to give the "iron curtain" speech, 1946. Harry Vaughan and an unidentified British officer in back. *(UPI Photo)*

James F. Byrnes *(right)*, retiring secretary of state, congratulates his successor, George C. Marshall. Attorney General Tom Clark, with cigar, in background. *(Abbie Rowe, National Park Service)*

The President displays a tie chain presented to him upon his becoming an "honorary submarine skipper." The chain anchors one of his famous scrambled-egg ties. (UPI Photo)

At the Little White House in Key West. *(Left to right:* Matt Connelly, HST, and Charlie Ross. *(U.S. Navy)*

The President and Mrs. Truman fishing in Key West. *(U.S. Navy)*

Jimmy Roosevelt gets a rousing welcome as he arrives in Philadelphia to attend the Democratic National Convention. To the left of Jimmy, the chairman of the California delegation, John Shelly. The sign carriers seem confused about their allegiance, but one thing is certain—there are no Truman signs. *(UPI Photo)*

The nominees, HST and Alben W. Barkley, Philadelphia, 1948. *(Jules Schick, Wide World Photos)*

The whistle-stop campaign. (*UPI Photo*)

Three farmers have lunch at the National Plowing Contest, Dexter, Iowa, 1948. *Left to right:* Howard Walker (Dexter), the President, Ralph Mortimer (Dallas Center). (*Wide World Photos*)

and I met him at the airport. We reviewed the honor guard together and had pictures by the dozen. I gave him the best send off I could.

Bess, Margie and Mrs. Wallace came in at 7:30 A.M. Sat. Jan. 6.

Bess went to N.Y. yesterday, 9th, to go to a show with Margie.

Friday night, Jan. 5th, I went to the Gayety to see Edw. Arnold in the "Apple of his Eye." A great show.

Monday the 8th I went to Congress and gave them all I could in the Message on the State of the Union. Apparently it was all right. Telegrams and letters are running 15 to 1 favorably. Never worked so hard on a speech. All say it showed effort. Hope it does some good.

Received the Woodrow Wilson Award today. A wonderful medal with a grand citation on the back. Mrs. McAdoo, Mr. Sayre[2] and other highest of the high hats present. It was quite a ceremony. Didn't deserve it but that's the case in most awards. But not in those Congressional Medals of Honor I awarded yesterday to the survivors of five Korean heroes. Hope I'll not have to do that again. I'm a damned sentimentalist and I could hardly hold my voice steady when I gave a medal to a widow or a father for heroism in action.

It was similar to giving citations to the men who were shot protecting me at the Blair House—and I choked up just as I did then. What an old fool I am!

DIARY

Key West,
March 7, 1951

We came to Key West today in the Independence. Adm. Leahy, Matt Connelly, Joe Short, Bill Hassett, Don Dawson, Dave Stowe, Dave Bell, Joe Feeney, Gen. Vaughan, Adm. Dennison, Gen. Landry, Dave Lloyd, Irving Perlmeter were on the Independence.[1] We left Washington at 12:52 P.M., arrived at Key West at 4:34, 3 hours & 32 minutes.

Capt. Adell and all the officers of the base met us. The streets were lined with people and they gave me a welcome on this 11th visit, just as cordial as they did on the 1st one.

Inspected the Marine Guard. It is a great organization. All have battle stars on their ribbons and some have special medals and purple hearts. After the inspection we went to the Little White House, arriving at 5:10 P.M. Had dinner at seven and a conference with the staff.

---

2. Francis B. Sayre, President Wilson's son-in-law.

1. Joseph Short was Charlie Ross's successor as press secretary; Dawson, Stowe, Bell, Feeney, and Lloyd were presidential assistants; Perlmeter was assistant press secretary.

On the way down in the plane we discussed Presidents and their troubles. Collier's published an article about military Presidents. It is most interesting and in the main as accurate as could be expected. Most of the special writers make a three day research and write profound treatises on what they know nothing about. This Collier's article on our military Presidents was very nearly correct. We discussed it and found some errors, but not serious ones. If Collier's editors had found errors one fourth as great in any statements I make, they would write a vicious editorial on them.

My good friend William Hillman has been editing and making a continuity of some of my personal diaries for publication in a book which will come out March 18, '52.

Mr. Hillman has been the foreign editor of Collier's. When they found that he was putting this book together, they discharged him! They told him that they thought that there is nothing good about me and Bill had no business to help me get the truth to the people of the United States. That is "Free Press" in reverse! They will be sorry for that attitude because the good people of this great Republic do not like a below the belt approach to anything.

DIARY

April 6, 1951

MacArthur shoots another political bomb through Joe Martin, leader of the Republican minority in the House.

This looks like the last straw.

Rank insubordination. Last summer he sent a long statement to the Vets of Foreign Wars—not through the high command back home, but directly! He sent copies to newspapers and magazines particularly hostile to me.

I was furnished a copy from the press room of the White House which had been *accidentally* sent there.

I ordered the release suppressed and then sent him a very carefully prepared directive dated Dec. 5, 1950, setting out Far Eastern policy after I'd flown 14,404 [miles] to Wake Island to see him and reach an understanding face to face.

He told me the war in Korea was over, that we could transfer a regular division to Germany Jan. 1st. He was positive Red China would not come in. He expected to support our Far Eastern policy.

I call in Gen. Marshall, Dean Acheson, Mr. Harriman and Gen. Bradley before Cabinet to discuss situation. I've come to the conclusion that our Big General in the Far East must be recalled. I don't express any opinion or make known my decision.

Direct the four to meet again Friday afternoon and go over all phases of the situation.

DIARY

April 8, 1951

I see the Chief Justice and Sam Rayburn. Barkley in hospital but I talk with him on phone.

The situation in Far East is discussed but I do not disclose my intentions.

DIARY

April 9, 1951

Meet the Big Four, Barkley, Rayburn, McFarland,[1] McCormack and explain Far Eastern situation. Receive comments suggesting certain actions.

Meet with Acheson, Marshall, Bradley and Harriman. Go over recall orders to MacArthur and suggested public statement. Approve both and decide to send the orders to Frank Pace, Sec. of the Army, for delivery to MacArthur and Ridgway.[2] Send message to Korean Ambassador. Message to be sent tomorrow at 8 P.M. our time. It will arrive at 10 A.M. Wednesday in Korea.

Gen. Bradley called about 9 P.M. Said there had been a leak. He, Dean Rusk,[3] Mr. Harriman came to see me. Mr. Murphy was also present.

Discussed the situation and I ordered messages sent at once and directly to MacArthur.

DIARY

April 10, 1951

Quite an explosion. Was expected but I had to act.
Telegrams and letters of abuse by the dozens.

---

1. Senator Ernest W. McFarland of Arizona was majority leader of the upper house.
2. After the dismissal of General MacArthur, Ridgway took command of the U.N. forces.
3. Then assistant secretary of state for Far Eastern affairs.

TO RALPH E. TRUMAN

June 2, 1951

Dear Ralph:

I can't be present in Topeka for the 35th reunion. Things are getting worse and worse here. I had to cut the cruise on the Potomac short.

The Congress had passed a bill that may stop rearmament of Europe. The "great" Missouri Senator, Kem, caused the trouble. I've been working on a statement about it all day.[1]

Now this is completely confidential and the reason I can't come. The Secret Service have received more than the usual number of threats to rub me out at the reunion. You know I never worry about those things because you and I have been shot at by experts. But what worries me is that some good fellow who has three or four kids may get killed—to keep me from that fate. You've no idea how it feels to have a grand man killed and two more badly wounded protecting you. So I'm not coming.

I never felt as badly for missing a meeting in my life.

You can only say that public business kept me away. My best to Olive.

Sincerely,

Harry

DIARY

June 21, 1951

My day has been a strenuous one, as usual. Met the President of Ecuador yesterday afternoon at 3:00 P.M. Gave him the usual honors, 21 guns, inspection of the honor guard at the airport, parade in downtown Washington, stop at the Municipal Bldg., key to the City and response by the Ecuadorian President, continue on to Blair House, pictures on the front steps, tea in the garden, State Dinner at the Carlton, toasts etc.

The President departed the Blair House at 9:20 A.M. today. I arose at 5 A.M. and tried to catch up with my reading, document signing, dictation etc. Almost made it.

Had a session with the Sec. of State and Sec. of Defense on a *most* important matter. Russians are tired of the Korean affair and want to quit. Well we'll see.

Had a most important session with the Chiefs of Staff. Ground, Navy,

---

1. Senator James P. Kem had sponsored a rider on a deficiency appropriations bill, which barred United States economic aid to any government shipping strategic materials to communist countries. The President signed the bill but strongly criticized the rider.

Air and Gen. Bradley gave me a report on the lessons and the improvement as a result of Korean "War."

Had a speech session with the staff. Buttoned up a health speech for tomorrow (22nd) afternoon. Must write another Saturday for Monday delivery in Tennessee. Then another for July 4th at the Washington Monument celebrating 175th birthday of the Declaration of Independence.[1] It is a Nation Wide Celebration. Ch. Justice Vinson is the National Chairman of a committee made up of the Vice President, the Speaker of the House, and the Floor Leaders of the Senate and the House of Representatives. Looks as if it will be an epoch making affair. Hope it will hook Vinson for the next President!

MacArthur is now a "drug on the market" with the Senate Republicans. His Texas trip was a dud. And the witnesses by telling the truth have left the joint committee with[out] a real headline for weeks. The committees put out a most interesting report today on how they would turn the "bear" loose.[2] The facts are too much for the opposition Democrats and the Chiang Kai-shek Republicans. Too bad too bad. Their official mud slinger and Goebbels liar also made a bad blunder when he attacked General Marshall.[3] He is trying another Nazi-Communist trick today by trying another lying attack on people already cleared earlier. What a low ebb for the G.O.P. Well we'll see.

TO BESS W. TRUMAN

June 25, 1951

Dear Bess:

It was grand to have you and Margaret on the telephone yesterday. She is still going at a grand pace for our public relations in Europe, and I think she is also having a good time.[1]

After I talked to you, I went for a drive. Picked up the Vinsons and drove to Leesburg. Gen. and Mrs. Marshall and Mr. Baruch and Mr. Baruch's secretary and nurse were there. The old man has had an operation on his face. Gen. Marshall thought it was cancer. So do I—it looked

---

1. Almost all the Presidents in the twentieth century have used speechwriters, and so did Truman. By "writing" a speech he usually meant outlining it orally and going over a draft or two and annotating final copy.

2. Truman thought the MacArthur hearings had given Congress a bear to hold by the tail —for MacArthur, he believed, made a fool of himself, and how would Congress report that?

3. Senator Jenner of Indiana, in a long diatribe in 1950, had told fellow senators that Marshall was not only willing but eager to play the role of front man for traitors and that this was no new role because Marshall was a living lie.

---

1. Margaret together with two friends had left on a trip to Europe, sailing on May 26 on the *America*. They returned early in July on the maiden voyage of the *Constitution*.

like it. The old man wept and said he hoped our misunderstanding would be something in the past and not happen again. Of course I agreed to it. He left shortly after the Chief, Mrs. Vinson and I arrived.

We had a most pleasant afternoon and a good supper with the Marshalls. Fred and the General told a lot of good stories about their careers and experiences. It was most interesting.

Mrs. Marshall's son was there, offered to take me for a swim in one of the neighbors' pools. I didn't go. He had a date for supper somewhere else, and when he left, he said goodbye Colonel to General Marshall. The General said all the family called him Colonel—that he said seemed to be his first name to them.

I'm leaving for Tennessee shortly to speak at the dedication of an air research center, named for Gen. Arnold. I'm going to tear the Russians and the Republicans apart—call a spade just what it is and tell Malik if Russia wants peace, peace is available and has been since 1945. This is the anniversary of the flight from Independence a year ago that has been quite a day in history. All the papers except the sabotage sheets gave me the best of it yesterday.

This week contains another very important—most important—anniversary. Thursday will be thirty-two years. What a thirty-two years! I've never been anything but happy for that anniversary. Maybe I haven't given you all you're entitled to, but I've done my best, and I'm still in love with the prettiest girl in the world.

Hope all are well. We'll talk to Margie in Rome next Sunday.

Lots of love.

                                                            Harry

TO NELLIE NOLAND

                                                    August 8, 1951

Dear Nellie:

Your good letter of July 27th was most highly appreciated. I was more than pleased at what you wrote about "grit." I hope your diagnosis is correct. Never a day passes that some scalawag or some so-called high class publication doesn't take a swipe at my character, integrity and ancestry.

As "Father" Divine says "ain't life wonderful." Bill Hassett and myself have decided to start a new religious sect when we are done saving the country in this job. Bill's my correspondence secretary. He furnishes me with acceptances to resignations, handles religious and sectarian correspondence, writes 100 year old congratulations to old ladies and old gentlemen whose relatives think the President of the United States should take notice of such contributions to the public welfare. He also takes notice of the annual meetings of D.A.R.'s, Colonial Dames, U.D.C., Sons of the Revolution, Knights of Columbus, Elks, Eagles, Shriners, B'nai B'rith, Jewish Welfare Society, etc. etc. ad lib. We always discuss whether we'll pull out all the stops, ring the bells and give 'em a full treatment or whether we'll just be coldly formal. It's quite a game.

We also have to decide on the days and weeks to celebrate—such as Foot Happiness Week, Thanksgiving Day, Virginia Dare Day (the gal not the wine) etc. ad lib on that. We have more than six hundred requests for proclamations on days, weeks and months—enough to run in celebrations for a hundred years!

There's nothing like being President of these United States. I've been offered a million dollars for my memoirs! They are not for sale at any price. But I intend to set 'em down and leave 'em to Margie.

Hope you and Myra[1] had a grand time over 3 score and 10! I'll catch you in a couple of years. Hope you and Ethel are both well and that I'll see you both soon.

Sincerely,

Harry

About that new religious racket that Bill and I are working on—we haven't yet decided whether we'll sell medicine, ideas or another New Testament or Book of Mormon. . . .

DIARY

August 30, 1951

The President of the Republic of the Philippines met with the signers of the mutual defense treaty at the Labor Dept. Auditorium, where the Atlantic Pact was signed.

He and I stood behind the signers. Sec. Acheson signed first. Then General Romulo[1] signed and turn about until all had signed.

I introduced the President of the Republic of the Philippines, who made a beautiful speech, ending with a pledge of everlasting friendship.

As President of the United States I replied.

We then went to a luncheon at the Blair-Lee House.

As usual I toasted the Guest of Honor and he replied in a wonderful tribute to the United States.

---

1. Colgan.

---

1. President Romulo had been a U.S. brigadier general during World War II.

As usual old Tom Connally, Texas Senator and Chairman of the Senate Foreign Relations Committee, tried the best he could to insult one of my guests. That has been the usual procedure for the last four years.

If old Tom isn't raising hell about protocol and where he sits, he is insulting one of the guests!

TO BESS W. TRUMAN

September 1, 1951

Dear Bess:

I have been resisting an impulse to call you, to call Margaret, to call Vivian, to call Mary Jane.

Went to the 50th anniversary celebration of the American League at the ball park this afternoon. Joe Short, Charlie Murphy, Dave Stowe, Adm. Dennison, Gen. Landry with a dozen or so secret service, police, F.B.I. and others saw that I arrived at the game and departed safely. The Chief Justice and his younger son James sat with me in the front row in our box. Fred knew all the old players and all the new ones, and he saw to it that I did a land office business autographing baseballs for them. Old Griff[1] sat on my left and told me what the various players on the Washington team should have done and didn't do. Nick[2] was sitting in the aisle on the other side of Griff and pulling for the home team to beat the Yanks because that would put Boston Red Sox closer to the top. Washington lost 5 to 0. Old Clark said Washington lost because you were not present. I agreed with him.

Charlie Murphy was here a while ago and gave me some papers for use in San Francisco.[3] I've been working on the bond drive speech for Monday evening and my Jap Peace Speech for Tuesday, an "off the cuff" speech for the Democratic luncheon in Frisco on Tuesday and a dedication speech for the Reserve Armory in K.C. on Thursday and one for the Tirey Ford Post on Wednesday or Friday. Wish I could come home like anybody else and do as I please.

You should see the Shah's rug. It is beautiful. 12 × 16. Never saw a prettier one. The Harrimans brought a grand evening bag. I'll bring it with me.

You ought to see the scimitar old Ibn Saud sent to me. It is 350 years old, belonged to his Great-great-great-grandfather. It is in a solid gold sheath incrusted with pearls and rubies. He told Doc it was his most prized possession, and he sent it to me because my doctor had saved his

---

1. Clark Griffith, owner of the Washington team.
2. Nicolas Bez, an old friend.
3. Where the Japanese Peace Treaty was to be signed.

life! Doc performed an operation on his esophagus. Took out a tumor that was slowly choking him to death. He wouldn't let Doc have a helper because he didn't want anyone to know what was the matter with him. So Doc gave him a local and pulled it out. Luckily it wasn't malignant. Then the specialists Doc took with him gave the old man a complete going over and left him sound and in good health.[4]

Hope you and Margie are having a nice evening—not as lonely and homesick as mine. I have your groceries all assembled. If we stop for gas in K.C. on the way out, I'll unload them and send them to you.

Lots of love from your all time "sweetie."

Harry

DIARY

September 2, 1951

The Lord Mayor of London is supposed to call on me today.

He didn't show up!

I find that he is in Ottawa, Canada, and that his call is to take place on Sept. 16th!

Well, it is hell when things at the top get balled up.

Justice Douglas visited Indonesia on the way back from the Himalayas and had a long talk with President Sukarno, who had "tremendous admiration" for Ambassador Merle Cochran. The ambassador, Douglas wrote, was about to be removed, and he advised the President to stop it, for Cochran was doing the best American job in all of Southeast Asia. Meanwhile, the justice had made a press-conference statement in San Francisco advising a political settlement and recognition of Red China.

TO WILLIAM O. DOUGLAS

September 13, 1951

Dear Bill:

I have your note of the eighth regarding Indonesia and I appreciate it very much.

I also appreciate highly your continued interest in politics and foreign affairs. I was somewhat embarrassed by your statement on Commu-

---

4. The President had sent Dr. Graham to assist Ibn Saud. All these gifts, including the Shah's rug, became by protocol possessions of the people of the United States. The rug presently is on display at the Truman Library in Independence. As for the scimitar, alas, see footnote, p. 109.

nist China. As long as I am President, if I can prevent it, that cut throat organization will never be recognized by us as the Government of China and I am sorry that a Justice of the Supreme Court has been willing to champion the interest of a bunch of murderers by a public statement.

I am being very frank with you Bill because fundamentally I am very fond of you but you have missed the boat on three different occasions if you really wanted to get into politics.[1] Since you are on the highest Court in the land it seems to me that the best thing you can possibly do would be to give your best effort to that Court and let the President of the United States run the political end of foreign and domestic affairs.

Sincerely yours,
Harry S. Truman

The irresponsibility of the press in publishing vital military infor-mation bothered the President, and another Soviet nuclear explosion, which occurred late in September or very early in October inspired him to lecture his press conference—all the Russians had to do, he said, was read the newspapers. His comments had not been appreciated by the Washington correspondent of the Times.

TO ARTHUR KROCK (UNSENT)

October 7, 1951

My dear Arthur:

I've just read your column about my security press conference. You give me credit for the responsibility of the men who were the sources of the information about which I talked. I wish that were true.

You see the Generals and the Admirals and the career men in govern-ment look upon the occupant of the White House as only a temporary nuisance who soon will be succeeded by another temporary occupant who won't find out what it is all about for a long time and then it will be too late to do anything about it.

You newspaper men have a complex that anyone who tells you of any of your many shortcomings is either ambitious to be a dictator or else he is an ignoramus. But you should take into consideration that we are no longer in the gay nineties of Ben Harrison, William McKinley or Teddy the Rough Rider.

We are faced with the most terrible responsibility that any nation

---

1. The President had twice asked Douglas to be secretary of the interior—in 1946 when Ickes resigned, and in 1948 when Krug resigned. Both times Douglas refused. In the interval between these two offers came Truman's invitation to Douglas to join the ticket as vice-presidential candidate in 1948.

ever faced. From Darius I's Persia, Alexander's Greece, Hadrian's Rome, Victoria's Britain, no nation or group of nations has had our responsibilities. If we could spend one year's military appropriation to develop the Euphrates Valley, the plateau of Ethiopia, the table land of South America—if we could open the Rhine-Danube waterway, the Kiel Canal, the Black Sea Straits to free trade, if Russia would be a good neighbor and use her military expenditures for her own economic development, I would not have to scold the publishers for giving away our military secrets. Wish you'd do a little soul searching and see if at *great* intervals the President may be right.

The country is yours as well as mine. You find no trouble in suppressing news in which I'm interested. Why can't you do a little safety policing?

TO ETHEL NOLAND

December 12, 1951

Dear Ethel:

I've been a long time answering your good letter of Thanksgiving Day. I have a good excuse—but I also hate alibis! The business of the Government began to pick up to such an extent, the last week I was in Key West, that I had to come to Washington to get on top of it. What with firing tax collectors and asst. attorneys general, the budget, the message on the State of the Union (by the way it's in a hell of a state!) and the economic message I have very little to do between now and January 8th.

Princess Elizabeth is a very grand person and so is the Duke. They made a grand impression here.

It has been suggested that the King & I fire all our ambassadors and let Margaret and the Princess act for the two countries. What do you think about that?

There's another headache I didn't mention before—Mr. Churchill. He'd probably object to any such procedure. He's going to cause me plenty of trouble just before my top headache—the Congress—gets back to town.

Yes Dr. Graham took care of old man Mossadegh and that sent him home in a good humor. But it hasn't helped the Iranian Oil Situation much.[1]

---

1. Dr. Mohammed Mossadegh, the quixotic prime minister of Iran, had been in Washington for treatment by Dr. Graham. Mossadegh disguised his essential cunning behind a behavior that amused and annoyed Westerners, for he was accustomed to receiving them while in bed, and frequently he would burst into tears, and sometimes he fainted. He was a large landowner but a natinoalist, and opposed the young Shah. Had Mossadegh received more support, perhaps American aid funds, he might have proved an instrument of increasing democracy in Iran. Instead, the Americans were preoccupied with the Korean War and the

Hope you liked Hillman and Wagg.[2] They are nice people.

Bess leaves for home tonight and Margaret and I will come out Dec. 24th weather permitting.

Hope the eye came out all right and that Nellie is fully recovered.[3]

Had a letter from Myra. She wrote in a gay spirit so I hope all's well.

Sincerely,

Harry

TO DWIGHT D. EISENHOWER

December 18, 1951

Dear Ike:

The columnists, the slick magazines and all the political people who like to speculate are saying many things about what is to happen in 1952.

As I told you in 1948 and at our luncheon in 1951, do what you think best for the country. My own position is in the balance. If I do what I want to do I'll go back to Missouri and *maybe* run for the Senate. If you decide to finish the European job (and I don't know who else can) I must keep the isolationists out of the White House. I wish you would let me know what you intend to do. It will be between us and no one else.

I have the utmost confidence in your judgment and your patriotism. My best to you and Mrs. Ike for a happy holiday season.

Most sincerely,

Harry S. Truman

[Eisenhower, then in command of N.A.T.O. troops, answered in a handwritten letter on January 1, 1952, cautiously disclaiming any political ambition.]

MEMORANDUM

Hotel Muehlebach, Kansas City
December 26, 1951

The facts about recent discharges for malfeasance in office. The collector of internal revenue in San Francisco was discharged for ineffi-

---

communist menace. Mossadegh enraged the British government by nationalizing the Anglo-Iranian Oil Company early in May 1951, and the British were doing their best to cut off Iran's oil sales abroad and bring down Mossadegh's government.

2. Alfred Wagg, a photographer, was collaborating with Hillman on his book about HST.

3. Nellie had been ill since midsummer, apparently in part with gall bladder trouble. In early July she underwent an operation.

ciency. He was afterward indicted by a California Federal Grand Jury at the behest of the Atty. General.

The collector in Boston was fired because of irregularities in his office. The collector in St. Louis was asked to resign because he did not attend to the duties of his office. He was afterward indicted for irregularities in his office. The collector at Nashville was fired because he is a drug addict. The New York office was cleaned up because of irregularities.

Caudle was discharged because he did not handle his office efficiently and Oliphant was allowed to resign for the same reason.

All these operations were carried out after investigations by the Treasury. In each instance Committees in Congress and individuals in Congress made great displays in the press after the fact trying to gain credit for themselves publicly which is a natural and usual procedure with some Congressmen, not all. In every instance executive action had been taken to meet the situation.

When the President came back from Florida a meeting was called of the Attorney General, the F.B.I. Chief and the Chairman of the Civil Service Commission. It was suggested that these three gentlemen form a commission and clean up the situation. There were loud outcries against the suggestion by all three of the gentlemen.

Then I decided at their suggestion to set up an independent commission and ask Judge Murphy of New York to head it, with Dr. Dan Poling of Philadelphia[1] and Dan Bell of the American Trust, former Asst. Sec. of the Treasury and former head of the Philippine Commission, as members.

Judge Murphy agreed right away to do the job for me. Then I called Dr. Poling and he agreed. Mr. Bell turned me down on account of his health and his bank board.

Murphy went back to New York and talked to the press, which he should not have done. Then he had a meeting with his colleagues on the Federal Bench and wrote me a letter asking to be released from his commitment. I didn't answer his letter because he gave out an interview which was very misleading and a stark misstatement of fact.[2]

This procedure on Murphy's part caused me some embarrassment. I had asked Arthur Flemming, a former member of the Civil Service Commission, to act in Bell's place. After Murphy's wild statement to the press I did not hear from Flemming.

I then decided I'd use a new approach. Give the Atty. Gen. an ambas-

---

1. A prominent clergyman.

2. From newspaper reports it is difficult to be sure of what Judge Murphy may have said, but he perhaps was put out that the proposed commission might not have the power to subpoena witnesses.

sadorship and put Wayne Morse, Senator from Oregon, in as Atty. Gen. and have the clean-up from that angle. Wayne thought it over for twenty-four hours and said "No" to it. I have asked Justin Miller, former Appeals Court Judge, former law school dean and an all round go getter, to do the job. I think he'll do it.

In the mean time we are reorganizing the Internal Revenue Department and I hope will get the job done.

TO ROY ROBERTS (UNSENT?)

December 30, 1951

Dear Roy:

On the day I came back to Washington, there was a very heavy headline in the Star-Times about a cave near Atchison, Kansas, which is to be used for storage in case of emergency. Some time back the Luce publications printed a list of *all* our atomic plants, and maps showing exactly where they are located. Pictures have been published showing the location of the White House bombproof shelter. Articles have been written and published about our proposed communications center in the mountains west of Washington. Air photographs of Washington, New York, Cleveland, Detroit and other key cities have been published in the Scripps-Howard papers all over the country.

Stalin needs no spy system to tell him our "top secrets."

Can't you as our home town editor get the managing editors of our responsible publications together and bring home to them that such publicity as I have referred to is an invitation to total destruction?

It seems to me that this is of such vital importance that something should be done about it.

I had a session with a bunch of editors about my security order and asked them to make some constructive suggestions. They agreed to do it —and then backed out!

If Stalin attains his objective every editor and publisher in this country will be shot or placed in a labor camp from which he'll never return.

I want no kowtows to me—but I do want to save this Republic.

1952

In the last full year of his presidency, Truman found his routine as chief executive of the United States returning to normal. The President could not easily locate his clothes or his books in the magnificently rebuilt White House, but it again was possible to enjoy some privacy and manage the necessary social functions, such as receptions and putting up visiting firemen for the night.

The politics of the country were out of kilter—that was the main problem in 1952 and Truman was unable to do much more than watch them rock along. His candidate for the presidency, Adlai Stevenson, behaved in an appallingly coy manner. A candidate had to display modesty, but Stevenson—whom the President invited to run as early as January—did not seem to know his mind. As the convention approached, Truman momentarily reconsidered his own decision not to run, and then decided that he was getting too old—he was sixty-eight in 1952—and at the last moment turned to Vice-President Barkley, a fine man but even older. What so annoyed the President about this situation was that right down to the Republican convention there was a shoo-in opportunity for the Democrats to win, for the Republicans seemed to have gone for Senator Taft.

In this election year matters turned downward when Eisenhower took the Republican nomination; that meant that almost any Democrat would lose. Pushed into the race, Stevenson and his vice-presidential running mate, Senator John Sparkman of Alabama, ignored the President, and Stevenson even referred to "the mess in Washington," appearing to run against Truman rather than Eisenhower. For a while the President was so annoyed by these tactics that he thought of sitting out the campaign, letting the Democratic candidates lose by their sheer ineptitude. Then his abiding faith in the Democratic party, together with the candidates' sensing that they acted injudiciously, brought him into another whistlestop trip, the sort that he dearly loved. But of course *it was not enough in the year 1952, when a majority of the American people liked Ike.*

In the spring of the year the steel crisis occupied much of the President's time, as almost frantically he sought to bring together the steel managers and workers, the latter represented by the United Steelworkers of America. Just a few hours before the planned strike, Truman seized the mills, in accord with the Constitution, he wrote in his memoirs—the provision that says that "the executive power shall be vested in a President of the United States of America." The Supreme Court, the chief justice dissenting, felt otherwise, and on June 2 declared the seizure unconstitutional, whereupon a strike began that lasted until July 24, with 600,000 workers out more than seven weeks, right in the middle of the Korean War. The President was furious, but there was little he could do with the court; with Congress, which was uncooperative in producing legislation; or the American people, who did not seem to care.

Internationally no new crises arose, although the Korean War refused to come to an end. In Iran the failure of the British-owned Anglo-Iranian Oil Company to pay enough for Iranian oil had helped bring to power the nationalist Mossadegh, but the mess that followed—the Shah's departure from the country, a revolution against Mossadegh that brought in Major General Fazlollah Zahedi as prime minister, the Shah's return—came the next year, 1953, when Truman had left office.

In 1952, the President's friend William Hillman brought out his book about the Truman era entitled Mr. President, *an extravagant collection of black-and-white and color pictures, with selected (but not infrequently bowdlerized) diary entries, memoranda, and public and private statements. The book reflected Truman's increasing sensitivity to the historical importance of the world's greatest elective office. Meanwhile the President wrote compulsively in his diary about the experiences of his predecessors and himself in trying to get Americans to help themselves.*

DIARY

January 1–2, 1952

What a New Year's Day!

I have talked to Bess. She has a sore throat in Independence. I have talked to Vivian and to Mary Jane. My baby was out until 3 A.M. in Kansas City, so—I couldn't talk to her when I called her mother.

What a New Year's Day! 1952 is here and so am I—gloomy as can be. But we must look to the program of world peace, and keep on looking. I talked to Bill Hillman on the subject last night and tonight. If that peace program can go through we face the greatest age in history. I wish I was seventeen instead of sixty-seven, with the same urge I had at seventeen to learn and to know world history. I spent a lot of time reading about the World's Great. Moses, Joshua, David, Solomon, Darius I and Cyrus the Great his uncle. Alexander, Hannibal, Caesar, Antoninus Pius, Hadrian, Titus, Marcus Aurelius Antoninus, Rameses III, Cleopatra, Mark Antony, Augustus Caesar, Thothmes III, Plato, Socrates, Pericles, Demosthenes, Cicero, Catos, both of them, and then Charlemagne, his father Charles Martel, Roland, John Hunyadi at Belgrade, Saladin, Suleiman the Magnificent, Jenghis Khan, Kubla Khan, Tamerlane, John Sobieski, Richelieu, Gustavus Adolphus of Sweden and Charles XII of Sweden, Alfred the Great, William of Normandy. The greatest of French Kings, Henry IV of France and King of Navarre, Francis I of France and Charles V of Spain. Elizabeth of England and Mary of Scotland. Sir Francis Drake and Captain Kidd, Martin Luther, Frederick the Great and Maria Theresa of Austria. Wellington and Lord Russell, Disraeli, Gladstone, Washington, Jefferson, Jackson, Lincoln, Grover Cleveland, Wilson, Franklin Roosevelt and the end!

DIARY

January 3, 1952

Margie came in this morning on the B & O from St. Louis. She had ridden the Missouri Pacific from Independence to St. Louis. I met her at Silver Spring. She was surprised to see me at the Station.

While I was waiting for the Diplomat to come in I looked around. The B & O station was new, on a double track. Great business houses were on both sides of the track, thick as they could be.

When I came to Washington on December 27, 1934, Silver Spring Station was in the midst of a beautiful park, with big trees all around it. It hadn't changed a great deal since Francis Preston Blair owned a farm there in Andrew Jackson's time. Blair also owned the house in which we live while White House repairs are made.

He bought the half block where the Blair House is for $6500.00 in the 1830's. He built the adjoining house on the west for his daughter, who married Adm. Lee. It is now the Blair-Lee House.

The corner lot east of the Blair House which now belongs to the General Services Administration sold for $700,000.00!

Margie looked very well except she's too thin. These damned diets the women go for are all wrong. More people die of dieting these days than of eating too much.

My good doctor is all the time trying to cut my weight down. Of course he's right and I should weigh 170 pounds. Now I weigh 175. What's five pounds between my doctor and me?

When I went into World War I, I weighed 145 pounds. After two years service I weighed 155. While I was in the Senate I was ten pounds heavier —165.

When I moved into the White House I went up to 185. I've now hit an average of 175. I walk two miles most every morning at a hundred and twenty eight steps a minute, I eat no bread but one piece of toast at breakfast, no butter, no sugar, no sweets. Usually have fruit, one egg, a strip of bacon and half a glass of skimmed milk for breakfast; liver & bacon or sweet breads or ham or fish and spinach and another nonfattening vegetable for lunch with fruit for dessert. For dinner I have a fruit cup, steak, a couple of nonfattening vegetables and an ice, orange, pineapple or raspberry for dinner. So—I maintain my waist line and can wear suits bought in 1935!

There has been a lot written about my clothes. Since I was twenty, I have worn suits made for me by my tailor! When I was in the Senate I was picked as one of the ten best dressed Senators. That was so after I became President. But—the dirty press, represented by Luce, Knight, Hearst and Roy Howard, decided that they couldn't hurt the President by dressing him as he should be, so this character assassination gang started to undress me! They went to the opposite extreme and said I was the worst dressed man in the United States! They lied one time or the other. (They lied both times—I'm neither the best nor the worst dressed man.)

DIARY

January 4, 1952

Mr. Churchill came today. I met him at the National Air Port. I'd sent the Independence to Floyd Bennett Field on Long Island to meet him and bring him to Washington.

When he came down the ramp from the plane I was at the bottom of the steps to greet him. He said "How do you do, Mr. President." I reminded him of an agreement we had made on the way to Fulton, Mo., in 1946 that I'd call him Winston and he would call me Harry—an agreement made at his suggestion. He replied that on formal occasions, such as the one taking place then at the Washington Air Port, he felt that he should be formal. But that the agreement was still in effect.

I gave him as cordial a welcome as I could after having him meet all our public officials—the Vice President, the members of the Cabinet and the Ambassadors of all countries—but Russia and her satellites. Russia has no word for courtesy in the Russian language. It is too bad.

Mr. Churchill and I boarded my car and proceeded to the Blair House. Many people along the way cheered him.

We had pictures taken on the steps, as usual on arrival at Blair House.

At 1 P.M. we had a reception for the luncheon guests, and cocktails afterwards. The Prime Minister took tomato juice, of all things. Said he wanted to show that "sometimes" he didn't take liquor.

It was a very nice luncheon. The P.M. sat on my right and Anthony Eden on my left. The Vice President was across the table from me with the Secretary of State on his right and Sir Oliver Franks, the British Ambassador, on his left. The other guests were arranged as Mr. *Protocol* said they should be.

At the end of the luncheon I proposed two toasts—not the usual procedure. One to the King of Great Britain and one to the Prime Minister, Mr. Churchill. The Prime Minister returned the toasts by offering one to the President.

We adjourned the meeting. I went to the Williamsburg at 4 P.M. Mr. Churchill and the team with him, together with Dean Acheson, Mr. Snyder and several others of my staff, came aboard at 5:30 P.M.

We had dinner at 7 P.M. Mr. Churchill and I went into the lounge on the upper deck and had a conference after dinner. We then sent for Mr. Acheson and Mr. Eden and continued our talks for some time and then went down to the mess hall where everybody was allowed to say his piece and express his opinion. It was a most enlightening meeting.

Mr. Churchill was highly pleased. We discussed everything. I listened and said very little.

TO THE NEW YORKER (UNSENT)

January 8, 1952

Dear New Yorker:

I've been reading your Jan. 5 Talk of the Town—and you've been taken in by one of Missouri's lovable old fakirs, Cyril Clemens—at one time there was a t before the s! He claims to be a seventh—it may be seventeenth—cousin of Hannibal's (Missouri not Carthage) well known humorist, Mark.

He has carried on a copious, one way letter writing for his I.M.T.S. for years & years. How I wish my lamented friend and press secretary, Charlie Ross, had lived to see you taken in!

He is the International Mark Twain Society and he merely puts people into it without a "by-your-leave" or any other formula. You'll get in now and no doubt be the recipient of nutty letters like the enclosed— which is my latest.

I don't know him, never saw him and don't want to. But of all the things to happen—the New Yorker to be hooked. It is almost as bad as the Nobel Board being hooked by that other old Missouri lovable fakir Ewing Cockrell, son of Francis Marion Cockrell, a Senator from Missouri for thirty years.[1] So you are in good company.

Mark, himself, was a kind of a charlatan and fakir—but all natives of Missouri love him—he was the lying columnist of his day. We have lots of 'em now but no Sam Clemenses.

This is a personal & confidential communication. You may publish it when I retire—which may be some time yet.

The problems with Caudle and Oliphant, with the Justice Department and the Bureau of Internal Revenue, and the difficulty of finding a sensible investigator were raising a stench in the newspapers early in January. There was the usual loose talk about Truman's association, years before, with the Pendergast machine.

MEMORANDUM
January 10, 1952

There has been much speculation about my relationship politically with T. J. Pendergast (Tom). He became a powerful political boss in Missouri after 1926. His career ended in the early 1940's.

I joined a new National Guard Battery of Light Field Artillery on June 14, 1905. It was Battery B, 1st Battalion Missouri Field Artillery.

When World War I came on April 6, 1917—that was the date the United States declared war on the Central Powers—Battery B in Kansas City and Battery C in Independence were expanded into a regiment of six batteries and Headquarters and Supply Companies. This regiment became the 129th F.A. 35th Division. It was trained at Camp Doniphan, Ft. Sill, Okla.

In Battery B at Camp Doniphan was a young man by the name of James M. Pendergast, son of Michael J. Pendergast, older brother of T. J. Pendergast.

---

1. Apparently Ewing Cockrell tried to put up his father, the senator, who after serving in the Confederate army got himself elected the successor of Carl Schurz, and after retirement became a member of the Texas-New Mexico boundary commission.

I became very well acquainted with young Jim during the war and when I came back I married and established my residence at Independence.

In 1922, it became necessary to elect an Eastern Judge for the County Court, an administrative body similar to County Commissioners in other States.

Along in July or August 1921 Jim Pendergast brought his father M.J. to see me at the little store Eddie Jacobson and I were operating on West 12th Street in Kansas City.

Mike Pendergast was head of the "goat" organization in the old 10th Ward of Kansas City and was recognized in the country part of Jackson County as the head of the Pendergast organization outside Kansas City.

M.J. asked me if I would consider the nomination to the County Court from the Eastern District. I told him I would. I had been road overseer in Washington Township where the family farm is located and Postmaster of Grandview before World War I came along.

Well, to make it short I filed for Eastern Judge at the proper time in 1922. There were four other candidates.

A banker at Blue Springs, Lyman Emmett Montgomery, a fine man, was endorsed by the "rabbits," another Democratic faction in the City and County headed by Joseph B. Shannon, afterward Congressman from the 5th Mo. District for a long time. A road building contractor by the name of George Shaw was another candidate. He had no factional backing. Tom Parent, a road overseer at Oak Grove, had the backing of Miles Bulger, Presiding Judge of the County Court, and a number of road overseers. James Compton, an Independence real estate man, was the fifth candidate.

I made a house to house canvass, went to every political meeting and won the nomination. Even the "goat" organization didn't think I could do it. When it came time for reelection in 1924 the "rabbits" bolted the ticket because of differences over patronage and I was defeated by a nice old Republican harness maker in Independence, who afterwards became locally famous for that feat.

I went to work after my defeat but kept up my political contacts. In 1926 the factions patched up their difference. In the spring Kansas City adopted a new city manager style charter and the Democrats elected five of the nine councilmen and appointed Henry McElroy City Manager. He had been my colleague on the County Court from the Western District which was Kansas City.

I was nominated and elected Presiding Judge of the County Court in the fall election and took office Jan. 1, 1927.

Then I had my first contacts with T. J. Pendergast and Joseph B.

Shannon. They were interested in county patronage and also in county purchases. The Court appointed the purchasing agent, a county welfare officer, a county auditor, heads of homes, approved the budgets of elected officials of the county, such as Treasurer, County Clerk, Circuit Clerk, County Collector, County Assessor, County Highway Engineer. The Court also appointed road overseers and various other officials. There were about nine hundred patronage jobs and they could be the foundation of a political organization.

T. J. Pendergast was interested in having as many friends in key positions as possible but he always took the position that if a man didn't do the job he was supposed to do, fire him and get someone who would. I always followed that policy and I never had a cross word with him. T.J.P.

In 1928 the "city" decided to ask for an election to authorize a bond issue for traffic ways, an auditorium, a city hall, a sewer system and several other things including a water plant and the purchase of a bridge across the Missouri River.

I decided to ask for a County bond issue, at the same time for a road system, two new Court Houses, and a County hospital. Pendergast told me that a County bond issue would not carry. I told him that if I told the voters how I would handle it that it would carry.

I went to the people and told them that I would appoint a bi-partisan board of engineers to oversee the road construction and that I would employ the two best known firms of architects in town to handle the building program, with a consulting architect from out of the State.

The county bond issue carried by a three fourths majority instead of the required two thirds. I appointed the engineers and the local architects. Then I took my private car—not a county one—and drove to Shreveport, Denver, Houston, Racine, Milwaukee, Buffalo, Brooklyn, Lincoln, Baton Rouge and several other places and looked at the new public buildings, met the architects and contractors, inspected the buildings and finally decided to employ the architect of the Court House at Shreveport as consulting architect for our county buildings.

When the Court was ready to let the first road contracts Mr. Pendergast called me and told me that he was in trouble with the local road contractors and would I meet and talk with them. I told him I would. I met them with T.J.P. present. They gave me the old song and dance about being local citizens and taxpayers and that they should have an inside track to the construction contracts.

I told them that the contracts would be let to the lowest bidders wherever they came from and that the specifications would be adhered to strictly. T.J. turned to his friends and said "I told you that he's the contrariest man in the County. Get out of here." When they were gone he said to me "You carry out your commitments to the voters." I did just that. But there was a three man Court and the two bosses, Pendergast and Shannon, could have ruined me if they'd wanted to. Tom Pendergast was a man of his word and he kept it with me. My handling of the County business became an asset to the Democratic Organization.

After 8 years as Presiding Judge I left the County with a road system equal to any in the country, refinanced its floating debt and a set of public buildings that the people could be proud of.

I was elected to the Senate in 1934 over severe opposition in the primary.

Two distinguished Congressmen ran against me. [The] Hon. John Cochran of St. Louis, the Post Dispatch candidate, and the Hon. Jacob L. Milligan of Richmond, Mo., the Kansas City Star and Bennett Clark candidate.

By going into sixty of Missouri's 114 counties I won the nomination by a plurality of over 40,000 votes and was easily victorious in the general election on a support Roosevelt platform—which I did when I arrived in Washington.

T. J. Pendergast never talked to me about my duties as County Judge except in matters of patronage but the one time on the bond issue contracts and then he supported me. He only talked to me once about my work in the Senate and that was when Senator Alben Barkley was running for floor leader. Jim Farley called Mr. Pendergast and asked him to call me and "tell" me to support Barkley. Well he called me from Colorado Springs and I told him that I was pledged to Pat Harrison of Mississippi because Pat had asked me to vote for him and that Pat had made some speeches for me in the Missouri campaign, that I'd stand by Senator Harrison. T.J. said "I told Jim that if you were committed you'd stand by your commitment, because you are a contrary Missourian." I voted for Pat and told Barkley in advance that I would. When Barkley was elected I supported him loyally.

On no other occasion did T. J. Pendergast ever talk to me about my actions in the Senate. He was an able clear thinker and understood political situations and how to handle them better than any man I have ever known. His word was better than the contracts of most men and he never forgot his verbal commitments. His physical breakdown in 1936 caused all his trouble.

I never deserted him when he needed friends. Many for whom he'd done much more than he ever did for me ran out on him when the going was rough. I didn't do that—and I am President of the United States in my own right!

Because Pendergast was persecuted over his financial difficulties and was convicted of income tax fraud and went to federal prison at

Leavenworth, he has been used by people opposed to me in an effort to discredit me. The opposition people whether in the Democratic Party in 1940 or in the sabotage press or the lying columnists or the poor old wrecked Republican Party and its present day character assassination methods have never been able to hurt me politically by slander and abuse. They never will.

After I was through in the County at home several Grand Juries both State and Federal went over my career as a County Judge with a fine tooth comb, and they could only give me a clean bill of health. That's the answer.

Donald Dawson, a big, handsome air force veteran, joined the White House staff in 1948, and did a superb job of organizing Truman's whistle-stop visits by nudging local regulars along the route. If something needed expediting, Don could do it.

MEMORANDUM TO DONALD DAWSON

January 10, 1952

Don Dawson:

Mrs. Ricketts was the manager of 4701 when we lived there. She has become invalided and needs a place to stay.

She is an Eastern Star, who has kept up her dues. She wants to go to the Eastern Star Home, which is the only place she can go. Make them take her. She's one of the 153,000,000 who have no pull except the President. She has the right to go to the home.

If this damned District of Columbia had old age homes where a paid old age retirement could be arranged the "boss" & I could take care of the situation. But there is none. So only the Eastern Star Home is left. If the good old lady was not eligible, I wouldn't raise hell about it. But *they* are cheating her. Stop it.

H.S.T.

[Mrs. Nancy Ricketts was admitted to the Home.]

DIARY

January 14, 1952

Mr. Hassett has just called me at 9:50 P.M. to report that the Secretary of the Interior, Oscar Chapman, has had a heart attack. I've had a lot of trouble with Interior. I had to accept the resignation of Harold Ickes because he wanted me to be a Franklin Roosevelt—and I could not be. He fell out with me because I sent Ed Pauley's appointment to the Senate as under-secretary of the Navy! The President (Mr. Roosevelt) had asked me as Vice President if I'd help Mr. Pauley to confirmation in the Senate. Of course I said I would. Yet when Pauley's name [went] to the Senate "honest" Harold had a spasm and Pauley was not confirmed.

I called in William O. Douglas and offered to make him the Secretary of the Interior. He hummed and hawed about the offer and then I appointed Julius Krug, who made a great secretary for some time and then I had to ask for his resignation.[1] Again, I called on Douglas, again he hummed and hawed and I appointed Oscar Chapman, as fine and efficient [a] Secretary of the Interior as we've ever had.

In the interval between these two offers to Douglas I called him at his home in the State of Washington while the Democratic Convention was in session in 1948 and offered to make him the Vice Presidential nominee —again he hummed and hawed. I found that my dear and good friend Barkley wanted it and I endorsed him.

I did not support Barkley when he was a candidate for leader of the majority in the Senate and I told him frankly that I was pledged to Pat Harrison. After he was elected I supported him loyally even in his tiff with Roosevelt.

He has made a great Vice-President. No President and Vice-President have been as cooperative as Barkley and I.

MEMORANDUM

January 18, 1952

"Top Secret"

Every day I receive an envelope from the military establishment. It is of heavy "butcher" paper sealed with tape with another one of the same sort of paper inside it.

I open the outside envelope, which is about 8 × 10—I open the inside one and read—of all things—what I've already read in the Washington Post, the "sabotage sheet," the N.Y. Times, Herald Tribune, Baltimore Sun and what I will see later in the snotty little "Howard" paper, the Washington News and the Star. The sabotage sheet is the Washington

---

1. Krug had been forced to resign in 1948. He got into trouble for several reasons. For one thing, he proved faint-hearted in a politically awkward year. For another, newspapers reported him involved in a lawsuit over a $750,000 loan, and his name was found on the expense account of a lobbyist.

Times-Herald. It is Bertie McCormick's lie outlet in the capital city. His Chicago Tribune and New York Daily News are his lie outlets in those two great cities.

Roy Howard's chain and the Knight layout are Hearst imitators, but not quite up to the dirtiest Hearst technique. But they are coming along. . . .

MEMORANDUM TO ARTHUR KROCK

January 24, 1952

I notice this morning that you refer to elegies for my good friend Bob Patterson.[1]

Now I really don't believe anyone wrote a funeral dirge about him. I am very sure that you are speaking of eulogies. Now it is a terrible thing for an ignorant country boy to call the attention of the greatest word artist on the New York Times to an error like this but I just couldn't help doing it.

[unsigned]

David H. Morgan was an old friend in Eureka, Kansas, who special-ized in oil and gas drilling in the eastern part of the state. Years before, in 1916–1919, Morgan and Truman had engaged in a leasing and drilling speculation that came very close to discovering the Teter Pool, a famous Oklahoma oil field. In January 1952, Morgan's daughter Eleanor had been two weeks in Washington without an assignment from the State Department. Morgan asked his friend Harry to do something for her. Quietly, however, because Eleanor was a bit independent. Morgan said it would be "betwixt you & I."

TO DAVID H. MORGAN

January 28, 1952

Dear Dave:

I appreciated very much your letter of the twenty-third. I am glad you liked the Congressional Messages and the article in the Washington Star of last Sunday.

I hope your project works out all right.

I wish you, yourself, would tell Eleanor that the best way in the world for her to progress in this situation, in which she is now placed, is to

---

1. Robert P. Patterson, former secretary of war, had been killed in a plane crash.

attend strictly to business and be very careful not to bring outside influences to bear until she has been there long enough to know what it is all about.

The State Department is a peculiar organization, made up principally of extremely bright people who made tremendous college marks but who have had very little association with actual people down to the ground. They are clannish and snooty and sometimes I feel like firing the whole bunch but it requires a tremendous amount of education to accomplish the purposes for which the State Department is set up. In a great many key places I have men of common sense and we are improving the situation right along.

The present Secretary of State is one of the best that has ever been in the office, but on lower levels we still have the career men who have been taken out of the colleges without any experience with the common people. I'll give you one particular instance to show you just how the situation works.

Alben Barkley, when he was United States Senator, was in Egypt with a bunch of Congressmen and Senators on a parliamentary union meeting. The Chargé d'affaires in Cairo escorted them. He wore a checked suit, carried a cane, wore a cap and talked with an Oxford accent. Barkley kept looking at him and wondering if the gentleman could have been reared in Egypt. Finally he asked him what his antecedents were. The man said he was a native of Topeka, Kansas.

Of course, if he dared go back to Topeka wearing that checked suit, the cap and carrying a cane, he would have lasted about ten minutes in the Kansas Hotel lobby.

So you tell Eleanor to attend strictly to her job and let the situation take its course for the time being.

Sincerely yours,
Harry S. Truman

Cousin Grace Summer, who lived in Dallas, wrote that it seemed to her everybody had more money than ever before, although they hated to pay taxes. She said she told them to quit wanting so much, or else "hush." She had taken a drive on a Sunday and could not believe her eyes, because of the many large business places being built, and houses; and "still more needed so they say."

TO GRACE SUMMER

January 28, 1952

Dear Grace,

I certainly appreciated your letter of the twenty-second. I am sorry that you have not been feeling so well. I hope it is only temporary and that you will shortly be up and around again.

You are right that everybody has more to buy with than they ever had before in their lives. There were times when you know they didn't even have money to pay the taxes they are hollering about now. The human animal reacts that way. When he is prosperous he spends his time kicking at the Government and when he is not prosperous he does the same thing. That is just part of the game.

Please remember me to all the family. Margaret was home for the weekend and we spent a very happy Saturday and Sunday.

Sincerely yours,

Harry

TO ETHEL NOLAND

February 2, 1952

This is "ground hog day." Here it looks as if the little beast will not see his shadow, and therefore we'll have a mild and early spring.

You know I like these old superstitions. Remember my "turnip day" Congress? It was Nellie's birthday too and that no doubt added to my good luck as well as the "turnips"—Republicans to us.

I was most pleased to have your letter about Alex Doniphan. I sent the outline of his career to our Ambassador to the Court of St. James and asked him to have someone of his numerous staff look the old gentleman up. Soon as I hear from Walter Gifford you'll hear from me.[1]

I wonder if you realize that an old farmer from Jackson County, Missouri, is asking the former president and chairman of the board of the A.T. & T. to do something he can't refuse to do.

I had an experience with Winthrop Aldrich, son in law of John D. Rockefeller, while I was in the Senate. I was making an investigation of a company with an account in the Chase National Bank. The vice president (and there are forty or fifty of them) who gave me the information

---

1. Colonel Alexander Doniphan was one of the heroes of the Mexican War, and came from Liberty, Missouri, near Independence; Ethel thought there was some chance that Doniphan was related to the Youngs and Trumans.

I wanted, asked me to go with him and meet Mr. Aldrich, the president. Being polite I said OK and we went to the great man's outer office. My poor V.P. fidgeted and squirmed and I being a Missourian was highly amused. Finally I said to him "You tell the old S.O.B. to go to hell. I didn't want to see him anyway." He was abject in his apologies. But when I became President of the U.S. the great Mr. Aldrich came around for an appointment. I let him cool his heels for about an hour, which, I'm sure, was no lesson to him, while I saw a half dozen *common* people ahead of him. Us Missourians are not vindictive, no, not at all. When he finally got in I said nothing doing to his proposition.

You know Josh Billings once said, "Always be nice to your poor relations, it will be hard to explain!" Winthrop probably never heard of Josh.

We've just received a beautiful portrait of Margaret from the lady who made my "stuffed shirt" official White House picture. It is lovely. Wish you could see it.

Hope Nellie is all right. Soon as I hear from our Ambassador you shall have the information you want.

Love to you both.

Harry

DIARY

February 9, 1952

The political pot boils incessantly. Never a press conference that does not finally end up with—"When are you going to tell us what you intend to do about running for President?" There are many astute approaches to the question and there [are] some very smart boys among the White House Press representatives.

I have known what I am going to do since April 1950 and it is on record. But, at the beginning of a session of Congress, it does not seem to me to be the proper time to make the announcement of "to run or not to run."

At an opportune time, which should not be very far in the future now, I shall announce that on such and such a date at a certain public gathering I intend to make known what my purpose is at the Democratic National Convention in July at Chicago. Merely make that bald announcement, cause so much suspense that everyone in the country will have his radio or television set turned on and then make a riproaring statement of the principles for which the Democratic Party stands—in other words state the platform for the Party at Chicago, make the announcement as to whether I'll run or not and then stop. In that way I can nail the lies of the sabotage press and the lying air commentators and the columnists whose business it is to prostitute the minds of the voters.

TO ETHEL NOLAND

February 17, 1952

Dear Ethel:

I have a letter from our Ambassador to the Court of St. James, that he has put someone to work on the Doniphan ancestry request you made of me. Ethel, can you imagine the former chairman of the A.T. & T., the American Representative to Great Britain, taking a request from a Missouri clod hopper seriously? But there you are.

We are happy to have the greatest republic in the history of the world headed by what I hope will turn out to be a true follower of Cincinnatus, Marcus Aurelius Antoninus, Jefferson, Wilson and those other great [men] who wanted the best for the most people. That of course may not happen. If it does you and I won't be alive to know about it.

You know how indifferent I've been to ancestry. I told you once in a sort of teasing, bragging mood that I didn't care a hoot about my own ancestors. I was going to be somebody's ancestor. Well it looks like I'm stymied except for my brother's and cousin's children.

Margie seems to be following the line of her aunts and her cousins! But what I started out to suggest is that I really wish you'd go to work in dead earnest on the Truman tree. Even if you find a gibbet I'd like to know about it. We've tracked the Tylers, the Holmeses, the Doniphans, the Greggs, the Youngs, the Nolands and many others, but Ethel where in hell did my seventh great grandfather come from and what caused a President of the United States accidentally to happen?

There are Trumans in Connecticut, New York, Maryland, South Carolina, Tennessee, Kentucky, Illinois, Canada and you know those in Missouri.

Did our ancestor start the big British brewery, did he misspell his good English name in the time of Bill the Norman to keep his head on his shoulders, or what happened? Did he come originally from Northumberland, Scotland, Wales, Normandy or Cornwall?

I hope you can find out for your cousin, because he's to be lied about, misrepresented and misquoted for the next 100 years, I fear.

My best to Nellie. Hope she is entirely recovered.

Maybe I'm getting Potomac Fever! It is a terrible disease. But I'll *cure* it before April 24, 1952.

Sincerely,

Harry

DIARY

February 18, 1952

The President's Duties.

1. By the Constitution, he is the Executive of the Government.

2. By the Constitution, he is the Commander in Chief of the Armed Forces.

3. By the Constitution, he is the responsible head of Foreign Policy and with the help of his Secretary of State implements Foreign Policy.

4. He is the leader of his Party, makes and carries out the Party Platform as best he can.

5. He is the Social Head of the State. He entertains visiting Heads of State.

6. He is the No. 1 public relations man of the Government. He spends a lot of time persuading people to do what they should do without persuasion.

7. He has more duties and powers than a Roman Emperor, a Gen., a Hitler or a Mussolini; but he never uses those powers or prerogatives, because he is a democrat (with a little d) and because he believes in the Magna Carta and the Bill of Rights. But first he believes in the XXth Chapter of Exodus, the Vth Chapter of Deuteronomy, and the V, VI, & VIIth chapters of the Gospel according to St. Matthew.

8. He should be a Cincinnatus, Marcus Aurelius Antoninus, a Cato, Washington, Jefferson and Jackson all in one. I fear that there is no such man. But if we have one who tries to do what is right because it is right, the greatest Republic in the history of the world will survive.

DIARY

February 20, 1952

Today has been one to read about. I was up at 5:40 A.M. Shaved and dressed by 6:05. Listened to a news broadcast at 5:55 and at 6:10 was reading documents by the wholesale—so many of them and so much "fine print" I missed my 7 o'clock walk.

The "Boss" and I had breakfast at 8:30 and about 8:50 I went to the White House office. Since the assault on the police and the secret service, I ride across the street in a car the roof of which will turn a grenade, the windows and sides turn a bullet and the floor will stop a land mine! Behind me in an open car ride six or seven men with automatics and machineguns. The uniformed police stop traffic in every direction—and

I cross the street in state and wonder why anyone would want to live like that. When I take my morning walk at 7 A.M. a guard walks beside me and he's always a fine man and a congenial conversationalist. Behind me are three more good men, athletes and *good shots,* across the street is another good man and a half block behind me is a car with maybe five or six well equipped guards. It is a hell of a way to live. But after the assault on the Blair House I learned that the men who want to keep me alive are the ones who get hurt and not the President. I'd always thought that I might be able to take care of an assassin as old Andy Jackson did but I found that the guards get hurt and not the President. So now I conform to the rules without protest.[1]

Well we get across the street and I begin to dictate answers to my personal mail, to my dictation secretary. When that is done I sit for an artist who is making a model for a medallion. But I read documents all the time too.

Then I send for the Chief Clerk of the White House and sign whatever documents have accumulated. Sign on an average 600 a day, 365 days in the year. It is 10 o'clock by now and I call in the staff. The press secretary tells me what he expects to be asked at his 10:30 press reception, gives me articles and editorials to read.

The Assistant to the President then gives me the results of Senatorial and Congressional interviews and requests; tells me what the boards and bureaus are doing and makes recommendations for decisions.

The Appointment Secretary submits requests for appointments and recommendations as to which ones should come to see me. He hands the invitations to make speeches and public appearances and the whole staff takes part in the discussion.

The Legal Counselor to the President discusses interviews with the Atty. Gen. Counselors of the Depts. suggest the signing or rejection of executive orders, discuss the legal aspects of legislation etc.

The executive assistants report one at a time on special matters, appointments to office, disgruntled minority groups, labor problems and whatever else needs the attention of the President.

The able correspondence Secretary makes suggestions on messages to be sent to various meetings over the country, birthdays and special

---

1. The attempted assassination of President Jackson occurred on January 30, 1835, when the President visited the house chamber to attend funeral services for the late Representative Warren R. Davis of South Carolina. After Jackson had filed past the casket and, with the cabinet, descended to the rotunda of the Capitol, a stranger aimed and fired two pistols at him, one after the other, at pointblank range. The President clubbed his cane and lunged for the man, but a young army officer reached the assailant first. Jackson was unharmed, for only the caps of the pistols exploded, though the weapons had been properly loaded. An expert on small arms afterward calculated the chance of two successive misfires as one in 125,000.

days to be remembered and remarked. Heads off eager beavers who want to use the White House for personal promotion. He is indispensable to the President.

Then the Army Aide is consulted. He reports on selective service medals and citations, complaints of mammas, court martials etc. The Naval and Air Aides follow the same procedure. Sometimes the aides have special duties assigned to them and then they make reports and recommendations.

The Chief Clerk presents more documents and papers to be signed.

Soon as the staff is dismissed the Intelligence service reports what goes on all around the world. It is all "Top Secret" and most interesting. It helps the President to make decisions on foreign and domestic policy.

Then comes the appointment list, Senators, Congressmen, visiting preachers, prize winners, Cabinet members and anyone else who can get by the Appointment Secretary. There is from one to forty every fifteen minutes until 1 P.M. Then lunch, a thirty minute nap, and at 3 P.M. more appointments, maybe a press conference, sometimes a session in the White House pool—but not often—then the armored car and across the street to spend the evening on papers getting ready for another day.

It really is a great life—if you like it!

DIARY

February 26, 1952

The top Bishop of the Episcopal Church came to see me at 5:30 P.M. yesterday. He wanted to protest the sending of a representative to Vatican City. His argument was Church and State. A Nuncio from the Vatican, he said, would cause all Protestants a bad time.

He didn't know, of course, and I didn't tell him that the Cardinals of the Papacy felt the same way about a Papal Nuncio. The Nuncio would rank them all and would have to make their dates with the President!

I told the High Bishop Episcopal that I did not give a damn about protocol—that all in the world I wanted to do was to organize the moral forces against the immoral forces. I told him that Stalin and his crowd had no intellectual honesty and no moral code, that they had broken 30 or 40 treaties they'd made with us and the free world and that all I wanted to do was to organize Exodus XX, Matthew V, VI & VII to save morals in the world.

Sorry he couldn't see anything but the Totalitarian Catholic Church of Rome as anything but a menace to free religion! What a travesty. If a

Baptist can see what's toward—why not a high hat Church of England Bishop?

No one can understand such a question, I suppose.

But if I could succeed in getting the world of morals associated against the world of no morals, we'd have world peace for ages to come. Confucius, Buddha, Moses, our own Jesus Christ, Mahomet, all preached: "Do as you'd be done by." Treat others as you'd be treated. So did all the other great teachers and philosophers.

But along comes Marx, Lenin, Trotsky, Stalin to upset morals and intellectual honesty and a lot of "crackpots" want to follow them.

The Great Creator of the Universe won't allow it! I am sure of that.

DIARY

[March 2,] 1952[1]

The doctor says that my mother-in-law is very sick. Yesterday I called the wife of Mrs. Truman's oldest brother, Frank Wallace. Bess had called earlier in the day. Frank had decided to come on to D.C., so had George, the second son.

After I called Natalie, Frank and George called Fred in Albuquerque. He managed to board the same plane which picked up Frank and George in Kansas City.

I met them at the Washington Air Port at 1:30 Sat. March 1, 1952. They were a solemn trio—so was I. But their mother had survived. She improved noticeably when the three sons arrived at Blair House. Sunday Bess and I showed all three brothers the renovated White House. We discussed the original 1792–1798 building; the 1816–18 rebuilding, the 1902 renovation by Teddy Roosevelt with McKim, Mead and White as architects. A botch job, by the way. Some of the most beautiful chandeliers were sent to the Capitol and I can't have them returned. The old burned and scorched timbers were put back into the building. Teddy was evidently using his Big Stick somewhere else.

Coolidge put a concrete 3rd floor on top of Teddy's botched rebuilding, adding 180 tons to the old brick pillars' carrying capacity.

It was just too much. In 1947 the old House began to fall down.

One Sunday in 1948 I was working in the Study on the family floor, which is directly above the Blue Room and the Diplomatic Reception Room.

Fields, the head butler, brought my lunch to my desk in the Study.

---

1. The President dated this diary entry February 29, but it was obviously written on Sunday afternoon, March 2.

Fields is a big man—and a grand man too. The floor sagged and moved like a ship at sea. The next day I had a survey made and the engineer moved the President into the Lincoln Room in the S.E. corner of the House.

They supported the Study, the bathroom of the President, the sitting-room of the 1st Lady and the hallway of the second floor with iron rods connected to the roof support. Then in the late fall of 1948 moved the whole family to Blair House.

I asked the Congress to authorize the President to reconstruct the White House, without changing the exterior appearance except the north porch. I was turned down. A Congressional Commission was authorized by law to rebuild and renovate the President's House.

And did they rebuild and renovate it! I'll say they did, to the tune of 5½ million dollars.

They took the insides all out. Dug two basements, put in steel and concrete like you've never seen in the Empire State Bldg., Pentagon or anywhere else. Only an earthquake or an atomic bomb—one of our latest, not the phony Russia talks about—could wreck the old building now.[2]

If Teddy or Coolidge had done the job we now have done, the President of this day could have stayed in the President's House until the end of his terms.

When finished it will be a great building and will last a very long time.

We came back to the Blair House after the inspection, Bess, Frank, George and Fred children of my mother-in-law. She was very ill.

We sat down and discussed the situation. I'd ordered my doctor to come home from Arabia where he had gone to help the old King recover from a severe case of arthritis.

TO ETHEL NOLAND

March 3, 1952

Dear Ethel:

I was most happy to have your letter of Feb. 25. Ralph was in to see me Friday about the 35th Division meeting in Springfield some time in June. He wants to start the proceeding on the afternoon of my arrival and far into the night, get up and attend a breakfast for 1500 people the next morning, march in a four mile parade, have a special luncheon for my old—and I mean *old*—comrades of Bty. D. 129th F.A. as of 1918, dedicate

---

2. By 1952 the United States was moving rapidly toward achievement of an H-bomb, and the Soviets claimed they were too, except they moved toward a scientific dead end and did not achieve a true H-bomb until some years later.

a couple of damned dams in north Arkansas, look over his home in Springfield, shake hands with all the people in S.W. Missouri, S.E. Kansas, N.E. Oklahoma and N.W. Arkansas and do various and sundry other chores. Last year the list was so long at Topeka and the Kansas Governor is such a screwball that I didn't go.

I won't have the Kansas Governor as an excuse this time. The Governors of Ark. & Okla. are decent people. You notice that I'm not mentioning a certain chief executive of my own state.

Then Ralph brought me a coat of arms marked Tremaine. Now, Ethel, I think that this Tremaine thing is a lot of bunk. I am sure that the good old Saxon name Tru Man is just what it purports to be and nothing whatever to do with Normandy or what spewed out of it. Maybe I'm wrong. Anyway as I've told you so long as we don't find Captain Kidd, Morgan the Pirate or J.P. either for that matter in "the line" I'm satisfied.

Hope Nellie is well and all is well with you. Mrs. Wallace is very sick. I wired the boys to come, but she is better today.

Sincerely,

Harry

DIARY

March 4, 1952

My daughter left for Arkansas tonight at 7:45. She sings at Conway. Her pal Drucie Snyder Horton went with her. She was hesitant about going. Her grandmother is in a very precarious condition. The grandmother will be 90 years old August 4th. At that age the slightest thing can bring the end. But I told Margie that she had a contract and that she had to meet it.

Her three uncles, her mother's brothers, were here over the week end and they went home last night, at their mother's direction. That is what they should have done. Everything possible is being done. I hope that the mother can survive to return to the White House and then for the return to Independence. I have been through the present situation twice in my life and it is heartrending. I was with my father the night he died and I spent two weeks day and night with my mother when she was on her death bed—and then was not present when she passed on. I was in a plane over Cincinnati and I knew what the message would say when it was handed to me. Just two hours away!

I'd had to return, after spending two weeks at home, because of the pressure of public business. Then I was too late on the return.

Tonight I had a long visit with Gov. Stevenson of Illinois. Some weeks ago I asked him to come to see me. At that first meeting we talked of the Presidency and what it meant; the burden of it and the constitutional amendment limiting the term to eight years.

I told the Governor at that time that I'd been in public elective office for thirty years or would be Jan. 1, 1953, that I'd been defeated once in 1924 for two years but that I'd spent two years in the army in World War One from Apr. 22, 1917, to May 6, 1919, so I counted myself a thirty year service man in elective office and never had I won one that I wanted! That is hard to believe. Some time I'll set the facts down.

Tonight the Governor came to see me at his request to tell me that he had made a commitment to run for reelection in Illinois and that he did not think he could go back on that commitment honorably. I appreciate his view point and I honor him for it. He said he would not want to have people believe that he was announcing for reelection in his great State just as a stepping stone to the White House. He is an honorable man. Wish I could have talked with him before his announcement. He is a modest man too. He seems to think that I am something of a superman which isn't true of course.

He was overcome by my first talk with him in which I had offered to have him nominated by the Democratic Convention in July. I had explained to him that any President can control his party's convention. Then I cited Jackson, Hayes, Teddy Roosevelt, Wilson, Franklin Roosevelt and myself at Philadelphia in 1948. I reminded him that Washington picked John Adams, that Jefferson did the same with Madison and Monroe before conventions were used for the purpose of selecting nominees. I told him I could get him nominated whether he wanted to be or not. Then I asked what he'd do in that case. He was very much worried and said that no patriot could say no to such a condition.

Then he argued that only I can beat any Republican be he Taft, Eisenhower, Warren, or anyone else! My wife and daughter had said the same thing to me an hour before. What the hell am I to do? I'll know when the time comes because I am sure God Almighty will guide me.

DIARY

March 27, 1952

Arrived from Key West at six this afternoon. Had good sunny vacation. Wrote and rewrote a speech for the Jefferson Jackson Dinner Saturday 29th. Had a chance to read all the piled up documents and file most of them.

Mrs. Truman was on hand to meet me, as was Dean Acheson, Charlie

Sawyer, Charlie Brannan, Oscar Chapman, Frank McKinney, Bill Bray, Com. Donohue and newsmen, photographers and visiting young people.[1]

The "boss" and I were formally received at the Pennsylvania Ave. entrance to the renovated White House by all four ushers, the butlers, doormen and by Mr. Larson & Mr. Reynolds. Mr. Larson gave me a gold key to the House, which Mr. Crim assured me would *not* open any door on the place.

Bess & I looked over the East Room, Green Room, Blue Room, Red Room and State Dining Room. They are lovely. So is the hall and state stairway. I had dinner alone in the family dining room—Bess had to go to the Shoreham to a Salvation Army affair.

I spent the evening going over the house. With all the trouble and worry it is worth it—but not 5½ million dollars! If I could have had charge of the construction it would have been done for half the money and in half the time!

DIARY

April 3, 1952

The lovely Queen of Holland arrived yesterday. She is a grand person. So is the Prince. He had an American sense of humor.

We gave them 21 guns at the airport, a cordial welcome speech, expressed regret that Margie could not be present and then rode through the usual Washington welcoming crowds.

It was all we could hope for. At the District stand the sidewalks and building windows were as full of people as was possible. John Russell Young[1] made a welcoming speech with which no one, including Billy Hearst and Roy Howard, could find fault. The City gave the Queen a key and it rained. The rain was blamed on the Federal, not the City Government!

I'm told that Mrs. Wm. H. Taft telephoned the Weather Bureau in April and asked if a certain day in June would be a clear, pleasant day. She was told it would be. She was having a garden party. The heavens opened and spilled gallons of water on the party. Mrs. Taft wanted the weather man fired. I can't say that I blame her for that wish. I've wanted him fired many a time!

But the weather man needs someone to come to his defense. We've

---

1. Charles Sawyer, successor to Harriman in 1947 as secretary of commerce; Frank McKinney, chairman of the Democratic National Committee; William J. Bray, special assistant in Dr. Steelman's office; F. Joseph Donohue, commissioner of the District of Columbia.

---

1. A newspaperman, commissioner of the District of Columbia.

made wonderful strides in our understanding of what goes to make up weather conditions. The Bureau has information on temperatures, pressures and high air conditions that can give the right information on general conditions. No one can accurately predict *local* conditions. I know—because I've been plowing in a field on the farm, the sun would be shining on me, and a half mile away the rain would come down in sheets on the same farm!

Well anyway the welcome to the Queen and the Prince of the Netherlands was great. People stood in the rain to cheer. I was very happy that they did.

DIARY

April 13, 1952

Jefferson's birthday. Bess & I walk across Lafayette Square to St. John's Church for 8 o'clock service. Mr. Searles, one of the White House ushers, tells Mrs. T. she's done a good deed—taking a Baptist to an Episcopal service! I've gone with her time and again to her service—and she has gone with me to the 1st Baptist Church.

I've never been of the opinion that Almighty God cares for the building or the form that a believer approaches the Maker of Heaven and Earth. "When two or three are gathered together" or when one asks for help from God he'll get it just as surely as will panoplied occupants of any pulpit. Forms and ceremonies impress a lot of people, but I've never thought that The Almighty could be impressed by anything but the heart and soul of the individual. That's why I'm a Baptist, whose church authority starts from the bottom—not the top. So much for churches.

Charlie Sawyer came to see me about the steel situation. I told him to sit tight and run the plants until settlement failed and then I'd direct him to take further action.

After Mr. Sawyer left, Tom Connally came to see me and told me that he did not intend to file for re-election in Texas. Said he would be 75 years old this year and he'd decided to quit. He said he wanted me informed before I saw it in the papers. I appreciated his telling me about it. He said that he felt as I did—that he should quit while he had time to live happily a few years. Wise man.

At 12:20 I went to the Jefferson Memorial and had my Military Aide, General Vaughan, and my Air Force Aide, General Landry, lay a wreath in front of Thomas Jefferson's statue in the memorial that bears his name.

I've been present at wreath layings at Lincoln Memorial for seven years—and I decided that Jefferson, who made the greatest contribution to our system of government, should have the same sort of recognition from the President. Noted by their absence were the Lincoln zealots—but those present at the Jefferson ceremony had always been present at the Lincoln ceremony. Sometimes "broadmindedness" is a one way street.

DIARY

April 15, 1952

Yesterday I welcomed the last Displaced Person and his family to the United States. The law allowed 339,000 to come to this country. He was No. 339,000. He had a lovely wife and two sweet little girls. He came from Poland. The Russians drove him out. . . .

When I was at Potsdam I looked into the displaced person situation. At that time there were 1,200,000 of them from all the countries named in Eastern Europe. After I arrived at Washington, I asked Dick Russell, who was the chairman of the emigration committee in the Senate, and his opposite number in the House, who came from Texas, to go to Germany and then to come and see me to talk about a plan for taking care of them.

Well these two great Chairmen went to Europe and came back. They both reported that we already had enough "furriners" in this country and we needed no more! I reminded them that "displaced" persons made this great nation what it is.

The idea I had was that we take 400,000, South America take 400,000 and the Commonwealth countries take 400,000.

After most bitter legislative fights we finally took 339,000.

I hope we will agree to 300,000 more. They are fine people and may be an addition to our blood stream that we need right now.

TO ETHEL NOLAND

May 11, 1952

Dear Ethel:

Your letter of the 6th was a dandy. Now whatever you do you go to Rob's wedding. You and Nellie are really in loco parentis to those two boys and I'm sure he'd be a most disappointed young man if one of you at least does not appear. They are both fine boys and I'm glad to have them in our family circle.[1]

---

1. Rob was Robert Allen Southern, grandson of the brother of William Southern, Jr., grand-nephew of Ethel. Rob married Cynthia Drews of Chicago. The "two boys" were Rob and his younger brother, John Tilford Southern, who were looked after by their great-aunts, Ethel and Nellie.

Of course I can't be there, much to my regret. Bess went down town for a wedding present. I've not seen it yet but you know Miss Lizzie knows how to do those things. You know what would happen if I came? The Wedding would be so submerged in the visit of the Presidente that the young people wouldn't know they'd had a wedding. First, advance secret service men would "case the joint"—house or church, wherever it takes place. They have to have the guest list and be sure no one of them had a knife, a gun or a bomb. They'd be stationed at every corner of the house or church and the whole town police force would be on duty and as jittery as if the Russian Army were coming. So you can see it would spoil the event. Bess must stay with her mother and Margie has a T.V. show or something in New York. Ain't it hell to have a head of the State in the family?

Helen Souter and Margaret Ott Barnes were overnight guests last night and I believe enjoyed it very much. Bess just now took them to the airport to catch planes for Chicago and K.C.

You tell Nellie to be patient and obey orders and she'll be all right. She comes of tough stock as you well know.

I'm having the usual hell and repeat performances, steel, oil and Chile copper. But we'll live through them as usual. It has just been [one] crisis after another since I've been here and we've met them and are still going strong.

Love to you both.

Harry

DIARY

May 15, 1952

Just had a note and an editorial from a Wyoming Republican paper at Casper. One of my neighbors in Independence had written the editor a letter asking him why he didn't present both sides in his so-called independent Republican sheet. That letter caused him to write an editorial which is a confession.

He is against a bipartisan foreign policy! He hates Trumanism. Everyone of good sense knows that the greatest Republic in history must have a continuing and a firm foreign policy. Even Vandenberg was converted to that theory. Only Taft and the old time isolationists are against that sort of foreign policy.

Let us define Trumanism.

One, we have found by hard earned experience that the Soviets respect only force. So we have built up our armed forces. . . .

Two, we have held the economic front in balance at home. The farmer, the laboring man, white collar workers, industry and industry management are in the midst of the most prosperous era in the history of the world.

Three, the public interest comes first in the mind of the present occupant of the White House.

Four, we prevented Tito from taking Trieste right after the German foldup, we forced Stalin out of Iran, we saved Greece and Turkey, we stayed in Berlin, and we knocked the socks off the communists in Korea, we gave the Philippines free government, we gave Puerto Rico its first native Governor, we gave that beautiful island a constitution and home rule, we appointed the first native governor of the Virgin Islands. If that's Trumanism, I confess judgment and I'm proud to have my name attached to that program by the lousy, unfair, controlled press even if that controlled press tries to make me look like a dub!

DIARY

May 18, 1952

The conferences on the Korean Armistice are propaganda sounding boards for the Commies.

Charge them with murdering our soldiers and civilians who are prisoners of war against every rule of the Geneva convention. Charge them with kidnaping children in South Korea just as they are doing in Berlin and as they did in Greece. Thousands of German children have been deported in the last seven years and have never been heard from. 1500 Greek children were taken from their homes and their parents while the Commies occupied northern Greece. Where are these Korean, German and Greek children? Have they been murdered? We believe they have.

What has happened to the 1,000,000 German prisoners the Soviet holds or have they also been murdered as the Poles were murdered at Katyn?

Where are the million Japs who surrendered to the Russians? Are they murdered or are they in slave labor camps?

How many South Korean and Allied prisoners have you shot without cause? You claim you hold only 12,000 prisoners. Where are the other thousands of civilians and soldiers you carried off from South Korea?

If you signed an agreement it wouldn't be worth the paper it is written on.

You've broken every agreement you made at Tehran, Yalta and Potsdam. You have no morals, no honor. Your whole program at this conference has been based on lies and propaganda.

Now do you want an end to hostilities in Korea or do you want China and Siberia destroyed? You may have one or the other, whichever you want. These lies of yours at this conference have gone far enough. You either accept our fair and just proposal or you will be completely destroyed.

Read Confucius on morals to them. Read Buddha's code to them. Read the Declaration of Independence to them. Read the French declaration, Liberty & Fraternity. Read the Bill of Rights to them. Read the 5th, 6th & 7th Chapters of St. Matthew to them. Read St. John's prophecy on Anti Christ and have your own interpreter do it.

You've enough real truth here to last you a month. Be sure the world press is briefed on every meeting where you follow these instructions.

The C. in C.

DIARY

June 1, 1952

A couple of golden crowns with all kinds of expensive jewels have been stolen from a Roman Catholic shrine in Brooklyn. The crowns were on images of Jesus Christ and Mary his mother.

I've an idea if Jesus were here his sympathies would be with the thieves and not with the Pharisees who crowned him with gold and jewels.

The only crown he ever wore was one of thorns placed there by the emissaries of the Roman Emperor and the Jewish Priesthood. He came to help the lowly and the down trodden. But since Constantine the Great he has been taken over by the Despots of both Church and State.

The High Church rulers both Roman and English are for the rich and the privileged. Martin Luther pointed out some of the reasons for reform in the Roman Church. So did Knox, Calvin and Hus.

Roger Williams, William Penn, John Wesley and others did the same for the Church of Henry VIII and Cardinal Wolsey. All these reformers were vilified by those who were economically in the class where they could look down on the ordinary man.

Cotton Mather hoped that Wm. Penn on his first trip to the New World would be captured by the Caribbean pirates and sold into slavery or hanged! A very modern and present day Christian approach.

If Jesus Christ were to return he'd be on the side of the persecuted all around the world. He would not be wearing a golden crown and fine raiment, he'd most likely be wearing a ready made sack suit and be standing on a street corner preaching tolerance, brother love and truth. He'd be stoned and persecuted by the most liberal of our modern day followers of the man with the golden crown. He'd probably be placed in a sanitarium in the free countries. He'd be shot, hanged or sent to a slave labor camp behind the iron curtain.

He'd no more recognize his teachings in St. Peter's or Canterbury Cathedrals than he would in Riverside or Trinity Churches in New York or the First Baptist or Foundry Methodist Churches in Washington. He was a reformer and a protestant against organized, priesthood-controlled religion.

He taught that every man is the creation of a merciful God, that men are sinners and that he had come into the world to teach sinners how to approach His Father—and the way was not through Caiaphas the High Priest or Augustus the Roman Emperor. The way is direct and straight. Any man can tell the Almighty and Most Merciful God his troubles and directly ask for guidance. *He will get it.*

TO ETHEL NOLAND

June 4, 1952

Dear Ethel:

I have treated you like a step child of a mean step parent. You are long overdue for a reply to your good letter of May 21.

I am so glad you went to Rob's wedding and that you took to air to do it. As I told you once before, she was at the White House with some other students and told me that Robert was a friend of hers. I am glad you liked her and her family.

Had a letter from Mary in which she said she'd been to see Nellie. I hope that Nellie is well on the road to recovery. I won't be able to stop in Independence on this trip home on Friday. I have to go to Springfield to attend a 35th Division Reunion. I am going to quit reunions when I step out of this office and associate myself with the rising generation. No one can live in the past and do his country any service. These old stiffs who get together and talk about how brave and great they were forty years ago are a pain in the neck to me. They should be using experience to meet present day problems.

That's what is the trouble with the Senate and the High Court! Those two bodies are controlled by the past.

I'm glad the kids liked the notes I sent them. It is the habit of men in high office to kowtow to the so-called big shots and to neglect the little people with no pull. When a guy comes to me with endorsements from

Senators and House members and letters and calls from Governors and Wall Streeters, it leaves me rather cold. But when some old lady or a boy in the army tells me what's troubling them I go to work.

We had a lawn party for Vets yesterday. Bess and I were at the head of the line with Mrs. Woodrow Wilson next and then all the Cabinet & their wives and then Generals and Admirals and Asst. Secretaries galore. The boys had a chance to shake hands with all the big shots in the Executive Depts. There were 1430 of them and it took two solid hours to pass them by. Then they were given ice cream, cookies, prohibition punch, cigarettes etc. and a beautiful concert by the Marine Band.

I spent the rest of the day discussing ways and means to keep the country and the world off the skids as a result of the awful court decision. But we'll make it.

Take care of yourself and tell Nellie to keep a stiff upper lip.

Sincerely,

Harry

DIARY

June 8, 1952

Friday, at noon, Mrs. Truman, her mother, Vietta, Dr. Graham and two of my aides, Gen. Vaughan and General Landry, along with Joe Short, Mrs. Short, Matt Connelly and Ted Marks,[1] took off on the Independence for Grandview and Springfield.

We landed at Grandview Air Port at 1:40 Central Standard Time— 3:40 Eastern Day Light Time—a monstrosity in time keeping.[2]

Bess, her mother, Dr. Graham and Vietta went to Independence. My brother Vivian and sister Mary met me at the airport and went on to Springfield with me. It took us 35 minutes to fly the 200 miles which usually takes 4½ hours to drive and 7 or 8 hours on the train.

Capt. Allen, of the Corps of Engineers, in charge of construction, insisted that I take a look at what is being done to the Grandview Air Port. It was an interesting tour.

Vivian's wife, Luella, and Harry's wife were at the airport with Harry's two daughters—one of them brand new. Both lovely children.

Arrived at Springfield about ¼ of an hour ahead of schedule. We could see at least five acres of cars parked around the airfield before we landed. It was estimated that 5 or 6 thousand people were there to meet me. Actually there were between 10 & 15 thousand. The first es-

1. Fellow officer in the 129th Field Artillery, best man at Truman's wedding in 1919.
2. Truman hated Daylight Savings Time.

timate was by a hostile local newspaper—but very liberal indeed from that source.

Drove into Springfield in an open car with Vivian & Mary in the back seat with me. It was like 1948. There were at least 100 thousand people on the streets yelling as usual "Hello Harry," "There he is" and "We want you again." But, I am sorry to write, "They can't have me again."

At the Colonial Hotel the streets were jammed in every direction with enthusiastic fans.

Had dinner with the family, in a room next door to my suite. Gen. Ralph E. Truman was host. Olive, his wife, Henrietta Davidson, his daughter, Anna Davidson, his granddaughter, Mary & Vivian and Roma Colgan who is the wife of Rochester Colgan, a grandson of Aunt Emma, one of my father's sisters, were present.

Soon as dinner was over we went to the Shrine Mosque where a wonderful entertainment was given by the 35th Division Committee. The winners of the Square Dance contest danced for us. They were wonderful.

A team of children, all under six, danced a beautiful square dance with a pretty little girl also under six as the caller.

Then Ronald Reagan and his wife Nancy Davis with Gene Nelson, Virginia Gibson and Mrs. Grover Cleveland Alexander came over from the premiere of "The Winning Team" and gave us a half hour of grand entertainment.

We then adjourned to Ralph's new home and had a most pleasant evening. Went back to the Colonial Hotel about 11 P.M. and went to bed.

Was up and around at 5:30 A.M. on the 7th. My brother had the adjoining bedroom in the Suite. He was up about the same time and we discussed Missouri politics, the farm at Grandview, the proposed Cultural Center I wanted to set up, the price of land, roads etc.

Before I went to bed Matt Connelly, Vivian and Ralph tried to argue me out of the march in the parade. I wouldn't be convinced. Most every morning I take a two mile walk at the rate of 128 steps a minute and I just knew that the two mile parade at a 120 steps a minute would be easy. It was although it was 100° in the shade—and we marched in the sun!

Went from the hotel to breakfast in the basement of the Mosque. The two Batteries, D & F, with which I served in World War I were well represented. I was pleased and highly complimented that so many in each organization turned out.

I was presented with a medal and made a member of the Hill Billy organization. A person is not eligible unless he's witnessed a fox hunt, hillbilly style. I've been present at several but for the purposes of the show they put on a recorded one. Started with roosters crowing and then the hounds barking in the chase. They presented the medal and the certificate.

It was up to me then to accept. I thanked them for the honor and told them that I would suggest that they have a game rooster to do the crowing instead of the Shanghai because the game would do the crowing more expeditiously. Told them that I recognized the voice of "Old Blue" and "Old Bob," two of the hounds, and explained to them that I received hardly any medals but that I was the target for a lot of bricks!

Then I told them that my most pleasant duty is conferring medals on men who earn them. Reminded them that on last Monday I had given Gen. Eisenhower his fourth Medal. That I'd given Gen. MacArthur one at Wake Island and conferred a large number on various leaders in World War II, that I had handed out more Congressional Medals of Honor than all the Presidents before me put together had done.

Then I told them of my experience in giving Gen. Wainwright a Congressional Medal of Honor in the rose garden of the White House. He had become very emotional and told me he had expected to be courtmartialed instead of receiving the highest military award.

Then I told them about the big Captain on whom I'd conferred the Cong. Medal of Honor. He captured or killed a great many Germans in a little village on the drive to Berlin. When he ran out of grenades he threw rocks at the houses and the Germans came out and gave up because they thought the rocks were grenades.

When I placed the medal on him I told him I didn't want him to throw rocks at me. He said "Oh no, Mr. President, I wouldn't do that. I'm more scared now than I was in that village."

After breakfast we went upstairs to a very solemn and impressive memorial service. When that was over we went to Ralph's home and sat until the parade started.

I rode in the car for a couple of blocks and then walked the 2.2 miles to the reviewing stand. Stood and reviewed the parade for an hour, as wet as a rat in the ocean.

We then went to the Shrine Mosque to await the broadcasting time for the speech. It seemed to go over in a big way. Editorials in various metropolitan papers were favorable—for a wonder—and the speech was rebroadcast on a number of stations.

From the Mosque, we went to the airport and took off for the Capital City. As usual shook hands with all the police, local, state and national.

As soon as the plane was under way I took a bath, changed clothes from the skin out and never felt better! If I had not walked—oh my.

Arrived in Washington at 6:09 eastern day light time.

Margie was at the airport.

DIARY

June 15, 1952

Well here I am, Sunday evening all alone. Margaret came to the Great White Prison for the week end on Friday 13th. I went by train to Groton (rhymes with rotten) to speak on atomic energy for peace time use. Should have flown both ways but my staff decided that it would be bad weather going up. It wasn't.

The speech was semi political and evidently made a hit. I've never made a speech, since I became President, that didn't have a political flavor. It can't be done.[1]

I've been prowling around the House trying to find my music books which were on the piano at the Blair House. The contractor who remodeled the White House gave me a gold master key to all the Yale locks. It opened all of them tonight but the one I wanted to get into! Just about the time we have things in shape to find what we want, we'll move out and then we'll never find anything. Lesson: Don't raise your boy to be President of the United States.

It is the greatest office in the history of the world. Not one of the great oriental potentates, Roman Emperors, French Kings, Napoleon, Victoria, Queen of Great Britain, Jenghis Khan, Tamerlane, the Mogul Emperors, the great Caliph of Baghdad had half the power and influence that the President of the United States now has. It is a terrifying responsibility. But the responsibility has to be met and the decisions made—right or wrong.

I make them as they come, always prayerfully and hopefully.

Former Representative Maury Maverick of Texas was a great advice-giver, but Truman liked him and always answered his letters. This time Maverick complained about treatment of Americans of Chinese extraction by the Hong Kong consulate.

TO MAURY MAVERICK

July 3, 1952

Dear Maury:

I read your memorandum of June nineteenth regarding the State Department with a lot of interest. The State Department has been so

---

1. The President on June 14 laid the keel for the first nuclear submarine, the U.S.S. *Nautilus,* and said that new ships cost money, that some members of Congress did not realize the fact, but that the two senators from Connecticut, by chance Democrats, did.

THE WHITE HOUSE
WASHINGTON

June 15 '52

Well here I am, Sunday evening all alone. Margaret came to the Great White Prison for the week end on Friday 13th. I went by train to Groton (rhymes with rotten) to speak on atomic energy for peace time use. Should have flown both ways but my staff decided that it would be bad weather going up. It wasn't. The speech was semi political and evidently made a hit. I've never made a speech, since I became President, that didn't have a political flavor. It can't be done.

roundly abused and so thoroughly misrepresented by the Congressmen of the United States that they are in a state of being "cowed" as
you would say in Texas. They are in the same condition as a pet dog
after he has been whipped by the person of whom he thinks the most.
Of course, down on the third and fourth levels in the Department
there are people who do not understand exactly what this whole situation is all about. They are still living in the time when Great Britain
represented us in world affairs, and they have not yet awakened to
the fact that we are the leader now in world affairs and must assume
that position.

There never has been a more able Secretary of State than Dean
Acheson but he has exactly the same trouble that I had when I first came
into this office. Everybody knew what ought to be done and tried his best
to keep me from doing it but I finally got it straightened out. It will take
four, five or six years to put the State Department in the right sort of
condition. The same thing is true of the Justice Department and two or
three other departments that I could name but these things can't be done
in fifteen minutes.

The individual cases you mentioned are just samples of what I hear
every day.

This terrible McCarran-Walter Bill has made things much worse.
That bill was nothing in the world but approval of all the mistakes
the State and Justice have made in the last ten years in the administration of the immigration laws. It is now the law of the land and
there is nothing we can do about it. It was made the law of the land
by as many Democrats as Republicans voting to override my veto and
that vote was in the Senate and the House. I think you ought to read a
copy of the veto message and you will find that you are stymied at
every turn of the road in everything you are trying to do, just as I
am.[1]

> Sincerely yours,
> Harry S. Truman

---

1. Senator Patrick A. McCarran (Nevada) and Representative Francis E. Walter (Pennsylvania), both Democrats, had introduced a bill codifying and revising U.S. immigration, naturalization, and nationality laws. The bill passed in late May 1952. While it eliminated race as
a bar to immigration and naturalization, it retained the principle of national origins, using
the census of 1920 to allocate quotas. Critics said it cut down on admission of Asian and
eastern, central, and southern Europeans, who were not present in great numbers in 1920, and
for this reason Truman vetoed it.

DIARY

July 6, 1952

Mr. T. & I went to the ball game between Washington & Boston last night. The Senators won 4 to 3. On the 4th of July we went to what we supposed would be a double header. It rained at the end of the 3rd and the beginning of the 4th inning. We waited an hour and it kept raining. Finally we went back to the White House—and it cleared up so that Mr. Griffith was able to have his two games. He lost the first one 9 to 4 and he also lost the second one.

On Saturday night July 5th we went to the game and the Senators won 4 to 3. They also won on Sunday 6 to 1. I won't go to a Sunday game —for no good reason—but I'd rather go to church, but Sundays don't have an impression today.

I tried to go to a church on Sunday and listen to the sermon, but the preacher became a National Figure because I appeared at his church. I quit appearing. And I'll never appear at his church again. Wish he'd had common sense. I could have helped him behind the scenes very much. But he could not resist the temptation to take advantage of a situation for a headline. He had the headline and lost a customer who had been very fond of him.

I should have known better. He was a Virginian and looked very much like Harry Byrd. And I'm sorry to say that Harry Byrd is not what the sabotage press try to make him. He and Bennett Champ Clark had the best and most important opportunities in the Senate of the United States that any two men ever had. Both of them muffed their opportunities!

Now why would two such wise men do that? No one knows.

Byrd is still in the Senate, for how long no one knows. Bennett Champ is on the D.C. Court of Appeals—to which court I appointed him because he begged me to do it! What a mistake I made! He had been 100% against any policy I have advocated! He is still against anything I am supporting —but I'm soft hearted and he is the personification of ingratitude. He is not in a class by himself, I'm sorry to say.

MEMORANDUM

July 6, 1952

The Republicans are meeting today in Chicago to select a candidate. Taft has control of the organization and will no doubt seat enough delegates to have himself nominated.

In 1940 Wall Street took on Willkie, an Indiana Democrat, and by the same methods that Taft is using at Chicago today kept Taft out of the race.

Willkie was beaten by F.D.R. and Henry Wallace. He was a bad loser. Cried like a baby over a national hookup—figuratively I mean. The defeat was too much for him.

In 1944, the same big business gang took up Dewey. F.D.R. and I gave him a drubbing as bad as Willkie's was in 1940.

In 1948 Taft was sure he would be the nominee. Again the same Wall Street gang gave the nomination to Dewey. He failed again in the campaign, due to a special effort on the part of the Democrats to tell the people the truth.

Now Taft has control of the machinery and the "kept press" is yelling thief and robber. I'm very happy over the situation. But I'm not happy over the situation with which the Democratic Convention is faced.

There are five candidates. Three from the South, one from Kentucky and one from New York.

Senator Russell is an able and an intelligent man. He has been Governor of Georgia and is now Senator from that great State. He has all the qualifications as to ability and brains. But he is poison to Northern Democrats and honest Liberals. I doubt if he could carry a single State north of the Ohio River or 36°30'. Too bad he had to be born in Georgia, home of the modern Ku Klux Klan and the most vicious of anti-Catholics. There is no chance for Dick.

Then there is Kefauver, the Junior Senator from Tennessee. He served in the House from his home State and had no reputation for anything in particular but his being unable to understand what was going on when the House was in session. He has the same sort of reputation in the Senate.

He had a crime committee, started in Kansas City with great headlines, and finally he told Roy Roberts that the Atty. Gen. had already cleaned up the town. It was placed on page nine in *very fine print.* Then the great crime investigator went to St. Louis.

He found something in *East* St. Louis, Illinois—nothing in Missouri. But *St. Louis, Mo.,* was used for the *headlines.* So the President of the United States had all the credit for Illinois crime.

The "great" investigator went to Chicago, found some rotten situations as is always possible in that sprawling town. He succeeded in beating a good Senator, Scott Lucas.

Philadelphia was the home of the crookedest city administration in the country. Did the great crime investigator go to Philadelphia to make an investigation? He did not.

Polk County, Tennessee, is the sinkhole of iniquity and it lies south and adjoining the home country of the "great investigator." Did he look into it? He did not.

When the time came for a report to the United States Senate the "great crime investigator" took his report, copyrighted it and sold it as a book over his own name! Talk about ethics—well he has none. He has made speeches to all the "economic royalist" organizations in the country at from $500.00 to $1500.00 an appearance. More ethics!! What a President this demagogic dumb bell would make!

Now we come to a grand man, a good administrator, former governor and United States Senator from Oklahoma. He is a great speaker—a convincing one on the platform. But he has a gas record and a cloture record. Labor, liberals and New Deal–Fair Deal Democrats won't support him.[1]

Then comes Alben Barkley—Congressman, U.S. Senator, floor leader of the majority in the Senate longer than any other man, Vice President for four years—75 years old Nov. 24, 1952! He wants to be President more than he wants anything else in the world. He can't see, he shows his age. I wish he could be 64 instead of 74 at this date! It takes him five minutes to sign his name and, as President, he'd have to sign it 600 times a day—and no one can do it for him. It is a felony for anyone to sign the President's name. My good friend Alben would be dead in three months if he should inherit my job!

Harriman is an active candidate. He is the ablest of them all. But he has been a Wall Street Banker, is the son of one of the old time pirates of the first score of years of this century. Can we elect a Wall Street Banker and a railroad tycoon President of the United States on the Democratic Ticket? Ask someone else. I can't answer!

TO ETHEL NOLAND

July 11, 1952

Dear Ethel:

I was most happy to have yours of July 6th. The enclosure gave me quite a kick—"There's Nothing Like Confidence." Well, maybe there isn't!

It looks very much like my candidate for the Republican nomination has beaten himself. Of all the dumb bunnies—he is the worst. Son of a

---

1. Robert S. Kerr, of the Kerr-McGee oil interests, had aggressively sponsored a bill to remove independent gas producers from federal regulation, and Truman vetoed it. Kerr was a powerful figure in Senate debate and voting, and thereby also made enemies.

President and a Chief Justice, in the Ohio Legislature, U.S. Senator, three times candidate for President—and look what he's done to himself. When a fellow is not honest intellectually, what can we expect.

I'm surely sorry that Nellie has had to go back to the hospital. What a bunch of robbers they are! Why can anyone be against my health program? We'd be able to meet situations such as Nellie's if we had it.

You know, speaking of Myra, when we lived on the farm where the sons of Vivian are now, your Uncle John let Aunt Emma have a couple of degueratype (the word's not in my desk dictionary, so I can't spell it!) of our Truman grandparents. Myra has found them and has promised to return them. The promise was made 6 months ago and I haven't seen them yet. But no doubt I'll eventually get them. Your remark about her April letter caused me to think of the pictures.

I talk to *"Lizzie"* every day and she keeps me informed about you and Nellie. Take care of *yourself* and try to get Nellie on her feet.

Sincerely,
Harry

DIARY

July 24, 1952

I just had a telephone conversation with Governor Stevenson at 3:30 o'clock. He called me and asked me if the situation developed to the point where he would be put in nomination would it embarrass me. If it would, he would not allow it to happen. I told him it not only would not embarrass me but that it would please me in every way, that I have no commitments and if he is nominated I would put forth every effort possible to see that he is elected and he will never hear from me after the election is over unless he sends for me. He expressed happiness and appreciation for this statement and said that he would not be at the airport to meet me tomorrow when I arrived in Chicago because the Chairman of the National Committee had advised him it would be better if he were not at the airport. I told him not to worry about that because those things didn't bother me in the slightest. He seemed to be in a very happy frame of mind and I told him that I was very sure that he would not only be put in nomination but that he would be nominated.

TO ADLAI E. STEVENSON

The Blackstone, Chicago
July 26, 1952, 6:40 A.M., C.D.T.

Dear Governor:

Last night was one of the most remarkable I've spent in all my sixty-eight years. When thousands of people—delegates and visitors—are willing to sit and listen to a set speech and an introduction by me, and then listen to a most wonderful acceptance speech by you, at two o'clock in the morning, there is no doubt that we are on the right track, in the public interest.

You are a brave man. You are assuming the responsibility of the most important office in the history of the world.

You have the ancestral, political and the educational background to do a most wonderful job. If it is worth anything, you have my whole-hearted support and cooperation.

When the noise and shouting are over, I hope you may be able to come to Washington for a discussion of what is before you.

Sincerely,
Harry S. Truman

The President invited both candidates, Democratic and Republican, to come to Washington for briefings on the organization of the White House and the state of the Union. The Republican candidate refused to be briefed; his advisers evidently thought it would hurt his campaign.

TO DWIGHT D. EISENHOWER

August 16, 1952

Dear Ike:

I am sorry if I caused you embarrassment.

What I've always had in mind was and is a continuing foreign policy. You know that is a fact, because you had a part in outlining it.

Partisan politics should stop at the boundaries of the United States. I am extremely sorry that you have allowed a bunch of screwballs to come between us.

You have made a bad mistake and I'm hoping it won't injure this great Republic.

There has never been one like it and I want to see it continue regardless of the man who occupies the most important position in the history of the world.

May God guide you and give you light.

From a man who has always been your friend and who always wanted to be!

Sincerely,
Harry S. Truman

DIARY

August 19, 1952

I have quite a day. Eric Johnston came in at 11:00 A.M. and told me about the troubles of the Motion Picture Association.[1] He told me how much Eisenhower hated Point IV. That was no surprise because Ike had told me when he made his last report to me on his return from Europe that he didn't understand Point IV and that he thought *birth control* is the answer. I asked him if he'd do me a favor. He said he would—if he could. I told him to make speeches on birth control in Boston, Brooklyn, Detroit and Chicago. He did not get the point at all. He is not as intelligent as I thought. Evidently his staff has furnished the intelligence.

Eric told me that he intended to support my candidate! Eric is for Point IV. He is also against the idea of forcing the Movie Producers to furnish their productions to T.V. before the Movie Theaters can show them. So am I.

Talk to Joe Keenan, A.F. of L., about the coming campaign, and Robt. Ramspeck[2] about his troubles.

Had a grand meeting with Harry Seay[3] and his friend from Texas.

Saw Albert Greenfield[4] about an appearance Nov. 11, 1952, at the Mayflower Hotel, D.C., to receive a gold medal.

Saw the Sec. of Defense about the distribution of Atomic Bombs, Ike and other things.

When I came back to my study in the White House after some other appointments at the office I saw Dr. Graham who pronounced me O.K. as usual.

Call the Boss (Mrs. Truman) at six as usual. All's well at home. Had dinner as usual on the south porch at seven and then trouble began.

Joe Short, Press Secretary, called and said that Margie's guards had

---

1. Johnston was president of the Association.
2. Ex-congressman from Georgia.
3. Democratic committeeman from Texas.
4. Philadelphia real estate broker and banker.

caused an incident in the Swedish Capital.[5] I called the Sec. of the Treas. and the Sec. of State to find out what the hell was wrong. They called Stockholm and finally reported to me that nothing is wrong. Some damn fool reporter wanted a headline, just as the same sort do here. I was relieved when the Sec. of State and the Sec. of the Treasury informed me that the Swedish Foreign Minister had issued a statement saying that the whole thing is a hoax.

Wish Margie was home! Called Bess and told her what had transpired, so she would not hear it over the news broadcasts. All seems to be well and so's your old man!

TO HARRY H. VAUGHAN

August 28, 1952

Harry:

In 1852 General Winfield Scott was nominated by the Whigs for President.

In 1840 William Henry Harrison and John Tyler were nominated by the Whigs and won the election. Harrison died in a month and Tyler, a Virginia Democrat, became the President. He was not popular.

In 1844 James K. Polk was elected President. He was one of the great Presidents. George M. Dallas was his Vice President. The Texas city is named for him.

In 1848 the Whigs nominated Zachary Taylor & Millard Fillmore. The Democrats were split into two factions and Taylor was elected. He died of a stomach infection a year and four months after his inauguration. Fillmore finished out his term.

So in 1852, the Whigs, feeling that their success with Generals in two campaigns would bring another General to the White House, placed Old Fuss & Feathers before the people. It took 53 ballots to do it. Daniel Webster and Millard Fillmore were the other Whig Candidates.

The Democrats forgot their differences and nominated a former Senator from New Hampshire, son of a New Hampshire Governor and a Brigadier General in General Scott's Army in Mexico on the march from Vera Cruz to Mexico City.

It is said that Pierce had the stomach ache whenever an engagement was imminent. Anyway he was absent at Chapultepec.

Scott was cartooned in his uniform, cartooned eating soup as a result of his statement that he must eat a bowl of soup when he was wanted for

5. Margaret and Drucie Snyder Horton had sailed for Europe on the maiden voyage of the *United States* on July 3, and the itinerary included England, Ireland, Scotland, Wales, Switzerland, France, Austria, Germany. Denmark, Sweden, Finland, and Norway.

a political conference of some sort. Anyway when the votes were counted Scott had 42 and Pierce 254.

Pierce was the best looking President the White House ever had—but as President he ranks with Buchanan and Calvin Coolidge.

A general—5 star—is now the candidate of the Whig Party's successor, the Republican. He was tops as a commander in a great war. So was Scott.

So What.

[unsigned]

TO ADLAI E. STEVENSON (UNSENT)

[Early August 1952]

Dear Governor:

I have come to the conclusion that you are embarrassed by having the President of the United States in your corner in this campaign.

Therefore I shall remain silent and stay in Washington until Nov. 4.

You understand that I had decided in 1949 that I would not be a candidate for this greatest office in the history of the world, again.

In January 1952 you came to the Blair House at my request and we discussed a successor to me in the White House.

You were coy and backward, advancing various reasons why you had to be the candidate for Governor of Illinois, your divorce, your belief that you did not have the qualifications etc.

Again a month later we had the same sort of a discussion.

When the time for the Democratic Convention approached I sent the Chairman of the Democratic Committee to see you. Frank McKinney was the ablest chairman the Democratic Committee had produced in my recollection. You stalled and gave him the same answer you had given me.

Then I called the Vice President to the White House along with Mr. McKinney and a number of other able national politicos and told him that we would support him for the nomination for President.

You of course know the rest of the story. Barkley became discouraged and withdrew. He was intending to leave Chicago a whipped man. I called Mr. McKinney and Barkley's farewell speech was the result.

On Friday morning you called me and told me that your friends—among them the Governor of Indiana, who is now running on the Republican ticket—wanted to nominate you. You wanted to know if I would be embarrassed by that procedure. I told you that I would be highly pleased.

That afternoon I boarded a plane and landed in Chicago in the middle of the afternoon. The Convention had recessed with no nomination.

Kefauver had some 360 votes, you had 330 odd, and favorite sons had the balance.

I sent one of my aides to see Mr. Harriman, one to see Gov. Dever of Mass., one to see the Minnesota and the Michigan delegations with instructions to switch to you. Harriman and Gov. Dever switched, the amateurs didn't until later.

You were nominated and you made a grand acceptance speech.

Then you proceeded to break up the Democratic Committee, which I had spent years in organizing, you called in the former mayor of Louisville [Wilson Wyatt] as your personal chairman and fired McKinney, the best chairman of the National Committee in my recollection.

Since the Convention you have treated the President as a liability. You brought in Beardsley Ruml[1] as finance chairman, who is in the Wilson Wyatt class as an amateur. You had your Chicago lawyer[2] made chairman of the National Committee. He is a fine man but has no political contacts and is completely ignored by both you and Wyatt.

I have tried to make it plain to you that I want you elected—in fact I want you to win this time more than I wanted to win in 1948.

But—I can't stand snub after snub by you and Mr. Wyatt.

When the President after much thought (from a political point of view, which may be beneath *high level* consideration) asks the Democratic Candidate to come to a strategy conference and is coldly turned down and referred to a crackpot, it seems to me that the Democratic Candidate is above associating with the lowly President of the United States.

I shall go to the dedication of the Hungry Horse Dam in Montana, make a public power speech, get in a plane and come back to Washington and stay there.

You and Wilson can now run your campaign without interference or advice.

The amateurish nature of Stevenson's campaign became clearly apparent when on August 16, in a "letter to Oregon," he allowed himself to be mousetrapped into answering for the Oregon Journal *the "oft-heard question": "Can Stevenson really clean up the mess in Washington?" Stevenson foolishly replied: "As to whether I can clean up the mess in Washington, I would bespeak the careful scrutiny of what I inherited in Illinois and what has been accomplished in three years." He was just*

1. A foundation executive and an official of R. H. Macy and Company.
2. Stephen A. Mitchell.

going over the question before answering it, but he had said it! He dou-
bled his error by going on to say: "As you well know, I did not want the
nomination and received it without commitments to anyone about any-
thing—including President Truman. As evidence of my directions, I
have established my headquarters here in Springfield, with people of my
own choosing, rather than in Washington. The new national chairman,
instead of an old line politician, is a close personal friend whose most
recent public service has been as counsel to the Congressional committee
investigating the Department of Justice."

TO ADLAI E. STEVENSON (UNSENT)

[Late August 1952]

My dear Governor:

Your letter to Oregon is a surprising document. It makes the campaign rather ridiculous. It seems to me that the Presidential Nominee and his running-mate are trying to beat the Democratic President instead of the Republicans and the General of the Army who heads their ticket.

There is no mess in Washington except the sabotage press in the nature of Bertie McCormick's Times-Herald and the anemic Roy Howard's snotty little News.

The Dixiecrats and the Taft Republicans along with Nixon, Knowland, Harry Byrd and the seniority chairmen of the Key Committees of the House and the Senate make the only mess in the national scene.

You seem to be running on their record and not on the forward looking record of the Democratic Administration as represented by the President, the Vice President and the Speaker of the House.

I've come to the conclusion that if you want to run against your friends, they should retire from the scene and let you do it.

When you say that you are indebted to no one for your nomination, that makes nice reading in the sabotage press, but gets you no votes because it isn't true.

There are more votes on "skid row" than there are on the "North Shore" for the "Party of the People." New York, Illinois, Missouri, California, Ohio and the farm belt are worth more to you than Texas and the Dixiecrat States.

You fired and balled up the Democratic Committee Organization that I've been creating over the last four years.

I'm telling you to take your crackpots, your high socialites with their noses in the air, run your campaign and win if you can. Cowfever [Kefauver] could not have treated me any more shabbily than have you.

Had I not come to Chicago when I did, the squirrel headed coonskin cap man from old man Crump's State, who has no sense of honor, would have been the nominee.

Best of luck to you from a bystander who has become disinterested.

DIARY

September 9, 1952

I have, as usual, a real day. Talk with the staff at ten A.M. Then have a session with Max Lowenthal. The Chargé d'Affaires on Formosa spends a quarter of an hour telling what is happening on that island. It is an interesting story.

The Secretary of Defense then comes in and we discuss the coming Atomic Explosion[1] on Eniwetok on Nov. 1. It will be an explosion of all explosions. Wish I could be present. I can't of course.

Had a Memo from Mr. Lovett on plane production, prepared by the Sec. for Air, and a Munitions Report, which were most encouraging.[2] Bob gave me a definition of a statistician—"a man who draws a straight line from an unwarranted assumption to a foregone conclusion"! I gave him one for a consultant Washington style—"an ordinary citizen away from home."

Came over to the House after a long session with the new Chairman of the Dem. Committee.

Bess & I talk to Margie at 6:30 on a three way hookup. We go down to the south porch at seven for dinner—a good dinner too—tenderloin of some kind, really tender, asparagus, and a cooked stuffed tomato, then a large piece of thick, light yellow cake with caramel sauce.

One of our squirrels comes up to the table and asks for a bite to eat. Turns up his nose at a crumb of bread soaked in cooked tomato juice. We send for some crackers and he accepts pieces of cracker and goes under a chair each time, sits up and eats. Bess hands him the pieces one at a time until he has eaten three whole crackers. Then, without a bow or a thank you he walks down the steps and disappears. But he'll be back tomorrow night as usual for more to eat.

Tomorrow he'll take the attitude of the "You ain't done nothin' for me lately" of Barkley's Kentucky constituent in 1938.

Barkley was campaigning in 1938 along the Ohio River in a small town. He noticed an old fellow with whom he was well acquainted cross

---

1. Of the prototype of a hydrogen bomb.

2. Lovett, undersecretary of defense, became secretary on September 12, upon Marshall's resignation.

the street to avoid meeting him. Alben asked another friend with whom he was talking at the time if old man so & so was at outs with him. Barkley was informed that old man so & so was "mad" at him. So Barkley crossed the street and stopped old man so & so and asked what the trouble could possibly be.

Barkley reminded the old man that as soon as the Armistice of 1918 was signed he had succeeded in having his boy returned so the old man could run his farm. "Yes," said the old man, "you did that." "Well," said Alben, "didn't I get your daughter made postmaster of this town?" "Yes," said the old man, "you did." "Then," said Barkley, "didn't I get you a disaster loan a few years ago when the Ohio washed you out?" "Yes," said the old man, "you did." "Then," said Barkley, "why are you against me?" "Well," said the old man, "you ain't done nothin' for me lately"!

It is a good story and it makes a hit when told, but there are very, very few like old man so & so. The vast majority of the people for whom favors are done do not forget.

Well, to finish the day I am expecting to listen to Ike at ten P.M. and to Adlai at 10:30. Ike at Indianapolis, Adlai at Frisco.

Mr. Hopkins, the chief clerk, informed me when I signed the documents and letters this afternoon that the mail had fallen below 5000 letters today for the first time since I've been President. I asked him a foolish question—why?

The diplomatic chief clerk informed me that the mail always decreased in volume at the end of an Administration, particularly when the White House Occupant was not coming back. Well it is "The King is dead —Long live the King."

It is fortunate that I've never taken an attitude that the kudos and kowtows are made to me as an individual. I knew always that the greatest office in the history of the world was getting them and Harry S. Truman as an individual was not. I hope I'm still the country man from Missouri.

TO ARTHUR KROCK (UNSENT)

September 11, 1952

Dear Arthur:

In your column this morning, you speak of gross and costly blunders of the Truman Administration in foreign policy. Wish you would be specific and name them.

Was the salvation of Greece and Turkey a blunder? Was the Berlin Airlift a blunder? Was the economic recovery of free Europe with our assistance a blunder? Was the military rehabilitation and strengthening of the free world a blunder? Was the European Alliance (N.A.T.O.) a blunder? Was the rehabilitation of the Philippine Republic a blunder? Were the Japanese Treaty and the Pacific Agreements blunders?

Chiang Kai-shek's downfall was his own doing. His field Generals surrendered the equipment we gave him to the Commies and used his own arms and ammunition to overthrow him. Only an American Army of 2,000,000 men could have saved him and that would have been World War III.

Now where and what are the blunders?

Foreign policy has been costly. But World War III would be ten times as costly.

The appropriations for Greece and Turkey and the Marshall Plan and also for the Military Plan[1] were voted by bipartisan majorities in Congress, which made them approved National Policies.

The Treaties were overwhelmingly approved.

I've always thought Arthur Krock to be intellectually honest. But when you contribute to the breakup of the foreign policy of the United States, you help bring on World War III. When you do it by misleading and untrue statements—well it is almost as bad for the country as McCarthyism.

You can disagree all you want on any subject, farm, labor, monetary, debt control or foreign policy and I won't care at all—if you tell the truth.

DIARY

September 23, 1952

I'll never forget my first appearance on a political platform. It happened in 1922 in the American Legion Hall in Lee's Summit, Jackson County, Missouri. I had filed as candidate for Judge of the County Court for the Eastern District of Jackson County. . . .

I had been in the National Guard, commanded a battery of light artillery overseas in the World War, been in business on 12th St. in Kansas City and failed.

So it was a busted merchant, an ex soldier and farmer who had no political experience against four good men.

That first meeting was a flop for me. I was scared worse than I was when I first came under fire in 1918.

The Hall was full. Various candidates were introduced by Col. Stayton, who presided. Then came my turn. I had stage fright so badly that all I could say was, "I hope you'll vote and work for me in the primary," in a trembling voice and then I sat down.

---

1. The Mutual Defense Assistance Program, grants to N.A.T.O. and other allies for military equipment.

TO NELLIE NOLAND

September 26, 1952

Dear Nellie:

I was most happy to have your letter of Sept. 22. Had one from Mary dated the same day. She told me that she had a most pleasant visit with you and Ethel and Ruth, Robert and his wife.

I am glad you are getting around even if it is on crutches. That is much better than sitting or staying in bed. You see I can speak from experience. Back in 1909 or 1910 I fell on the frozen ground in the cow lot and broke my left leg. Was on crutches and walked with a cane for months. A 400 pound calf threw me when I was trying to take him to his pen from his breakfast. He was robbing his partner. Both were being raised by an old cow that gave enough milk for two calves. Gluttons are alike be they cats, pigs or men.

I am starting on a campaign tour but without much enthusiasm. My own candidate has charged me with a "mess" in Washington and now turns out to have secret political funds up his sleeve. Ike has taken up with McCarthy and Jenner, the proponents of the Big Lie, and has himself completely distorted the truth on Korea, R.R. strikes and the European Foreign Policy. He has also discriminated against our Missouri Senator. If he takes McCarthy and Jenner to his bosom along with Nixon he surely ought not to discriminate against our counterfeit. Kem is just a big liar and just as low down as McCarthy and Jenner, but not so clever. Ike ought not to mistreat him though, just because he's dumb.

The Senate Press Gallery took a poll on which Senator is the worst Senator in this Congress. McCarthy was winning overwhelmingly and did win, but Pete Brandt of the Post Dispatch told me that out of state pride he voted for Kem!

When I was in the Senate the same press outfit took a poll on the ten men who had made the greatest contribution to the war effort. I was the only legislator in the list. How times change. In times past Missouri wins a best Senator—now she competes for the worst. Take care of yourself and please don't fall any more.

Sincerely,

Harry

Remember me to Ethel and all the family. You probably won't hear from me for some time.

DIARY

Since Nov. 4 things have moved very fast. The office work of the President has almost doubled. The President-elect has been coy about co-operating for the turnover. All that the present incumbent wants is an orderly transfer of authority. Ike and his advisors are afraid of some kind of trick. There are no tricks.

Affairs, foreign and domestic, must be discussed and the new President should be in a position to take over a going program.

I am very much afraid that Ike's advisors have convinced him that he is dealing with a man who wants to embarrass him. That is not true. All I want to do is to make an orderly turnover. It has never been done.

So I sent him messages urging that he have a representative to familiarize himself with the budget, and one to acquaint himself, and Ike, with foreign affairs, defense and finance.

The General finally awoke to the necessity and appointed Mr. Dodge, a capable Detroit banker, and Cabot Lodge, Jr., as his representatives.

The General made a number of commitments in his campaign speeches, among them a trip to Korea.[1] I wish he had not done that. I have arranged for him to use the Presidential Plane, the Independence, for the trip. He will find things just as he has been briefed. What he can do to ease the tension among the mothers, the wives, the sisters and cousins and the aunts, I don't know. I sincerely wish he didn't have to make the trip. It is an awful risk. If he should fail to come back I wonder what would happen. May God protect him.

It seems that the people think I have lost an election and have been discredited. I wonder.

My good for nothing, highjacking, blackmailing Kansas City Star has decided that "Truman was a Drag" to Stevenson. Republicans and the Republican-controlled press agree. The Governor and Democrats do not. I do not know. I was paying my debt to the Party for being so good to me. Most top politicos in both parties fail to understand such an unheard of attitude.

---

1. At the height of the campaign, Ike made a speech in Detroit, traditional Democratic territory inhabited by auto workers, and promised to go to Korea if elected, the presumption being that he could do something to end the Korean War. The speech infuriated Truman.

DIARY

November 20, 1952

The President Elect came to see me day before yesterday, Nov. 18 '52. When he came into the President's office he had a chip on his shoulder. Only one photographer was allowed to take pictures in the office. He made three exposures. Two were good, one looked grim. The grim one was used by the N.Y. Times and one or two other Ike papers. The two good ones were used by some of the metropolitan dailies.

The press is still in a bad fix. Only attacks on the administration sell papers. When Ike has to take unjustified attacks by his fair weather friends I wonder what effect it will have.

I told him when he came into the Presidential office that all I had in mind is an orderly turnover to him. . . . I offered to leave the pictures of Hidalgo, the Mexican Liberator, given to me for the Presidential office, San Martín, given to me by the Argentine Government, and Bolivar, given to me by the Venezuelan Government, in the President's office. I was informed, very curtly, that I'd do well to take them with me—that the governments of these countries would, no doubt, give the new President the same pictures! Then I gave him the world globe that he used in World War II which he had given me at Frankfurt when I went to Potsdam. He accepted that—not very graciously.

I told him that I wanted to turn the administrative branch of the government over to him as a going concern and that I had instructed my White House Staff and all Cabinet Officers to cooperate in this undertaking.

Ike asked me if I had a chief of staff in the White House. I told him that there is an assistant to the President, Dr. John Steelman, who coordinates the differences between Cabinet Officers and between the President's Secretaries, but that any member of the Cabinet and any secretary or administrative assistant is at liberty to see the President at any time on any subject.

I advised him that his appointment secretary would be his personal contact with the public. I told him that this man must be a real diplomat, able to say "No" nine tenths of the time and make no one angry. I told him that his press secretary must be able to keep press and radio-television in line. He must be familiar with reporters' problems and be able to stand between the President and the press & radio. I advised him to obtain a correspondence secretary who could suggest answers to 75% of the mail, keep track of birthdays, special days, proclamations and be able to write letters he could sign after reading the first paragraph.

I told him he must have assistants who could talk to State, Treasury, Commerce and Labor, that he must have one to act as personnel officer to head off job hunters and to investigate and make recommendations for all positions filled by Presidential appointment. I informed him that he should have a "minority group" assistant to hear complaints and assuage the hurt feelings of Negroes, Mexicans, Puerto Ricans, Indians and any other groups, including Poles, Lithuanians, Irish and what have you. I think all this went into one ear and out the other.

Then I took him back to the Cabinet Room and had the Sec. of State, the Sec. of the Treasury, the Sec. of Defense and Averell Harriman brief him and answer questions. Gen. Eisenhower was overwhelmed when he found what he faced.

He had Sen. Lodge and Mr. Dodge with him. Dodge is an able, honest man.

I also told him in my office that he must have a counselor who knows legislative procedure and who could write bills and analyze laws which came up to him to sign.

DIARY

November 24, 1952, 5:00 A.M.

The White House is quiet as a church. I can hear the planes at the air port warming up. As always there is a traffic roar—sounds like wind and rain through the magnolias.

Bess's mother is dying across the hallway. She was 90 years old August 4th. Vivian's mother-in-law passed on Saturday at eleven thirty. She also was ninety just a month after or before Mrs. Wallace. When you are sixty-eight death watches come often.

In 1947 my mother lay for weeks on a rocking bed suffering no end. When she finally passed on I was over Cincinnati and instinctively I knew she'd gone. I'd been dozing and dreamed she'd said "Goodbye, Harry. Be a good boy." When Dr. Graham came in to my room on the Sacred Cow I knew what he would say.

I'd stayed by her for days and then had to come back to the Capital. Public business has to be cared for when a man is President of the United States.

Since last September Mother Wallace has been dying—even before that, but we've kept doctors and nurses with her day and night and have kept her alive. We had hoped—and still hope—she'll survive until Christmas. Our last as President.

This old House is a most remarkable one. Started in 1792 by George Washington's laying of the corner stone. Burned in 1814, by the British. Occupied by John and Abigail Adams. Abigail left some most interesting stories about its bleak cold interior, the unfinished East Room. Using the East Room as a laundry dryer, complaining of lack of servants' bell pulls and other things.

Jefferson receiving diplomats in house slippers and a dressing gown. Dolly Madison loading pictures and books and documents into a wagon and escaping just two jumps ahead of the British when they applied the torch.

Then Monroe refinishing the rehabilitated old place with his own and some imported French furniture. And catching hell because he sent to Paris to buy things he could not obtain in the primitive U.S.A.!

Old John Quincy Adams who went swimming in the Chesapeake & Potomac Canal every morning. A certain eager lady sat on his clothes on the bank one morning and interviewed him! Rather embarrassing I'd think—especially to old John Quincy.

Then old Andy Jackson and his rough, tough backwoodsmen walking on the furniture with muddy boots and eating a 300 pound cheese, grinding it into the lovely Monroe and Adams carpets!

I've an idea that Martin Van Buren restored some of the Monroe and J. Q. Adams elegance. Then came William Henry Harrison and Tyler. Harrison lived only thirty days after his being sworn in. Another sad day in the old House. Then Tyler and his lovely second wife. She was Miss Gardiner. There is a lovely picture of her in the White House. Old Tyler had a lot of nerve. He established the precedent that the Vice President becomes the President in fact when he succeeds to the office. Tyler had his troubles with Congress, his cabinet and the country, but he succeeded in annexing Texas. Now whether that accomplishment was an asset or not I'm unable to say.

Texas walked out of the Union against the advice of Sam Houston in 1861. The State has become oil rich and supports some of the worst newspapers in the country. But it has a great many good patriotic people as citizens who do not own oil wells, cattle ranches or newspapers. Thank Almighty God they are in the vast majority.

Polk came along next. He was the first "dark horse" candidate nominated and elected. He announced that he only wanted one term and he kept that promise. Died a short time after he retired. Not much White House lore about him.

Then came Zach Taylor, a professional military man. The old man was not familiar with politics or government. He was not a good administrator. Died from eating cherries and watermelon at a 4th of July celebration on the monument grounds. Another White House tragedy.

Millard Fillmore took over. First President from Buffalo. Cleveland was the other one.

Then came the campaign of 1852. The 1952 campaign was a repeat, without the same result.

DIARY

November 28, 1952

Margie came down from N.Y. Wednesday morning. She was to come on Thursday—Thanksgiving Day. I'm sure she was uneasy about her grandmother and her mother—so she came a day sooner.

We had a grand dinner in the State Dining Room, with Mrs. John Snyder, John & Drucie Horton and Lynn, the two year old daughter of John & Drucie.

Lynn is a precocious child. She took all of us into camp. We had a double bill picture show in the projection room on the ground floor—a cartoon comedy and a colored Irish romance—and the 2 year old stayed awake and commented on the scenes.

The next day, Friday, I dispose of much paper work, quit at noon and hope for the rest of the day off. It doesn't happen. Dave Lloyd comes over at 3 P.M. and we compose an article for the Democratic Digest. The Atty. General comes over and we discuss "shoes and ships and sealing wax and things." Suits and indictments and secret files ad lib.

We have dinner in the family dining room. My good old mother in law is very, very sick. We've had nurses and doctors with her day and night for almost a year. She has had the best of treatment, I'm happy to say. . . .

Margie has the northwest bedroom and sitting room. There is a fireplace in the corner of her bedroom. When there is no fire in it, there is a down draft and when the wind is northwest it is not comfortable for Margie in that bed room. So this afternoon she and Vietta Garr, our old cook and general factotum at Independence and the White House since we've been here, hunted up a bridge table and set it up in front of Margie's fireplace in her bed room.

Well we had dinner at seven as usual discussed ghosts and who'd died in the White House and then dress up and go across Lafayette Square to celebrate the anniversary of the new U.S.O. in the old Belasco Theater building. Mrs. T. had and has been interested in U.S.O. work so they wanted her to cut the birthday cake. Well we all, Mrs. T., Margie and the Presidente, dressed up and went over to the U.S.O. The Boss cut the birthday cake, they drew a number out of a box for the one to get the first slice that the first Lady cut and a Marine won! The President made some asinine remarks and we came back to the White House.

It was agreed we'd go to bed at once because Margie & I had to board the train for Philadelphia at 8:15 tomorrow to go to the Army-Navy football game—our last appearance officially at this function. Mrs. T. can't go because of her mother's condition.

Well I went to bed and read a hair raiser in Adventure. Just as I arrived at a bloody incident, the madam bursts into my bedroom through the hall door and shouted "Did you hear that awful noise?"

I hadn't and said so—not a popular statement. So I put on my bathrobe and made an investigation.

What do you think I found after looking all around? Why that Margie's bridge table had fallen from in front of the fireplace in her bedroom and knocked over the fireguard!

It must have made a grand ghost sound where Margie and her mamma were sitting in Mrs. T.'s sittingroom!

I didn't hear it. What a relief when the cause of the noise was discovered by me. I left two very happy ladies and went back to bed.

DIARY

December 4, 1952

Last night Adlai Stevenson was here for dinner. Mrs. Truman had asked Mrs. Lasker[1] and Mrs. Mahoney. We discussed public health, Dr. Magnuson,[2] Military Training, the Presidential campaign and other things before and during dinner.

From 9:00 P.M. until 10:30 P.M. the Governor and I talked about the Democratic Party, his part in the future, what he would do from now on and the composition of the National Committee. Agreed that Mitchell should stay on for some months, raise money to pay the deficit and set up an organization for research, publicity etc. That he should try to arrange a policy committee in the Senate and the House and then let the Committee itself decide on the new Chairman.

---

1. Mary W. Lasker, philanthropist, the widow of Albert D. Lasker, a public relations executive.

2. Dr. Paul B. Magnuson, surgeon, was head of the President's Commission on the Health Needs of the Nation, and had announced that his group would report to the President on December 18. He spoke of a private program of health insurance, some of it underwritten by the federal government.

The Governor has decided to take a trip around the world and write a travelogue about it. He is going for his own education. A good thing I think.

Wanted to know what I would do. Told him I didn't know.

DIARY

December 6, 1952

Yesterday at 12:30 my mother-in-law passed away. She was a grand lady. When I hear these mother-in-law jokes I don't laugh. They are not funny to me, because I've had a good one. So has my brother. My mother was a good mother-in-law to Vivian's and my wife. It gives me a pain in the neck to read the awful jokes that the so-called humorists crack about mother-in-law.

Today we go to Missouri to bury her. Four years ago, 1946, I was on the same errand for my mother.[1] The sabotage press—Bertie & Willie—made it appear that I was wasting public money to be decent to my mother. May God forgive them, I can't and won't.

The same lice will do the same publicity job when I take Mrs. Wallace, Bess and Margaret home to bury the mother-in-law.

To hell with them. When history is written they will be the sons of bitches—not I.

Look at old Medill, Horace Greeley et al. in Lincoln's time. Biddle in Jackson's and old man Pulitzer in Cleveland's.

It isn't Jackson, Lincoln and Cleveland who were wrong!

MEMORANDUM

December 22, 1952

Consideration of the Nov. 4th election is interesting. The majority of the Republican candidate was 6,600,000 odd votes.

27,300,000 cast for the Democrats and 33,900,000 for the Republican Dixiecrat, Shivercrat, anti Korean Bible-belt coalition.[1] It was the greatest turnout of votes in the history of the country. It was an appalling campaign made up of lies, misrepresentation and bald demagoguery mixed with a holy approach in a long faced Cotton Mather manner by the Republicans. No effort on the part of the Democrats to have the

---

1. The President, of course, erred—Martha Ellen Truman died in 1947.

---

1. The term "Shivercrat" derived from Governor Allan Shivers of Texas, who went off the Democratic reservation.

people understand the real issues was successful. Military hero glamor, character assassination (McCarthyism) and promises of world peace (which are impossible of fulfillment) gave the Catholics, the Protestant Bible Belt and the "sisters and the cousins and the aunts" along with the mammas, the sweethearts and the wives of the fighting men an incentive to go out and vote "agin the government."

Massachusetts, which gave the Democrats a majority of 242,000 in 1948, gave the coalition 200,000 in 1952. Missouri gave the Coalition a majority of about 30,000 in 1952. The Democrats carried it in 1948 by 262,000. New York, Ohio, Indiana, Illinois, Kentucky, Tennessee, Texas were all swayed by a quasi-religious, anti-administration feeling, based on the ideas mentioned.

The country from an economic standpoint was never in better condition. The gross national product runs in the neighborhood of 344 billion dollars, national income 290 billions, both records for all time.

There are 63,300,000 employed in civilian pursuits and only 1.4 million out of work, another all time high record for holders of jobs.

More farmers own farms, have more conveniences than ever before in this or any other country. Wages for all workers are at an all time high. Business profits are at record rates. Yet Propaganda, character assassination and glamour overshadowed these hard facts.

For seven years the country had faced the Soviet threat—in Iran, in Greece and Turkey, in Berlin and in Korea and Indo-China—and faced it successfully. Yet one demagogic statement made the people forget![2]

Had the election of the President been close, the Democratic loss could have been laid at the door of the management of the situation from Jan. 1 '52 until the election.

The Governor of Illinois was urged in Jan. and Feb. to agree to be the Democratic candidate. He refused and kept refusing until the day came around for the nominations of candidates for President by the Democratic Convention.

In the meantime a fakir from Tennessee who had made some glamorous investigations of local crime conditions was openly campaigning from one end of the country to the other for the nomination. There were native son candidates from Oklahoma, N.Y. & Mass. A meeting of some leading Democrats had been held and it was decided to put the name of Vice President Barkley before the Convention. This meeting was held in June [July] after the Gov. of Ill. had again refused the support of the leading Democrats who would control the Convention.

---

2. Eisenhower's promise to go to Korea.

The Convention met, was welcomed by the Mayor of Chicago and the Governor of Illinois. The Gov. made a fine speech.

Barkley held a meeting with some labor leaders on Monday, was refused their support and withdrew over the protest of his friends.

On the morning of the day for the nominations for President the Governor of Illinois called the White House and asked if the President would be embarrassed if he allowed his friends to nominate him. He was informed that there would be no embarrassment. But he let the old counterfeit fence straddler, the Governor of Indiana, do the nominating.

The Tennessee Senator had been nominated, as had the Senator from Oklahoma, the Governor of Mass., who had been the keynote speaker, Mr. Harriman from New York and one or two others—Dick Russell from the South being one of them.

The Convention had been very skillfully handled by its National Committee Chairman, together with its temporary Chairman and keynote speaker, the Gov. of Mass., and by the permanent chairman, the Speaker of the House of Representatives, who has no equal as a presiding officer.

The balloting began. On the third ballot the Sen. from Tenn. had 360 votes, the Gov. of Ill. 330, the Sen. from Georgia 267, Harriman 87, the Gov. of Mass. the Mass. delegation etc. The Convention recessed as the President arrived in Chicago for the purpose of presenting the nominee to the Convention.

At a dinner at the Saddle and Sirloin Club it was decided that Mr. Harriman and the Gov. of Mass. would withdraw in favor of the Gov. of Ill. When the Convention reconvened this was done and the nomination of the Governor of Illinois was assured.

After the acceptance speech a conference was held behind the stage and Senator Sparkman was agreed to as the candidate for Vice President. Those present were Sam Rayburn, Adlai Stevenson, Frank McKinney and the President.

Then the Governor set up a headquarters in the City of Springfield, presided over by Wilson Wyatt of Louisville, Kentucky, former Mayor of Louisville and former President of A.D.A.

The Governor then fired Mr. McKinney and had Stu Mitchell made National Chairman of the Democratic Committee. That made the National Headquarters in Washington and the Governor's Hqtrs. in Springfield, both to be presided over by amateurs. This is no reflection on either Mr. Wyatt or Mr. Mitchell but merely a statement of fact. The Chairman of a great political party must know what it is all about and he can't learn it in three months and from the top place.

There have been many Chairmen of the National Committee and

there have been some very good ones. Frank McKinney was one of the very good Chairmen, in fact there has never been a better one. The organization was set to go as it had never been set before. When McKinney was fired the organization fell apart and the best efforts of all concerned were not up to making a going concern out of the two-headed arrangement.

That did not cause us to lose the election. I doubt if anyone could have won on the Democratic ticket in 1952. But we did not get all the votes we were entitled to, even in a losing year.

Had Stevenson agreed to go when he was urged to do so in January or February he could have been sold to the country *before* the Convention. There would have been no other candidates with the possible exception of Russell of Georgia and it is doubtful he'd have let his name be used at the Convention with the Governor of Illinois. It would have been easier to finance the campaign—which the Committee was unsuccessful in doing.

The Governor wrote a letter to an Oregon paper and referred to "the mess in Washington." Of course the opposition pounced on that phrase and made a campaign slogan out of it.

The Governor found it very difficult to believe that a life-long politician can be an honest man. He did not and does not yet understand the necessity of organization from the precinct to the National Committee.

He and Franklin Roosevelt had experienced contact with two rotten, money grabbing machines—Kelly-Nash and Tammany Hall. It did not occur to the Governor or to the President that even these terrible machines usually present honest men for public office. Republican machines like Vare's of Pa., Pratt's of N.Y., Green-McCormick and Big Bill Thompson's and the notorious Cox Machine of Cincinnati placed the crooks in office. There were never worse personal and political crooks than Pratt, Vare, Penrose, Bill Thompson, Green and the later Philadelphia City administration.

The Press—the vaunted "free" press—supported all these iniquitous Republican Machines. The outstanding crooks were all Democrats according to the "free press."

There are more honest men who are professional politicians than there are honest bankers and business men. The word of a successful man in politics is worth more than the bond of a banker, of a big business man.

So the Governor distrusted the President, the Chairman of the National Committee and the Democratic Party. He had read Bertie McCormick's awful Tribune and Hearst's Chicago sewer sheet until he more than half believed what they had to say about Roosevelt's New Deal and the President's Fair Deal. A half hearted approach never won in a political campaign. That approach did not win for Scott Lucas in Illinois, for Ernest McFarland in Arizona, for the old white hatted counterfeit in Indiana nor for various Congressmen and Senators who tried to play both sides of the street.

A man running for office must believe in his cause and make the people believe [in] it and in him.

Had the election of 1952 been close, the discharge of the National Committee Chairman, the lack of faith in the Administrations of Roosevelt and Truman would have lost that election even to Robert Taft.

1953-1971

Retirement may be a problem to many Americans, but it was no problem to Harry Truman, at least at first; in fact, he could not find time to do all the things he wanted, until, in the late 1960s, the pace of his life slowed down because of increasing ill health.

The Truman retirement was simply a translation into other activities, and because they all tended to run along simultaneously, it is difficult to describe them. In accord with the ease of travel for twentieth-century Americans, and having accustomed himself to moving about during the presidency, Truman made a great many trips, some of them vacation trips but most of them for purposes, mostly good political purposes. He and Bess went off to Hawaii in the early summer of 1953, staying at Coconut Island on the estate of his friend Ed Pauley, and in the summers of 1956 and 1958 the Trumans went to Europe, cutting a wide swath the first time, a narrow one the second. All the while the retired President was going by plane to Chicago and New York and Phoenix and San Francisco and once in a while to Los Angeles ("nut city"), cheering up the Democrats, smiting the Republicans, often returning to Independence dragging a few Republican carcasses behind, as he described his activities.

In the interstices of his trips Truman devoted himself to two educational enterprises, the first of which was production of his memoirs, published in two volumes in 1955–1956. The memoirs were no hack literary job accomplished by a few editors sent out by Doubleday to Kansas City. The President dictated them himself, with the assistance of Bill Hillman and Dave Noyes and Francis Heller, the latter a young professor of political science at the University of Kansas. When finished, and polished up a little, the result showed the author of record as the author in fact, for the memoirs moved along in the same brisk, cheerful, logical way that Truman moved.

No sooner were the memoirs finished than the President threw all his energies into arranging for construction of the Truman Library at

Independence. He had been collecting money during some of his trips around the country, and it proved possible to build the library entirely from private funds, after which he gave the building to the people of the United States and it was taken over by the General Services Administration and run by professionals of the National Archives and Records Service. The library was opened in 1957, with suitable dedication by the Kansas City Catholic archbishop. It became Truman's pride and joy, where he maintained his private office and kept his private papers and displayed the gifts presented to him during and after the presidency. In the small library auditorium he lectured visiting schoolchildren on the duties and importance of the presidency.

No former President like Truman could be expected to stay out of the hustings, and he not merely watched the ups and downs of national politics but actively took part in them. Often his former counsel Charlie Murphy got up the speeches, in Truman style, and the President worked them over. At first, in 1954, there was a Democratic success in the congressional elections, but generally speaking, the country had turned to the Republicans and for a while perhaps no one, not even the whistle-stop speaker from Independence, could do much good. In 1956 at the Democratic convention, the President came out for Averell Harriman, a hopeless cause when Stevenson chose to run again. In 1960 it was a Democratic year, but to Truman's annoyance the occasion was captured by a young man whose father put up the money. When John Kennedy won, Truman looked forward to better things, but then the administration's accent on youth, and its obvious embarrassment in dealing with nineteenth-century Democrats such as Truman and Acheson, took the shine off the Democratic victory. In 1964, Truman watched his friend Johnson win, but it was not much of a race. In 1968, the retired President was not in good enough health to think about the victory of the man whom he despised more than all his political enemies of the 1950s and 1960s.

As the years passed, the President took increasing pleasure in his family, and no event gave so much happiness as the marriage of Margaret to the newspaperman Clifton T. Daniel in 1956 and the appearance of four grandchildren, all boys, beginning with Clifton Truman Daniel in 1957.

There were the increasing illnesses of friends, and the funerals, and the lessening correspondence because of inability to get around. A gall bladder operation in 1954 hardly fazed the President, but a fall in the bathroom ten years later proved impossible to get over, and there was an almost shocking loss of weight and increasing debility. Death came on December 26, 1972, when Harry Truman was eighty-eight.

It had been a long passage since the birth of Harry S. Truman in the antediluvian year 1884, in the era of President Chester A. Arthur, in the little town of Lamar, Missouri, at a time when the people of the United States had hardly anything to do with the affairs of Europe, not to mention any other part of the world; a time when little boys could look forward to a long life without wars, when they could still help with the taming of the American West, when the industrialization of the country beckoned with chances to get rich; or they could choose (as the young Truman initially chose) to stay on the farm and plow the rich soil of states like Missouri and on occasion work in township and county elections and help keep the Democratic party in power in western Missouri, and send the right sort of senators to faraway Washington.

TO ETHEL NOLAND

January 2, 1953

Dear Ethel:

Yours was a grand letter. Of course I am sorry that your door bell could not have the three rings on Dec. 25th. I hope Nellie put enough sugar in the cranberry sauce! I'll live to be 90 and not forget.[1]

I'm glad you had a "high old Christmas." Wish I could have "dropped in" on that dinner.

Isn't it too bad that people have to carry a "cross" all their lives. I am thinking of Trumie.[2] When I get home I want to see them.

We've been knee deep in relatives lately. Had Frank and George and Fred and their wives and families and Mary Jane and Martha Ann and her new husband and now Fred and Audrey. The farm boys, Harry and Gilbert, can't come, for which I'm sorry.[3] When you think of the situation you wonder how on earth the present occupant of the White House ever arrived.

I was telling Fred Truman about the evenings Bess & I spent with you and Nellie over Caesar and Cicero. Neither of us would have made the

1. At a family dinner just before Truman went into the army during the First World War, Cousin Nellie served cranberry sauce, and had forgotten to put in the sugar. The impossible-tasting cranberries became a source of kidding for years thereafter; indeed Ethel received a postcard from France in 1918 asking about the sugar in the cranberries. [*Ed. note:* The above story is from Cousin Nellie's niece, Mrs. Ardis Haukenberry, who presently lives in the Noland house.]

2. Robert Truman Ragland, whose wife had been in the riding accident more than two years before.

3. The three Wallace brothers, Mary, and two of Vivian's children (Martha Ann, Fred); three of Vivian's sons were not present—John C. and the farm boys.

grade if we'd stayed away. And now look at us! The First Lady of the land and the Presidente!

No one knows what responsibility the Presidency puts on a man.

He is the chief executive, the commander in chief of all the armed forces, the top man in his party, the social head of the State and the President of the United States.

Alexander the Great, Augustus Caesar, Jenghis Khan, Louis XIV, Napoleon nor any other of the great historical figures had the power or the world influence of the President of the U.S.A.

It bears down on a country boy. But I'm coming home Jan. 20th, 1953, and, I hope, pull a Cincinnatus, who was old G. Washington's ideal.

There are three things that get a man. No. 1 is Power—Alexander, Julius Caesar, Jenghis Khan, Tamerlane, Napoleon 1. No. 2 is ambition for high social recognition. That is all tinsel and fake. No. 3 is appetite or inability to exercise physical restraint.

Alexander—too much wine at the wrong time.

Caesar—too much trust in ladies and what he thought were friends.

Napoleon—ideas of grandeur, his "star" and no control over his passions.

What a letter!

Happy New Year.

Harry

DIARY

January 20, 1953

Inauguration Day—a beautiful day. I spend from 8:45 to 10:30 in the office winding up odds & ends and telling the clerks & secret service boys goodbye.

The Cabinet and their wives are in the Red Room when I arrive back at the House. We have a most pleasant visit until the General and his entourage arrive. Then we leave for the Capitol. I ride with Ike in car No. 1 along with Joe Martin & Styles Bridges. Bess & Margie ride with Mrs. Ike.

Conversation is general—on the crowd, the pleasant day, the orderly turnover etc. Ike finally said that Kenneth Royall tried to order him home in 1948 for the inaugural ceremony but he wouldn't come because half the people cheering me at that time had told him they were for him. I said, "Ike I didn't ask you to come—or you'd been here." Bridges gasped and Joe Martin changed the subject.

Ceremony came off as scheduled. Mrs. T., Margaret and I left the platform, entered a car on the south side of it and drove to Georgetown to the home of Dean Acheson, where we met the other members of the Cabinet and their wives along with John & Mrs. Steelman the stabilization director, Mr. Fowler[1] & Mrs. Fowler, Charley & Mrs. Murphy and Matt and Mrs. Connelly. It was a grand luncheon. The Chief Justice was there and received a good ribbing for alleged disrespect to the former President.

The street in front of Dean's house was full of people who cheered as if I were coming in instead of going out. Went to Matt's apartment and had a nap, then went to the train at 5:30 P.M. An immense crowd—some 9 or 10 thousand by police estimate. Took four policemen & 3 secret service men to get us to the car. Never anything like it, so it is said. Train pulled out amid cheers & tears. Crowd at Silver Spring, Md., some three or four hundred. Crowd at Harpers Ferry, Grafton, and it was reported to me at every stop all night long. Same way across Indiana and Illinois.

DIARY

January 21, 1953

Three or four thousand people at the station in St. Louis, a grand reception. Crowds at Washington, Hermann and more than a thousand at Jefferson City, California, Tipton and all along the line the same. Mr. Younty at Tipton gave me a haircut.

Arrived at Independence one hour late, 8:15 [P.M.] instead of 7:15. There were more than 10,000 people at the station—such a crowd and such a jam no one could get through. Never was such a crowd or such a welcome in Independence. There were 5000 more at the house at 219 No. Delaware St. Mrs. T. & I were overcome. It was the pay-off for thirty years of hell and hard work.

DIARY

March 20, 1953

We left K.C. last night, Mar. 19th at 9:45. We were 15 minutes late! Some two months ago it was decided, after various and sundry conferences with Bess & Margie, that we'd go to the Hawaiian Islands for a rest and vacation. Well we are on the way there.

I bought rail tickets and bedrooms on the U.P. to San Francisco a month ago. Averell Harriman had called me from Hobe Sound, Florida,

1. Director, Office of Defense Mobilization.

and told me he would be in K.C. on the 19th and would then go on to Sun Valley.

The Ex V.P. of the U.P.R.R. called me and informed me that Mr. Harriman's business car would be attached to the U.P.'s City of St. Louis, the train on which I had the bedrooms and would I ride it to Ogden, Utah. Well, of course I would.

Bess and I had been sure we'd never ride a special car again after we arrived in Independence Jan. 21, 1953, on the Ferdinand Magellan, the Private Car of the President of the United States. Ike had asked us to use it. We appreciated his courtesy. He had also offered the Independence to us. The Independence is a DC-6 with every gadget and safety device there is on it. It had the first T.V. set, on which we saw ourselves take off for Chicago on Thursday of the Democratic Convention of 1952.

My sister, Mary Jane, and Bess' brothers, Frank and George, and May and Natalie (May & Natalie are the wives of Frank & George) came to the K.C. Union Station to see us off. So did Art Ball, Fred Ralphs [?], Tom Evans and a lot of news men and many others.[1]

DIARY

[April 1953]

The trip on the President Cleveland of the American President Lines from San Francisco to Honolulu by way of Los Angeles was a most pleasant one.

We sailed from San Francisco Bay at 11 o'clock in the morning of March 22, 1953. It was a very beautiful day, sunny and pleasant. A great crowd was at the dock to see the ship off, the outline of the city's skyline from the bay side was a sight to remember.

We arrived in Los Angeles at breakfast time and had a session with the press boys and the photographers.

Dave Noyes, Anna Roosevelt, her son and husband came aboard and stayed for luncheon. We had a most pleasant visit. The evening of the 23rd the Wine and Food Association gave a dinner aboard which was a very pleasant affair.

We sailed at noon on the 24th for the beautiful islands in the center of the Pacific.

Not a good sailor, I spent the first day out in bed but recovered on the second day and enjoyed the whole cruise from that day on.

Many very agreeable people were on the ship, most of them on board

---

1. Tom L. Evans, owner of station KCMO in Kansas City and a chain of drugstores in the Kansas City area, was a long-time friend of the President.

for the whole trip around the Pacific, Japan, Formosa, Hong Kong, Manila, Japan and then Hawaii and home.

We arrived off Oahu early on the morning of March 29th. It was a lovely day. Diamond Head and then Honolulu with the Pali in the background, rainbows, clouds, sunshine and a beautiful city all in one scene.

We docked at 8 A.M. amid a noisy reception. Officials of all ranks were present. Admiral Radford, Commander in Chief of the Pacific, escorted us off the ship and to our destination. Photographers, news men and numerous reception committees came aboard and covered us with leis and smothered us with questions and flash bulbs.

We finally boarded cars and were escorted through the crowds by the Hawaiian police, and over the Pali to Kaneohe Bay, where Mr. Pauley met us. We boarded the Admiral's launch and arrived at Coconut Island, where Mrs. Pauley and all the children met us and escorted us to the beautiful house on the hill.

Admiral Radford returned to Pearl Harbor and we began one of the most pleasant vacations we ever experienced! A grand dinner was ready for us and four Hawaiian girls danced the historical dances of ancient Hawaii for us, explaining the meaning of each movement in the lore of the wonderful people who had inhabited the Islands before Captain Cook came and spoiled the situation.

We went to our quarters after the grand midday dinner, took a nap, put on vacation clothes afterwards and went to the swimming hole, after which we had another dinner, a pleasant evening under the palm trees and went to bed at ten o'clock.

I was up early as usual and walked over and around the island. I found afterwards that there are 10,000 coconut palms, hibiscus, oleander, orchids and all sorts of plants and beautiful flowers which bloom all year around. There was the wreck of the old Seth Parker which was a famous Oceanographic Cruise Ship and the remains of a zoo (just the pens) which a former owner had maintained.

The University of Hawaii and the University of California maintain a fish experiment station on the island now and Mr. Pauley furnishes the endowment for it. It is a most interesting plant.

A couple of days after we arrived we let the press boys come over and look things over. The picture men had a field day and after that one time they let us enjoy ourselves.

After we had been on the island a few days I sent word to Admiral Radford that [I] would like to visit the Island of Hawaii and see the great volcano Mauna Loa. The Admiral sent me a C-47 in charge of two fine Navy Commanders and we were airborne at 7 A.M. It is a 200 mile flight from Oahu to Hawaii. The weather was perfect. I had a good view of

Molokai the leper island and at an elevation of 11,200 feet saw the Island of Maui with its 10,500 foot extinct volcano. The Navy men told me that we had the first clear day in two years at that time of day. The weather was perfect when we arrived at Hawaii. We flew over the saddle between Mauna Kea and Mauna Loa. These volcanoes are snow capped and rise to heights above the sea level of 13,800 and 13,700 feet respectively. The sea at a distance of 3 miles out is 18,000 feet deep so that from base to top these volcanoes are more than 32,000 feet high!

We landed at Hilo at about 10:30 and they gave us the usual all out reception. We drove around the city and then to the Interior Dept's building in Volcano Park where Dr. Macdonald showed some pictures of the eruptions of Mauna Loa in 1949 and 1950. These pictures are remarkable in color and show just what happened. Looking at them and with the explanations of Dr. Macdonald I felt as if I were witnessing the eruption.[1]

He told me that more than 600 million cubic yards of lava had overflown the side of the volcano and gone down to the ocean in a molten river. Thousands of fish were killed and a great many new varieties from the depths came to the surface. They were still hunting for scientific names for some of them when I was there.

We had a luncheon at the Volcano House, an Interior Department Hotel which is run by a Mr. Lycurgus. He is 93 years old and he told me he claimed to be a son of the Spartan King. He entertained us royally and showed his picture gallery with a lot of distinguished people in pictures shaking hands with him, playing cribbage with him etc.

After lunch we drove on around the Island to the Navy Air Field on the west side of it. We passed various lava flows which were pointed out to me and the dates given to me.

We passed a house in a little town where Mark Twain spent some time after he was fired from a Sacramento, Calif., paper.

When we arrived at the air field it was raining and I mean it was pouring down. A couple of Hawaii native ladies thanked me for the rain. They said that Peli the Goddess of the Great Volcano was weeping because I was leaving! But they surely needed the rain. They said that Peli was happy when I came and gave us clear weather and sorry when I left, hence the rain.

On the flight back to Kaneohe Bay we took off in the terrific rain and in ten minutes were in sunshine. We saw a school of whales below us off Maui. The navy men said that meant good luck. Well we landed safely in time for dinner.

---

1. Dr. Gordon A. Macdonald was Director of the Hawaiian Volcano Observatory, Hawaiian National Park.

[The President's notes on the trip break off here. The stay in Hawaii came to an end with departure from Honolulu on April 29. The ship arrived in San Francisco on May 3, the Trumans left by rail for Kansas City next day, and they arrived back home on May 6.]

DIARY

May 20, 1953

This morning at 7 A.M. I took off for my morning walk. I'd just had the Dodge car washed a day or so ago and it looked as if it had never been used.

The weather man had said it would rain so I decided to put the washed car in the garage and use the black car which was already spotted and dusty. My sister-in-law, watching me make the change, which required some maneuvering due to the location of several cars in the drive way, wanted to know if I might be practicing for a job in a parking station!

I went on down Van Horn Road (some call it Truman Road now) and took a look at the work progressing on the widening for a two way traffic line through the county seat. A shovel (automatic) and a drag line were working as well as some laboring men digging in the old fashioned way. The boss or the contractor was looking on and I asked him if he didn't need a good strawboss. He took a look at me and then watched the work a while and then took another look and broke out in a broad smile and said "Oh yes! You *are* out of a job aren't you."

Went on around the block and came up to Maple Ave. and River Blvd., where a couple of women and a man were getting into a car preparatory to going to work. The man and one of the women came over and stopped me and said they wanted to shake my hand and tell me they had left Washington on Nov. 8th when they knew I wouldn't be there longer. But they said they had lived in Alexandria and not on Pennsylvania Avenue!

A day or two ago I was walking down Farmer Street about 7:30 A.M. when a nice old lady and gentleman standing in a door way that opens directly on the sidewalk asked me if I would please cross the street as they wanted to talk to me. I crossed over and the nice grey haired lady said to the man "You tell him, I'm shaking so I can hardly talk." The old man told me that his wife wanted me to write my name in their granddaughter's note book. The granddaughter lived in Detroit and was very sure that anybody in Independence [could] get me to do whatever was wanted. I'd never seen the old people before but I signed the granddaughter's autograph book.

A day or so before that I was walking up the hill at Union and Maple and was stopped by a bunch of boys and girls for the purpose of having a picture made with a young man named Adams who was running for President of the Student Council. I wonder how he came out. That stunt may have beaten him.

DIARY

July 8, 1953

I went walking this morning as I usually do when the weather permits and my mail reading is not overwhelming.

It was a beautiful sunny morning. I left the backporch where I was reading piles of mail and walked out the gate behind the old barn— which is now a two car garage. It was a four car garage but these new wide cars have halved its capacity.

As I walked out of the alley into Delaware Street a young man jumped [out] of his car on the west side of the street and said that he and his wife had been waiting for a chance to see me. He was from Strateor (look it up), Ill., said he'd seen me from the station there on my campaign tour.[1] He was a nice looking man and his wife was a pretty young woman. Both looked sleepy. They'd evidently arisen early so as to be sure they had a chance to see me and shake hands.

I always try to be as pleasant as I can to the numerous people who want to see and talk to me. They, of course, don't know that I walk early to get a chance to think over things and get ready for work of the day. But they come from every State in the Union and I must consider that they've made a special effort to see me—so I treat them accordingly even [if] it does sometimes spoil a train of thought.

Well I went to Maple Ave., turned left "toward town" and spoke to several people, turned south on Pleasant Street. After I'd passed the light at Lexington I met a young man, Frank A. Reynolds, who introduced himself as John Strother's son-in-law. We talked a few minutes and I thought of the Strother family—one of the best old families in the County.

John was Democratic Committeeman from Blue Township (Independence) from the time I was road overseer in Washington Township until I went to Washington as U.S. senator from Missouri. He was a grand man—but wouldn't tell his age! He was in my father's generation and he

---

1. As the President suspected, he had misspelled the name. It is Streator.

always wanted to be young with the young men. He was a good lawyer and an honest one too.

Just as I started to leave Mr. Strother's son-in-law—and there were other great Strothers: Sam, who was a pillar of the Democratic Party in Kansas City; a second generation Judge, Duvall, and many others—as I say, just [as] I started to walk again a car stopped across the street and a man jump[ed] out and came over to shake hands and said "I'm sure you can't remember me—it's been so long since you've seen me." I did though. I told him whose son he is and who his grandfather was! Some feat for a man who has met millions of people.

He belonged to the Pugh family. His grandfather, Noah E Pugh, was one fine man. He came out to Missouri in 1894 or 1895 and settled on my mother's part of her father's estate, 160 acres south east of the present home farm about three miles. Mr. Pugh had several sons and daughters older and younger than I. Conley Pugh was a few years older than I and was married to a nice Grandview girl when they were very young. It was a happy marriage and the man who stopped me is Conley's oldest boy. He told me that he had four children. It is remarkable indeed how time flies and makes you an old man whether you want to be or not.

I finished my walk and went back to work on the mail and my memoirs. I suppose I'll always be busy as the proverbial bee from morn to night.

MEMORANDUM

July 8, 1953

When you contemplate a career think only of the service you can render to your fellowmen.

Study the lives of great men—the truly great men. Men who have made sacrifices for the betterment of the world and their individual countries and communities.

There are all sorts of men and women who have made history. Abraham, Isaac, Jacob, Joseph, Moses, Joshua, the Great Prophets of Israel. Hammurabi the great Sumerian law-giver, Solon, Lycurgus, Aristides, Cyrus the Great, Darius the Great, Alexander, Hannibal, Caesar, Jenghis Khan, Tamerlane, the Great Mogul, Saladin, Suleiman the Magnificent, Charles Martel, Charlemagne, Napoleon to name a few.

Then there were Buddha, Jesus, Cincinnatus, George Washington, Abraham Lincoln, Woodrow Wilson.

Some men of great name were destroyers of mankind, some were law-givers, some were just plain patriots, some were philosophers, some left the world worse off than they found it, some left it better off.

The moralists and philosophers left the world a much greater heritage than did most of the rulers and conquerors.

Marcus Aurelius, Antoninus Pius and Justinian were rulers and also law-givers and moralists. Their successors were no good. I wonder why?

In that connection I often think of Plato and his report of the teachings of Socrates, one of the really great teachers and philosophers of all time. Then I think of Alcibiades and Aristides. One a first class demagogue and rounder and the other a great ruler of Athens. But the Athenians didn't appreciate the honorable Aristides. They banished him for one reason, because they were tired hearing him called the just. They loved Alcibiades because he was no good!

I've always been a very great admirer of three great men in government, Cincinnatus the old Roman Dictator, Cato the Younger who was the Republican Romans' greatest and most honorable administrator. And then George Washington our own first President.

Cincinnatus knew when and how to lay down his great powers. After he had saved the Republic he went back to his plow and became the good private citizen of his country. Cato, in an age of grafters and demagogues, ran the great Roman Republic for the people. He audited and handled the finances of the Roman Provinces and of Rome itself honestly—something unheard of in that day of the declining Republic.

Washington knew when and how to quit public office and lay down the immense power he wielded with the people, as did Cincinnatus. After he'd won the war to create this United States, presided over the Constitutional Convention, and set the country on the right road to greatness, he returned to his farm and became a model citizen of his country. He could have been king, president for life if he'd been ambitious for power.

I've given you an outline of a course of study. Take the men I've named. Find out what they did and how they did it and why they did it. What effect did their acts have on their countries and on the world.

The President worried about the condition of the Democratic party, especially after Stevenson had disbanded its organization by replacing Chairman McKinney, and arranged a meeting in Detroit of the factions, including Chairman Mitchell. Stevenson had gone abroad on a trip, and the idea was to give him an enthusiastic welcome back to Chicago.

DIARY

The Blackstone, Chicago
[September 6, 1953]

3:25. Left the airport at Kansas City. The wheels left the ground at 3:29 Kansas City time, 4:29 Chicago time. Wheels hit the ground at 6:03 Chicago time, 1:34 hrs flight time.

A little seven year old girl with two front teeth missing was in the seat just in front of mine. Her grandmother had brought her to the plane and had told her she was sitting in the seat ahead of mine. . . . She looked out of the window most of the time and called my attention to the fact that we were above or below the clouds and that the automobiles looked like bugs crawling along the roads.

I told her that if she hadn't put her tongue in the place where her front teeth came out she would probably have had two gold teeth. I told her that my grandmother had told me that.

A couple of small boys were on the plane too going from California to Pittsburgh. The nice stewardess brought them to my seat to shake hands. None of these children had any relative with them! Can you imagine Mrs. Truman and myself allowing Margaret to ride a plane by herself when she was seven? I can't.

The T.W.A. people had arranged for me to be met by a car to take me to the Blackstone, but at that I was recognized and waved and asked questions. But the arrival at the hotel was all right, as quiet as could be. The manager met me at the door and told me he'd have had a brass band to meet me if I'd let him do it. He would have done just that too.

I called Mrs. T. as soon as I arrived at my room, and then answered a call from Matt Connelly in Detroit. He was worried about Steve Mitchell's coming to Detroit. But I'd told Steve to come there to talk to me about the Chicago meeting of the Democrats to welcome Stevenson. It is a ticklish business. But I have only one road to tread—a straight one to retirement!

TO DEAN ACHESON

October 2, 1953

Dear Dean:

I failed to send you a telegram last night for the simple reason that I was out in the midst of the Caruthersville Fair Grounds making a speech on the educational necessities of the next generation. I left in a hurry to drive eighty miles in an hour and a half in order to catch a train to be home this morning. . . .

I have been going down to Caruthersville for twenty or twenty-five years because that southeast corner of Missouri has always been in my corner politically and I went down there this time since I was out of office and not running for office to show them I was just interested in them. I had one of the biggest crowds they ever had when I addressed the meeting and I got a bigger ovation than I did when I was President of the United States. They gave me a great big silver cup engraved—

Harry S. Truman
From your friends and admirers in Caruthersville.

They had to take me eighty miles to a city down in Arkansas, Jonesboro, to catch the train for home. There had been no previous announcement that I was to go there but when I got to the station there were two thousand people there. It took two policemen and a Deputy Sheriff to get me on the train. I don't know what the world is coming to when people in Arkansas and southeast Missouri, which is about the same as the deep South, turn out like that for an Ex-President, who has told them where to get off on Civil Rights. Maybe the world is turning over. I think I'll put up a tent and charge admission!

Sincerely,
Harry S. Truman

Vic H. Housholder was an old member of Battery D, with whom the President exchanged dozens of letters.

TO VIC H. HOUSHOLDER

The Blackstone, Chicago
November 29, 1953

Dear Vic:

. . . Sometime I wish I'd done what Pete Allen did and stayed in the Army in 1919. But I guess fate had a hand in what you and I did at that time. Maybe it has been for the best. I hope it has.

I'd give most anything to pay a visit to Arizona, go to Becker's place[1] in the White Mountains and visit Tombstone, see the Grand Canyon on

---

1. Julius Becker was a friend of twenty years' standing, interested in good roads and associated with the National Old Trails Roads Association.

the ground and do a lot of other things you want me to do. But Vic I'm a nuisance to my friends. I can't seem to get from under that awful glare that shines on the White House.

Mrs. T. and I thought we'd solved the problem when I bought a Chrysler car and we started for Washington.[2] When we'd crossed the Missouri River at Waverly on highway 24 on our way to Hannibal the "Boss" said to me, "Isn't it good to be on our own again, doing as we please as we did in the old Senate days?" I said that I thought it was grand and that I hoped we'd do as we pleased from that time on.

We stopped at Hannibal, Mo., for lunch at the junction of highways 61 & 36. Everything went well until a couple of oldtime County Judges came in and saw me. They said "Why there's Judge Truman" —and then every waitress and all the customers had to shake hands and have autographs. We went on to Decatur, Ill., and stopped for gas at a Shell station where I used to stop when I was a Senator. The old man kept looking at me as he filled up the gas tank and finally he asked me if I was Senator Truman. I admitted the charge and asked him if he could direct me to the good Motel in the town. We'd never stayed at one and we wanted to try it out and see if we liked it. Well he directed us but he told everybody in town about it. The Chief of Police got worried about us and sent two plain clothes men and four uniformed police to look after us. They took us to dinner and to breakfast the next morning and escorted us out of town with a sigh of relief.

Well that happened at Wheeling, W. Va., Washington, Pa., and Washington, D.C. It happened in New York, in Pennsylvania on the fast highway where a Pa. highway cop stopped me so he could shake hands and the papers said I was stopped for a traffic violation! So, Vic, we've decided that until the glamour wears off we'll only do the official things we have to. Take last night, I spoke to 23,000 people in the auditorium where I was nominated for V.P. in 1944. They gave me a present of a silver seven branch candlestick like Moses used in the Tabernacle, and did everything but elect me President of the USA and Israel! What the hell am I to do? I hope sometime this glamour will wear off but until it does I can't inflict myself on my friends.

Be patient and let's hope for the best, because I want to visit you and Arizona.

Sincerely,
Harry S. Truman

2. On June 19, 1953.

Late in November the President went to New York to participate in the announcement, during a dinner at the Waldorf, of the Weizmann scientific awards, named after the first president of the State of Israel.

DIARY

The Waldorf-Astoria, New York
November 30, 1953

Been reading an article in the New Republic on Art with a capital A. It is a review of a book by André Malraux called Voices of Silence. After reading it I felt as if I'd read a third level State Department monograph on the Cold War. But the reviewer wound up with an understandable sentence, he advised the reader to buy the book for $25.00. Most modern readers dislike to pay 25 cents for a Western or a Murder Mystery. Can you imagine any one of them paying $25.00 for a book on "Art"?

Well the vast majority of readers will not pay $25.00 for any book, let alone one of capital A Art.

I am very much interested in beautiful things, beautiful buildings, lovely pictures, music—real music, not noise.

The Parthenon, Taj Mahal, St Paul's Cathedral in London, York Minster, Chartres Cathedral, the Dome of the Rock in Jerusalem, the Capitol buildings of Mississippi, West Virginia, Utah, Missouri, the New York Life Building, N.Y. City, the Sun Insurance building, Montreal, the Parliament Building in London, the Madeleine in Paris, the lovely Palace of Versailles, St Mark's and the Doge's Palace in Venice.

Pictures, Mona Lisa, the Merchant, the Laughing Cavalier, Turner's landscapes, Remington's Westerns and dozens of others like them. I dislike Picasso, and all the moderns—they are lousy. Any kid can take an egg and a piece of ham and make more understandable pictures.

Music, Mozart, Beethoven, Bach, Mendelssohn, Strauss Waltzes, Chopin waltzes, Polonaises, Etudes, Von Weber, Rondo Brilliante, Polacca Brilliante. Beautiful harmonies that make you love them. They are not noise. It is music.

Early in the Eisenhower administration, the chairman of the House Un-American Activities Committee, Harold H. Velde, sought to make capital out of the case of Harry Dexter White, an assistant secretary of the treasury, who according to allegations had been under the influence of communism and perhaps was even a member of the Communist Party. According to the interpretation placed upon his actions by his

detractors, White had foisted off on Secretary of the Treasury Morgen-
thau the plan for the pastoralization of Germany known as the Morgen-
thau Plan, the proposal given by the secretary to Churchill and Roose-
velt at the second Quebec conference in 1944. The plan was deemed a
"Communist plot," because if it had gone into effect, the result would
have been the economic collapse of the Continent—Germany was the
economic center of Europe, and pastoralization would have meant no
economic center. On November 9, 1953, Congressman Velde audaciously
subpoenaed former President Truman to appear before the committee
on Friday, November 13, in Washington. Truman angrily refused to
comply, and issued a forthright statement accusing Velde of seeking to
violate a "long line of precedents commencing with George Washington
himself in 1796."

At stake in the Velde affair, the President said, was the doctrine of
separation of powers. Also at stake was the reputation of the Truman
administration, for White had served in the administration—after leav-
ing the treasury, he became United States executive director of the Inter-
national Monetary Fund—until shortly before his death in 1947. It was
clear to Truman that the Republicans, in the person of Attorney General
Herbert Brownell, Jr., were out to get him. Truman released his letter to
Velde on November 11, and followed it five days later with a blast di-
rected straight at Brownell, whom he was careful to describe as the
former chairman of the Republican National Committee. Brownell had
announced that "Harry Dexter White was known to be a communist spy
by the very people who appointed him," and the President lashed back
that Brownell had "degraded the highest function of Government—the
administration of justice—into cheap political trickery." Truman said
it was evident that the Eisenhower administration, for political advan-
tage, had fully embraced McCarthyism, the corruption of truth, the
abandonment of devotion to fair play, the abandonment of due process,
and gone over to use of the big lie, the spread of fear, the destruction of
faith. The President pulled out all the stops. For his own private record
Truman made the following account of the situation.

MEMORANDUM

[November 1953]

Asst. Sec. of the Treasury White

Mr. White was Asst. Secretary of the Treasury under Secretary of the
Treasury Mr. Morgenthau [who] made a plan for the elimination of the
industrial section of Germany. Mr. White helped him draw up the plan.

It was discussed at Quebec when President Roosevelt and Mr. Churchill met there to discuss a number of things.

When Mr. Roosevelt died and I became President a conference was agreed on by Stalin, Churchill and me. The conference was to be held at Berlin. It is known as the Potsdam Conference.

Mr. Morgenthau wanted to go. I told him he could not go and he resigned from the Cabinet.

After Mr. Vinson became Secretary of the Treasury a bank conference was called for Savannah. It was decided that Mr. White should not go to the conference and he resigned.

There had been some question about White's friendliness to Russia and the F.B.I. had made a report on him based we afterwards found on statements made to the F.B.I. by a crook and a louse, Mrs. Bentley and Whittaker Chambers. Statements by these people are about as reliable as to facts as are those of any communist and a communist isn't supposed to tell the truth, not even under torture.

Mr. White appeared before one of the Committees of Congress and swore that he was a loyal citizen and that the Bentley and Chambers report of the F.B.I. was untrue.

Mr. White then died of a heart attack and Mr. Vinson has also passed away.[1] Convicting a dead man of treason on a communist F.B.I. report is in line with present administration policy.

MEMORANDUM

[1953?]

I'm thinking of a program for youngsters of senior high school age and first and second year college. My plan is to address assemblies of high schools and colleges on citizenship, political responsibility and the duty a citizen owes to the Republic of which he is a citizen.

I want to give high schools and small colleges preference. I have an idea that 100 schools with 1000 students are of much more value to the country than two schools with 50,000 students.

The objective is to build character, find brain power and make responsible citizens to keep the freedom of the individual intact.

Personal contact with instructors of character is absolutely essential to these objectives. Mass production of college graduates is not the answer to an educated citizenship.

When the pioneers came into the Ohio-Mississippi-Missouri valley the first thing they thought of after shelter and safety for their families

---

1. The chief justice died on September 8, 1953.

was education for the children. In every settlement a church was built and then a school house—sometimes one building for both purposes.

Some of the greatest men of the 19th century in our great nation had to make the hardest kind of struggle for education. The fundamentals, reading, writing and arithmetic, were hard to obtain.

As the settlements grew and communications improved great schools both religious and secular grew also. I am anxious to see that thirst for knowledge encouraged at the base.

The GI Bill of Rights proved conclusively that young men from 18 to 26 after some experience thirst for learning and that they are willing to work hard and at some disadvantage for an education.

My definition of an education is the lighting of that spark which is called a "thirst for information or knowledge." A college graduate with the right sort of instruction should find at his graduation that he is only at the door of knowledge. He should have learned in going through his schooling *where to find the information on the subjects that make for scholarship.*

If he hasn't learned that, the time spent in school has been wasted for no good purpose.

If, when he comes out of school, that thirst for learning has been brought out he never ceases to find fields for study that open up endlessly before him.

The old idea that grammar, rhetoric, logic, arithmetic, geometry, music and astronomy constitute the basis of an education is just as true now as it always has been.

Archimedes, Aristotle, Euclid, Galileo, Leonardo da Vinci, Sir Isaac Newton, Einstein all started from these fundamentals, as did the great literary lights and the great musicians.

So let's not forget basic principles based on character.

Early in January Truman went to New York for a luncheon given by the Radio and Television Executives Society, at the Roosevelt Hotel.

DIARY

The Waldorf-Astoria, New York
January 9, 1954

This visit to New York has been an eye opener as other visits have been. When the plane Bill Hillman and I were on arrived at the N.Y. Airport photographers and reporters met us as they had done in the past.

Fifteen or twenty of them took pictures as we descended from the plane.

Inside the building T.V. and News Reels were set up and the men in charge asked me the usual questions about things in general and Eisenhower's State of the Union Message. I told them that Ike's New Deal recommendations merited support, that his political statements had the usual demagogic sound. I was thinking particularly about his statement that he is against "Socialized Medicine." So is every one. The American Medical Association in 1952 had a mild case of hydrophobia over my suggestion that a health tax be levied by the Federal Government so the ordinary fellow could pay his doctor and hospital bills when an emergency arose in his family.

Most people can't pay $12.00 to $25.00 a day for a hospital room and $500.00 for a minor operation in addition to nurse hire and incidentals. So I thought and I still think that a nest egg held out of the regular pay as is social security might meet the situation. If the propaganda of A.M.A. is studied you'd find the doctors don't want guarantee payments for fees. Why I'll never know.

Ike received a great hand from the Republican side on this piece of demagoguery. He offered nothing and suggested no real program.

I've had the usual reception here. Wish my "glamour" would come off so I can be a "regular citizen" again. Looks now as if it never will.

MEMORANDUM

April 24, 1954

I have often thought of the situation when the Chinese marched into Korea in late 1950. General MacArthur had assured me at Wake Island a month or two before the "Volunteers" came over the Yalu that it wouldn't happen. Apparently his information service was not what it should have been. High ranking military men usually surround themselves with trained "yes men" so that they may hear how good and great the Commander is and how well his guesses afterward turn to facts.

The Great General was not the same man he was at Wake after the Chinese came from the north. He began writing letters to Republican Congressmen and giving interviews to such sheets as Dave Lawrence publishes in Washington. He even went so far as to crib the two main paragraphs from a message I had expected to send to Mao, at Peking, and use them himself as an ultimatum to the Chinese–North Korean Commander in the field.

After he was relieved he spent some time discussing the fact that the President of the United States and his Commander in Chief would not allow him to carry on a war in Manchuria. General Mark Clark in his book "From the Danube to the Yalu" implies that the "police action" in Korea could have been a victorious "war" in the Far East if he and his predecessors had been given a free hand to bomb Manchuria.

These able field Generals see only the front they work to hold and win. The Commander-in-Chief must see not only Asia and the Pacific Ocean, he must see Europe, Africa, the whole Southern Hemisphere, the Arctic, and the Antarctic.

Now suppose, for speculative purposes, the C in C had yielded to his locally minded and in most cases locally misinformed field Generals. What would have happened? The Generals say that a few bombs on airfields in Manchuria would have caused a Korean victory to the Yalu.

To have been effective Peking, Shanghai, Canton, Mukden, Dairen, Vladivostok and Central Siberia at Ulan-Ude on Lake Baikal would have had to be destroyed. It would have been a unilateral action by the U.S.A.

On the European side of the Soviet Empire the Russians would have marched to the North Sea and the Channel. We had six divisions of our own and about that many of our allies to oppose them. They had over 4,000,000 men in their ground forces. They could not have been stopped.

On the east we would have wiped out those great Chinese cities and have killed some 25,000,000 innocent women, children and noncombatants.

We'd have had World War III on our hands and no allies. All Central Europe and perhaps Turkey, Greece, Italy and North Africa with the great Near East oil field would have been under Russian control.

In the first place I could not bring myself to order the slaughter of 25,000,000 noncombatants. In 1945 I had ordered the A Bomb dropped on Japan at two places devoted almost exclusively to war production. We were at war. We were trying to end it in order to save the lives of our soldiers and sailors. The new bomb was a powerful new weapon of war. In my opinion it had to be used to end the unnecessary slaughter on both sides. It was an entirely different situation from Korea. We stopped the war and saved thousands of casualties on both sides.

In Korea we were fighting a police action with sixteen allied nations to support the World Organization which had set up the Republic of Korea. We had held the Chinese after defeating the North Koreans and whipping the Russian Air Force.

I just could not make the order for a Third World War. I know I was *right*.

President in his own right. Mr. Truman has just taken the oath, 1949. Chief Justice Fred M. Vinson *(left)*, Rep. Sam Rayburn, Speaker of the House *(far left)*; Charles E. Cropley, Clerk of Supreme Court holding the Bible *(center)*; Vice President Alben Barkley *(far right)*. *(Wide World Photos)*

At a state banquet for His Imperial Majesty, the Shah of Iran. *(Abbie Rowe, National Park Service)*

Blair House. The President and First Family lived here from 1949 to 1952, while repairs were being done on the White House.

Taking no chances after the assassination attempt, the President rides in a bulletproof limousine, followed by heavily armed secret service men, maneuvering the short distance between the White House executive offices and Blair House. *(Wide World Photos)*

Marching in the 1949 reunion parade of the 35th Division in Little Rock, Arkansas. *Left to right:* Frank Spina, Louis Johnson, HST, Sid McMath, and Harry Vaughan.

President Truman and General Douglas MacArthur greet each other for the first time on Wake Island. *(UPI Photo)*

Leaving Washington, 1953; "...went to the train at 5:30 P.M. An immense crowd—some 9 or 10 thousand by police estimate. Took four policemen & 3 secret service men to get us to the car. Never anything like it, so it is said. Train pulled out amid cheers & tears." (Diary, January 20, 1953) *(UPI Photo)*

The Truman home in Independence, Missouri. *(Independence Examiner)*

With no one else in sight, the
former President crosses a street,
alone and quite happy about it.
(St. Louis Post-Dispatch)

HST addressing a high-school audience.

HST walking with F. Forlati in San Marco Square in Venice, Italy, 1956.

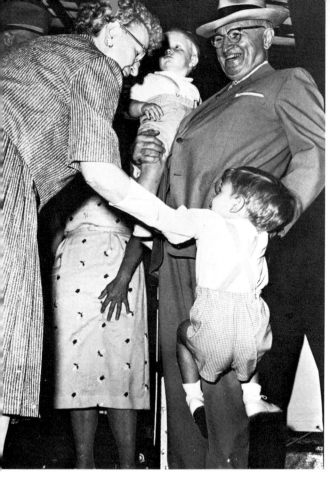

The former President and
Mrs. Truman with grandchildren.

Mary Jane, Harry S., and J. Vivian Truman, in the office at the Harry S. Truman Library, 1963.

Fiftieth wedding anniversary, 1969. *(Ken White)*

MEMORANDUM

June 2, 1954

Reading over the minutes of Potsdam: the agreement over the Black Sea Straits and the recognition of Rumania and Bulgaria took two whole sessions. Stalin was anxious to have the de facto governments of the two Balkan countries recognized. I refused because our representatives were not allowed freedom of movement by the puppet governments set up by the Soviets.

Molotov did a lot of talking at Potsdam. He and Stalin along with Trotsky and Lenin were among the old Bolsheviks of the 1917 Revolution.

Molotov would take the bit in his teeth and talk as if he were the Russian State until Stalin would smile and say a few words in Russian and Molly would change his tune.

When Molotov came to the United States he acted like a balky mule and the only way I could build a fire under him was to send Harry Hopkins to Moscow to tell Stalin what was happening. When Stalin was approached directly by Harriman, Hopkins, or myself we usually obtained what we wanted.

We all thought that Molly never gave Stalin all the facts unless he was forced to do it. I always felt that Molotov was a complete demonstration of a perfect mutton head.

MEMORANDUM

July 1954

Most men when they reach the age to begin to think, that is from 17 to 24, want to come to an immediate conclusion as to their future place in the world. Some have been good students of history and biography—most have not. Some accept the "get by" theory, a great many honestly want to make good on merit and ability. Some become great financiers and big business men by sharp practice, some work through the great professions, medicine and law, by the same methods.

But there are honorable men in all walks of life; in fact honest men far outnumber the men of sharp practice. Honest men in the legal and medical professions have arranged a code of ethics which, if followed, there would be no sharp practice in either of those professions.

In politics which is the science of government men have been discussing right and wrong and the rights of the individual since the time of the great Babylonian law giver Hammurabi, Moses the great law giver of the Hebrews, Aristotle whose essay on politics has scarcely been equaled, St. Paul and the Gospels, St. Thomas Aquinas, Marcus Aurelius Antoninus, Justinian, Machiavelli, the origins of the British Common law and the Code Napoleon.

There has been much chaff and a lot of gobbledegook written and discussed about the ethics of a politician. If the young man chooses politics as a profession he'll find it to his advantage to study the lives of all the great leaders throughout history starting with Greece and the great leaders of the city republics and the great leaders of the heyday of the Roman Republic. He should study carefully and thoroughly the rise and the leaders of the American Government from 1776 to date.

He should carefully study the lives of the leaders of the Continental Congress, the Constitutional Convention, and he should know the lives and motives of every President of the United States. Congressional leaders in every Presidential Administration should be carefully studied along with their ethics and their motives. Then he should know his State History from its colonial or territorial beginnings as well as his county history. If he lives in a town or city he should know his city government and its workings just as he should know how his county government works.

It takes seven years of hard study and an equal number of practice to make a doctor. Then he must have the desire to be one. Equally as much time is required to make a good lawyer. Some doctors and a great many lawyers never get out of the mediocre class.

It takes a life time of the hardest kind of work and study to become a successful politician. A great doctor is known by the size of his practice and his ability as a diagnostician. A great lawyer is known by his knowledge of the law and his ability to win cases and properly advise his clients. A great financier is known by the money he controls.

A great politician is known for the service he renders. He doesn't have to become President or Governor or the head of his city or county to be a great politician. There are mayors of villages, county attorneys, county commissioners or supervisors who render just as great service locally as do the heads of the government.

No young man should go into politics if he wants to get rich or if he expects an adequate reward for his services. An honest public servant can't become rich in politics. He can only attain greatness and satisfaction by service.

My political career

I had studied history, read everything I could get my hands on, including some of the encyclopedias in the Independence Library. I was particularly interested in the individuals who had made the history that the professional historians wrote and distorted to suit their own views.

If all the historians of the past wrote as Henry Adams and old man Beard and his wife did in modern times, there is very little of past history to be believed from Thucydides, Herodotus, Tacitus to Greene and Guizot. But when the lives of great men are studied from the records they leave some real idea of what happened.

My mother bought a four volume set when I was about ten years old called Great Men and Famous Women. That book with Abbott's Lives of Great Men and the Encyclopedias gave me some idea of how men attained places in history.

In reading the lives of American Presidents, Generals and Legislators I attained a knowledge of how they rose to the top. It seemed to me that farmers, military men, financiers, lawyers and school teachers usually began at the bottom, did good jobs in whatever they undertook and finally reached the top.

As soon as I was twenty-one I joined the militia. I was working in a bank, studying finance at the time I became a member of Battery B of the Missouri National Guard.

After three years in the bank at the bottom of the ladder the family moved back to the 600 acre farm which belonged to my grandmother on my mother's side. I joined the family on the farm in 1906 and with my father and brother helped to run the farm. My father was always interested in local politics wherever he happened to be.

He was appointed road overseer in a large district which included the small village of Grandview. In helping him on the road between farm work I became acquainted with everyone in the Township. In 1908 my father was reappointed a Judge of Election in Grandview Precinct and I became the Democratic Clerk. There were about 150 to 200 votes in the precinct at that time and all the judges and the two clerks knew every one of the voters. I served as clerk and my father as judge of election until his death in 1915. Then I succeeded him as road overseer. I became interested in a mining deal along with a neighbor and a promoter from Harrisonville. I learned a lot about hard rock mining and received a lot [of] experience but made no money.

In the meantime my brother had married and moved [to] another farm and I continued to run the home farm by hiring a couple of men.

In 1917 President Wilson was forced into the war by the German submarine policy. I had been very much interested in his nomination in 1912 and became one of his great admirers. All of us in the Democratic line-up were very highly pleased with his re-election in 1916.

When the war came, due to my 12 years experience in Battery B I pitched in and helped to expand Batteries B and C into a regiment. I had hoped to become a sergeant in one of the new batteries but became a 1st Lieutenant in Battery F, went through [a] strenuous training period at Ft. Sill School of Fire and Battery Administration at Camp Doniphan at the same time. Was examined for promotion in March and sent overseas on March 30th, 1917, to another School of Fire. When that was finished I became a Captain and Bn. Adjutant and then Bty. Commander and Bn. instructor in firing.

After some three months on the front the Armistice came and in February we were moved to Brest as a Port of Embarkation for home. Arrived at Camp Funston, Kansas, May 5th and was discharged May 6th, 1919.

Returned to the farm but could not settle down on it. Opened a furnishing goods store in Kansas City which was prosperous for two years and failed in 1922.

That year I ran for a County Court place and won it. In a five man race for the nomination I out campaigned the other four and became the Judge of the County Court for the Eastern District of Jackson County. Learned an immense amount about public administration in two years and was defeated for re-election in 1924 because of a split in the Democratic Party.

In 1926 was elected Presiding Judge of Jackson County's Court and took over the running of the administrative end of the County Government. I became thoroughly informed on every phase of County administration, suggested reforms on procedure which were not adopted, became acquainted with the Missouri Legislature and all the County Judges in the State. I caused the whole road system of the county to be rebuilt, rebuilt its public buildings and put it on a sound financial basis. I organized a regional planning system for the metropolitan area which included three counties in Kansas and three in Missouri.

In 1934 I became a candidate for the Senate. Carried on the same kind of campaign I had for Eastern Judge and won the nomination. I knew all County Judges and County Clerks in the State, had been very active in State Legion affairs and was on my way up in the Grand Lodge A.F. & A.M. of Missouri.

Was elected in the fall of 1934 and went to Washington in December to be sworn in as the Junior U.S. Senator from Missouri.

I became a member of the Appropriations Committee, the Interstate Commerce Committee and the Public Buildings and Grounds Committee. I worked my best in all of them, carrying documents and bills home with me to work on.

In Appropriations I became acquainted with every phase of the immense structure of the Federal Government. In Interstate Commerce I became familiar with every phase of transportation. On Public Buildings and Grounds I learned about Government buildings and their upkeep.

In 1940 I had the primary fight of my life against the Governor and the brother of one of my opponents in 1934. I made a strenuous campaign and won.

In 1941 I organized an investigating committee to watch expenditure of the military after the draft act was passed. That committee made a good reputation and is credited with saving the taxpayers fifteen billion dollars.

In 1944 I was nominated at Chicago by the Democrats for Vice President. I was elected with Franklin Roosevelt on a platform I helped to write. I was sworn in as Vice President Jan. 20, 1945, on the south portico of the White House. On April 12th, 1945, President Roosevelt died and I became President of the United States.

In all this long career I had certain rules which I followed win, lose or draw. I refused to handle any political money in any way whatever. I engaged in no private interests whatever that could be helped by local, state or national governments. I refused presents, hotel accommodations or trips which were paid for by private parties.

There were opportunities by the wholesale for making immense amounts of money at the county level and also in the Senate. I lived on the salary I was legally entitled to and considered that I was employed by the taxpayers, and the people of my county, state and nation. I made no speeches for money or expenses while I was in the Senate, or as V.P. or as President.

I would much rather be an honorable public servant and known as such than to be the richest man in the world.

MEMORANDUM

November 11, 1954, 5:30 A.M.

Thirty-six years ago today at 5:30 A.M. standard time at Verdun the operations office, Major Newell T. Paterson, Hqtrs. 129th Field Artillery 35th Division, called me at my Battery Headquarters on a bluff facing Metz and told me that at 11 A.M. French standard time the Germans would sign an Armistice; that the drive then in progress would proceed and that I would fire certain barrages in support of the 81st Infantry Division which the 129th had been supporting since the drive toward Metz had started on Nov. 7, 1918.

Major Paterson told me that I was to say nothing about the cessation of hostilities until 11 A.M. My battery fired the assigned barrages at the times specified. The last one was toward a little village called Hermeville eleven thousand meters from my position. My last shot was fired at 10:45.

When the firing ceased all along the front line it seemed not so. It was so quiet it made me feel as if I'd been suddenly deprived of my ability to hear.

The men at the guns, the Captain, the Lieutenants, the sergeants and the corporals looked at each other for some time and then a great cheer arose all along the line. We could hear the men in the infantry a thousand meters in front raising holy hell. The French battery behind our position were dancing, shouting and waving bottles of wine. That battery was made up of four six-inch Napoleon guns with no recoil mechanism. When fired with a lanyard they ran back and up an oversized carpenter's horse and then ran back into position. Celebration at the front went on for the rest of the day and far into the night. Very pistols, rockets and whatever else was handy were fired.

I went to bed about ten P.M. but the members of the French Battery insisted on marching around my cot and shaking hands. They'd shout "Vive le Capitain Américain, vive President Wilson," take another swig from their wine bottles and do it over. It was 2 A.M. before I could sleep at all.

The next day the men began to think of home, mother and sweetheart.

We moved back to the echelon and then to Le Mans and then Brest and home. It was April 9, 1919, before we embarked on the U.S.S. Zeppelin, a German boat taken over by the U.S.

We landed in N.Y. on April 20, 1919, Easter Sunday morning. It was a beautiful day and New York City gave us a great welcome.

MEMORANDUM

[1954?]

I wonder how far Moses would have gone if he'd taken a poll in Egypt? What would Jesus Christ have preached if he'd taken a poll in Israel? Where would the Reformation have gone if Martin Luther had taken a poll? It isn't polls or public opinion of the moment that counts. It is right and wrong and leadership—men with fortitude, honesty and a belief in the right that makes epochs in the history of the world.

The President's tolerance did not extend to the art of Thomas Hart Benton, native to his own Missouri. When Abraham Bernstein, a representative of United Artists Corporation and a promoter of Benton, in-

quired if Truman would pose with the artist in Kansas City, the President refused.

TO ABRAHAM BERNSTEIN (UNSENT)

January 7, 1955

Mr. Bernstein:

Your letter of Jan. 6: In the first place I know nothing about Art with a capital A, particularly the frustrated brand known as Modern.

I don't like Mr. Benton's Kentuckian. It looks like no resident or emigrant from that great State that I've ever seen. Both of my grandfathers were from Kentucky as were both of my grandmothers. All of the four had brothers and sisters most of whom I saw when I was a child. They did not look like that long necked monstrosity of Mr. Thomas Hart Benton's.

I won't encourage him to do any more horrors like those in Missouri's beautiful capitol.

[Truman later came to appreciate Benton and commissioned him to decorate the entrance to the Truman Library in Independence with a large mural, "Independence and the Opening of the West."]

The Eisenhower administration's efforts to get the government out of business, apparently by dismantling or weakening some of the New Deal programs, dismayed Truman, and the administration's attitude on offshore oil—that it belonged to the states rather than the federal government—confirmed his fears. Gingerly opposition to Senator Bricker's proposed amendment to the Constitution limiting the President's right to make treaties did not make him feel better, and every now and then some loose pronouncement from Washington made him see red. He sent off a telegram to Wayne Morse in the Senate asking for action, and in the telegram's first draft, subsequently amended, he scribbled: "Coolidge, McKinley and Grant are to be made great Presidents. Stop it now." He followed the telegram with a letter.

TO WAYNE MORSE

January 28, 1955

Dear Wayne:

I am enclosing a copy of a telegram which I sent to you yesterday. I have been worried almost sick over the manner in which the assets of the

United States have been thrown away and are intending to be thrown away. Perhaps given away would be more accurate. One of the things that worries me tremendously is the fact that the President doesn't seem to appreciate his prerogatives.

I thought your colleague set the tone to some of the things that have been done when he compared the campaign tactics of Knowland and Nixon. Some of the things that were sent out in that campaign to the various States were really the worst brand of criminal libel I have ever seen. That was particularly true in Illinois, Michigan, Montana, Wyoming and Oregon. I don't think we ought to sit idly by and let paid advertisers make those of us who have spent our lives in patriotic service be termed murderers and traitors as was done in the campaign of 1954. That program was started in 1952 [1950] when Jenner called General Marshall a traitor. If Marshall is a traitor there are no loyal citizens.

I am so wrought up about the situation that I just thought I had to do something about it and you are the victim!

Sincerely yours,
Harry S. Truman

DIARY

St. Louis
February 2, 1955

Ice and sleet so thick on the streets I didn't go to the office. Had made arrangements to come to Dr. Harold Reader's 10th anniversary dinner at the Scottish Rite Temple on Lindall Blvd. So I stayed at the house, went over the Washington and New York papers, yesterday's mail and took a good morning nap from 10:15 to 11:15. Packed my brief case with shaving case, clean shirt and a folder of reading material on the memoir, had lunch with Bess and started for the station. Got stuck trying to negotiate the alley gate and had to back up and go out the north or Truman Road gate.

The G.P.A. of the Mo. P. RR was down to see me off. Parked the car behind the station and boarded the Omaha Eagle. Read papers and documents all the way from home. Shook the hands of forty or so passengers and signed as many autographs.

Arrived at Tower Grove Station and was met by one of my best friends, Roy W. Harper, Federal Judge, and by Judge Aronson of the St. Louis Circuit Court, a member of the Grand Lodge of Missouri, reporters, photographers, and members of the St. Louis Police Department and driven to the Temple. Met dozens and dozens of Masons, signed cards, patents and just plain paper until dinner was announced.

It was a very nice affair. The Club sponsoring the dinner handled the program. Rabbi Sam Thurmond pronounced the invocation and the benediction and did his usual solemn and reverend job. I'm sure the Lord loves him as He undoubtedly does Harold Reader, the Lutheran Bishop of Germany, Sweden and Norway, the Patriarch of Istanbul, the present Pope Pius XII, the Archbishop of Canterbury and millions and millions of honest everyday so-called "common men & women."

I've never thought that God gives a damn about pomp and circumstance, gold crowns, jeweled breast plates and ancestral background. When the Gates of Heaven are reached by the shades of the earth bound, the rank and riches enjoyed on this planet won't be of value. Some of our grandees will have to do a lot of explaining on how they got that way. Wish I could hear their alibis! I can't for the probabilities are I'll be thinking up some for myself.

The Club gave Dr. Reader a scroll that was covered with a beautiful sentiment and properly framed. They gave him some lovely roses for Mrs. Reader and then asked me to say a few words.

I told them of my long acquaintance with Dr. Reader, our World War I association, our Masonic association and then launched into a world peace appeal on the basis of the Fatherhood of God and the Brotherhood of Man.

They gave me an ovation and almost mobbed me after the meeting. I had to be rescued from the handshakers and the autograph hounds.

Rabbi Thurmond, Judge Harper, Judge Aronson, the representative [of] the St. Louis Police Department and several good members of the fraternity sat around and talked about Missouri political history, personal happenings and many other things which made me think of "shoes, and sealing wax etc."

I was surrounded and rescued from the handshakes and the autograph hunters and brought to the Pullman on which I was to go to Independence.

It was a most pleasant and profitable evening for me. Not profitable financially because I paid my transportation charges, tips and all. But profitable because I saw and talked to friends who are real. They know, like and approve of me and my actions, win, lose or draw.

A great Baptist preacher, a Jewish Rabbi who prayed for me when I most needed it, 800 men from all walks of life who are not sure what they believe or what they are for—well they decided all of them that they wanted world peace after I'd talked to them—and who doesn't?

For some years during the 1950s, Senator Bricker of Ohio, a stalwart Republican, got a great deal of political mileage out of a proposed amendment to the Constitution that would have limited severely the President's treaty-making powers. Former President Truman had little use for the proposition.

TO THOMAS C. HENNINGS, JR.

March 25, 1955

Dear Senator:

Since you are on the Committee on Judiciary I am expressing my views on the proposed amendment to the Constitution limiting the treaty making powers of the President of the United States.

Paragraph 2 of Section 2 of Article II of the Constitution of the United States provides that:

"He (the President) shall have Power, by and with the Advice and Consent of the Senate, to make Treaties, provided two-thirds of the Senators present concur; and he shall nominate and by and with the Consent of the Senate shall appoint Ambassadors, other public Ministers and Consuls" etc.

Sections 2 and 3 of Article II provide the powers of the President, most of which are limited, with regard to the Foreign Policy of the United States. If the powers of the President are further limited by amendment as suggested, the country may as well readopt the Articles of Confederation and go back to a Greek city state.

The men who wrote the Constitution knew history, were familiar with government as practiced in their day and had become experienced in the shortcomings of the Articles of Confederation.

It is my opinion that any Senator of the United States who wants to abolish the Constitution and create a Confederacy is a dangerous citizen and should be checked and balanced so he cannot accomplish his purpose.

It required eighty years of experience, a John Marshall and a Civil War to establish and confirm the greatest document of government in the history of the world.

Sincerely yours,

Harry S. Truman

We should retain by every means possible the separation of powers: The Congress to make the laws, the President to make them work practically, the Judiciary to interpret them.

After a return to power, Sir Winston Churchill became too old to continue as prime minister—arteriosclerosis was affecting his memory —and he retired in favor of Anthony Eden.

TO SIR WINSTON CHURCHILL

April 6, 1955

Dear Sir Winston:

I feel as I know the whole world feels—that something has gone that will be most difficult to replace.

We all know that we cannot go on forever. I wish you could have gone on indefinitely.

My association with you was one of the high lights of my life. Your contribution to the salvation of the free world from totalitarians and tyrants has never been equalled in history.

May your retirement be no retirement but a happy relief from responsibility and a continued contribution to the safety and welfare of this old world.

Most sincerely,
Harry

The tenth anniversary of the opening of the conference that drew up the U.N. Charter brought the President back to San Francisco.

DIARY

Fairmont Hotel, San Francisco
June 24, 1955

Mike Westwood[1] was at the house in Independence at 6 A.M. just as the Independence Municipal Power Plant whistle blew, the town clock on the Court House struck and the bell on the Catholic Church began to ring good Catholics to prayer. Mike evidently had made a great effort to be on the dot at six, because I could see he'd been celebrating the night before. He finally told me, as he always does, what he'd been doing. He'd been over to Liberty to a rodeo the night before. From what he said there was a celebration and how!

We left home immediately. Bess was at the window waving goodbye to me, the old yard rabbit was looking at me as were two neighborhood cats—a black one and a yellow one from under the spiraea bushes at the

---

. Bodyguard.

back door. Pigeons, jay birds, robins, a thrush and a cat bird were on hand for a drink and a flutter in the bird bath.

Mike and I picked up Charlie Murphy who was at the Kansas City Club for the night. He and Dave Lloyd had come out from Washington to talk with me about my U.N. speech. Dave had gone on to San Francisco on the morning of the 23rd. He'd ridden the same Continental scheduled plane that Charlie and I were to take this morning. Mr. Smith of the Continental Co. met us at the airport and rode with us to Denver. Tom Gavin came down to see us off too. Tom's a grand fellow. He was my alternate at the Convention of the Democrats in 1952—a very ticklish position. I was living in the White House then. There's always a spot light on that residence and all connected with it. Tom did a perfect job at Chicago for me and he's still always trying to help me. No man has had as many and as loyal friends as I have. Tom Gavin is one of them.

The plane was off on time. The wheels were free from the runway at 7:04. We circled the city and headed for Denver at 14,000 feet. Arrived in that city at 9:38 by Denver time, 10:38 Central Time.

News men, photographers, United and Continental Air Line officials met us and took us to the office of United in the terminal, gave us coffee, doughnuts and cakes. We'd had bacon, eggs, coffee and milk for breakfast after we left the K.C. airport.

My former Secretary of Agriculture the Hon. Charlie Brannan and Mrs. Brannan were at the station to meet Charlie Murphy and me. What a pleasant visit we had with them while we waited for the United Air Lines plane to be readied for flight. We left the ground at 10 A.M. Denver time, just one hour late.

Right here let me say that the Brannans are the finest of fine people. They had entertained me a couple of weeks earlier at a Library dinner and had given the fund a big check. It was like seeing members of the family to meet them again.

We arrived in Salt Lake City only a quarter of an hour late although we left Denver nearly an hour behind time.

We took off from Denver toward the north west, passed Long's Peak, with Pike's Peak in the distance to the south and all those tall Rocky Mountains lined up south of us. We were flying at 14,000 feet when we leveled off and turned west. The Rockies to our left and the Wyoming plains to our right. We could see Estes Park on our left and the Pass to our right where the U.P. Railroad crosses the Continental Divide. In a short time the pilot of the plane told us we were passing Dinosaur National Monument to the south. I reminded Charlie Murphy that, in 1952, we'd called that place Republican Party headquarters. I told Charlie that I think it still is!

As we flew along I couldn't help but think of my old Grandfather Young who'd driven wagon trains from the home farm in Jackson County, Missouri, to Colorado, Utah and California from 1846 to 1860. We'd left home at seven A.M. and at 11 A.M. were well past the high mountains. Grandpa would have left home at what is now Grandview at four A.M. and in all probability would have been ten or twelve miles west of the Missouri line. What an age we live and have our being in! We had a mountain trout luncheon and before we realized it were descending into the Great Salt Lake Valley. We could see it much better than Brigham Young and his Mormon followers could when they trekked from Council Bluffs, Iowa, in the 1830's. From the air it looks like a paradise and from the eminence from which Brigham Young saw it, it must have looked like heaven indeed.

We landed at Salt Lake City Air Port, were met by Cal Rollins, National Democratic Committeeman, newspaper men and a crowd which was estimated by Randall Jessee a K.C. Star reporter at 300 people. I held a press conference, met a husky young man of two years who was named for me by his enthusiastic father and mother and then took off again a half hour late.

We flew over the remains of the Great Salt Lake, the saltiest of the salty seas, which is slowly and gradually drying up. Then we came to the great gambling and marriage destruction hell, known as Nevada. To look at it from the air it is just that—hell on earth. There are tiny green specks on the landscape where dice, roulette, light-o-loves, crooked poker and gambling thugs thrive. Such places should be abolished and so should Nevada. It never should have been made a State. A county in the great State of California would be too much of a civil existence for that dead and sinful territory. Think of that awful, sinful place having two Senators and a Congressman in Washington, and Alaska and Hawaii not represented. It is a travesty on our system and a disgrace to free government.

Well we finally passed the hell hole of iniquity by flying over one of the most beautiful spots in the whole world—Lake Tahoe. It is a lovely picture from the air and it must have affected the old pirates of the Comstock lode, the whores and the gamblers of Mark Twain's time also because some very wonderful descriptions of it have been written in those times.

We landed in San Francisco on time at 2:55 P.M. Pacific Daylight Time. The Mayor of San Francisco, Secretaries of the U.N., photographers innumerable, and Democrats by the dozen were on the ground to meet me. Never had a more cordial welcome anywhere but in the same city time and again. We were driven up town behind a screaming police escort to the Mark Hopkins Hotel for an appearance before the Committee for the United Nations. Addressed a few words to them on the U.N. and told them about the Library we are placing at home to contain my papers. Then went over to the Fairmont across the street and met a lot of people. Took a bath and a short nap and at 6 P.M. S.F. time went down stairs to meeting of a Library Committee. Had a very good dinner and an organization meeting for funds for the Library. A committee from the Junior Mechanics presented me a citation, a gold medal and a check for $5,000.00 for the Library. Had to hurry to my room to meet the President of the U.N. Assembly and the Secretary General. They escorted me to the Auditorium where I was to speak.

We entered the General Assembly meeting at the time set. The President, Von Kleffens, the Secretary General, Dag Hammarskjold and Mr. Cardon[2] escorting me to the Platform in the same auditorium where I had closed the U.N. meeting in 1945. What a reception I received as we walked across the stage to our seats. I had to stand twice and acknowledge the cheers. A speech was made by Mr. Cardon on the various activities of the U.N. He was introduced by the Sec. General. Then the President of the U.N. took the rostrum and started an introduction of me. He was stopped when he mentioned my name and I had to go to the speaker's place and stand beside him so he could finish the introduction. When it was time for me to step in front of the microphones there was another more vociferous ovation.

When the speech was finished there was another ovation of several minutes. I had been interrupted at least a dozen times in the delivery of the speech.[3]

After it was over I went back to the Fairmont, appeared a few minutes at a labor meeting which Senator Humphrey was addressing and then went to a reception for the foreign ministers.

Mr. Molotov was there and was very cordial to me. Rumor had it he would not come. The foreign ministers of France, Iran and all the rest came as did numerous delegates and visitors.

The President of the General Assembly and the Secretary General escorted me to my room and told me to go to bed. It is 10 P.M. S.F. time.

My host in Tennessee was in the hallway. Mr. McSween and his friend came in and we rehearsed the meeting at the Ramp Festival.[4] Had a lot of laughs, talked politics and I went to bed.

---

2. Philip V. Cardon, director general of the Food and Agriculture Organization.

3. Truman's speech was a rousing tribute to the U.N., the rule of which, he said, was an alternative to anarchy and possible destruction. He looked forward to greater understanding and agreement among the great powers, and especially to disarmament, the hope of peace.

4. Donald M. McSween was one of the sponsors of the annual festival, which Truman attended in Cosby, Tennessee, on April 24. A ramp looks like a slender onion, and has been described as a super-garlic, ten times as powerful as an onion.

In November, nearly three years after the end of the Truman presidency, the first volume of the memoirs was ready, and the second was published in March 1956. Entitled simply Memoirs, *the volumes bore subtitles—*Year of Decisions *for the initial presidential year, and* Years of Trial and Hope *for the remaining period to January 1953. Preparation for bringing out the memoirs was thorough, with pre-publication in the* New York Times, St. Louis Post-Dispatch, *and* Life *magazine. Not all the arrangements were to the President's taste, as when the editor in chief of Doubleday and Company, Ken McCormick, proposed a $35 limited edition of the memoirs. Truman balked at the very idea. McCormick then proposed to give the President five hundred sets of the book.*

TO KEN McCORMICK

July 1, 1955

Dear Ken:

I am very sorry that there was a misunderstanding about the autographs for the book. I want five hundred copies of the edition to which you referred in your telegram, but I will not accept them as a gift. I want you to bill me for them at the publisher's price, and I will send you a check immediately.

I will then proceed with the autographing program, about which we talked, for the book dealers in Kansas City. I will set aside one day near the book's publication date, and I will autograph as many as I can. I am not an expert with a machine, and I would rather do it by hand. As you know, I am accustomed to signing my name a great many times a day.

I have also told Stanton Griffis of Brentano's, who was my ambassador to Poland, Egypt and Spain, that I would do the same thing for him sometime when I happened to be back east.

I cannot possibly enter into a program which would look as if I were selling autographs instead of a book. I want the book sold on its merit. If it cannot be sold that way, then it's not worth having. I have a very strong feeling about any man, who has had the honor of being an occupant of the White House in the greatest job in the history of the world, who would exploit that position in any way, shape, or form. I hope you understand the situation.

We will go on from here, and I am sure developments will work out to your interest and satisfaction.

Sincerely yours,

Harry S. Truman

[As of June 28, 1955, the advance sale among the Kansas City book-
shops was 14,250 sets. A big autographing party was arranged for Octo-
ber at the Muehlebach, to which the owners of all the Kansas City book
outlets were invited, and McCormick, sure he would need more than
5,000 signed books, asked the President if it would be possible to have
10,000.]

The antipathy of the President for Eisenhower's secretary of state,
John Foster Dulles, went back to the special election of 1949 in New York
State when Dulles was running for the Senate (he had been serving a
brief appointive term) and lost to Herbert H. Lehman; at that time
Dulles made a statement that seemed anti-Semitic to Truman, and the
President never forgot it. Because of Truman's irritation, Secretary
Acheson could not at first get the President to agree to admit Dulles's
virtues as a negotiator. When Dulles finally did come into the depart-
ment, to work on the Japanese peace treaty, it was only as a "consul-
tant." Eventually Dulles received the rank of special ambassador, but
the President never liked him, and when he became secretary of state
under Eisenhower the old animus reappeared.

Henry F. Grady had been Ambassador to Greece and later to Iran
during Truman's second administration.

TO HENRY F. GRADY

July 9, 1955

Dear Henry:

You don't know how very much I appreciated your letter of July 1st.
Of course, I was sorry to miss you on this trip, and I was also sorry for
the confusion which caused the cancellation of the dinner you had organized, but it had to be done under the circumstances.

I had a most pleasant conversation with Mrs. Grady and showed her
my correspondence with our Secretary of State. I was intrigued with the
statement that he kept his hands behind his back during the ovation
given me by the United Nations Organization.

Mr. Molotov came to the reception given by the Secretary General for
the foreign ministers and for me. Mr. Dulles did not come; but then,
perhaps, I do not know all I should about State Department protocol.

Sincerely yours,

Harry

DIARY

July 24, 1955

A couple of red birds decided to build a nest on the back porch. Grape vines and rose bushes climb over the south exposure and there is an ideal place for a nest. A few days after the nest was finished four beautiful speckled eggs appeared. And in due time four little naked birds came to life. In a few days these four little birds were able to make hungry noises and the mama and papa birds were busy all day and late in the evening furnishing food to four apparently insatiable appetites.

DIARY

July 31, 1955

The four little birds finally opened their eyes and began to have feathers appear. We watched them grow and wanted to see them fly away at the proper time. The old birds became very tame. We could walk right up to the nest and they would keep right on taking care of their children.

Our next door neighbors on the south across the alley have a great big black cat. He used our yard to walk around and cool off. He would have nothing to do with us individually, except that he'd allow my good brother-in-law George to pet him.

One evening we saw him start up the back steps to the porch where the red birds had their nest with the four little birds. We ran him off but the next morning we heard the mama & papa birds making a great fuss about five o'clock. When we arrived at the porch about 5:15 the nest was upside down and the four little red birds were inside the big black cat. Too bad the cat couldn't have been caught in the act. It would have been too bad for him.

The President did not admire his putative ancestor, President John Tyler, and said so in his memoirs. Stephen F. Chadwick had married Tyler's granddaughter, and in a letter enclosed a copy of a speech by Claude Bowers, who served as Truman's ambassador to Chile, extolling Tyler at the unveiling of a bust of the late President in Richmond, Virginia, in 1931.

TO STEPHEN F. CHADWICK

December 10, 1955

Dear Mr. Chadwick:

I certainly appreciated your good letter of November 25th and the copy of the speech by our great ambassador, Claude Bowers. I enjoyed reading them both.

We all get peculiar slants on historical figures. One of my complexes —I guess you could call it that—is that loyalty to the party which creates your public career is fundamental.

No one can charge John Tyler with a lack of courage. He resigned from the Senate because he did not agree with Andrew Jackson, but I could never forgive him for leaving his party to join the Whigs, or for leaving the Union in 1861—although I must admit he did make an effort to hold the Union together.

Grover Cleveland's family left the party also, and his descendants are all economic royalists and far-right Republicans. How that happened I cannot understand, but perhaps my education has been neglected along that line.

Sincerely yours,
Harry S. Truman

General MacArthur obtained a set of advance proofs of the passages of the memoirs dealing with himself and prepared an intemperate reply. The proofs came from the New York Times, *and the managing editor of* Life, *Edward K. Thompson, reluctantly decided to publish the reply, since the* Times *otherwise would have had a scoop. Thompson sent a draft of the general's remarks to Truman. MacArthur had said that because other individuals already had had to respond to Truman's allegations about themselves (here he mentioned the names of Byrnes, Wallace, former Attorney General Biddle, former Foreign Aid Administrator Crowley, and Admiral Leahy) he, MacArthur, had been forewarned, and had decided that to remain silent would be a disservice to the nation. The President, he said, was quite wrongheaded. "I will not be so brash," he began, "as to attempt to diagnose the animating impulses which have led him into such a labyrinth of fancy and fiction, distortion and misrepresentation. Suffice it to suggest that a well known quotation may provide a clue to the answer: 'Everything looks yellow to a jaundiced eye.' For such does seem peculiarly applicable to Mr. Truman's memoirs in the writing of which he has been unable to rise above those petty instincts based upon spite and vindictiveness which have so fre-*

quently led him into violent and vulgar public controversy." MacArthur blamed Truman and the Department of State for refusing to give the South Koreans enough heavy arms to repel the North Koreans, and said that it was all done under an erroneous fear that the South Koreans, properly equipped, might invade the north. The President then refused to unify South and North Korea and the result was Red China triumphant. *"Red China promptly was accepted as the military colossus of the East. Korea was left ravished and divided."* The general said that his dismissal was not merely uncalled for, but when it came it was totally without tact, without warning: *"No office boy, no charwoman, no servant of any sort would have been dismissed with such callous disregard for the ordinary decencies."*

TO EDWARD K. THOMPSON

January 6, 1956

Dear Mr. Thompson:

I certainly appreciated your letter of December 29th regarding the MacArthur reaction to my statements in the book.

His blowup was expected, of course, and it seems to be more personal than factual. When an egotist is punctured, a lot of noise and whistling always accompanies the escaping air.

I am not at all worried by what the great general has had to say, and don't let it worry you. If he had stuck to facts, he would be in a much better position. The statements in the book can be supported by the documents themselves, and I fear very much that he understands that and does not really like to see the facts stated. That makes no difference to me, however.

There will be no reply on my part. What is in the book is based entirely on records and facts and my memory—which I think is much better than his.

Sincerely yours,
Harry S. Truman

TO HARRY H. VAUGHAN

February 10, 1956

Dear Harry:

I certainly appreciate your sending me the copy of the background of Point IV.[1] Of course, I would like to have a bound copy for the Library.

---

1. Bertha Coblens Joseph, "The Background and Scope of Point 4," an address to the Shanghai Tiffin Club, Town Hall, New York, on Lincoln's birthday, 1952, printed as senate document 102, 82d cong., 2d sess. (Washington, 1952).

I wish you would tell Carl Hayden that. In fact, I would like to have 4 bound copies because I would like to place one in the library of the University of Missouri, one in the University of Kansas, and one in the University of Kansas City.

Our great bald-headed General, with the dyed hair, seems to have had quite a spasm in yesterday morning's paper. They called me to comment on it and I told them my comment was in the statement of the facts in the Memoirs.

I hope you are in good health and that all is going well with you.

I just received a sheet off the ticker which says a Polish born electrician, by the name of Andreas Malz, has decided he would like to go through life with the name of Harry Solomon Truman, so he had his name changed. He took on the middle name of my grandfather Young, which all the Anti-Semitics tried to give me. If I had the family name I would be proud of it, but I haven't.

Sincerely yours,
Harry S. Truman

[The President's middle initial, which, legally, stood for nothing, caused endless confusion. For example, when Truman was being sworn in as President on the evening of April 12, 1945, Chief Justice Stone began, "I, Harry Shippe Truman . . ." and the new President responded, "I, Harry S. Truman . . ." In the senatorial election of 1940, his opponents listed his middle name as Solomon, trying to make it appear he was Jewish.]

The President had his friends among the Republicans, the most notable, of course, being former President Hoover, and some of them were on the far right. On occasion he was glad to recommend them for public appearances, in part out of friendship, in part out of certainty that they could do no political harm.

TO DONALD H. McSWEEN

February 20, 1956

Dear Don:

I am very sorry that President Hoover has decided he cannot come to the Ramp Festival, and I have been trying to think of someone who would be agreeable to both you and Carroll Reece.

It seems to me that Carroll could persuade Joe Martin, the Minority Leader in the House and its former Speaker, to come. He's in the same far-right class as Carroll and President Hoover, and he makes an excellent speech. When I made appearances in Massachusetts during the 1948 and '52 campaigns, he always came to pay his respects, and I think he would fill the bill here from a bi-partisan viewpoint. Besides, and I am not being disparaging, I do not believe he'll gather many votes for the Republican ticket among the Democrats, or the Republicans, either, for that matter. But he does make a good speech.

Sincerely yours,
Harry S. Truman

Truman made his first post-presidential trip to Europe in the summer of 1956, and the following diary account shows what the former chief executive encountered. The trip resulted in a series of ten articles, distributed by King Features Syndicate, in which the President used his diary entries but changed them considerably, after which William Hillman in New York again did rewriting before releasing the articles to the syndicate. The original entries give Truman's frank impressions of the moment.

DIARY

S.S. United States
May [11–15], 1956

In which a trip to Europe is arranged after long deliberation.

After we left the White House, Mrs. Truman & I along with our daughter were invited by my good friend and former Reparations Ambassador, Ed Pauley, to spend a month on Coconut Island just off the north coast of Oahu in the Hawaiian Islands. We had a wonderful time, spent a lot of time sleeping, swimming, sunning and resting.

When we arrived at Independence from that trip I found an invitation from Lord Halifax to come to Oxford for an honorary degree. Due to the fact that I'd signed a contract with Life Magazine to write a memoir of my Presidential experience in the White House I asked for a postponement. The invitation was again extended in 1954. An operation for the removal of an obstreperous gall bladder prevented the trip again. The invitation was renewed in 1955 and was accepted for June 1956.

Preparations began and then Margaret informed us that she had found a grand man—and she had—and that she expected a wedding at home in Independence on April 21, 1956. That affair was accomplished to the satisfaction of her mother, her father, Clif Daniel's mother and father and apparently the entire nation.

Soon as the wedding was over Mrs. Truman and I began our preparations for the trip. When it was announced that we would go to Europe on May 11 by the great ship United States, invitations from the wonderful people who had visited us officially and unofficially while we were at the White House began to arrive from across the Atlantic.

I persuaded the Honorable Stanley Woodward and Mrs. Woodward to go along with Mrs. Truman and me and give us the same sort of help he had given us as Chief of Protocol in Washington. The Woodwards are wonderful people. He had also been Ambassador to Canada during my tenure of the Presidency and is thoroughly aware of the standards of approach to the visit of a former President of the United States.

Well we began to assemble the necessities and the trimmings and to visit and talk with our friends. The last few days were rather hectic. We had to write letters to people who had written us about Margie's wedding, assemble hats and dresses, stockings, sox and shoes, tails and tuxedoes and all sorts of things you never worry about at home or in the White House either because there you have someone to do it.

In assembling my individual luggage I was coming down stairs, missed a step and rolled a half dozen steps to the landing and pulled a ligament loose in my right ankle. It was seven o'clock in the morning and by noon I had an ankle as big as two should be. Dr. Graham who has been my personal physician bound it up and I managed to get around.

We packed madly Friday, Saturday and Sunday but made very little impression on the chore in hand, what with phone calls, errands and being sure to see or call up all the members of both our immediate families.

[The following account, until a bracketed notation showing its end, was added to the original diary entry by dictation.]

On May 5th, Saturday, about twenty-five of my close personal friends in Kansas City gave me a birthday party at which I was presented with all metal money from nearly every country in Europe. It was a wonderful party, and I enjoyed myself immensely. A fine model of the S.S. *United States* had been set up with small figures representing Mrs. Truman and me waving through a rain of colored streamers from the upper deck. Another ship model served as centerpiece on the large square table. There was a beautiful birthday cake which they insisted on my taking home. And to see that everyone would have a taste of the cake, individual cup cakes decorated with the numeral "72" were given to all.

After the luncheon my cousin, Major General Ralph Truman, and I drove to Kansas City, Kansas, to help dedicate the new Armory there. This building is one of a series to be built around the United States as a result of the re-organization of the Coast Guard and the Marine Corps. I had already had the privilege of dedicating the new armories at Marysville, Missouri, and Independence, Missouri.

On my way home I stopped off at my office to gather up the huge pile of mail that had arrived that morning. [End of dictated text.] I receive an immense individual mail, probably the largest of the kind in my home city, and I answer and acknowledge nearly all of it. I have two very efficient ladies working for me, Miss Rose Conway and Miss Frances Myers, who work every day and Saturday too to help me keep up. I have also a very able young man by the name of Eugene Bailey with me who took all the dictation on my two volume book—some million and a half words to publish five hundred thousand. These three good and able people worked almost day and night that last week to get me ready to leave on the morning of May 8, my 72nd birthday.

Our train left Independence at 7:15 and we had sixteen pieces of luggage to be loaded with us.

All our neighbors, the Mayor of Independence and his family and our families, as many as could come, were at the station to see us off. We delayed the train at least ten minutes while we said goodbye and placed the baggage so it would be least in the way. Before the train came the news photographers of the local papers and broadcasting stations gave me a birthday cake. It was cut up and passed around and we had a grand party before seven A.M.

At St. Louis, where we transferred from the Missouri Pacific's Colorado Eagle to the Pennsylvania's Spirit of St. Louis, reporters, photographers and friends met us and helped us change trains. The people who run the railroads, agents, conductors, enginemen, porters, station masters, redcaps and all are always extremely helpful and courteous to us. The head man of the Pennsy finally told us to please get aboard or the Spirit of St. Louis would never get out of the station on time.

At Indianapolis we were met by Hon. Frank McKinney and the Indianapolis reporters and photographers and most cordially treated by them. The train stays there ten minutes, it was ten minutes ahead of time and we had a grand twenty minute visit.

When dinner time came we had another birthday cake which was cut and distributed to those who were in the diner at the time.

At the Penn Station in N.Y. we were almost mobbed with kindness by news men, photographers and patrons of the station. Finally arrived at the Carlyle Hotel where Margie had made reservations for us. She had quite a time getting us through the station even with the efficient help of New York police. I had a press and radio conference, shook hands with everyone who could get to me and had a good time generally.

At the hotel, Mr. Lloyd, Mr. Murphy, Mr. Don Dawson and Mr. Bill Hillman took turns answering two phones, making appointments and finally loading us in the New York City greeter's cars for the pier and the good ship United States. The Hon. Dick Patterson, three times Ambassador while I was President, always sees that N.Y. City treats me as if I were a big shot visitor.

We had to come to N.Y. on the 9th because the Governor, Honorable Averell Harriman, was receiving the Four Freedoms Award and they wanted me to present it. It was a grand party and the Governor certainly deserved the honor. Received another beautiful birthday cake which was cut and passed around as far as it would go.

Now here we are in mid Atlantic, really having a grand cruise. The old Atlantic, for a wonder, is as smooth as the Pacific and the sun shines as brightly as in Honolulu. [The following also added by dictation.] It is quite different from my first trip to Europe in 1918. I was a member of the overseas detail of the 35th Division which was sent over in advance of the division to go to school in France. We left New York on the old *George Washington* at midnight on March 30th, which was the day before Easter Sunday. There were very few lights, just a few showing here and there, but we were able to see the Statue of Liberty as we went by. I was billeted on D Deck with four other first lieutenants, and we decided that if we managed to come back from the war, Miss Liberty would have to turn around if she wanted to see us again. This is the first time I have seen her since then.

In the summer of 1945 I left Norfolk, Virginia, on the U.S.S. *Augusta,* which took me as far as Antwerp. At Antwerp I was flown in the old DC-4 known as the *Sacred Cow* to Berlin and the Potsdam Conference. This trip, I know, will be a much more pleasant one.

TO TOM L. AND MAMIE LOU EVANS

Hotel Excelsior, Naples
May 23, 1956

Dear Tom and Mamie Lou:

We've had a fantastic trip. You should both be along to wave as in 1948. We were met at St. Louis, Indianapolis, mobbed in New York at the train and the ship. The jam at the Paris, Rome and Naples stations was like Washington in 1948 after the election.

Went to the American Cemetery in Paris and placed a wreath on the slab marking the graves of 24 unknown American soldiers. Stanley's brother was buried there in World War I. It is a beautifully kept place.

Went to Salerno and to an old Greek town south of there to see some ruins. We'll go to Pompeii today then to Florence and Venice. I'm not a good sightseer and I'd rather be home. Can't see what I want to for the reporters & photo men.

Hope you & the Mrs. are well and that we'll see you when we arrive in Independence on July 8th.

Sincerely,
Harry S. Truman

I'm already being misquoted!

DIARY

[En route from Florence]
May 27–28–29, 1956

A scenic ride from Arezzo to Firenzi (Florence). The usual cordial reception. The Mayor and the Prefect called to pay respects and welcome us. It was election day and everyone was excited about it. We drove around the city, visited the home of the Hon. Myron C. Taylor[1] which is now a girls' finishing school in music and art. It is a lovely place and is a gift to the Catholic Church in the name of Pope Pius XII as a non-sectarian school. Mr. Taylor has endowed it. He is an Episcopalian. After visiting the gardens and the piano studios and the painting and sculpture studios, we had a cup of coffee and listened to some of the young ladies play the piano and sing to us. The young ladies were excellent in their renditions and some of them will be professionals undoubtedly.

We had luncheon the same day with Mr. Bernard Berenson at his villa on the outskirts of Florence. He is a most remarkable man 92 years old and as clear headed and mentally alert as a man of 35 or 40. He is considered the greatest authority on Renaissance Art and is noted for his epigrams, one of which struck me forcibly. We were discussing world affairs and he remarked that modern diplomacy had degenerated into "Open insults openly arrived at." We discussed the causes of the first World War, the Austrian Prime Minister of that time, the Serbian situation and the whys & wherefores of the Austrian ultimatum which started the war.

Stanley Woodward & I visited a number of the famous places in Florence, discussed Florentine Art and Architecture and Italian politics, the elections then going on and a lot of things—"shoes and ships and

---

1. Taylor had been Truman's personal representative to the Vatican.

sealing wax and things and whether the ocean is boiling hot and whether pigs have wings."

On the evening of our arrival we went to dinner with Mr. Giorgini[2] to whom we had been recommended by B. Altman's Mr. Haight. Mr. Haight had been responsible for the refurnishing of the White House after its reconstruction when Mrs. Truman and I were living at the Blair House.

The dinner was a small family affair and most enjoyable. After dinner other guests were invited, among them Miss Frances Perkins and Miss Gladys Swarthout.[3] There were also present a large number of the leading citizens of Florence. Mr. Giorgini has some beautiful and rare art treasures which we persuaded him to show us.

I had most happy and pleasant conversations with Miss Perkins and Miss Swarthout. Meeting them in Italy was almost like a family reunion because both of them had been a part of the Truman Administration in days gone by. Both had been very kind to Margaret—and that's the shortest way to the old man's heart.

We had a most pleasant afternoon reception at the American Consulate with Mr. & Mrs. Service.[4] They are lovely people and they have a most interesting family—two boys and a girl. At this reception we met the top government employees of the consulate and several leading Florentines. Judge Learned Hand was present with Mrs. Hand. We had a grand visit. The next day at 12:12 [?] P.M. the Mayor, the Prefect, the Chief of Police and several other citizens and the American Consul and his wife escorted us to the train.

The mayor had just been reelected and of course he was very happy. He is a remarkable man and lives a private life that causes him to be called "the Saint."

The Prefect is an officer similar to our State Governors, except that he is appointed by the President of the Republic of Italy and is a career official. I was very much impressed by these officials—we have been met by them in every city—particularly the Prefect of the Florentine Province. He was a large man who reminded me of the picture of Grover Cleveland in the White House. He was born in Fiume across the Adriatic and could speak, read and write a half dozen languages.

---

2. G. B. Giorgini, associated with Altman's department store in New York, had a house in Florence.

3. Formerly a Metropolitan Opera contralto.

4. Richard M. Service was American consul in Florence.

DIARY

Saturday morning, June 2, we regretfully left Venice. We always leave the cities we visit with regret because there are so many art treasures and historical monuments to see that it is impossible in the limited time we have to see everything.

We'll no doubt feel the same way about Salzburg, Austria, where we arrived at 5:30 P.M. Saturday. Leaving Venice in the rain reminded me of a flight it was my experience to make from the Island of Oahu to the Island of Hawaii to see Mauna Loa. The day was perfect and the visibility as far as you could see. . . .

When we departed from the Naval Air Base on the west side of the Island of Hawaii, it was pouring rain. Two good old Hawaiian women came up to me and said, "Pali was most happy when you came, now she is weeping because you leave." Pali is the goddess of the volcano.

We came to Venice in sunshine and we left Venice in pouring rain. I do not know which Roman Goddess or Italian Saint wanted us to stay. I hope it was San Mario or San Francisco.

Our train trip to Salzburg through northern Italy and southern Austria was a most pleasant one through the beautiful and fertile plain of Italy and the scenic foothills of Austria. We stopped at many stations and were recognized through the car window and cordially received.

Our arrival in Salzburg was a pleasant one. The rain had ceased and we were most cordially received in the railroad station by a great crowd of smiling people.

We were driven to Mr. Woodward's farm, which is about eight miles from Salzburg at a little Austrian village, St. Jacob by name. The American Ambassador to Vienna, Mr. Thompson, and his beautiful wife came to tea at the Woodwards' and I discussed the Russian occupation and the evacuation of the occupying forces of the Allies with him. He is of the opinion that American-British forces made a very favorable impression on the Austrians. His opinion was confirmed later in the evening by the Governor of Salzburg at a musicale and supper, given by him at the former palace of the Prince Archbishop of Salzburg.

I've never attended a happier or more pleasing musical event. The conductor, Dr.———, was superb. A beautiful Mozart number was rendered by the orchestra, followed by vocal duets and trios of Mozart songs.

The two young men and three young ladies who sang had lovely voices and knew how to use them.

The vocal part of the program was followed by another beautiful Mozart Minuet & Minuetto. We then went in to supper, cold meats, fish, salad, ice cream, just a light repast according to Austrian standards.

The acoustics of the concert hall were perfect, the rendition both by the orchestra and the vocalists was as fine as I've ever heard—and I've heard most of the great ones.

The Governor made a speech thanking the U.S. for the Marshall Plan and Point 4 which was heart warming.

The next day [we saw] the exclusive uniform guard of the district similar in their social and uniform equipment to the Ancient and Honorable Artillery of Boston and the Washington Artillery of New Orleans, only the Salzburg outfit use blunderbusses and black powder to fire a salute.

They came up to Mr. Woodward's beautiful place with a brass band and lined up, giving me and Mr. Woodward each a salute. Then Mr. Woodward and I and the commanding officer inspected the outfit and they marched back to St. Jacob for beer & skittles. We followed them to the village and were shown through the ancient church. Dr.———, organist for the Salzburg Cathedral, played Mozart's 9th Sonata (16th by new numbering) on the 250 year old organ. It was fantastic the way that old organ worked and most beautiful the way it sounded. The organist's wife had to pump the bellows, which she did by standing on the pump handle to bring it down. It was arranged for that purpose.

The good old Father in charge of the Church showed us all the relics and explained them in a most interesting manner.

We then went down the street where the band was playing and the saluters and the villagers were drinking beer and eating cheese and hard rolls.

When I sat down everyone there wanted an autograph and I must have signed at least 150 post cards. We had to leave before everybody obtained an autograph.

Monday morning all of us went to Mozart's house and birthplace. We were shown the room where he was born and the instruments on which he played and for which he composed.

Dr. ——— of the great music school here played the theme to my two favorite sonatas, the 9th & the 18th (old numbers). Then they let me try out the old Mozart instrument. I found that it was somewhat different from the modern piano but that it makes beautiful music. This Mozart town has certainly been a joy to me and it is hard to understand all the troubles & vicissitudes it has been through in times past.

The Austrians are very lucky that the Russians are gone. They robbed the country of everything they could get their hands on and forced a reparations agreement from them for more loot. Their destructive attitude in Poland, Rumania, Hungary, Czechoslovakia and Manchuria is based on the teachings of Jenghis Khan and Tamerlane.

Their treatment of the satellites is fantastic. They suppress all opposition, use slave labor camps and shoot those who have culture and influence. This information I've gathered by conversations with those who have had contact and association with displaced persons from the Balkan and Baltic countries.

The government of Russia may be really putting on a new front.[1] I hope they are, but the men who are doing the job were tools of Stalin just as Stalin was the tool of Lenin. When Stalin became the dictator he didn't hesitate to eliminate his associated comrades, by both Russian legal and any other means at hand.

Russia is a great country and the Soviet Union is made up of sturdy people but they have been oppressed and downtrodden by dictatorships from the time of Ivan the Terrible and Peter the Great to this very day. Sometime, and I hope this is the beginning of that time, the Russian people will awaken to the meaning of liberty and world peace and the world can live happily ever after.

Until that time comes the United States must maintain its position of defense and its friendship and cooperation with the free world.

DIARY

[Paris?]
June 6 [16?], 1956

We drove out of Paris at 10 A.M. and arrived at Versailles to see the palace and the gardens. It is the extravaganza of King Louis XIV, the "Grand Monarque," whose statement "I am the State" is one of the historical sentences expressing the Bourbon attitude toward government. It is the exact opposite of "Government of the people, for the people and by the people," the statement of Abraham Lincoln.

While the Grand Monarque was spending the revenues of France on small wars here and there he was also squandering the hard earned savings of the people, squeezed from them by almost blood-letting meth-

---

1. As a result of the Austrian State Treaty, signed in 1955 by the Allies of the Second World War, the occupying powers departed—including the Russians. The Geneva Summit Conference of that year gave promise of détente between the Soviet Union and the Western democracies. In February 1956, the then general secretary of the Russian Communist party, Nikita Khrushchev, gave his famous speech denouncing Stalin to the Twentieth Party Congress.

ods, on palaces for mistresses and this most famous of palace gardens.

It is beautiful to look at and to rave over but I was thinking as I looked that the heads of his great-grandson Louis XVI and his beautiful Marie Antoinette paid for the Grand Monarque's extravagance in the Revolution.

We drove on to Chartres for a visit to the Cathedral said to be the best example of Gothic Architecture in France. The windows are of stained glass of the 12th century and are the most beautiful and famous in the world. I've always wanted to see this great Cathedral from the inside. I passed within sight of it in 1918 but was not close enough to see its beauty even on the outside. The architect in charge explained the origin, the windows and the sculpture to us in a most entertaining and instructive manner. We did not go up into the spire nor walk around the building on the outside for the reason that it was pouring rain.

After the visit to Chartres we proceeded to a small village, Jouy by name, where we were most cordially received and had a wonderful luncheon. I had an opportunity to talk to an English-speaking Frenchman who informed me that the rank and file in France still loved Americans from the United States. I have watched the faces of the people in all the cities and towns we have passed and have noticed happy smiling faces of welcome. I'll have further comment on this later.

We arrived at Chenonceaux in the middle of the afternoon where we put up at a beautiful little hotel, Chez Ottoni by name. The host, whose name is on the hotel, was a perfect one and gave us a most cordial welcome.

After a short rest we drove to the famous Chateau, about a half mile from the hotel, where Catherine de Medici, Mary Queen of Scots, Diane of Poitiers and Madame de Guise spent a lot of time. I was told that the place was built by the wife of a finance minister of France whose husband robbed the King's treasury to furnish the funds for his wife's building project.

The famous Catherine spent her time here and exercised her authority over her three sons, who were Kings of France after the death of Francis I, by sending messages to the government in Paris.

Of course, there are all sorts of traditions and stories about the happenings of the days of Catherine but she was a remarkable woman and a Medici, all of whom believed in government by deviation as set out in The Prince by Machiavelli. Catherine was the mother of ten children, three of whom became kings of France and two of whom became queens. Quite a record for a tough conspiratorial old woman.

We were invited to dinner by the Marquis of Vibray who lives in a beautiful Chateau some 30 miles from our hotel. The place has been in the family for 700 years, the house is 325 years old and very beautiful and very livable which can't be said for most of the much talked about Chateaux of France.

I lived in one at Montigny-sur-Aube in 1918 for six weeks in April & May. It was built with walls six feet thick and cold tile floors. It had a water tank up at the top of one of the towers and a shower of the needle variety. The water stayed at a temperature of about 32° F. and when you pulled the lever for water after you shut yourself in you sincerely wished you were an Eskimo and did not have to take an ice cold needle bath. The torture chambers of old had nothing on that bath.

I had a conversation with each of several people at the dinner which the Marquis gave and I asked the same questions I had of the working Frenchman. I was informed by these very well to do people that the anti-American propaganda was organized by some people who had gotten rich as a result of the Marshall Plan and Point 4 and who were not pleased with our attitude of a fair distribution of income to all the people; that the rank and file of the French people loved us and always would as a result of our efforts in their behalf in both world wars. I told them that the American people had never forgotten La Fayette and his contribution to the founding of our Republic.

The Marquis and his brother had two ancestors in Washington's Army. Both are members of the Order of the Cincinnati[1] and very proud of it.

I took a walk early on the morning of the 11th before we started for Paris and met another old Frenchman who had been following me around. The chief of the security attached to our party translated his remarks for me. He said that all Frenchmen loved Americans and that they always would.

I am of the opinion formed from my experience in the receptions I've received that the press in France is a controlled press just as the Republican propaganda press at home is, and that if the majority of the people from the economically well to do to the taxi driver and the elevator man could express themselves they'd be unanimous in their feeling of friendship for the U.S.A.

I fear very much that our economic privilege public relations have helped the French propaganda press to give us a bad name. That shouldn't happen. France is and always has been a great nation. France

---

1. Named after Lucius Quinctius Cincinnatus, a hero of the fifth century B.C., who traditionally saved Rome from two threatened hostile invasions and then returned to his farm, the Society of the Cincinnati enrolls descendants of Revolutionary War officers. It was founded in 1783.

from the French Revolution has been for Liberty, Equality and Fraternity. So have we.

In Italy, in Austria, in Germany I find that the people on the street love us. I find that they want peace in the world. We must not lose any opportunity to cooperate with them now or in the future.

DIARY

[London]
June [21?], 1956

Had a very pleasant and informative visit with Holland's lovely Queen. The Netherlands are prosperous and the people are happy. Saw a flower market auction. It works like the N.Y. stock exchange and the Chicago wheat pit. Never saw as many beautiful flowers and they told us the first grades had been sold before we arrived.

Visited the Mauritzhaus, a small art gallery in The Hague. It has some Rembrandts and some of the best of the Dutch landscape painters. These Dutch painters of portraits and landscapes were artists and geniuses.

They make our modern day daubers and frustrated ham and egg men look just what they are. It is too bad that our age has forgotten those things that make real art appealing—or they are too lazy to take the pains to do real work.

I saw a bronze monstrosity in one of the art galleries and asked the director if it was meant to be a bronze picture of a devil's darning needle, a vicious-looking bug that's scary to look at. The director turned pale and told me it was a modernist conception of love at first sight! Then *I* fainted.

We were lucky to arrive in Amsterdam while a world-wide Rembrandt exhibition was on. It was beautiful and heart warming. There were loans from the Hermitage in St. Petersburg, from Minnesota, Boston, the Met in N.Y. and from the Louvre and other great galleries.

A ride on the canals of Amsterdam gave us a good back door view of the city and the harbor.

We crossed the Channel on a night boat and landed at the English side in beautiful sunshine. We've had very little sunshine but rain, rain, rain, day after day, with sometimes a peep of sun—in Italy, France and Holland.

I was most happy to see London. Never been here. It is a wonderful city. Oxford is all that tradition and history says it is. A most colorful, solemn and dignified educational institution.

Visited the House of Commons and watched a questions period.

It is most interesting. It was Home Affairs Day and the opposition asked questions about every thing from roads to bawdy houses and gang-sters. Visited the House of Lords and listened to a long-winded speech as boresome as any U.S. Senator could make in a filibuster. So you see what and how we inherited that procedure!

England is prosperous, cordial and courteous. From Lords to taxi drivers and policemen they recognize and wave and bow to the former President. When they have a chance they show by word and deed that they still like us and appreciate our friendship. It is heart warming.

DIARY

[London]
June 24, 1956

Had luncheon with Winston Churchill at his country place. Lord Beaverbrook,[1] Sarah and Mary and her husband were present. Sir Winston and Lady Churchill met us at the door. We stopped for pictures. Many of the neighbor people were at the gate. They gave a wave and a cheer as Mrs. Truman & I entered.

Sir Winston and I had a most pleasant conversation about Potsdam, its agreements and Russian perfidy. I walked around the place with him, feeding the gold fish in two ponds and sitting in the garden watching his three grand children play. It was a scene long to be remembered and an experience never to be forgotten. ·

Mr. Churchill is as keen mentally as ever. He still has the ability to meet quip with quip and to turn a phrase in his own inimitable manner. But his physical condition shows his 82 years. He walks more slowly and he doesn't hear well.

He told me that he could do whatever had to be done as he always did but that he'd rather not do it. He walked around and up and down steps with no more effort than would be expected of a man his age. He remarked that it would be a great thing for the world if I should become President of the United States again. I told him there is no chance of that.

Lord Beaverbrook impressed me very much. I had quite a conversation with him. He is a great admirer of Sir Winston. He also told me that, on this European trip, he thought I'd made the greatest ambassador of good will the U.S.A. had ever had here. Quite a statement from that source. He also said that Margaret had done a wonderful piece of work

1. Minister for aircraft production, minister of supply, and lord privy seal during the Second World War.

along the same line. He may have been pulling my leg but I don't think so.

It was all over too soon and we had to return to London. Chartwell is a beautiful place. The House faces a hill covered with rhododendrons, which were in full bloom. Behind the House is a beautiful garden and below that a valley containing a lake in the distance, a lovely view which Sir Winston called the Wheels of Kent.

He showed me a large number of his paintings in the House and told me he had some 400 more in his studio in the valley below the House. We didn't have the time to visit the studio. It was a very pleasant visit and a happy one for me.

[The Truman party embarked again on the United States *on June 28, at Southampton, and arrived in New York on July 3.]*

At the Democratic convention in July, Truman, supporting for Averell Harriman, stated explicitly why he thought Harriman would be better than Adlai Stevenson, who, of course, won the nomination. He meant it, too, as Stevenson well knew; Truman believed that the United States needed a President who wanted the job, not someone who just toyed with the idea of the presidency, and a man who would surround himself with professionals and not amateurs. After it became clear that Stevenson would get the nomination, Truman called off the campaign for Harriman and dutifully offered to help in any way, and he meant that too.

TO ADLAI E. STEVENSON

August 19, 1956

Dear Governor:

I hope that the next time I send you a letter of congratulation I can say "Dear Mr. President." I do sincerely congratulate you on your great victory in the convention.

Something had to be done to wake up the Party and I undertook to do it. I was in deadly earnest, as a Democratic Politician, to put some life and leadership into the Party. It was the purpose in 1952 to do just that for you. I am sure that you did not understand that the Democratic Party and the United States of America never needed a leader as badly as it does at this time.

You have all the qualifications for that position if you will just let them come to the top. In the California and Florida primaries it began to come out—but complete satisfaction did not come to me until the Convention fight and your victory there.

I was not putting on a show at that Convention. The principles of the Democratic Party and the welfare of the nation and the world, I felt, were at stake. The Democratic Party can not exist as a "me too" Party. It must exist for all the people rich & poor, privileged and underprivileged. It must be ever ready to see justice done to those who can't hire expensive representatives to look after their welfare in Washington.

Only the President can do that. He must be a fighter and one whose heart is in the General Welfare.

I have never had a desire to be a Party Boss or to be the No. 1 Democrat. I tried to abdicate in 1952. The happenings at Chicago gave you the leadership *on your own.* Now I'm ready to do whatever I can to help the Party and its Leader win.

It is up to you to decide what that will be. I do hope you'll have a central headquarters and someone in charge who understands leadership in politics.

I wouldn't blame you if you'd never speak to me again—but let's win this campaign and think of that afterwards.

Sincerely,
Harry S. Truman

On September 3, Truman said in a speech in Milwaukee that he had convincing evidence that Vice-President Nixon once charged him with treason. "It was done at Texarkana, Texas, on the twenty-seventh of October, 1952," he told a questioner on a television panel show broadcast by a local station in Milwaukee. "You read that speech carefully." In the speech Nixon was quoted by the Associated Press as having told a cheering crowd that the then President Truman, Dean Acheson, his secretary of state, and Adlai E. Stevenson were "traitors to the high principles in which many of the nation's Democrats believe." He said "real Democrats" were "outraged by the Truman-Acheson-Stevenson gang's toleration and defense of communism in high places." Nixon afterward denied that he ever called Truman a traitor or the Democratic party the party of treason, and Leonard Hall, the Republican national chairman, offered $1,000 to charity for proof that Nixon ever did so. Hence the following letter.

TO LEONARD W. HALL

September 11, 1956

My dear Mr. Hall:

Some time ago you made a statement to the press that you would contribute one thousand dollars to any charity I might name if it could be proved that the Vice President had called this former President a traitor.

Because it has been proved rather conclusively, may I suggest that this contribution be made to the Red Cross of Korea, a country in which the Republicans have professed such a deep interest during the past few years.

Sincerely yours,
Harry S. Truman

[Hall refused to pay the money.]

The author (with Walter Hehmeyer) of Harry Truman: President *(New York, 1948), Frank McNaughton was campaign manager for Richard Stengel, who was running for the Senate in Illinois. He had written asking Truman's advice.*

TO FRANK McNAUGHTON

October 18, 1956

Dear Frank:

In reply to your letter of the fourth, I think you are on the right track when the candidate for Senator, the Honorable Richard Stengel, sees just as many people as he possibly can.

It is personal contact that really gets the votes—at least that was my experience in 1948—and, without trying to tell Mr. Stengel what he ought to do, the more people he can see in his State the surer he is of election.

I went through four such campaigns in Missouri when I was running for Senator—two primary campaigns, and two election campaigns. The people want to see the man they are voting for and they want to know what he stands for. My approach to the thing was always to explain the principles on which I was running. Don't attack your opponent. Whenever you do, it only gives him free advertising and another chance to attack you. Let him attack you if he will, but you will be all right if you stick to the issues.

Sincerely yours,
Harry S. Truman

TO DWIGHT D. EISENHOWER (UNSENT)

November 28, 1956

My dear Ike:

You are elected again and this time without a Congress of your own choosing. A record with only one precedent, back a hundred and eight years ago—1848 when old Zach Taylor, another professional General, was elected with Millard Fillmore, who was the Know Nothing Candidate in 1856. Your V.P. is not that far advanced.

I sincerely hope you'll wear a homburg hat and a short coat as you did in 1953 at the inauguration. You'll no doubt have your son present, as you should, but you won't have to scold me for having him there. You can now order him to be present yourself.[1]

I am sincerely hoping you'll pray as loudly and as long as you did in 1953—January 20th. I also hope you'll go to Egypt and Palestine and perhaps to Hungary and Poland in order to surrender to the Kremlin as you did in Korea in 1953.[2]

With Eastland, Thurmond, Talmadge, Holland, Byrd and McClellan,[3] you should be able to really inaugurate your so called New Republicanism.

By all means consult Lausche of Ohio, Revercomb of W. Virginia and your two boys from old Kentuck.[4] With that crew you should be able to wreck T.V.A., give away the balance of our national resources, completely ruin our foreign policy and set the country back to 1896 and 1929.

Best of luck and may the honest Democrats and Liberal Republicans save you from disaster.

---

1. In preparation for the inaugural of 1953, Truman ordered President-elect Eisenhower's son John home from Korea, thinking that such an act would be a gesture of thoughtfulness, although relations between the President and the President-elect had cooled noticeably, as was evident during the ride from the White House to the Capitol. When the two men reached the Capitol they went to the sergeant-at-arms' office to wait for the summons to the platform, and Ike turned to Truman and said, "I wonder who is responsible for my son John being ordered to Washington from Korea? I wonder who is trying to embarrass me?" To which Truman answered: "The President of the United States ordered your son to attend your inauguration. If you think somebody was trying to embarrass you by this order, then the President assumes full responsibility." (Margaret Truman, *Harry S. Truman* [New York, 1973], p. 557.)

2. For the Suez crisis and Hungarian and Polish rebellions, see below.

3. Conservative southern Democrats in the Senate.

4. More Senate conservatives.

TO CLARK CLIFFORD

December 6, 1956

Dear Clark:

Thank you very much for your letter of the 4th and the cartoon from the Washington Daily News. I really do not understand why Roy Howard permitted such a thing to be published in one of his papers. It is highly improbable, but do you suppose he is beginning to accept the truth?[1]

I understand that Dean Acheson is under the weather with a virus infection, and I hope that he's not seriously incapacitated. Although he is customarily very prompt in answering letters, he still has two or three of mine to acknowledge.

Paul Butler[2] notified me this morning of my appointment as a member of an advisory committee to the Democratic National Committee, along with Governor Stevenson, Governor Battle of Virginia, Mrs. Roosevelt and Senator Kefauver. I refuse to speculate on the outcome of a meeting of our minds.

Sincerely yours,
Harry S. Truman

The Suez crisis of October–November 1956 was deeply embarrassing to the government of the United States, for it involved an almost obvious collusion of the British and French governments—N.A.T.O. allies—with the government of Israel. Prime Minister Anthony Eden and Premier Edgar Faure also did not bother to keep the United States informed of their plans to invade Egypt, although the Americans probably informed themselves; the U-2 pilot of later fame, Francis Gary Powers, was to write in his autobiography that he made a surveillance flight over the eastern Mediterranean in the early autumn of 1956 and photographed the Anglo-French build-up. The invasion came just at the time of the presidential election in the United States. It also was at the time the Russians were having great trouble maintaining control of two of their European satellites, Poland and Hungary; the invasion masked Soviet troubles in Europe and allowed the Russians to snuff out the Hungarian revolutionary government. The Anglo-French-Israeli invasion was no military success, for the British and French moved ponderously, giving the impression they were invading France in 1944 rather than Egypt, which should

---

1. The cartoon, by Talburt, showed United States foreign policy as a sphinx, with Britain and France standing in front of it and with Britain holding a "riddle" book.

2. Chairman of the Democratic National Committee.

have been a military pushover. The issue was taken to the United Nations, where the United States and Russia ganged up on the errant N.A.T.O. allies, a saddening spectacle. Former President Truman, who had presided over the formation of N.A.T.O., was outraged by the way in which the Eisenhower administration had allowed itself to be involved in this mess and wrote plainly to the majority leader of the Senate, Lyndon B. Johnson.

TO LYNDON B. JOHNSON

December 11, 1956

Dear Lyndon:

I do not know when I have received a letter I appreciated more than yours of the seventh. Your speech at Whitney was a very progressive one, and you did succeed in getting most of our suggestions put through.[1]

I have never wanted to pose as a prophet, nor do I intend to be one now, but I do want to keep the Democratic Party a party of the people. We can never win unless it is.

In our long telephone conversation the other night Sam explained why he felt that he should not serve, officially, on the advisory committee to the Democratic Executive Committee, and I understand his viewpoint. When I was President and asked him to attend Cabinet meetings, he refused on the basis of his belief that the Legislative Branch of the Government should not be a part of the Executive Branch. Nevertheless, he and I discussed every subject that came up in Cabinet meetings and other places, and we understood each other completely.

All that I am interested in is getting an effective program based on constructive ideas for the welfare of the country and the world. I am just as sure as I sit here that it will not come from the other end of the street—unless there is some great, and unlikely, change of attitude there. . . .

Another thing that worries me is our falling out with our real, honest-to-goodness friends, Britain and France. What the remedy for that is I don't know. Dulles is over there now making new errors and compounding old ones, in his usual fashion.

---

1. A year before, at Whitney, Texas, on Lyndon Johnson Day, November 21, 1955, the senate majority leader set out a program for "the party with a heart" that included extension of social security, tax revision for low-income groups, aid to medical research, school construction, public roads, restoration of 90 percent of farm parity, a natural gas bill, housing, a water resources program, federal support for depressed areas, fair immigration and naturalization laws, a constitutional amendment eliminating the poll tax, and disaster insurance. Johnson told Truman that he then had marshaled the Democratic majority, which passed most of the above measures.

It does seem to me that the foreign relations committees of the House and the Senate and their chairmen and the Majority leaders of the House and the Senate ought to investigate this thing thoroughly, and force the man at the other end of the street to come up with a program to prevent a third world war. I am speaking from experience. If I had sat still and let the Russians take Berlin, or had let them take Iran and Greece and Turkey as they proposed to do, we would have been isolated and already in another world war.

Now is the time, too, to achieve friendly relations, on an active basis, with India. Nehru has discovered that his friends are not in the same corner that he and Gandhi occupied. Hungary proved that to him rather conclusively.

I am going on at length here, and probably shouldn't, but I am terribly disturbed, not only about our foreign affairs but our domestic situation. This tight money program of the special-interest people has almost put a stop to home construction and industrial expansion. The powers that be abolished the Reconstruction Finance Corporation because it prevented a tight money market, and unless Congress takes some constructive action in the matter, we will continue down the road to another 1929.

I do not believe that the Executive Department understands national finance, international relations, or national defense. If Congress held a series of hearings—and it should—you would find exactly how little they do know.

It is really incredible when one considers the gentleman—born in Texas and raised in Kansas, educated at West Point—his service as Chief of Staff to Douglas MacArthur, and the wealth of training he had under two Presidents who knew where to lead the world.

I say it is incredible. Millard Fillmore, Franklin Pierce and Calvin Coolidge are paragons of energy and decision alongside him. Lyndon, for God's sake, get hold of Sam and John McCormack and do something!

> Sincerely yours,
> Harry S. Truman

The old Pickwick Hotel building in Kansas City, at Tenth and McGee, was next to a bus station, and on top of the bus station was a clock.

MEMORANDUM

December 17, 1956

Pickwick:

You have a clock over your bus depot that gives me a case of time-ophobia. I look at that clock every time I go to the Federal Reserve Building's privy, on floor 11.

When my watch and all four of my clocks say it is 9:25 A.M. Central Standard Time, that damned clock of yours will say it is 6:40. I don't know whether it is afternoon or forenoon or just halfway between Eastern Daylight Time and no time at all.

Just because you are named for Charles Dickens' Mr. Pickwick doesn't give you authority to mess up our local time.

It is bad enough when these municipalities like New York, Chicago, St. Louis and some others ball up the Standard Time Zones. It took almost forty years to attain a sensible time zone set up for this round globe of ours and now we might just as well go back to meridian time of the 1820's.

You shouldn't contribute to that confusion.

Being a former President was an expensive business, as Truman discovered after he left the White House. There was an immense correspondence and he was expected to appear here and there and pay his travel and hotel expenses, and many causes expected cash contributions; it was just not like being a private citizen. The former President needed money to keep the mechanism going. Of the two living ex-Presidents, Hoover was a millionaire and could easily afford the office help and other expenses. Truman had never made much money, and indeed had been deeply in debt throughout the 1920s and 1930s and found himself forced to put Bess on the payroll during the Senate years—she was listed as a member of his office staff. After leaving the presidency he had plenty of chances to make money by selling his name, and he turned them down with scorn, for he vividly remembered the antics of the Roosevelt family. He hoped to pay his office and travel expenses from his writings—he enjoyed writing and looked forward to expressing himself in print—but then the memoirs proved very disappointing financially. By the late 1950s he was ready to see enactment of an "ex-Presidents law" that would pick up the public part of his office expenses and travel.

TO JOHN W. McCORMACK

January 10, 1957

Dear John:

I can't tell you how much I appreciated your letter of the sixth.

It certainly was a pleasure to have the opportunity to sit with you and Sam again and discuss things that are for the welfare of the country.

I was talking to Sam about the difference in the net result of the sale of my Memoirs and the sale of Eisenhower's book. As you remember, we obtained for him a capital gains tax which gave him a net return, including the State Tax, of $437,000.00 for his book.

When my program came up the Internal Revenue, without any interference from the President, wanted to take 80% of the same figure that Eisenhower got for his book. Sam Rosenman and two or three tax experts finally worked the thing so it was paid over a five year period and a 67½% tax was charged, which included the State tax.[1]

In order to be able to transact the business of writing the Memoirs and to meet the tremendous burden of handling the largest volume of mail in the State, I had to rent an office in Kansas City and the total overhead for the period from February 1953 until about November of last year, 1956, amounted to a sum over $153,000.00. Had it not been for the fact that I was able to sell some property that my brother, sister and I inherited from our mother I would practically be on relief but with the sale of that property I am not financially embarrassed. However, it does seem to me in all fairness that part of the overhead should be met. I would say 70% of the $153,000.00 that I have been out for office help, rent, postage, telephones and everything else that goes with the expense of an office for a former President should be paid.

I don't want a pension and do not expect one but I do think 70% of the expenses or overhead should be paid by the Government—the 30% is what I would ordinarily have been out on my own hook if I hadn't tried to meet the responsibilities of being a former President.

---

1. Eisenhower sold the rights to his Second World War memoir, *Crusade in Europe* (Garden City, N.Y.: 1948), for a lump sum of $635,000 and obtained a ruling from the Internal Revenue authorities that becaue he was not a professional author the sale could be treated as a capital gain, with a 25 percent tax. Because of the resulting outcry, Congress in 1950 passed the so-called Eisenhower amendment, which forbade any use of capital gains for writers whether professional or amateur. Doubleday paid Truman the same package-deal, no-royalties amount for his memoirs that Ike received for *Crusade*. Truman then had to pay out 67½ percent for federal and state income taxes, plus the cost of researchers and typing and hundreds of presentation copies that he had to buy at publisher's cost.

As you know, we passed a Bill which gave all five star Generals and Admirals three clerks, and all the emoluments that went with their office when they retired.

It seems rather peculiar that a fellow who spent eighteen years in government service and succeeded in getting all these things done for the people he commanded should have to go broke in order to tell the people the truth about what really happened. It seems to me in all justice a part of this tremendous overhead should be met by the public.

I don't want any pension and never have wanted any because I'll manage to get along but I am just giving you the difference in the approach between the great General and myself on the Memoirs. My net return will be about $37,000.00 total over a five year period! It was a package deal. I receive no royalties.

I would never have given you this information if you hadn't asked for it.

Sincerely yours,
Harry S. Truman

When in the midst of the Suez crisis the Russians suppressed the Hungarian revolution, a flood of refugees crossed the border into Austria and there was a huge outpouring of sympathy for the Hungarians. The President received a telegram asking that he sign a petition to the government of the Soviet Union asking for justice for the people of Hungary.

TO WILLIAM J. DONOVAN

January 11, 1957

Dear General:

I received the telegram this morning signed by you, Mrs. Roosevelt, Norman Thomas and François Mauriac.

I've always made it a point never to sign a petition of any sort. I got into trouble when I first got into politics by signing a petition.

I think you are on the right track but I am just as sure as I can be that getting up a petition will only get the Hungarians into trouble rather than do them any good. The only person able to help is the head of the Government of the United States. I know from experience that carloads of petitions came to the White House and very few of them were ever of any use to anybody except to get the names of the people who signed them in the papers.

I am anxious to see something concrete done for Hungary but I don't think you can do it by a petition.

Sincerely yours,
Harry S. Truman

Early in 1957, the former State Department official, turned historian, Herbert Feis inquired through Dean Acheson if it would be possible to see Truman's private papers pertaining to the Potsdam Conference— Feis was writing a book which eventually received the Pulitzer Prize in history. Acheson spoke with Truman, who mulled over the possibility of Feis's use of the papers and eventually decided against it. In the course of the mulling, the President composed a handwritten letter to Acheson about his experiences at Potsdam. He kept the letter around for a while, uncertain what to do with it, and almost a month later, on April 12, wrote of his uncertainty ("I wrote you a longhand letter after I had talked to you about the Potsdam papers but I haven't made up my mind to send it"). Then he put the letter away.

TO DEAN ACHESON (UNSENT)

March 15, 1957

Dear Dean:

It was certainly a pleasure to talk with you about Potsdam and the Doctor who is interested in that phase of our foreign policy.

I hardly ever look back for the purpose of contemplating "what might have been." Potsdam brings to mind "what might have been" had you been there instead of the Congressman, Senator, Supreme Court Justice, Presidential Assistant, Secretary of State, Governor of Secession South Carolina the Honorable James F. Byrnes!

At that time I trusted him implicitly—and he was then conniving to run the Presidency over my head! I had Joe Davies, at that time a Russophile as most of us were, Ed Pauley, the only hard boiled hard hitting anti-Russian around except the tough old Admiral, Bill Leahy. Certainly things were presented because Russia had no program except to take over the free part of Europe, kill as many Germans as possible and fool the Western Alliance. Britain only wanted to control the Eastern Mediterranean, keep India, oil in Persia, the Suez Canal and whatever else was floating loose.

There was an innocent idealist at one corner of that Round Table who wanted free waterways, Danube-Rhine-Kiel Canal, Suez, Black Sea Straits, Panama all free, a restoration of Germany, France, Italy, Poland,

Czechoslovakia, Rumania and the Balkans and a proper treatment of Latvia, Lithuania, Finland, free Philippines, Indonesia, Indo China, a Chinese Republic and a free Japan.

What a show that was! But a large number of agreements were reached in spite of the setup—only to be broken as soon as the unconscionable Russian Dictator returned to Moscow! And I liked the little son of a bitch. He was a good six inches shorter than I am and even Churchill was only three inches taller than Joe! Yet I was the little man in stature and intellect! So the Press said. Well we'll see.

Wish you [had] been there. Tell your friend I'll help him all I can. My best to Alice.

Clark Clifford wrote two letters to the President under the date March 12, 1957, the first thanking Truman for a letter about the passing of his, Clifford's, mother, and the second remarking the tenth anniversary of the Truman Doctrine. The name Truman Doctrine did not sit well with the President, but there was little he could do about it; the American people are fond of large statements of principle, as their political leaders observed long ago, and hence the multitude of doctrines and other such pronouncements in American history.

Ten years after the doctrine of 1947, the Suez crisis had just come to an end, and the Eisenhower administration was seeking to quiet the Arab nations of the Middle East with an appropriation of $200 million which was known, elaborately, as the Eisenhower Doctrine.

TO CLARK CLIFFORD

March 18, 1957

Dear Clark:

Thank you very much for your note of the 12th about your mother. As you know, I have been through the same experience and can appreciate your feelings.

I was also highly pleased with your other letter concerning March 12, 1947. I will never forget that day. If the present administration had stepped in and used the same methods in connection with Suez, there would have been no trouble there either.

The editorial you enclosed was a good one. I never was very much impressed that that policy was named the Truman Doctrine. Like the Marshall Plan, it too was only a part of the foreign policy of the United States, and that is how history should refer to it. If this administration's advertising people have their way, its latest travesty on the Middle East will go down in history as greater than the Monroe Doctrine.

I hope we can see each other before too long and, like the Walrus and the Carpenter, talk of many things, of shoes and ships and sealing wax, and even maybe prove that the sea is boiling hot and that pigs have wings.

Please give my best to "Grandma" Clifford and tell her that it looks as if Mrs. Truman will join her in that great association of grandmothers. I cannot understand why no one has organized them for protection against baby-sitting.

Please tell Randy[1] hello for me too.

Sincerely yours,
Harry S. Truman

TO JAMES A. FARLEY

April 6, 1957

Dear Jim:

As it always is, one of the highlights of my visit to the metropolis of the United States was the pleasure of having breakfast with you. I certainly did enjoy it.

I had a good time, too, with the cab driver who took me back to the hotel. He told me a story which I'll pass on to you. When Winston Churchill was in New York on one of his visits to the United States, his car broke down, and he was in danger of missing a speaking engagement at the NBC broadcasting studios. He flagged a cab and on arriving at his destination asked the driver if he would wait until he came out. The driver, not recognizing Churchill, said, "Johnny, I can't wait for you because I want to get back to headquarters to hear Winston Churchill talk on the radio." Churchill was rather intrigued and asked him what he thought of Mr. Churchill. "Johnny," he said, "he's just the greatest Prime Minister Great Britain ever had." Churchill took out a twenty dollar bill and gave it to him. The driver, still not recognizing him, said, "Johnny, for twenty dollars I'd wait for anyone."

I am counting on your being present for the library dedication ceremonies on July 6th. Please don't fail me.

Sincerely yours,
Harry

---

1. Randall Clifford, Clark's son.

The former White House staffer David Lloyd, operating out of Washington, was in the business of raising funds for building the Truman Library in Independence, and the great occasion loomed when the library could be dedicated. Problems arose. The Truman relatives were not well known to the fund raiser and failed to receive invitations. And there was the matter of getting a Catholic archbishop to do the dedication, rather than a good Baptist; the President sensed the time was right for a Catholic, but he could hardly prove that fact to his Baptist friends.

TO DAVID D. LLOYD

April 22, 1957

Dear Dave:

In reply to your letter of the 17th, I have written a letter to Joe Martin asking him to come to the dedication.

It pains me to say this, but you have got me into quite a family storm. A large number of the good ladies of the bridge club, who like to put it over on one another, have received invitations, but my two sisters-in-law who live right in back of us and who are members of the club did not receive invitations. My sister and my brother and my nephews and nieces have not received theirs. Only two members of my office staff have received invitations.

Mrs. Truman is in close daily contact with the sisters-in-law, and if you don't watch out, you will be the principal witness in a divorce case. I'll have Sam Rosenman as the lawyer for both sides, and you will be cross-questioned until you are cross-eyed.

Of course, I understand the situation, but I have no explanation to offer to the folks at home. I am going to call on the Archbishop tomorrow. I know he is willing to do the job, but I believe it would be better if I went to see him. All of this is going to put me in bad with some of my Baptist friends, but I don't see why they can't get over it. That's what their teachings tell them they are supposed to do.

Rabbi Thurman from Saint Louis will be the chaplain for the corner stone laying ceremony. That will take care of him, and he is the only one I care about.

Sincerely yours,
Harry S. Truman

Ralph Ginzburg, the enterprising articles editor of Esquire, *wanted an article by the President, apparently with the President's assistance, and Truman was uncertain, for two reasons.*

TO RALPH GINZBURG

October 4, 1957

Dear Mr. Ginzburg:

I have been a long time writing you after I heard from Bill Hillman on the Esquire proposition.

I have been reading the four recent issues that you sent to Bill, which he turned over to me, and, of course, I have always liked Esquire, but I never could agree with Esquire on the publication of the undressed ladies in most of the magazine.

That piece by James Roosevelt, a copy of which Bill gave me, didn't help matters very much either.

Sometime later I will be glad to talk with you on the proposition and maybe we can get together.

Sincerely yours,
Harry S. Truman

TO EDWARD K. THOMPSON

October 9, 1957

Dear Mr. Thompson:

You don't know how very much I appreciated your going to all the trouble to make those 200 proofs of the color picture of me in my Masonic regalia.

I have been trying my level best as the people, in the time of Mark Twain, would say out West, not to be in a position of asking favors for no good reason, except the reason that I was in the White House, so I am going to take you at your word and enclose you a check for $200.00 on the Riggs National Bank of Washington.

If there is anything in the world that I dislike, it is a man who is always mooching things, based on some service he may have rendered publicly. Sometime when we get together in New York, I'll tell you a story on the subject that I think will just fill the bill.

Again, I appreciate most highly your going to all that trouble to fix the pictures up for me because I have quite a demand for them.

Sincerely yours,
Harry S. Truman

The President delighted in children, and more than four years after the visit to Hawaii he remembered his little friends there, and made a

Christmas arrangement with the Vile-Goller Printing Company of Kansas City.

TO HY VILE

December 10, 1957

Dear Hy:

When I was at Coconut Island back in 1953 for a vacation Edwin Pauley's children were there with guests and I set up what I called a "Coconut Cabinet" on the Island.

I would like very much to have some engraved certificates made for these various children who were there—a certificate about 8 × 10, I would say, with engraved statements, and signature lines at the bottom for me, as a former President of the United States, and for Edwin Pauley, as the owner and Manager of the Estate.

I am enclosing the wording for the proposed certificates as we talked about over the telephone this morning.

I'd like to have these ready so I could send them for Christmas to these children, most of whom are now grown.

I'll appreciate it very much if you will get this done for me on the condition you be sure and send me a bill.

Sincerely yours,
Harry S. Truman

P.S. Please send me samples of the way you think they ought to look.

Susan Pauley, Secretary of State for Coconut Affairs and ranking member of the Coconut Cabinet, with authority to make obstreperous inhabitants behave and with authority to communicate with the Marines on the main island of Oahu for such police support as is necessary.

Penny Winkler, Secretary of Beauty with power to pick Queens of the Islands for looks, action and deportment. She has authority to go as far away as Los Angeles and Honolulu if she finds no qualified candidates on Coconut Island.

Ann Morrissey (Biddy). Secretary of Defense against short sheeting, frogs and animals from the deep Pacific. A very efficient member of the great Coconut Cabinet of Coconut Island of the Hawaiian Group is required for this program. She may call on the Secretary of State for Coconut for Marine support if necessary.

Stephen Pauley, Secretary for Mischief, whose authority runs to short sheeting, frogs and snakes in beds and whatever else causes laughter and ridiculous situations. His job is to persuade the Secretary of

Defense that all things in his department are necessary for the happiness
of the inhabitants of Coconut Island.

Dean Gargaro, Secretary for the causing of Many Laughs and good
times, with authority to cause such acts as will bring about conditions for
which he is responsible. His job is to make everyone happy by any means
he sees fit to employ.

Robert Pauley (Buzzy), Secretary of the Treasury of Coconut, with
power to collect all taxes in U.S. pennies, Coconut shell, sea shell, or any
other medium of exchange he may see fit to make legal including frogs,
snakes and marine animals as tax in kind.

*Some weeks after the Soviets sent up their Sputnik, Senator J. Wil-
liam Fulbright made a Senate speech remarking the strength of the
Soviet Union; it was a time, Fulbright said, for education.*

TO J. WILLIAM FULBRIGHT

January 28, 1958

Dear Senator:

I have just read a copy of your speech of January 23rd. Unfortunately,
the newspapers in this area did not give it proper coverage.

I do not know when I have read a statement I appreciated more. It
has always been my opinion that an improved approach to the education
of the rising generation is necessary if we expect to continue as the
leaders of the free world.

In this mimeographed copy, the first paragraph on Page 3 struck me
as being absolutely correct, as did the number of statements which follow
it.

All my Presidential papers were turned over to the Government,
along with every gift I received as President from world potentates and
other visitors to the White House. I went out and raised a million eight
hundred thousand dollars to construct a building to house these materials. Eventually, I hope to make the Library a center for the study of the
Presidency of the United States.

In the last session of the Congress a bill was passed authorizing the
indexing and microfilming of those Presidential papers now in the Library of Congress. There are about sixteen partial sets there. I now hope
that Congress will authorize the indexing and microfilming of all Presidential papers now in existence. Mine are being indexed, but the microfilming will have to be authorized by the government. If a comprehen-
sive job could be done, the history of the Executive Branch of the

government, together with the records of the Congress and the Supreme Court, would be available to every college in the country.

Sometime on your way to or from Arkansas, I hope you will stop by and let me show you just exactly what I have in mind. I am trying to get one of the big foundations to start a study of the Presidency and center that study here in the Library I have constructed. I have tried to prevent it from being, in any way, a memorial to me. I want it to be an educational institution, and I feel certain you would approve.

Sincerely yours,

Harry S. Truman

Governor Orville Freeman of Minnesota saw the President's filmed television interview with Edward R. Murrow and asked for assistance. In a very small way, Freeman wrote, he sometimes had to make decisions, and he always had admired the decisiveness of the President. He knew that Truman's reading had been exhaustive, and asked for "a couple of biographies or historical novels or histories about certain times and periods which you felt pointed up particularly the decision-making process."

TO ORVILLE L. FREEMAN

February 7, 1958

Dear Governor:

I do not know when I have received a letter I appreciated more than yours of the 4th. Thank you, too, for liking last Sunday's broadcast. I am highly complimented.

I have never given such a list to anyone before, but here are a few of the books I studied which helped to lend me confidence on many occasions.

There were the Marquis James books on Andrew Jackson, Claude Bowers' books on Jefferson, particularly his *Jefferson and Hamilton,* and a collection of Jefferson's letters called *A Jefferson Profile,* edited by a man named Padover. I think very highly of this last book.

There were all of Carl Sandburg's works on Abe Lincoln, the Memoirs of Thomas H. Benton and those of our former Congressman and Speaker from Missouri, Champ Clark; the Memoirs of General Grant which Mark Twain helped him write; the Memoirs of John Sherman and of William T. Sherman. Also valuable is Sol Bloom's accumulation of George Washington's papers which were published by the government.

When I was young, I read the Bible through many times. I read

Plutarch's Lives of the great Romans and, before that, a four-volume set entitled *Great Men and Famous Women* and Abbott's *Makers of History.* Later on I came across and read Gibbon's *Roman Empire.*

In fact, I read everything I could get my hands on about men who made history.

The simplest conclusion I reached was that the lazy men caused all the trouble and those who worked had the job of rectifying their mistakes.

It has been a life-time program for me, and if you start out on even this incomplete list, you will find it a lengthy study but well worthwhile. It will keep you out of mischief too.

Sincerely yours,

Harry S. Truman

Guy Lombardo wrote protesting a comment by the President on Ed Murrow's See It Now *program, during which Truman remarked that he did not like the "Missouri Waltz." "It's a ragtime song," the President said, "and if you let me say what I think—I don't give a damn about it. But I can't say it out loud, because it's the song of Missouri. It's as bad as the Star Spangled Banner so far as music is concerned." The orchestra leader contended that the "Missouri Waltz" was a "pleasant, relaxing, good piece of popular music . . . one of the finest popular melodies ever written."*

TO GUY LOMBARDO

February 11, 1958

Dear Guy:

Thank you for your letter of the third. Sammy Kaye wrote me a letter recently about another statement I made on music, and yours was just as highly appreciated.[1]

I cannot disagree with you that the Missouri Waltz may be a good piece of popular music, but in my opinion it is not a proper state song.

It is likely that I am prejudiced, but we both know that it takes a tenor, a baritone and a bass to sing the Star Spangled Banner. I have

---

1. In West Virginia at a Veterans Day celebration Truman had attacked rock and roll music, saying that "I was taught to appreciate good music, not this damn noise they play today." The bandleader Sammy Kaye protested that the former President did not qualify as a music critic, and in response Truman advised Kaye to read the Constitution, which allowed a citizen "to state a preference of expression in every field of endeavor, and as long as that document is the law of the land, no one can stop him."

never understood why it was not set to music that every single soldier in the Army could sing.

I always stand at attention for both songs and always with regret that I cannot appreciate the music of either of them.

Sincerely yours,
Harry S. Truman

To many people at the time, the plan of Congress to extend the east front of the Capitol some thirty-two feet, according to a proposal first made in 1905, seemed utterly ridiculous. Some advocates of the plan stressed the need for office space, which appeared a silly contention when the additional space was to cost about $17 million—the amount Congress had appropriated. Architects, and the D.A.R., stressed the destruction of the appearance of the Capitol. Truman's point—that the dome might come apart if there was no extension of the building and replacement of the sandstone blocks with marble—was lost from view. At the behest of friends, the solicitor general of the Truman administration, Philip B. Perlman, wrote to ask the President to oppose the extension, and must have been surprised at the response.

TO PHILIP B. PERLMAN

February 15, 1958

Dear Phil:

I read with interest your letter of the 7th regarding the program to finish the center front of the Capitol. Back in 1935 Tom Connally and I held hearings on the finishing of the center section of the Capitol, and the Senate passed a bill authorizing the completion [of] construction intended when the present dome was placed on the old building.

If you will go out and stand on the House steps or Senate steps of the addition which was finished in 1849, you will find that the dome is set seven or eight feet over the front portico of the Capitol. The old building was made out of red sandstone, and parts of the cornice fall every time there's a storm. It is a wonder no one has been killed.

The correct objective is to finish the building as was intended when the two Vermont marble wings were placed on it in the 1840's. The present dome was only half finished in 1863, and there are pictures in existence in the Capitol building showing the dome only half up, with all the machinery used to raise the parts and put it together.

In the basement of the Capitol building you will find a model of the building as it should be. All this hue and cry about spoiling the looks of the Capitol ranks with the wails and weeping I had to put up with when I carried out the original plans for a balcony on the White House.[1]

I am 100% for the completion of the center front of the Capitol to match the two wings, and I think everyone ought to get behind it and see that it is done. It is a disgraceful looking thing the way it is. The program which has been in existence ever since 1849 should be finished.

If these people who are crying about the Capitol now really think they are doing the right thing, they ought to continue their efforts by taking the present dome off and putting the old one back. I suggest that you make that proposal to the Damned Annual Row sisters and all the others who are raising this fuss, and I hope you will take the trouble to read the hearings held in 1935 by the Public Buildings and Grounds Committee together with the report Tom Connally and I made on the subject.

Sincerely yours,
Harry S. Truman

[The east front of the Capitol was extended.]

The President's physician, Dr. Graham, asked for a letter commending the head of Mercersburg Academy, Dr. Beachley, which was all right with Truman, but Beachley himself had made a suggestion that was unappealing.

TO DR. WALLACE H. GRAHAM

April 30, 1958

Dear Wally:

I am enclosing a copy of the letter I sent to the American Public Relations Association commending Dr. Beachley.

His suggestion that I make an appearance in Mercersburg is appreciated, but my difficulty now is to arrange my schedule so that I can do what you and Mrs. Truman have been trying to get me to do—stay at home a while. After this election year is over, maybe I will have better luck.

---

1. Early in his White House tenure, Truman took down the awnings on the south portico and put up a balcony, for the awnings looked droopy and also rotted out every year or two and had to be replaced. Moreover, a balcony was, as he wrote, in the original plans. But critics were outraged, and some of them inferred that a Missouri president would sit on the balcony with his bare feet hanging over the railing.

His idea of my dedicating the birthplace of President James Buchanan does not appeal to me, however. Sometime when we can sit down together, I will explain myself. If Buchanan had been an Andrew Jackson or an Abraham Lincoln, there would not have been a civil war. I would prefer not to endorse anything connected with him, but I am getting together a collection of information on all our Presidents in which I will try to be as impartial as the facts will let me. He is in the same class as Patrick Henry, whose monument I refused to dedicate, because, if he had had his way, we would not have had this Republic.[1]

Sincerely yours,
Harry S. Truman

Again, in 1958, the President and Mrs. Truman went to Europe, this time in the company of Judge Samuel I. Rosenman and Mrs. Rosenman. Unlike the earlier trip, this one was very quiet, almost private—little mail, few cables, only a couple of press conferences, no syndicated account of the trip. The President had no official things to do, and he and his wife were traveling as simply Mr. and Mrs. Truman from Independence, Missouri, come to see the Continent during a quiet summer. Even so, he was almost always recognized and pointed out, oohed and aahed over. The Trumans took the S.S. Independence, *leaving New York on May 26, destination Naples. They saw a bit of Italy and of southern France.*

Return was on the Constitution, *leaving Cannes on July 1, arriving in New York on July 9. The following diary entry was made on the stationery of the Château du Domaine St-Martin in Vence.*

DIARY

[June 1958]

To France
May 26, 1958

We leave on the Independence! It is a gallant and beautiful ship to see and is a good sailing ship, taking the rollers with very little discomfort to the passengers.

Hon. Sam Rosenman and Mrs. Rosenman are our traveling companions. They are most agreeable and pleasant people to be with. Both speak

---

1. In the Virginia convention of 1788 for ratifying the Constitution, Henry opposed its adoption as inimical to state sovereignty.

French fluently which is an asset to Mrs. Truman and me because we do not speak nor understand but few words of that language.

Our crossing was a most pleasant one. The sun shone nearly every day, the passengers were considerate and agreeable. Signed many autographs and posed for many pictures but altogether it was a pleasant trip. No telephone calls for political questions but a cable or two on the subject but they didn't have to be answered.

Arrived at the port on the Spanish coast across from Gibraltar. Had a press conference of no consequence, looked at the "Rock" and remembered the Insurance Company advertisement. It would be hard to recognize the place from the advertisement. But that is true of most ads. They are made to make a sale. Take pictures of resorts, California, Colorado, Arizona, Florida, Maine and Massachusetts. They have pictures to draw unsuspecting travelers just as do these Riviera French ads.

Never expect to see what the advertisements put in their pictures and there will be no disappointment. In this South of France there are many places worth seeing for their historical background. There are also some beautiful views if you can get yourself to forget the vandalism of the ignorant Christian Middle Ages before the Renaissance. Some of the most beautiful monuments of antiquity were used as quarries and some were willfully destroyed for propaganda purposes.

Athens, Rome, Alexandria, the great cities of the Nile and the Near East along with the historical cities of this southern France are only a few examples. My interest has been to see what a great civilization of the past could do and had done. It makes me wonder what may happen to our so-called modern set-up. Some three or four thousand years hence there will be wonder as to what we were trying to do. Maybe we'll end up as a lost Atlantis, a destroyed Knossos, a burned Rome and a maliciously destroyed Athens, Alexandria or the ruins in Vietnam and at Bokhara and Samarkand—who knows.

We may be able with the great scientific discoveries to make Gobi, Sahara, and all of the great American deserts bloom and support in luxury the billions yet unborn or we may use those same scientific discoveries to turn our planet into a fire ball again and fulfill the prophecy of Noah's time about a world destruction by fire instead of the purported destruction of that day. Who knows?

TO TOM L. EVANS

> *Château du Domaine St-Martin*
> *Route de Coursegoules*
> *à Vence, France*
> *June 21, 1958*

Dear Tom:

I've been procrastinating about writing letters, have sent only one to Margaret, one to Rose and one to Mary Jane in three weeks so you know I've been resting.

This is a lovely place up on a hill with rooms for only about a half dozen people. Most of the time we've had it to ourselves. It is 1500 feet above the Mediterranean Sea about 10 miles from Nice and the same distance from Cannes.

The ship stopped overnight in Naples, I was recognized soon as I went ashore and now everywhere they do as usual—"There he goes"— but it's in French and I can't understand it so it is O.K. When I stop to look in a store window or to buy a little H_2O flavored with bourbon I am an animal escaped from the circus known as the "Striped-Assed Donkey from Missouri." So you see I have to behave. I went into the Casino at Monte Carlo and couldn't bet a sou because everybody wanted to shake hands, French and U.S. citizens as well as British and Italians. I gave up and came out solvent. Guess it was a good thing.

Have been investigating Roman ruins in Nimes, Avignon and Arles. Will tell you and 822[1] about 'em when I come home.

Give my best to all our friends—822 and elsewhere and tell 'em I had no chance to learn any card manipulation at Monte Carlo. They know how—and how!

Mrs. T. joins me in best wishes to Mamie Lou and to you.

> Sincerely,
> Harry S. Truman

The Suez crisis of October–November 1956 marked a passing of responsibility for peace in the Middle East from the old-time imperial powers, Britain and France, to the United States, and it soon was apparent that America and Americans would have difficulty in the area. The Eisenhower Doctrine of 1957 had the unfortunate effect of sowing fur-

---

1. The 822 Club in Kansas City.

ther dissension, for the only Arab country to take money from the United States was Lebanon, afflicted with an almost impossible combination of religious, racial, and geographical problems—Moslems versus Christians, Arabs versus Greeks and other Westernized Middle Easterners, hill people versus city people. Lebanon was a rich little country and a prize to such have-not nations as Egypt, and the Egyptians under President Gamal Abdel Nasser appeared to threaten the Lebanese regime of President Camille Chamoun. Chamoun wished to be elected to an unconstitutional second term of office. He arranged to take American money under the Eisenhower Doctrine, and before long fighting broke out between Arabs and Christians, with Chamoun favoring the latter. At the same time a revolt erupted in nearby Iraq, where the king was murdered, and chaos also threatened in Jordan, where King Hussein was in trouble with Palestinians who were supporting Nasser. President Eisenhower sent marines into Lebanon, and British planes violated Israeli air space to fly troops into Jordan.

TELEPHONE CONVERSATION

July 15, 1958

The President [Truman]: Hello, Lyndon, how are you?

Lyndon Johnson: Very well, thank you, and I hope you are too. . . .

The President: I don't want to pry into your business, but no one in the world is any more interested in what's happening in the world to help keep the peace, and I'm worried to death about what I see in the papers. That's not the truth there, and I . . . [ellipsis points in original]

Johnson: Well, the fact is, the chickens are coming home to roost, and it looks as if someone is going to have to take a trip to Lebanon instead of Korea.

The President: It should have been done a year and a half ago.

Johnson: That's right. My mother was operated on yesterday, and I didn't get back until late last night. But the matter is . . . [original] I am told this, that the President felt he had to move with combat teams, the Marines and the fleet and act decisively at the moment. If he didn't, he would encourage possible action elsewhere, and he made that proposal. Rayburn felt that it ought to be done, and Russell thought it ought to be done—all except Fulbright. Mansfield suggested going through the UN, but it was felt that if we didn't act immediately, it might encourage the Russians . . . [original] but under the plan laid down it was felt that the least danger was in immediate action, and that's what has been done.

The President: It got Sherman Adams off the front page. . . .[1] [original]

Johnson: Yes. That's the best result.

The President: What I am worried about is the fact that we seem to be approaching closer to a complete break with this eastern outfit which may wind up with leveling the whole world. You know I have to go out and make speeches for the Democrats, and whatever I say I want to be right.

Johnson: It has great potentialities and great dangers, and I am told, after I got in last night, by those who attended the meeting that although it is fraught with great dangers and great troubles, at this moment, after what has happened in the last several months, it is fraught with less danger than it would be with more vacillation and hesitancy. He was encouraged to take action. Rayburn would know more, because he was in the meeting and the first man whose views were requested, and I am informed that he expressed them.

The President: Would you suggest I talk to Rayburn?

Johnson: Yes, I would.

The President: I will do it then.

Johnson: I think he can tell you. I gather from Russell, Benson[2] and Russell that Mansfield thought it should go through the UN, a police force action of the UN. Fulbright rather felt that they should not make a unilateral action, but when we are committed with these people that when they had intervention from the outside, we would go to them, we should go. If we didn't go, they would say we didn't mean anything.

The President: But you think I had better talk to Sam? The reason I am doing this is not that I want to interfere with Congress, I just don't want to go off half-cocked.

Johnson: The feeling is that the President of the United States [was right to send] the Marines in there. Forces went ashore to preserve independence. That action was taken on the appeal of the Lebanese government itself. The American forces have been committed, and at the present time no one can foresee the future, but the American people must be united, whatever the cost.

---

1. Eisenhower's chief of staff, former Governor Sherman Adams of New Hampshire, was on the front page because of accepting a vicuña coat and free hotel accommodations from a Boston textile manufacturer who was in tax trouble.

2. Ezra Taft Benson, secretary of agriculture.

TELEPHONE CONVERSATION

July 15, 1958

Speaker Sam Rayburn: Hey there, farmer!

The President: Hello, how's the farmer from Texas? I saw all this in the papers, and, you know, they're asking me to make some speeches, and I didn't want to go off half-cocked. I wanted you to tell me what the situation is. . . . [ellipsis points in original]

The Speaker: Well, we had a two and a half hour conference down there, like we used to have. Iraq went to hell yesterday. Lebanon is just about to go to hell, and Jordan is on the verge. They made up their minds that the best thing to do is to act quickly, before the Russians do something, and that it was all right if the President ordered troops in. He has authority under the Constitution to move troops. At my press conference this morning I said I thought it was the proper thing to do. It was pretty generally agreed—there must have been 20 or more members of the Senate there and the House, and it was pretty much the consensus, after we were told of the general situation after Iraq went to hell. Chamoun asked us to come, so we're not barging in. It's a civil war in a way, and with outside help coming in, but . . . [original]

The President: How about the UN approach?

The Speaker: The Security Council is in session this morning.

The President: In Korea I had the support of the UN Security Council before we went in, and I wondered if we were going to get it now.

The Speaker: We're supposed to get it today. But we made up our minds that if we were going to do anything, we ought to do it quickly. They like to argue up there you know. The consensus was that if we did not go in, after Lebanon had asked us to—they quoted Saudi Arabia that if we didn't do something, they would have to go in with Nasser. I think not only Lebanon, but Jordan and Iran are standing up, and of course Turkey will too, and I think that the British will come in any time we ask them to. But the idea now is, Harry, that we will do this thing until the UN makes up its mind to send in troops to relieve ours.

The President: What if Russia blocks the whole thing?

The Speaker: Well, I don't know . . . [original]

The President: They were boycotting the UN meetings when we got the Korean thing through . . . [original]

The Speaker: Or they would have vetoed it.

The President: That's right. We had the backing of the whole world.

The reason I wanted to talk to you, the press people are harassing me for an interview, and I wanted to say the right thing. I still don't know if I ought to make any comment. What do you think?

The Speaker: I don't know. I think . . . [original] I said in my press conference this morning that I thought the President, under all the circumstances, did the proper thing.

The President: That's what I wanted to know. Thanks, Sam. I will be there on Turnip Day, July 26th, and I want to see you. . . . [original]

TELEPHONE CONVERSATION

July 15, 1958

The President: How are you, Dean?

Mr. Acheson: I'm just being cross-examined by the Army.

The President: By whom?

Mr. Acheson: By the United States Army . . . [ellipsis points in original]

The President: What I was interested in . . . [original] I have talked to Sam Rayburn and Lyndon Johnson about the meeting last night authorizing the sending of the Marines into Lebanon, and, of course, I am being harassed by people who want statements from me, and I was anxious to talk to you before saying anything publicly. I would like to know your reaction, if you want to tell me.

Mr. Acheson: You mean the agreement that Dulles made? Is there a proposal for a joint resolution in . . . [original]?

The President: Yes, in the Security Council of the UN, just like the one we got for Korea, only this comes after the fact.

Mr. Acheson: But the United States Marines are not in there, are they?

The President: Yes, 6,000 of them are now in Lebanon, at the request of the President of Lebanon, and the reason I wanted to talk to you is that I didn't want to go off half-cocked or do anything to upset any policy affecting the peace of the world.

Mr. Acheson: Well, if that has been done, the only thing we can do is support it, but I think it's probably a mistake. I don't think they should have done it.

The President: I don't think they should have done it before the fact, either—I mean, before the UN approved it.

Mr. Acheson: I think the President having taken this step, all of us have got to see him through, that under the circumstances, the President had no other choice. The peace of the world is at stake.

The President: All I intend to say is that he had no other choice
. . . [original]

Mr. Acheson: I don't know if I would say "He had no other choice."
My suggestion is to say something to the effect that the President, as the
Commander in Chief and the head of the nation, is taking this step, and
you think it's the duty of everyone to stand by him. That just underwrites
what he has done. He is the one who had to make the decision. We don't
approve or disapprove, but we stand by him.

The President: I hope you're having a good time up there.

Mr. Acheson: I just came up to speak to the Army at their meeting on
weapon development. You know, this is a very surprising thing. I didn't
know we had landed Marines.

The President: I have talked to Sam Rayburn and Lyndon Johnson
about it. Sam was at the conference that authorized the thing at the
White House, and he made quite a statement that Chamoun asked us to
come in, so we are not barging in. . . . The Congressional leaders went
along with the President on the subject.

Mr. Acheson: Are they going to have a Congressional resolution?

The President: Neither Sam nor Lyndon said anything to me
about it. They are trying to get one from the UN, just as we did before
Korea.

Mr. Acheson: I think the whole thing's a terrible mess. Lebanon has
been left and probably the whole thing will blow up. I think if you make
this statement, it's the right one.

The President: I'll do my best to get one together. Don't worry about
this; it's not our responsibility this time. I will be back in Washington on
the 26th, and . . . [original]

Mr. Acheson: I am just here for today, and will be back tonight . . .
[original]

*[In an article copyrighted by the North American Newspaper Alli-
ance, released for publication on July 20, Truman said that President
Eisenhower had made a momentous decision and proclaimed a policy
that every citizen of the United States should support.]*

*The future chancellor of Austria, Dr. Bruno Kreisky, enlisted the
support of prominent Americans for Milovan Djilas, imprisoned by
Marshal Tito, and Clifton Daniel asked the President to send a letter.*

TO CLIFTON T. DANIEL

July 19, 1958

Dear Clif:

Your letter of July 15th regarding the message from Dr. Bruno Kreisky about the situation of Milovan Djilas:

Of course I'd like to help him, but if a letter to Tito from me were to be sent, Tito would probably hang Djilas.

In 1946 Tito informed me, in language easily understood, that he expected to march into Trieste. I invited him to come on, that there would be three American Divisions to meet him and the Mediterranean fleet would be there also.

He didn't march. You can see what might happen if I were to write him.

The former representative to Tito from the U.S., who is now public relations officer for Mayor Wagner, might be able to do some good.[1] He was very close to Tito—and I ordered him home.

Wish I could help.

I hear the young man is walking all over the place.[2] Tell Margie to behave herself.

Sincerely,

Grandpa

Mrs. Edward C. Acheson died July 25, 1958, in Washington, at the age of eighty-seven.

TO DEAN ACHESON

July 29, 1958

Dear Dean:

I have received a letter from Harry Vaughan dated July 26th enclosing a clipping from a Washington paper about the death of your mother.

I'll never forget my experience back in 1947. So you very well know that my sympathy is heartfelt. There is no supporter like your mother. Right or wrong, from her viewpoint you are always right.

---

1. Richard C. Patterson, Jr.
2. Truman's first grandchild, Clifton Truman Daniel, born June 5, 1957.

She may scold you for little things, but never for the big ones. Wish I'd known about it sooner. You'd have heard from me sooner.

Sincerely,

Harry S. Truman

TO SHERMAN MINTON

September 6, 1958

Dear Shay:

You'll never know how much I appreciated your good letter. Your postmaster is a gentleman and one of very few in public positions. I'm glad you had a good visit abroad. I took a trip myself in Southern France. I've tried for five years to return to my position of anonymity that I had in 1935 when you and I had such grand times together in the Senate of the United States with Joe Guffey, Nate Bachman, Pinkwhiskered Ham Lewis, Lewis Schwellenbach, and a lot of others including that man Bilbo, Hughie Long and Tom Connally. What a galaxy!

Your statements on the present situation at 1600 Penna. Ave. are so right. Why I don't know. Had a message from General Marshall the other day. He's been snubbed by the White House Bonehead just as I have. If Franklin Roosevelt were alive he'd be treated the same way. It is fantastic. How could a man be that way?

The people around the halls of the Great White Jail have succeeded in making General Grant and Warren Harding great Presidents!

The Dixon-Yates giveaway, the atomic power debauchery, and the giveaway of our forest reserves for fake mining claims rank almost with offshore oil in the use of public assets for payment of political debts to the special Republican interests.[1]

I can't help but explode once in a while on what has happened. I reduced the national debt by 27 billion dollars, balanced the budget for six of my eight years, met Tito, Stalin et al. in Yugoslavia, Persia and the Near East, kept Stalin out of Greece and Turkey and Berlin and put the United Nations into Korea and saved that Republic. Also kept crooked old Chiang Kai-shek from being mopped up by placing the 7th Fleet between him and danger.

Then what happened, they surrendered in Korea, unloosed Chiang by moving the 7th Fleet from Formosa Strait and like the 50,000 French-

---

1. The Dixon-Yates proposal by the administration involved the selling of electricity in the T.V.A. area by private entrepreneurs rather than allowing T.V.A. to put up a new generating plant powered by coal rather than water. The proposal failed when an embarrassing conflict of interest, involving the Dixon-Yates syndicate, forced the government to cancel the project in favor of a municipal facility proposed by the city of Memphis.

men at Agincourt they put it right back again! Lied to Indo-China, Britain and France on Suez and forgot the Near East and now where in hell are we? Landed in Lebanon, probably at war with terrible Red China, lost all our Western Hemisphere friends and searching desperately to blame Truman for the whole fantastic business!

Even Grant, Harding and Coolidge were not quite that bad.

Well to hell with it. I'm going to paste them hip and thigh in this '58 go around and then try to smash them in 1960—if we can find a candidate to do it with.

Take care of yourself and get into a position to help.

Sincerely,

Harry

Every now and then a request for information touched the President, and led to a good deal of thought prior to the writing out of a reply. Such was the case with an inquiry from Edward F. McFaddin, a justice of the supreme court of Arkansas, who had several questions. The President's answers dealt not merely with personal points but with the desegregation of the public schools in Arkansas, which then was much in the news because of the trouble in Little Rock.

TO EDWARD F. McFADDIN

September 29, 1958

Dear Justice McFaddin:

I am highly complimented by your letter of Sept. 23rd.

These memoirs of mine are not complete. I dictated over a million and a half words on the subject and we had to cut the number to about 520,000.

I'm leaving the balance to Margaret, hoping it will be of some value to her and also an addition to the truth and the facts of the time.

Now to answer your questions. I've had several moments of great joy, the end of two wars shortly after my going to the White House, the end of World War I while I was firing a battery of field artillery on the front at Verdun and one or two other great moments—the election night of 1948 for instance—but the greatest joy of them all was when my sweetheart from 6 years old on consented to become Mrs. Truman after World War I. She'd have been willing before the War but I thought I might be legless, eyeless or under some other handicap and we put it off until June 28th, 1919—just as soon as we could make arrangements after my discharge on May 6, 1919. When my daughter came that topped it.

My moments of greatest sorrow were when my mother and father passed away and when I had to officiate at the burial of some of my soldiers in World War I.

To contemplate changes for the past I think is an idle pastime. I've had a grand and full life from beginning to now. I like to look to the future and use the experiences of the past for its improvement. Wish I could live another 50 years at least and have a hand in the greatest future any Republic ever contemplated.

You see the future of this great country depends entirely on the coming generations and their understanding of what they have and what was done to create it, and what they must do to keep it.

It took "sweat, blood and tears" to create it and to maintain it. Unless the coming generations are willing to make the sacrifices necessary to keep it, this great Republic will go as did the city states of Greece, the Roman Republic and the Dutch Republic.

I suggest that you emphasize good will and common sense in your present crisis. That is all it takes. I know because I live in a county as unreconstructed as Arkansas and So. Carolina. Oklahoma and Tennessee have had no serious trouble. We must abide by the law of the land. We fought a war in 1861–65 to settle that question.

I hope you will join the effort to put some common sense into the public officials of your great state. Such actions as happened in your capital city will and have caused terrible repercussions abroad.

We were the leaders of the free world Jan. 20, 1953—now we are about to have no friends to lead. The future peace of the world depends on our being able to keep the friendship of our war-time allies France, Britain and the western hemisphere.

I've written you very frankly and I hope you'll make use of what I've put on paper for domestic peace and foreign unity.

This is a confidential communication and I hope you'll use it just that way. I have great admiration for you or I would not have answered your good letter.

Sincerely,
Harry S. Truman

The Treasurer of the United States during the Truman administration, Georgia Neese Gray, wrote that she was going to Kentucky to make a speech. Truman was reminded of the late Senator Barkley, who had died two years before. On April 30, 1956, the erstwhile "Veep" was giving a rousing address to 1,700 students and faculty of Washington and Lee University, and collapsed and died in the middle of the speech, just after he said that "I would rather be a servant in the House of the Lord than sit in the seat of the mighty."

TO GEORGIA NEESE GRAY

September 30, 1958

Dear Mrs. Gray:

I have been told that you expect to make an address in Louisville.

Senator Barkley and I were the closest of friends. He was one of the greatest Vice Presidents this country ever had and he and I worked out a program for the information of the Senate to be conveyed through the Vice President, which was a follow-up on what President Roosevelt had done with me.

He had a great many good stories which he used in his speeches around over the country. The one that impressed me most was about a meeting that he had in Ashland, Kentucky, which was limited in time because he had to catch a train. He took his watch out of his pocket when he started to speak and put it on the rostrum. After he had been talking for quite some time he looked at the watch, picked it up, shook it and held it to his ear—then some wild hillbilly Kentuckian in the back of the audience hollered in a loud voice, and I quote, "Senator there is a calendar behind you." I thought that was one of his best because when Barkley got started on a good speech he had no terminal facilities and that was a very good thing for the audience because they all appreciated his talks as long as he felt like continuing them and so did I.

I hope you have a grand meeting in Louisville and that Kentucky will have two Senators in the Senate when the election is over.

Sincerely yours,

Harry S. Truman

Bipartisan foreign policy as Truman understood it involved consulting with the "opposition" and informing them, not ignoring them and expecting them to go along.

TO DEAN ACHESON

October 14, 1958

Dear Dean:

I have been trying to get a chance to send you a longhand letter ever since I received yours of September 16th, and I am still going to write you in more detail than I am now.

I am enclosing you copies of the two last articles[1] which were gotten together on the foreign situation and while they are not exactly in conformity with the conversation which you and I had over the telephone, I did a lot of thinking after I talked to you, which no doubt I should have done before, and came to the conclusion that my fight for bipartisan foreign policy ought to be rather consistent and I think if you will read these statements you will find that you and I are not more than an inch or two apart on the subject. I am sure that the foreign policy of the United States is in the doldrums and has been ever since you and I left the White House.

When Eisenhower went to Korea and surrendered, that is what caused the present trouble. You remember the fiesta of the 7th Fleet when they pulled it out and in three weeks put it back. It was like the Frenchman marching up the hill and right down again.

I have been going around over the country listening to what people have to say. They are entirely confused by the procedure of the present administration on foreign policy and I have made press statements time and again if we ever could find out what the foreign policy of the present administration is, then we could decide whether we want to support it or not.

I repeat, the bipartisan foreign policy has never been in existence since you and I left the White House.

I was hoping that I would have a chance to see and talk with you personally in Washington the evening of the 17th, when Stanley Woodward is giving a small dinner for us.

We are going back there for the Women's Democratic dinner and then I am going to New Castle, Pennsylvania, Boston, Massachusetts and maybe to Delaware. After that I hope to spend two or three days with the young man in New York who is beginning to walk and talk. His mother says that he is just like his grandfather—he never walks—he runs—and talks all the time.

Please tell Alice to help me keep in the good graces of the former Secretary of State.

Sincerely yours,
Harry S. Truman

The Soviet army's suppression of the Hungarian rebellion in 1956 raised questions about the legitimacy of Hungary's representation in the

---

1. For the North American Newspaper Alliance.

United Nations, and a movement began to expel the Hungarians. The President refused to join.

TO ANGIER BIDDLE DUKE

October 29, 1958

Dear Mr. Duke:

In reply to your telegram of the 25th, which finally caught up with me in Independence, I think it is up to the United Nations themselves to settle the problem of the admission of Hungarian communist delegates to the U.N.

In the opinion of a retired farmer from Missouri, however, the communist treatment of Hungary equals the worst of history's barbarism, and, morally, Hungarian communist delegates deserve no recognition.

Sincerely yours,

Harry S. Truman

The congressional and gubernatorial elections of 1958 went generally in favor of the Democratic party, to the delight of Truman.

DIARY

November 5, 1958

I watched the election returns last night. I heard Governor Harriman admit defeat as I did the candidate for Senator, Mr. Hogan.[1] I heard the Governor of Connecticut accept victory modestly and tell his people that he represented all of them in his State. The returns were plain in the fact that people in this great country, when they discover the facts, are for the good of the country. In a political campaign it is hard work to keep facts and propaganda from becoming mixed. Smart advertising experts can make white look gray and then black. People seem to like verbal trimmings in ads and in speeches. But if the facts are repeated in plain language the propagandists get what's coming to them.

I always feel a sympathy for a defeated candidate and for his supporters and workers. No matter how wrong he may be on principle or record he is badly hurt by defeat. I know because I've been through it.

So a victor should be very charitable to the loser. Some are not and they never profit from it.

---

1. Harriman lost to Nelson A. Rockefeller; Frank S. Hogan was defeated in the New York senate race by Kenneth Keating.

Political writer Richard Rovere published a piece in Esquire, "The Last Days of Joe McCarthy," and the President liked it and wrote to the magazine's promotion manager who had sent it.

TO JAMES W. PINKSTON

November 17, 1958

Dear Mr. Pinkston:

I read with interest Richard Rovere's article about Joe McCarthy which you were kind enough to send me. Mr. Rovere has written a telling piece, and I wish he would do one or two or three others on the country's great demagogues—Huey Long, Tom Heflin and Pitchfork Tillman.

Then there was that period in the history of the United States, between 1824 and the late '30s, when the anti-Masonic affair came forward. Its proponents even got seven votes in the Electoral College. Shortly afterward, the same people began burning Catholic churches in the northeast part of the United States and tarring and feathering Catholic priests.[1]

Cotton Mather, with his fight against witchcraft in Salem, was, of course, our first really gifted demagogue. New England historians always try to put a muffler on that, and I would like to see Mr. Rovere do something on all of our periods of hysteria.

Sincerely yours,

Harry S. Truman

When Truman was in Uvalde, Texas, on November 22, 1958, helping former Vice-President John N. Garner celebrate his ninetieth birthday, a reporter asked what he thought of old Jack, whom someone once abused as "a whiskey-drinking, poker-playing, evil old man." The former President said Garner was the greatest presiding officer the Senate had ever had, including himself and the squirrel-head who presently occupied the post. Truman received the following telegram next day from W. L. Harriman of Detroit: YOUR INSULTS REGARDING VICE PRESIDENT HAVE GREAT MAGICAL EFFECT. MAY TRANSFORM REPUBLICAN ELEPHANT INTO SQUIRREL HEAD BUT MAY ALSO PROVE DEMOCRATIC DONKEY TO BE THE SAME OLD ASS. THIS TYPE OF INSULT COULD DESTROY THE DIGNITY AND RESPECT OF MEN OF HIGH OFFICE AND COULD ALSO CONVERT MANY DEMOCRATS TO REPUBLICANS BECAUSE OF YOUR DIMINUTIVE REMARKS. In response, Truman wrote out a draft telegram of his own.

---

1. The President refers to the anti-Masonic, anti-Catholic crazes epitomized by the Know-Nothing party of the 1850s.

TELEGRAM (UNSENT?)

[November 23, 1958]

Your nice wire was appreciated. None was received when Squirrel Head Nixon called the former President a traitor. Did you wire Jenner of Indiana when he called General George C. Marshall a traitor with the approval of Wisconsin's McCarthy?

Old line Republicans love character assassins. They are not assets to free government. Character assassins can not be insulted. If you love them vote the Republican ticket.

The President kept in touch with all his army friends who cared to write, and that was most of them. This meant a large correspondence, in addition to all the letters he had to write anyway, but "Captain Harry," as he was known with enormous affection, would not have had things otherwise. The following letter is typical.

TO J. A. DUCOURNAU

December 31, 1958

Dear Duke:

You do not know how very much I appreciated your good letter of the 19th. The program which you have outlined for your retirement is one which I envy, and I wish I could be with you.

I hope that you will go to the little village where you and I had quarters together when you first came into the Battery. We were sitting before a fire made of faggots, and you told me that your father always believed that a fire had a soul. I always think of that whenever I sit in front of an open fire.

When you visit all of those little towns where we stopped on our march across France, I hope that you will think of me. I have some pictures of those places, but they are almost faded out.

I have been hearing from John Thacher occasionally. In fact I just had a Christmas card from him. The next time I am in California I want to see him.

Please keep me informed on this trip of yours, and if you're traveling across land when you come back, please stop by to see me. I missed seeing you on my last visit to San Francisco.

Take good care of yourself. I want you to live a long time and leave me someone to talk to about events in France when we were there. Most of our associates have already passed on.

Sincerely yours,

Harry

Early in January the President went to Washington to attend a birthday dinner for Sam Rayburn.

DIARY

Mayflower Hotel, Washington
January 5, 1959

Arrived at Washington Air Port at 1:50 P.M. after a flight on T.W.A. leaving at 7 A.M. from Kansas City, Missouri. Flight 102. Stop made at St. Louis, also at Indianapolis. Had press and pictures as usual at D.C. airport—Mr. Ickes' bad dream.[1]

The Senator from Missouri, Honorable Stuart Symington, was with me all the way. He is a grand man and an honest straight thinking U.S. Senator. James Kemper, President of the Commerce Trust Company, also boarded the plane at Kansas City. In 1948 this Jim Kemper said that he thought highly of me personally—but that he could not waste money on a loser! He has married money a couple of times and has inherited a lot more from his money-loving dad. Old Bill Kemper was National Democratic Committeeman from Missouri in 1934 when the fight was made in Missouri for the nomination to the Senate, by Tuck Milligan, Jack Cochran[2] and me for the Senatorial nomination. After a most strenuous campaign in sixty or seventy of Missouri's 114 Counties I won by a plurality of 44,000. The lovely Post Dispatch was kind enough to say that the election in the primary had been stolen for me in Kansas City and Jackson County! Well the P.D. stole all the votes possible in St. Louis for Cochran—I received about 3300 in St. Louis & St. Louis County. Mr. Cochran received about that many (3300) in Jackson County and I the rest. But —I carried 40 Counties and ran second in 60. So I won. But the Pulitzer Paper in St. Louis had made arrangements for a fake nomination in Cochran's district in St. Louis for Congress. When he was beaten the fake nominee retired and Cochran was nominated for Congress by the local

---

1. As Secretary of the Interior, Ickes bitterly opposed construction of the Washington National Airport.

2. Congressman John J. Cochran was from St. Louis.

Post Dispatch Committee. What a scandal that would have been in Kansas City!

Senator Symington & I had a big time on the plane all the way to Washington reading Dave Lloyd's article in the Reporter on the national budget and Sidney Hyman's piece in the N.Y. Times Magazine for Sunday, Jan. 4th, on how Presidents are nominated and why! What an article!

Went down to the office of the Secretary of the Senate at 4:30 and saw several newly elected Senators—Maine, Alaska, Ohio, California and several others. All were interested in Senate filibusters. My opinion as expressed to them is that Senate filibusters are not so bad for legislation but that the air-tight Rules Committee in the House is the real stumbling block to forward-looking legislation.

DIARY

January 8, 1959

The weather is ideal for the flight to Phoenix and I hope it stays that way. Most people seem to think that special risk is taken in a flight. Many disasters have happened lately but the percentage is much better than automobile travel and above train travel. Of course if the increase in plane travel and the decrease in rail travel continues then the comparison will have to be made only with car travel on the roads. More people have been killed on the roads in the United States since automobiles came into use [in] 1915 than have been killed in all the wars in which we have been engaged since the French & Indian wars of the time when George Washington fought as a Lieut.-Colonel in General Braddock's Army.

This includes the French and Indian War of the 1700's, the Revolutionary War of 1776–1781, the War of 1812–1814, the Black Hawk War and the other Indian Wars of the period. It also includes the War between the States (Civil War), the Indian wars of the 60's & 70's, the Spanish American War, World War I and World War II and the Korean War of the United Nations.

The figures on these Wars and engagements will be furnished as will the deaths from the automobile.

It is really fantastic to think that man in his so-called progress should invent means for his own destruction. It seems that the old prophets had a line on what would happen when they made the statement that the next destruction of the world would be by fire and not by water.

Wonder how Noah would build an ark for that!

DIARY

January 16, 1959

Last evening I went to a little town in eastern Kansas called Louisburg for the purpose of giving a fifty year Masonic button to Mr. Hugh Lee. It was a grand meeting. Was there because my nephew Harry wanted me to be. Of course his brother Gilbert and my brother Vivian were all interested too. More than 300 were present for dinner and a thirty minute meeting.

I have been refusing invitations from every state in the Union for every sort of meeting from cat shows to State money dinner[s].

There are three four-drawer files full of refusals and enough acceptances to fill another one and a mulberry coffin too. When a notorious person is buried in a mulberry coffin he goes through "Hell a poppin'." It is the wood our forefathers avoided for fireplace use because it threw coals of fire all over the room.

I have prepared an article on Mikoyan, the Armenian Camel Thief of Stalin's regime, the murderer of the Hungarians and the new public relations man in USA for Nikita K.

Now work has to be done on Presidential lectures for Columbia.

TO STANLEY E. WHITEWAY (UNSENT?)

January 21, 1959

My dear Mr. Whiteway:

When I came to the office this morning at 8 A.M., through a blizzard that should have stayed in North Dakota, I found your wonderful letter which had been brought out to the Library special delivery.

Your statement about leaving something to the institution hit me where I live. It is my ambition to make the Library a center for the study of the Presidency. That great office has been neglected and misrepresented by so-called historians. It is the greatest executive office in the history of the world. I say that not because I held it but because I became acquainted with it by experience. I had read everything on it before fate passed it on to me. This Republic of ours is unique in the history of government and if the young people coming along in the future generations do not understand it and appreciate what they have it will go the way of the Judges of Israel, the City States of Greece, the great Roman Republic and the Dutch Republic.

These young people must understand that our great Government was obtained by "blood, sweat and tears" and a thousand years of effort on the part of the great thinkers over that period and blood-letting revolutions and sacrifices by the people. Why, we even had to spend four bloody years whipping ourselves to make the Constitution work. And we are still at it —trying to make it work!

Sam Rayburn has set up an institution at Bonham, Texas, which is the history of the Legislative branch of the Government from the first Continental Congress. The Chief Justice has succeeded in obtaining the approval of Congress for the use of the $300,000.00, which Mr. Justice Holmes left to the government, to write definitive biographies of the 88 Justices of the Supreme Court.

You see what I have in mind. A real history of the World's Greatest Government from the real sources.

Your contribution will go to the educational fund which will be set up to furnish scholarships for high school youngsters interested in government. I'll probably be in the past sure enough when your will is probated because I'm 74½ now but still "going good."

Thanks for your good letter. You see what you got yourself in for!

MEMORANDUM

February 10, 1959

Some definitions I've been asked to promulgate.

1. Liberal, a person who believes in the welfare of all the people— rich and poor, property owners and propertyless individuals.

According to the money class and the landed gentry, bankers and money lenders at 50% per year, a liberal is a person who believes in spending someone else's money for the welfare of all the people!

2. Conservative, a person who believes in the Status Quo. One who wishes for property and money control of government.

According to the so-called liberals, one who believes in exploitation of ordinary citizens by high interest rates on loans, who believes loan sharks—50% lenders—are justified because all poor people are dishonest and that a sales tax on food, clothing and other necessities is the proper way to obtain money for necessary government operations. Necessary government operations by this view is the enforcement of exorbitant interest rates and loan shark policies and the maintenance of government by the rich and the exploiters of the poor.

3. Republican, a member of the party that believes in No. 2. It was made up in the 1850's of the remnants of the Whigs, Federalists and Know Nothings. That organization was anti-Semitic, anti-Catholic and

drew the color line. It was revived in 1921 and 1922 and survived until 1932. It is most interesting to read the history of the 1854 Republican Party from John C. Fremont to Dwight D. Eisenhower. The name was taken at the suggestion of Horace Greeley from Thomas Jefferson's Democratic-Republican Party which stood for a democratic approach to a Republic!

4. Democrat: A believer in the people. Supposed to have come from the Greek City States. Jefferson used it as a prefix to the word Republican —one who believed in a Republic rather than a Monarchy. In Andrew Jackson's time the party's name was shortened to the Democratic Party. The party represents the ideas of all those who believe that all the people of a government have the right to an opinion on how it should be run. They should have a right to decide what taxes they should pay and for what purpose. They believe in property rights but they believe that the rights of the individual have first claim on a government whether he is a rich property owner or whether he is as poor as Job's Turkey.

TO CLIFTON T. DANIEL

July 3, 1959

Dear Clif:

You do not know how very much I appreciated your letter of June 29th with the clipping about the meeting at the Astor Hotel where Margaret accepted the Page One Award for me. If the mirror should break I can always read the citation standing on my head.[1]

I am very glad that Master Clifton Truman Daniel is learning about the birds and the bees. A fellow can't start too young, in my opinion.

I am happy that you like your new country place. If I can just get Grandma to behave herself and follow the doctor's instructions,[2] maybe we can get there to see you before you move back to New York. Her progress is slow, but she is getting along as well as can be expected after that terrific shock.

Sincerely yours,
Grand*father*

[P.S., handwritten] Tell Margie to make the kids—and their daddy—behave just as I *once* did with her and her mother!

---

1. Mrs. Daniel on June 26 accepted the award from the American Newspaper Guild's New York unit.

2. Mrs. Truman on May 18 underwent an operation for the removal of a benign breast tumor.

When it came to managing Democratic national conventions, the President had fixed ideas and disliked the national chairman's maneuvering on his own.

TO SAM RAYBURN

July 8, 1959

Dear Sam:

I noticed that Paul Butler is "firing from the hip," without any consultation with Democrats that count.

I don't like it and I know that you are as unappreciative as I am. It seems to me that when the time comes to lay out the Convention next year, some of us should get together and pick out the keynote speaker and the presiding officers of the Convention.

I want Sam Rayburn to preside and I'd like very much to have a keynote man who can put the Democrats on top for the election and then let the nominations take the regular course and end up with *two men* on the ticket who can lead us to victory.

I've no ax to grind, only the welfare of the United States of America and the Democratic Party. They are synonymous.

Sincerely,

Harry

TO DEAN ACHESON

August 22, 1959

Dear Dean:

I am in a very bad position. When Winston Churchill paid his last visit, it was not possible for me to be present at the White House, because the invitation came too late—as intended. Then he was in New York as the guest of our "old friend" Barney Baruch.

Averell Harriman called me at the last minute and asked me to go with him to Barney's house where Winston was a guest. I couldn't go because I was at that minute packing up to take a train home. Mrs. T. was due for an operation. So was Margie.

I wrote Winston and explained the situation. Haven't heard from him and probably won't. He thinks very much of old man Baruch and I don't. Of course he's fond of Ike because he thinks Ike saved the world in 1945. So I suppose I've lost a friend whom I have on record as just that. To hell with that. Now I have another problem.

You and I are on the advisory committee of the National Democratic Committee at the request of Paul Butler. I was never for him for National

Chairman of the Democratic Committee. He owes his position to Sam Rayburn and Lyndon Johnson. He is organizing the L.A. Convention for Stevenson. What can we do? If we do not have a winner this time, it will take another F.D.R. to put the country on the right track. We are on a switchback now.

Butler was elected at New Orleans on the basis of a statement which he made to the southern block. Now he says he didn't mean it.[1] He agreed to the Los Angeles site and now he says he didn't.

Seems to me the Chairman of the Democratic Committee should try to keep things in such shape as to nominate a man who can lead the people to believe that the Democratic Party will give them the best government, nationally and internationally.

Mr. Butler has not done that and as far as I can see does not intend to do it. I suppose we'll just have to let him lead the Party to defeat—but I don't want to be a party to it.

Ike's gone to Germany, France, Britain and Russia. He sent the Vice President ahead of him. Mr. Nixon's background is one of sabotage. By misrepresentation he was able to beat a good Congressman, a good Senator and make himself Vice President. As the representative of the President he ran up and down the country calling Democrats, me particularly, traitors. That was in 1954. Ike stood on the platform in Milwaukee and allowed Jenner and McCarthy to call Gen. George C. Marshall a traitor.

It was my privilege to peel the hide off of him for that in Colorado Springs.

Now Tricky Dicky and Alibi Ike are trying to take me into camp. I won't go. Maybe I'm wrong. But I'm one of these contrary Kentucky feudists by inheritance. We don't forget our friends and we remember those who lied about us—and I'm afraid don't forgive them—especially if the objective is to use us to get right with God!—for a purpose.

Should we quit the Advisory Committee or should we not? If Butler has his way we'll nominate a loser and elect Nixon for President!

I'm agin it!

Sincerely,
Harry

---

1. At a meeting of the National Committee in New Orleans in 1954, Butler supported a recommendation to drop the loyalty oath by which northern and eastern delegates to national conventions asked southerners to bind themselves to support the party's candidate for President as a condition of being seated. The election of Butler, from Indiana, marked a triumph of the South, Far West, Mountain, and Midwest states over Democratic states with big urban populations.

[Acheson responded that Churchill's memory was going, and suggested that the former prime minister had forgotten the President's letter, not ignored it. He proposed that Truman write a careful greeting upon Sir Winston's birthday on November 30 and again say how sorry he was to miss him. Acheson believed Kennedy could win in 1960, but only on an early ballot, and otherwise there were only two realistic choices, Stevenson and Johnson.]

Billy Taber, an eighth-grade student in the Rowe School of Conneaut, Ohio, wrote one day to ask the President what he should study in high school.

TO BILLY TABER

December 8, 1959

Dear Billy:

Replying to your letter of November 24 regarding a possible course of study to take in high school which would be beneficial to you, I will tell you what I think as a result of my long experience.

It would be well for you to take Latin because it is fundamental in the study of Italian, Spanish and French. There are thousands of words in the English language you can understand better if you know Latin.

A mathematical course including Algebra and Geometry is essential.

Both General History and a good History of the United States are most necessary.

In order to understand Composition and to learn how to read good literature intelligently you must study English and American Literature.

Also, you must have a basic knowledge of Physics before you finish your high school.

This looks like a great big load but if you arrange it right it will not work you too hard, especially if you are interested in these subjects; and it is good for a young man to improve his mind. I wish you luck in your studies but remember, it takes plenty of hard work and anxiety to obtain knowledge.

Sincerely yours,

Harry S. Truman

The editor of Civil War History, *published at the University of Iowa, received some observations from the President about the term "War Between the States."*

TO JAMES I. ROBERTSON, JR.

December 19, 1959

Dear Dr. Robertson:

I have always been interested in the "War Between the States." It has also been called the Civil War, the War of the Rebellion, the Border War and many other names.

Seems to me its proper name is the War Between the States, because it was a war to decide that the Government of the United States is a permanent entity and cannot be dismembered at the whim of either Massachusetts or South Carolina. Both tried to accomplish a Central American arrangement. Both failed, thank the good Lord.

We now have the greatest Republic in the history of the world. We must keep it just that. I'm spending the short remainder of my life trying to give the rising generation a clear idea of what they have and what they have to do to keep it.

When Roman citizens began to buy their way out of service to the Republic, when they became fat and lazy and depended on slaves to do what the Citizen should do—along came Caesar, Pompey and the great Augustus—the Roman Republic was at an end. The empire lasted some 330 years and disintegrated.

Along came Saladin, Jenghis Khan, the Hapsburgs, Richelieu, Charles V, Columbus, the great queen Elizabeth I and the rise and fall of the Dutch Republic.

We are their successors. What can we do to prevent our fate from going down the same road? We must—come hell or high water. We have control of the hell, and high water has gone by the board—unless the ice caps melt.

It is up to this great Republic to profit by history's mistakes.

Let's do it!

Harry S. Truman

TO THOMAS J. DODD

January 20, 1960

Dear Senator:

I appreciated your letter of January 12 very much with the "Orbis" Quarterly containing the article "If Coexistence Fails" enclosed.

I have never been a very strong "coexistence" man. That word was coined in an effort to make it appear that the world is safer than it is. The only language, in my opinion, that the Russians understand is "more

Divisions than they do." I sincerely hope, however, that an arrangement can be made so there can be peace in the world in spite of what the Russians do. I want you to understand very distinctly that you cannot trust them.

Sincerely yours,
Harry S. Truman

In the latter part of January the President went to Washington for the Democratic presidential campaign's kick-off dinner at the Sheraton-Park Hotel.

DIARY

Sheraton-Park Hotel, Washington
January 21, 1960

Arrived last night, Jan. 20, 1960, by plane from home. Charlie Murphy, Dave Stowe, Harry Vaughan were at the airport to meet me. It was like old times.

Called Bess soon as I arrived at the hotel. Dave Stowe did the calling. Mrs. T. was very happy to talk to Dave, Harry Vaughan and Charlie Murphy. I think she was sorry she wasn't here. Well, of course, so was I.

Been reading the Washington Post. How very anxious are they, the editors, to make a gentleman and a great Vice President of Nixon. They are having a great time trying. Which goes to show that the Vice President is a very important person. He should be chosen with care and consideration. A study should be made of the seven Vice Presidents who have succeeded.

While looking over the death notices of the Washington Post and the N.Y. Times along with those at home in the K.C. Star and the Independence Examiner, I began to think about what those notices mean to the descendants.

The children of the people who are in the death notices try to show just how good the former generation were. It is a great thing, for most second generations are sure that the preceding one undoubtedly was as ignorant and inefficient as could be.

But—when the older generation passed on, the descendants began to do a little thinking and wishing that great things had happened.

TO MONSIGNOR GEORGE W. KING

May 26, 1960

Dear Monsignor:

You do not know what a pleasure it was for me to sit with you at the funeral ceremony for my good friend, Roy Muehlebach.

I more than appreciated your saying a Mass for me. I think I can use several of them.

Sincerely yours,
Harry S. Truman

Truman did not feel that Senator Kennedy was ready to run for the presidency in 1960, and made no effort to hide his feeling. Agnes E. Meyer, the wife of the owner of the Washington Post, *wrote that the* New York Times *was printing every claim of Kennedy's, true or false, for support of additional delegates to the Democratic National Convention, and asked the former President if he could get a couple of researchers to work to spike some of the senator's propaganda.*

TO AGNES E. MEYER

June 25, 1960

Dear Mrs. Meyer:

Nothing is truer than the statement in your letter of June 18. I am doing all I possibly can do to head off this bandwagon psychology but our main difficulty is that the Democratic National Committee and its Chairman will do everything possible to contribute to it which is about as unethical an approach as a National Chairman could make. I have scolded him a time or two but it does not seem to do any good.

I am going to Los Angeles and make the best fight I can but it probably will not result in any concrete arrangement for the country. I am as sorry as you are that is the case. I am not a pessimist and always fight until the last dog dies as there are instances in the history of the Presidential elections that show the highly touted candidate is not always nominated. I can cite you several cases.

James Knox Polk was one and Franklin Pierce was another. The first one made a strong President and the second one was of no account as far as making decisions was concerned.

Then there was President Garfield and of course, as you know, the most famous one was when William Jennings Bryan was a candidate in 1896.

And if you remember, in Baltimore when it looked as if the New York kingmakers had Champ Clark, so they thought, nominated, Woodrow Wilson came to the top after a severe struggle and was nominated after Bryan made a speech on the subject. Then to top matters off Theodore Roosevelt split the Republican Party and Wilson was elected.

Just as a side comment, I count Woodrow Wilson among the five or six great Presidents of our country. Had he been a better politician his program would have gone over as it eventually had to go over under Franklin Roosevelt's administration.

I am calling your attention to these things because I know you are acquainted with them and also, I know that a situation is never over until the last vote is counted. That is true in national conventions and in elections. I am as happy as I can be that you are so vitally interested in this situation. We can't stand another four years like the past eight.

Sincerely yours,
Harry S. Truman

TO MIKE MONRONEY

June 30, 1960

Dear Mike:

I more than appreciated your letter of June 27.

I am very much worried about the present political situation. If we don't nominate somebody for President at Los Angeles who can be elected and who knows where he is going after he is elected, we are going to be in a very serious spot.

I am not impressed with Adlai but I do not blame you for being impressed because I am sure you do not know him as well as I do. But, for your information, Mike, whoever is nominated will be my candidate. I just hope we can nominate a man who can make a decision and make it quickly after he has all the facts. I wish you would read the articles which covered the situation between Adlai and myself during 1952 and 1956; then, you will find out exactly how I feel on the subject.

Sincerely yours,
Harry S. Truman

Truman refused to attend the Democratic National Convention in Los Angeles, because he believed that Kennedy supporters had every-thing sewed up.

MEMORANDUM

July 12, 1960

This will be the second day of the Democratic Convention in Los Angeles. I had hoped to be present but conditions prevented.

In 1900 I was present at the Democratic Convention in Kansas City when Bryan was nominated the second time. I was supposed to be a page. Mr. Kemper was the National Committeeman at that time. He and my father were very good friends and that was how I was able to be present. I'm afraid as a page I was a dud. But I ran many errands for Mr. Kemper.

In 1912 I was engineer for a binder with four mules and horses to make it run. The Convention was in Baltimore. A telegraph station was ¼ of a mile from the southwest corner of the wheat field where my two mules and two horses were glad to have a short breathing spell. They had been going round and round that 160 acre field since a quarter to six o'clock in the morning.

I'd stopped at the house at six and had breakfast. So I was as ready as the team for a breathing spell at two in the afternoon and hour after hour later.

When Bryan made his attack on August Belmont and the Champ Clark forces I was ecstatic but my father wasn't. He was [for] Champ Clark come hell or high water.

What a great thing for the welfare of the world when Woodrow Wilson was nominated at Baltimore in 1912. He was one of the greatest of great Presidents.

In 1917 I became a member of Battery F, 129th Field Artillery. On July 11th, 1918, was given command of Battery D, 129th F.A.

The Convention of 1920 in San Francisco nominated Governor Cox of Ohio and Franklin Roosevelt of New York. Harding and normalcy defeated them. I wonder what would have happened had they won.

In 1924 the Democrats held a convention in New York City. There were 102 or 103 ballots. This situation was caused by William G. McAdoo and Al Smith. It was thought that the Democrats had a cinch to win—and they had—but they threw it away. The Harding scandals were on a par with those of General Grant. The personal animosities of the top Democrats and their inordinate personal ambitions elected Calvin Coolidge. President Coolidge was of the opinion that leadership should be in the Congress. 1929 came as a result.

Franklin Roosevelt rescued the Republic from disintegration. Then came 1936, 1940, 1948.

I was one of Missouri's big four at the 1936 Convention and was assigned to the Platform Committee. Roosevelt and Garner were renominated as we all thought they would be. Garner made a great speech when he accepted.

The 1940 affair was Franklin Roosevelt's third try. He sent James F. Byrnes to Chicago to have Henry Wallace nominated. There was some dissension because some of us were afraid of Henry. He proved our fears justified four years later. A demonstration was organized for William Bankhead, father of Tallulah and at the time Speaker of the House of Representatives. Missouri joined that demonstration. It arrived nowhere. Henry Wallace was nominated and we started on another four year cycle. Henry went to Siberia to show the Mongols and the Manchus how to farm. He made several other trips for the President also.

In 1941 the Senate authorized a Committee to Investigate the National Defense Program. It received some favorable comment from the Senate and the House. The President finally decided it was an asset to the winning of the Second World War and made use of it.

When the Convention of 1944 met in Chicago, there were a number of candidates for Vice President. The President did not express a choice. He made the statement, in Chicago as he went through on the way west, that Henry Wallace or Bill Douglas would please him as nominees for Vice President. He mentioned Harry Truman incidentally and he was not a candidate.

On the date of the nomination of the candidate for Vice President, President Roosevelt expressed a preference from San Diego, California. That preference was for Truman and was made to Bob Hannegan, Chairman of the National Committee of the Democratic Party, and a number of party leaders who were present.

I was nominated and worked for the ticket as I should have.

In 1948 a lot of the left wing liberals including the Roosevelt boys (who by the way have promoted their father's position for financial reasons) were trying to nominate Eisenhower on the Democratic ticket. They didn't succeed. The Republican Convention had adopted a good platform. So—I called a Special Session of the Congress for July 26th (Turnip Day in Missouri) and invited the Republican Congress to enact their platform. That 80th Congress was dumb enough not to do it. If they'd passed only two bills I would have been up against real trouble. But they didn't.

In December 1951 I told my staff at Key West that I would not be a candidate. They were disappointed but did not report the statement to the press or public.

On Jan. 30, 1952, I asked Adlai Stevenson to come to the White House.

We were living in the Blair House at the time. He came and I urged him to let the organized Democrats support him for President. He refused. He came back the last week in February, at his request, and still refused!

He was talked to in March by the National Chairman, Frank McKinney, and still refused.

Sen. Barkley, Vice President, came to the Blair House and we decided to support him.

He went to Chicago and so arranged things to make the labor contingent refuse to support him. Then he withdrew, over my protest, after he had called me on Monday evening telling me what he was going to do. I urged him to stay in the race.

TO DEAN ACHESON (UNSENT)

August 26, 1960

Dear Dean:

Your letters of the 12th and the 23rd really gave me the lift I needed. I have been as blue as indigo since the California meeting in L.A. It was a travesty on National Conventions. Ed Pauley organized it and then Kennedy's pa kicked him out! Ed didn't consult me!

That Convention should have been helped immensely if it had been in Chicago, St. Louis or Philadelphia. But it wasn't held at any of those places. You and I are stuck with the necessity of taking the worst of two evils or none at all. So—I'm taking the *immature* Democrat as the best of the two. Nixon is impossible. So, there we are.

When I took the stand I did I hoped to help—but it didn't. I look at history and the period after Madison and then the one after Jackson. After Jackson we had Martin Van Buren, a smart fixer, and then William Henry Harrison, a "stuffed shirt" who insisted on riding a white horse to the Capitol—and a month later John Tyler was President. You know that old devil, who was my great grandmother's uncle, had some ideas of honor. He resigned from the Senate when he was not able to support Jackson's financial program. Then came James K. Polk, a great President. Said what he intended to do and did it. Then three months after leaving the White House, went home and died!

Then old Zach Taylor came along, father-in-law of Jefferson Davis. He became famous at the Battle of Buena Vista by telling Captain Bragg to "give them a little more grape." Winfield Scott "Old Fuss & Feathers" was as anxious as Grant and Ike to be President. Old Zach kept him out. But he ran again and was ingloriously defeated by one of his Brigadier Generals, Franklin Pierce—who always had the stomach ache or a pain in the neck when there was a shooting engagement in Mexico.

Franklin Pierce agreed to the repeal of the Missouri Compromise and signed the Kansas Nebraska Bill. With John Brown and his murders on the border between Missouri and Kansas these events caused the War Between the States—now officially called the Civil War, as was the War of the Roses in England.

I'm afraid I'm boring you but that is not the intention. I'm afraid that this immature boy who was responsible for picking out five great Senators may not know any more about the Presidency that he will occupy than he did about the great Senators.[1] Only one, Henry Clay, belonged in the list. I sent him a list of a dozen or so but it wasn't used. So, what the hell, you and I will take it and not like it but hope for the future.

Truman wrote to John T. Riley, manager of special projects for Look *magazine, which had published a piece called "If the South Had Won the Civil War."*

TO JOHN T. RILEY

November 17, 1960

Dear Mr. Riley:

I looked at the article to have the South win the war. It is a wonderful piece of imaginative writing, hardly based on cold facts.

Had Lee won at Gettysburg the war would not have been over even if Grant had not taken Vicksburg. Perhaps, England would have recognized the Confederacy and France would have stayed in Mexico with a French Empire from Panama to the Rio Grande.

Texas would not have joined Maximilian. But the Northwest would have seceded from the Northeast and taken over 54°–40′. Russia would have kept Alaska and in all probability have taken all Northwest Canada.

There would have been the Northwest Republic, the Northeast Republic, the Confederate Republic, the Mexican Empire, in the Southwest with California, Utah, Arizona and New Mexico as a part of that Empire.

And the Bolsheviks would have had the whole Northwest and what then. Maybe the Northeast and the Southeast could have created an alliance and held the Russians at the Mississippi. Isn't it great to contemplate?

My sympathies and all my family were on the side of the South. But I think the organization of the greatest Republic in the history of the world was worth all the sacrifices made to save it.

Sincerely yours,

Harry S. Truman

---

1. The President refers to John Kennedy's book *Profiles in Courage* (New York, 1956).

TO WESTERN UNION

November 25, 1960

Please come and take this crazy receiver you have set up in my office. It is nothing but a nuisance.

When messages are sent to me they are supposed to be delivered by you. I'm not supposed to be your delivery agent. I have other things to do.

I'm informing my friends and those who have business with me to write or phone me.

You had a delivery service here that was very satisfactory. Until you can restore it, don't bother with me.

Yours truly,
Harry S. Truman

[The district manager of Western Union moved quickly to soothe the President. He was deeply concerned that the Deskfax had caused inconvenience, but suggested that it remain. He would arrange for delivery of messages when Miss Conway was not in the office. In a letter of December 19, 1960, Truman was adamant: "I appreciated very much your letter but I am still of the opinion that our telegrams ought to be delivered in a manner in which we can read them." The manager capitulated and said he would deliver all messages by messenger.]

TO JOHN F. KENNEDY

January 24, 1961

Dear Mr. President:

You'll never know how very much I appreciated all the courtesies you extended to me at inauguration time.

I was invited into the White House for the first time in eight years.

I was shown through that great residence in a manner I'll never forget. I still hope you'll forgive me for being so impetuous at the Rose Room, and I hope the First Lady will forgive me.[1]

I want your administration to be most successful.

Sincerely,
Harry S. Truman

---

1. There is no record of the impetuosity at the Rose Room.

TO JOHN S. MONAGAN

April 21, 1961

Dear Congressman Monagan:

I have received a copy of your Bill introduced as House Joint Resolution 360, regarding the idea of the former Presidents becoming members of the Senate.

My idea on this subject has been forming since I first went to the Senate back in 1935, and after reading the Resolution which was introduced in 1889, it was my conclusion and the conclusion of several Senators who served with me, that former Presidents and former Speakers of the House, and Vice Presidents who had been Speakers of the House, should be allowed the privilege of the Floor of the Senate and the House, either one, for the purpose of discussing Bills and Resolutions which were pending.

It was my opinion that they should also have the privilege of sitting in Committees and discussing with the Committee members Bills and Resolutions which were pending before those Committees.

I do not think it is proper that the state balance in the Senate or the House should be in any way affected by this privilege, and it is my opinion that a Joint Resolution of the House and the Senate could arrange matters so that a President could appear on the Floor of either House in support or against any Bill or Resolution pending; but that he should not have a vote. The votes in the House and the Senate are arranged on a state basis and no state should have a vote that is not in keeping with the intent of the Constitution.

While your Resolution is a proposed Amendment to the Constitution, I am sure that it won't pass for the simple reason that no state wants to give up its present constitutional standing in either the House or Senate.

However, if an arrangement could be made so that former Presidents and Vice Presidents, who had served as Speakers in the House, could be allowed to sit with the great Legislative bodies in Washington, a basis where the constitutional equality of the state would not be affected, it seems to me that it would be a good thing.

I did not advocate it after I became President of the United States because it would have appeared as a special interest. Several Senators along with myself worked on it in the 1930's and if you look up the history on the situation an effort was made in 1889 to do the same thing, but when you introduce a Resolution that will impair the equality of the members of the states in the Legislative branch in either the House or the Senate you are up against an impossible situation.

I am very appreciative of what you have in mind. The end result is what we want. I thought you might like to have my opinion.

Sincerely yours,
Harry S. Truman

Russell L. Dearmont was chairman of the board of the Missouri Pacific, and passenger rail service was going downhill.

TO RUSSELL L. DEARMONT

July 3, 1961

Dear Russell:

Every time Mrs. Truman and I ride on the Missouri Pacific you always do something for us and we are always grateful. On the last trip from St. Louis to Kansas City the dining car steward would not let me pay for our dinner because you "set it up." That has happened time and again and I appreciate it and so does the "Boss."

Now, Russell, I am going to talk about something else—the Missouri Pacific trains across Missouri, the Colorado Eagle and the Omaha Eagle, have always been the most beautiful trains that cross the State and now I am downhearted because the new President of the Missouri Pacific seems to think that passenger morale is of no value to that great railroad. As you know, I was Vice Chairman of the Committee that investigated the receivership of the Missouri Pacific Railroad when it was in Judge Moore's Court and, if you will remember, when I was making the investigation the Missouri Pacific not only got a fair deal but justice.

I have always been a most ardent Missouri Pacific fan but if I have to continue to ride backward from St. Louis to Kansas City and from Kansas City to St. Louis, which I have had to do on two occasions, my feeling toward your great railroad will gradually decline. I can't understand how a man who has ruined the Rock Island Railroad can take over the Missouri Pacific and try to ruin it.

I sincerely hope that something can be done to restore the public relations situation between the Missouri Pacific Railroad and the people.

I have about come to the conclusion that the best thing for me to do is to take the Santa Fe or the Burlington to Chicago and ride on the New York Central Railroad to New York. I don't want to do that because I like to ride on the Missouri Pacific. The first recollection I have, as a youngster, was sitting on the coal shed at our house on Crysler Street, just about where the Missouri Pacific Depot is, watching the trains go by. As a result, I have always been a fan of the Missouri Pacific.

I don't know where in the world you found this fellow who wants to snub the public, who are his best assets. I wish you would send him back where he came from or somewhere else.

Sincerely yours,
Harry S. Truman

TO DEAN ACHESON

July 7, 1961

Dear Dean:

I am sitting here at the desk and wondering about things political, both nationally and internationally. It is a hell of a thought provoking situation.

Mr. Miles, his wife and the girls came in and I had a good visit with them. At least it was good from my point of view.[1]

There couldn't be any doubt how your commencement speech would turn out. Wish I could be as certain how my statements would come out. I have been calling off meeting after meeting on that account.

As you know, I wasn't for Kennedy at Los Angeles. But when the Convention decided that he was "the man," what could I do but work my head off to elect him. I did just that—and I'm still afraid of "Pop."

I have the same trouble with the "litter bugs" you wrote me about. They throw beer cans, pop bottles, lipstick wipers and anything else for the trash can into my front yard; from sidewalk and the street in front.

As an early riser I pick up the trash and take a walk with most unkind thoughts of the litter bug public!

As to Berlin and Laos and Indo-China and Cuba, we have problems and problems. May Almighty God help us to solve them! There have been times in the history of the world that I thought "He" was looking the other way. And I suppose "He" should have been!

The performance of our Chief Executive worries me, as the Chiefs of Staff do.[2]

You are making a contribution. I am not. Wish I could.

My best to Alice.

Sincerely,
Harry

---

1. William W. Miles, together with his family, visited with Truman upon request of Acheson; Miles was principal of the Sherwood High School in Sandy Spring, Maryland, and Acheson had given the commencement address to the graduating class there.

2. The President undoubtedly was referring to the abortive invasion of Cuba.

The President deeply regretted the decision of the Navy Department to anchor the mothballed battleship Missouri *in Bremerton, Washington, which locality he at one point described as a closet. He started a movement to bring the ship up the Mississippi and enshrine it in the state of Missouri—the battleship drew nearly forty feet of water and the navy would have had to take it apart and put it together, at which point it no longer would be the battleship* Missouri. *He blamed the Eisenhower administration for mothballing the ship in the "closet" and took up the matter again when the Democrats resumed office, writing to Secretary of the Navy John B. Connally.*

TO JOHN B. CONNALLY

August 29, 1961

Dear Mr. Secretary:

I am very much interested in a certain Battleship on which the surrender of the Japanese Empire was signed on September 2, 1945. I have copies of the plaques which are on the deck of the Battleship Missouri.

I don't know whether you understand it or not but the objective of the people who were in command from 1953 until the new President came in, in 1961, has been to cover up almost everything that was done in the Administration between 1945 and 1953.

My daughter christened the Battleship Missouri at the Brooklyn Navy Yard when it first started. I presented the Battleship with a United States Flag and a flag from Missouri and I have all the silverware that belonged to the original Battleship Missouri and the one which succeeded it.

For the purpose of having this Battleship in a position of approach by the public, it seems to me that it ought to be placed in the Navy Yard where it was built so everyone can see the most powerful battleship the Navy ever built.

I would like very much to hear from you on the subject and I hope that you will give the matter a lot of consideration.

Sincerely yours,

Harry S. Truman

[The battleship Missouri *stayed in the closet.]*

In a letter of September 21, 1961, Acheson wrote somberly of an imminent crisis: he believed Berlin was about to be given to the Rus-

sians. Everywhere he saw appeasement, and told Truman that he was, himself, about to go underground. He opined that eight years of Eisenhower and one of Kennedy were just about enough to produce disaster, and that the United States would quite possibly receive Barry Goldwater as a reward for governmental incompetence. The President, however, was not so sure.

TO DEAN ACHESON

September 25, 1961

Dear Dean:

Your somber note gave me the most depressing viewpoint I've had since Jan. 20th, 1953.

I can't agree with you. We saved Berlin once. We will have to do it again. The Russian Dictator is one of those who can't face issues when they are met head on.

You must remember that our head of State is young, inexperienced and hopeful. Let's hope the hopeful works.

Was good to talk to you. Let's keep working for the country. We, I hope, can do it. You know what I told you. I'm always in your corner.

Sincerely,

Harry

Monkey business anywhere was annoying to the President, and after talking with his sister, Mary, he wrote R. E. Wolfe, executive vice-president of the Tri-City Construction Company.

TO R. E. WOLFE

October 2, 1961

Dear Mr. Wolfe:

I was in Grandview Sunday morning and my sister handed me a copy of your form statement to the property owners along the street which runs in front of her house.

I notice, with very careful reading of the document, that you make no statement that you expect to put the driveways along the road back in the condition they were in before you started to work on them.

My sister had built her own driveway up to her house and garage, and now you have her completely shut off from it. She hasn't been able to get into her driveway with her car for three weeks and she is not physically able to walk for three or four blocks.

I have been visiting out there nearly once or twice a week ever since you started to build that curb in front of all the property owners and I have been wondering why you didn't build the curb straight across the street crossings as you did the driveways of the property owners.

I feel that my sister has been substantially damaged by what you have done, and I understand you are figuring on filling in back of the curb with chat.

I want you distinctly to understand that you will build a driveway to Miss Truman's place that fits her situation, as she had paid for building it before you messed things up.

Most of the property owners along that street have been very much damaged by what you have done. It seems to me that you could have handled this thing in a way in which no one would have been hurt.

I don't intend to have my sister suffer any damage in any way by what you have done.

The other property owners are in the same frame of mind.

> Sincerely yours,
>
> Harry S. Truman

The Daily Statement of the United States Treasury for December 13, 1961, was a mass of figures and columns, all footnoted for exceptions, and the reverse page of this finely printed single-page document was even more complicated, showing changes in the public debt, the effect of operations on the public debt, a memorandum on inter-fund transactions and U.S. savings bonds, series E and H.

TO THE TREASURER OF THE UNITED STATES (UNSENT)

December 26, 1961

Dear Sir:

I have been reading the statement of Dec. 13, 1961, the last one I have received.

I'd appreciate it if you could find a way to place debits and credits so an ordinary citizen like myself could understand what you are trying to show.

When I am through looking and figuring what you mean I have to set up my own statement.

Why don't you set up yours so any citizen who understands debits from credit can know what you are doing. I don't think that the financial advisor of God Himself would be able to understand what the financial position of the Government of the United States is, by reading your statement.

And I have been going through them and trying to find out what they mean for twenty-seven years! I found out but it took all day and half the night to do it. Make your statement a simple bookkeeping document so that any of us can understand it.

Walter P. Reuther, president of the United Automobile Workers, wrote the President on January 11, 1962, inviting him to be the principal speaker at a celebration of the twenty-fifth anniversary of the successful conclusion of the sit-down strikes in plants of the General Motors Corporation, and received what must have been a surprising response.

TO WALTER P. REUTHER

January 24, 1962

Dear Walter:

I appreciated very much your letter of the 11th, and I want to say to you very frankly that I don't like sit-down strikes.

I am sorry to say that it will not be possible for me to be with you on February 4th anyway but, between you and me and the gatepost, I don't think you would want me there because I would tell them exactly what I think about sit-down strikes.

I am for Labor and the right to strike but when you destroy a man's business, especially a little man, it just isn't right and you know it as well as I do.

Sincerely yours,
Harry S. Truman

TO J. EDWARD DAY

February 5, 1962

Dear Mr. Postmaster General:

Replying to yours of a few days ago (not dated) about the proposed cowshed addition to the Independence Post Office:

Back in the 1930's while I was United States Senator from Missouri, I obtained a lot at Osage and Lexington streets which contains 50,000 square feet. The objective was to obtain a post office and Federal Office Building for Independence, at that time a city of about 17,000 people. The city now has 80,000 inhabitants. Independence needs a Post Office and Federal Office Building.

The United States Government has owned the corner at Osage and Lexington Streets across Lexington Street from the present post office for about twenty-five years.

Look over the title to this lot which contains 50,000 square feet.

It was obtained for the Post Office Department and the title placed in the Government of the United States. That lot is worth about $2.50 or $3.00 a square foot—that is anywhere between $150,000.00 and $250,-000.00—and you are proposing a Dixon-Yates on it. To give away Government property and then pay rent on it!

Why don't you go ahead and build your substitute on the government owned lot in such a way that it can be used as a real post office and an office building in the future?

Why should the U.S. Gov't. give away property it already owns for the purpose we both have in mind—*and pay rent* on its own property?

I haven't exploded publicly on this—but if it is necessary I shall do it.

Yours truly,
Harry S. Truman

[The President sent copies of his letter to the two Missouri senators, the congressman from his local district, and the head of the General Services Administration. Postmaster General Day promised to do nothing until he and Truman talked over the problem. The United States Post Office and Federal Building of Independence, Missouri, at the corner of Osage and Lexington, was dedicated on May 8, 1966.]

TO JOHN F. KENNEDY

April 11, 1962

Dear Mr. President:

I am told that the 35th Division, along with three or four other National Guard Divisions, is to be broken up and disbanded.

In 1917, 1918 and 1919 the 35th Division, made up of Missouri and Kansas National Guard units, was one of the topnotch fighting units in World War I.

In 1942 to 1946 the 35th was made up of Missouri, Kansas, Nebraska and Arkansas units. But Missouri and Kansas units were the backbone of the fighting Division.

A statement attributed to George Washington about National Defense is this, "that the defense and welfare of the country is based on a well-trained militia."

The "Militia" of the present day is the National Guard of the various States of the Union.

Without any reflection on the bravery or ability of the Government paid and educated regular services, they have always been jealous of the "Militia."

The officers of the regular service of the Government are educated at the great service schools at the expense of the taxpayers. The officers of the various military units of the armed forces which make up the National Guard, the Naval Reserve and the Air Force Reserve are men who have had some service in war and who want to pass that information along, as civilians, to the volunteer forces of this great Republic.

Naturally, the "Regulars" want to eliminate the "Citizen Soldiers." If they succeed there will be room for many more "Regulars." It shouldn't happen.

The President, a *civilian,* is by the fundamental law of this great Republic, the Commander in Chief of the Armed Forces of the Nation.

Mr. President, I sincerely hope that you will take a good look at this suggestion that this great Division be broken up.

A smart aleck Regular Colonel in World War I inspected the 35th as it came out of the trenches. He hadn't been at the front! He expected "spit and polish" and of course it wasn't there. He made remarks reflecting on the National Guard. He got what was coming to him! He forgot that some of us who were civilian soldiers were in the Congress.[1]

I only ask you, Mr. President, to take a good look at what is happening to this great wartime Division. I was a member of it and so were most of my immediate family who were eligible. My first cousin, General Ralph E. Truman, became its Commanding General in the second World War. You have just now promoted one of his sons to a three star general.

The Division can be continued as a training unit in the States where it is presently located. Make it a training unit for civilians who want to learn something of military service.

Please give this situation a thorough going over before this great Division is abolished. It is a great fighting unit in the "Militia" referred to by the Great First President. He was a Militia Man.

Sincerely yours,
Harry S. Truman

[The 35th Division was broken up.]

---

1. Truman entered the Senate only in 1935, but he never forgot what he considered the stupidity of regular officers during the First World War.

*The individuals who persuaded the President to recognize the State
of Israel on May 14, 1948, eleven minutes after it had been proclaimed
in Tel Aviv, have never been convincingly identified. It is clear that the
State Department was against any immediate recognition. In April
1962, the President received a long letter from his former staff assistant
on the Interstate Commerce Committee of the Senate, Max Lowenthal,
asking permission to make a bequest in Truman's name to a fund for
needy children in the Negev, and the President's answer points to Lowenthal as a figure influential in the momentous decision.*

TO MAX LOWENTHAL

April 23, 1962

Dear Max:
    You don't know how very much I appreciated your good letter of the
7th. I have been a long time answering it. The reason is that I liked to read
your letter every once in a while.
    I know very well how you feel about me and that is one of the reasons
why I would not, under any circumstances, take away from you an honor
which you wanted to give me and for which you should have the credit.
Of course, if that is the way you want to do it I'll be glad to go along with
you.
    I know exactly how you feel about the idea of your not wanting to be
considered as benefactor to the State of Israel but I don't know why you
should because I don't know who has done more for Israel than you have.
In fact, you are the one I talked with when we were trying to work out
the recognition for the State of Israel, and you know how those Israelites
have placed me on a pedestal alongside of Moses, and that is the reason
I wrote you as I did because I wanted you to have the credit.
    I hope I will have a chance to see you the next time I am in New York,
which will be around May 9th or 10th, and we will have a discussion like
we used to have and you can give me all the hell you want to and it won't
make me mad at you.

Sincerely yours,
Harry S. Truman

TO JOHN F. KENNEDY

June 28, 1962

Dear Mr. President:
    It looks as if the Republicrats haven't changed a bit since 1936. Pres.
Roosevelt had his troubles with them—so did I.

Mr. President, you are on the right track. Don't let them tell *you* what to do—you tell them, as you have!

Your suggestions for the public welfare, in my opinion, are correct.

This is a personal and confidential statement for what it may be worth.

You know my program was "Give 'em Hell" and if they don't like it give 'em more hell.

Sincerely,

Harry S. Truman

MEMORANDUM

July 14, 1962

The Phone & the Privy

There are times when even a former President of the United States must go to the privy. Nothing can be done about that unless he is willing to do a childish thing and put on a clean pair of drawers! And when the drawers are six blocks away, he must go to the privy!

The phone kept ringing but the privy won. It had to!

And, believe it or not it is still ringing. From New York, from Florida, from San Francisco and Seattle. What the hell! Be nice to all.

Representative Kirwan of Ohio sent a copy of the New York Times *magazine of July 29, 1962, in which the Harvard historian Arthur M. Schlesinger, Sr., offered the results of a poll of seventy-five historians that rated the Presidents. Lincoln, Washington, Franklin D. Roosevelt, Wilson, and Jefferson received the accolade of greatness in the order given. After the top group came the half-dozen figures who were "near-great": Jackson, Theodore Roosevelt, Polk, Truman, John Adams, Cleveland.*

TO MICHAEL J. KIRWAN

August 13, 1962

Dear Mike:

Thank you for yours of July 30th, enclosing me a copy of the magazine which rated the Presidents. I don't know how they came to put me so high up on the list but I appreciate it nevertheless.

If I had been arranging the first five in the row of the great, I would have put Washington first, Jefferson second, Woodrow Wilson third, Lincoln fourth and Franklin Roosevelt fifth.

I, in all probability, would have moved Andrew Jackson into that row and made six of them but I didn't have anything to do with making it up. When I come up there you and I will talk it over.

Sincerely yours,

Harry S. Truman

Crosby Kemper, a member of the wealthy Kemper family of Kansas City, tried to exert financial leverage on the Missouri campaign of 1962, and Truman was especially bothered because Crosby went over to the Republicans.

TO CROSBY KEMPER (UNSENT)

September 5, 1962

Dear Crosby:

I have just been reliably informed that you have been putting pressure on and making threats to some of my good friends, regarding the campaigns in the state of Missouri, particularly the one for the Senate.

Now Crosby, I don't like that sort of thing. In one instance you have ruined the political prospects of one of our good young Democrats, by threatening to take his living away from him. You've got him working for a "Republican Kemper." That is something out of this world to me. Your father was my friend and the greatest part of his fortune came about because he was National Democratic Committeeman for thirty or forty years.

He was beaten for Mayor when he should have been elected. Your present friends the K.C. Star lied him into defeat.

Remember the Mexico & Orient deal when the Jackson County Democrats came to his rescue. I was there and I know.

Now I don't care a damn if one of the third generation of Kempers wants to go wrong because of the immense wealth of the family, but I do care if the second generation makes financial pressure a part of the campaign.

I have some forty thousand dollars in one account in your bank. I have twenty-five or thirty thousand in a Library account and I have forty thousand in your brother's bank. Do you want me to do what you did to my young friend? I can cut you both off now and for the future if I want to. And Mo. will have two Democratic Senators.

In the fall election in California, Truman's archenemy Richard M. Nixon was running for governor, and the prospect was enough to get the Missouri Democrat out to San Francisco to rally the faithful and smite down the unbelievers. But speechmaking had its problems, for the speech didn't turn up from the President's speech factory, which usually was headed by Charlie Murphy.

DIARY

Fairmont Hotel, San Francisco
September 11, 1962

Well the men around me are uneasy about tonight. So am I. Have no speech ready for release although Dave Noyes and a secretary to the state committee of the Democratic Party in California are trying to put some remarks in shape to give the press boys.

4:30 P.M.

Have a press conference. It seemed to go all right. Some dark complexioned guy with short black chin whiskers asked some loaded questions—and he received loaded answers. He evidently was a plant of Nixon's, I am sure.

Five o'clock P.M.

Called Mrs. Truman. Had a nice talk with her. When I make a call from a hotel to my house in Independence I always give the number at the house. That number is in the exchange at Kansas City. The smart gal on the phone for long distance always asks Missouri or Kansas. And she gets an instructive lecture on how things are set up phone wise in the suburb on the west side of Independence.

6:30 P.M.

No outline for tonight's speech has come back from the acting type girl, found out she had releases made for press releases and forgot to get the copy I needed ready!

7:00 P.M.

Went to the cocktail party and the line-up for the head table tonight. Believe it or not the notes for my remarks came just before dinner was ready! Well, I've had to meet emergencies and crises from 1903 to date. So I looked the copy over, scratched out about half of it, and told the dinner crowd what I believed in regard to the Government of the United States and Calif. Govt. in particular. I hope they liked it. They yelled and clapped their hands and stomped their feet as if they did.[1]

---

1. The speech obviously was incendiary. In preparation the President scrawled on a scrap of paper: "The people shut the *front* door on him. Watch out that they don't sneak him in

9:45 P.M.

Came back to this plush suite, which has a sign on the door "Presidential Suite." It has a living room big enough to have a "big four" or "big three" national conference or international conference, and crowd in all the staff, press and other hangers-on at such places, a couple of bed rooms and so many dressing rooms and bath and toilet places it is damned confusing to a "retired" farmer from the great State of Missouri!

DIARY

Fairmont Hotel, San Francisco
September 12, 1962

5 A.M.

I'm up, dressed and packed up for the trip to the U.S. No. 1 "crackpot city" in southern California. L.A. is No. 1 and New York City is No. 2 in the crackpot line in the U.S.A. The reason is that retired farmers from the Appalachians to the Rockies, government clerks on retired pay, busted little business men and other members of a class "who have nothing else to do" gravitate to N.Y. and L.A.

My home town, Independence, the County Seat of Jackson County, Missouri, is in my opinion the best place for a retired Missouri farmer to live. That state has had three "notorious" characters—Mark Twain, Jesse James and myself. The other two are shoveling coal for Pluto and I'm all that's left to appear for them.

MEMORANDUM

December 28, 1962

I've just been informed that the Democratic Party, of which I have been an active member since I was seventeen years old, has gone high

---

through the *back* door." And on an envelope: "Fine man [Governor Brown]. Clean fight. Character ass'n and dirty name calling. Choice between Brown good Gov. and a kindly man and the opposite in a mean, nasty fellow." And on another envelope:

That fellow couldn't get into the front door of the White House. Now he's trying to sneak in over the transom. Russian visit [of Nixon]. The Russian people wanted to learn something from him but Khrushchev taught him something. Khrushchev has been threatening to bury the free world and now that fellow [Nixon] boasts that he will bury the Democratic Party and its leaders here in California. Didn't come here to tell California what to do—but what not to do to the detriment of the great state. But the situation that has developed in Calif. has importance outside your borders. It affects the whole nation. An effort is underway to revive the man's political future. I am here to help prevent it.

hat and is charging one thousand dollars for the privilege of sitting with the President of the United States at a dinner!

The President of the United States represents 180,000,000 people who have no other person to look after their interests. The President and the Vice President are the only public officials elected by the 180 million.

It is my opinion that ten thousand Democrats at five dollars apiece for [the] privilege of sitting with and seeing the President as his guest would be worth ten thousand times ten or one hundred times that to the Democratic Party.

When the Party of the People goes high hat on a cost basis, it no longer represents the common every day man—who is the basis of the Democratic Party.

TO DEAN ACHESON

May 14, 1963

Dear Dean:

I understand that you are presiding at the dinner of the Washington Institute of Foreign Affairs, on May 28th. I certainly wish I could be with you but I just can't make it, much to my regret.

As you know, I am just as interested in what goes on now as I was when I was in the center of things but that old lady "Anno Domini" has been chasing me and I have to slow up a little bit, particularly since she has a partner in Mrs. Truman.

Please remember me to Mrs. Acheson.

Sincerely yours,
Harry S. Truman

TO PIERCE ADAMS

August 14, 1963

Dear Mr. Adams:

I appreciated very much your letter of the 12th, suggesting that I make a complaint to the owner of the Kansas City Baseball Team on their lack of winning.

I can't go along with you on that sort of approach for the simple reason that when I was President, every Tom, Dick and Harry tried to tell me what to do.

The President of the baseball team knows what to do and the best thing to do is to let him alone.

Sincerely yours,
Harry S. Truman

The President's old army friend Eddie McKim had a plan to advance the fortunes of Mutual of Omaha, with which company he was affiliated. Dr. Charles W. Mayo was retiring, and Eddie thought that Dr. Mayo and Truman might pose together, with Mayo presenting the President with two "senior citizen policies"—special hospital policies sold only to individuals over age sixty-five, and requiring no medical examination. Eddie said that as a result, a nice little check would be made out to either the President or the library fund.

TO EDWARD D. McKIM

October 15, 1963

Dear Eddie:

I more than appreciate your letter of September 19th, which I have been a long time in answering because I have been away from home so much of the time. I am glad Mary is doing well and has the infection whipped.

I was sorry to hear of the retirement of Dr. Chas. W. Mayo, but he will make a good consultant for the Insurance Company.

I don't object to a picture with Dr. Mayo—but there is one thing I don't like and that is to be called a "Senior Citizen." I still get around and when I get to be a "Senior Citizen" I hope they will put me in a pine box and cover me up.

Sincerely yours,
Harry S. Truman

The managing editor of Look *magazine sent the President the latest issue containing what he described as "an informative report on the controversial Central Intelligence Agency."*

TO WILLIAM B. ARTHUR

June 10, 1964

Dear Mr. Arthur:

Thank you for the copy of Look with the article on the Central Intelligence Agency. It is, I regret to say, not true to the facts in many respects.

The CIA was set up by me for the sole purpose of getting all the available information to the President. It was not intended to operate as an international agency engaged in strange activities.

Sincerely yours,
Harry S. Truman

TO LEONARD H. PASQUALICCHIO

July 22, 1964

Dear Mr. Pasqualicchio:

I read your letter of the 7th with a lot of interest and your reason for writing me was to support an Italian Delegate for the appointment as Judge of the United States Court of Appeals for the District of Columbia Circuit.

I don't recommend people for positions of that kind unless I am personally acquainted with them—[unless] I know their background and their ability to fill the position. With all the Italian background he has, it would seem to me that he should have gotten himself an appointment as Judge in Italy.

Sincerely yours,
Harry S. Truman

Sidney W. Souers, a business executive in St. Louis, rose to the rank of rear admiral in the naval reserve, and was executive secretary of the National Security Council during its first years. He kept in touch with Truman on political matters.

TO SIDNEY W. SOUERS

November 10, 1964

Dear Sid:

You don't know how very much I appreciated your letter of the 6th. It always gives me quite a lift to hear from you.

Goldwater caused a landslide, the like of which we haven't seen since President Roosevelt was elected, but this one seems to cover the whole round of things. The Republican Party is in a terrible fix. They are doing a lot of screaming to get out of it.

Of course, I would like to see a two-party system. A Democratic Party that knows where it is going and a Republican Party that thinks it does. I don't want the Republicans to get too strong, however, because the Democratic Party is the Party of the people and has been since the Civil War.

Sincerely yours,
Harry S. Truman

The columnist Joseph Alsop wrote the President on March 12, 1965, that on the advice of counsel (Dean Acheson) he was proposing, presumptuously, to apologize for the inexperience and bad judgment that had led him to underrate Truman's leadership when the President was in office. Alsop now saw the Truman era as a heroic period.

TO JOSEPH W. ALSOP

March 19, 1965

Dear Mr. Alsop:

Indeed, you could not have pleased me more. Nor need you have felt that you would be presuming in writing me on any subject.

It is true that I did not always react pleasantly to criticism—or derisive comments—but I never for a moment questioned the right of anyone to do so.

There is something in my make-up that rebels at the thought of exacting an apology from anyone who has publicly disapproved of me—and I surely would not expect to receive one from so talented an observer as yourself.

But I warmly welcome your reassessment of "the period" and dare hope that it might be sustained by the ultimate judgment.

Sincerely yours,

Harry S. Truman

TO SIDNEY W. SOUERS

January 23, 1967

Dear Sid:

I have been intending to write you for some time since receiving your letter in connection with Alsop's clumsy effort to equate the situation in South Vietnam with the Korean situation.

So far there has not been the remotest indication in any of the documents that we have searched, or any indication from the people who were then involved in shaping policy, that there is any basis for the allegation he made.

Your letter and your statement to Dave over the telephone proved very helpful.

With all best wishes and warm regards.

Sincerely yours,

Harry S. Truman

In Korea, Father Paul White sought to raise a million dollars for the Truman Memorial Hospital, and asked the President's permission to use his name.

TO FATHER PAUL WHITE

November 28, 1967

Dear Father White:

Thank you for your letter of October 15th, which I read with interest and admiration for your devotion to the welfare of the people of South Korea.

It has been, and is, my personal preference not to encourage the building of any memorials or monuments to me. I consider that whatever useful acts may have been performed during my administration were in fact the acts of the American people.

I hope that you will understand why I cannot do as you request. You have my best wishes in your chosen work.

Sincerely yours,

Harry S. Truman

Martha Ann Truman, the daughter of Vivian, married James F. Swoyer, and she and Jim and their son, Karl, lived on a farm near Oskaloosa, Kansas. She remained in touch with Uncle Harry and Aunt Bess as their horizons, once so wide, were constricting, as the letters from their end said less and less.

TO MARTHA ANN TRUMAN SWOYER

November 4, 1971

Dear Martha Ann:

Your Aunt Bess and I were delighted to have your newsy letter.

I don't see how you accomplish all that you do—with going to summer school, gardening, teaching, cooking and the usual housework. You had better take my advice and slow down a little.

We are glad that Karl is taking such a fine interest in his school work. I always tell the students who write to me, to obtain all of the education they can possibly get and to read as many good books as they can.

I know that your antique chairs will look very pretty when they are refinished and will be something nice to have in the years to come.

Aunt Bess and I are about the same. Reading is our main diversion these days.

With love and best wishes,
Uncle Harry

SOURCE NOTES

ABBREVIATIONS

HST *Harry S. Truman,* by Margaret Truman (New York, 1973)
MP *Mr. President,* by William Hillman (New York, 1952)
PPF Post-Presidential Files
PSF President's Secretary's Files

Apr. 11, 1945 : PPF, Memoirs, Box 47, letters to Mrs. John A. Truman and Mary
    Jane, set 2; part of this letter was published in *HST,* pp. 198–199. As mentioned,
    the voluminous correspondence between Truman and his mother and sister
    was mostly in the form of handwritten letters, from Washington as well as
    Grandview, and in the first years after the presidency, in preparation of his
    memoirs, the former chief executive had typed copies made, which presently
    are in the Harry S. Truman Library. Shortly before her death in 1978, at the
    age of eighty-nine, Mary took back the originals from the library and burned
    them.
Apr. 12, 1945 : PSF, Box 82, presidential appointments file, daily sheets, Apr. 1945.
    This diary entry appears in *MP,* pp. 109–111, and *HST,* pp. 209–210.
Apr. 13, 1945 : Ibid. With minor changes in *MP,* pp. 109, 111–112. This daily ap-
    pointment sheet and the next one, for Apr. 14, appear to have been written
    over and dictated as diary entries; no sheets seem to exist for the dates between
    Apr. 14 and May 14; beginning on the latter date they consist of annotations
    only.
Apr. 14, 1945 : Ibid. With minor changes in *MP,* pp. 112–113; small excerpt in *HST,*
    p. 220.
Apr. 15, 1945 : Ibid. With some changes in *MP,* pp. 113–114.
Apr. 18, 1945 : Ibid. (handwritten). This entry appears in *MP,* p. 109.
May 10, 1945 : Miscellaneous Historical Documents Relating to Harry S. Truman,
    Box 13, no. 394 (handwritten).
May 12, 1945 : ("The Courts") PSF, Box 333, longhand personal memos, 1945. In
    MP, p. 114.
May 12, 1945 : ("I should like") Ibid. In *MP,* p. 114.
May 13, 1945 : PSF, Box 322, S (handwritten).
May 14, 1945 : PSF, Box 82, May 1945. Most of this sheet in *HST,* pp. 250–251.

May 16, 1945 : Ibid.
May 17, 1945 : Ibid.
May 18, 1945 : Ibid. Small portion in *HST,* pp. 251–252.
May 19, 1945 : Ibid. Partly in *HST,* pp. 252–253.
May 21, 1945 : Ibid.
May 22, 1945 : PSF, Box 333, 1945. Mostly in *MP,* pp. 114–116.
May 23, 1945 : PSF, Box 82, May 1945. Last paragraph in *HST,* p. 254.
May 24, 1945 : Ibid.
May 27, 1945 : PSF, Box 333, 1945. Last two paragraphs in *MP,* pp. 116–117.
May 30, 1945 : Ibid.
June 1, 1945 : Ibid. Bowdlerized and excerpted in *MP,* pp. 117–118.
June 4, 1945 : Ibid. Mostly in *MP,* pp. 118–120.
June 5, 1945 : Ibid. Mostly in *MP,* pp. 120–121.
June 7, 1945 : Ibid. Excerpted in *MP,* p. 121.
June 13, 1945 : Ibid. Three sentences in *MP,* p. 122.
June 15, 1945 : PSF, Box 82, June 1945 (handwritten).
June 17, 1945 : PSF, Box 333, 1945. Partly in *MP,* p. 122, and *HST,* p. 260.
July 4, 1945 : Ibid. First paragraph in *MP,* p. 122.
July 7, 1945 : Ibid. Badly trimmed in *MP,* pp. 122–123.
July 9, 1945 : Ibid.
July 16, 1945 : PSF, Box 322, Ross, Mr. and Mrs. Charles G. (handwritten).
July 18, 1945 : Ibid.
July 20, 1945 : Ibid.
July 25, 1945 : Ibid.
July 26, 1945 : Ibid.
July 27, 1945 : Ibid.
July 30, 1945 : Ibid.
Aug. 5, 1945 : PSF, Box 333, 1945. Detail trimmed in *MP,* pp. 123, 125.
Aug. 10, 1945 : Ibid. Long section omitted in *MP,* p. 125.
Aug. 11, 1945 : Ibid. Last two sentences omitted in *MP,* p. 125.
Aug. 17, 1945 : PPF, Memoirs, Box 47, set 2. Partly published in *HST,* pp. 284–285.
Sept. 1, 1945 : Miscellaneous Historical Documents Relating to Harry S. Truman, Box 13, no. 394.
Sept. 5, 1945 : PSF, Box 82, Sept. 1945 (handwritten). Final sentence in *HST,* p. 290.
Sept. 11, 1945 : PPF, Memoirs, Box 47, set 2. Partly in *HST,* p. 299.
Sept. 18, 1945 : PSF, Box 82, Sept. 1945 (handwritten).
Sept. 20, 1945 : PSF, Box 333, 1945. Mostly in *MP,* p. 127.
Sept. 21, 1945 : PSF, Box 82, Sept. 1945 (handwritten).
Sept. 22, 1945 : PPF, Memoirs, Box 47, set 2. Partly in *HST,* p. 290.
Sept. 26, 1945 : PSF, Box 82, Sept. 1945 (handwritten).
Oct. 13, 1945 : PPF, Memoirs, Box 47, set 2. Partly in *HST,* pp. 289–290.
Oct. 15, 1945 : PSF, Box 82, Oct. 1945 (handwritten).
Oct. 23, 1945 : PPF, Memoirs, Box 47, set 2. Partly in *HST,* pp. 292–294.
Nov. 11, 1945 : Papers of Mary Ethel Noland, materials opened Dec. 1978 (handwritten).
Nov. 15 [?], 1945 : PSF, Box 82, Nov. 1945 (handwritten). Partly in *MP,* pp. 149–150.
Dec. 28, 1945 : PSF, Box 309, desk files, folder 2 (handwritten).
Jan. 5, 1946 : PSF, Box 333, 1946. In *MP,* pp. 21–23, and Harry S. Truman, *Memoirs: Year of Decisions* (Garden City, N.Y., 1955), pp. 551–552.

Jan. 16, 1946 : Miscellaneous Historical Documents Relating to Harry S. Truman, Box 12, no. 349 (handwritten).

Jan. 21, 1946 : Papers of Mary Ethel Noland, Box 2, HST to the Noland family, 1946 (handwritten).

Jan. 23, 1946 : PPF, Memoirs, Box 47, set 1. Partly in *HST,* pp. 304–305.

Feb. 14, 1946 : ("Just a statement") PSF, Box 333, 1946.

Feb. 14, 1946 : ("10:15") PSF, Box 83, presidential appointments files, daily sheets, Feb. 1946 (handwritten).

Feb. 25, 1946 : PSF, Box 323, Southern, William, Jr.

Feb. 26, 1946 : PSF, Box 332, Truman, Vivian.

Mar. 16, 1946 : PSF, Box 83, Mar. 1946 (handwritten).

May 21, 1946 : PSF, Box 320, Pendergast, James (handwritten).

May 29, 1946 : PSF, Box 120, Food—wheat data.

June 11, 1946 : PSF, Box 310, Duncan, Richard M.

June 13, 1946 : Papers of Mary Ethel Noland, Box 2, HST to the Noland family, 1946.

Aug. 22, 1946 : PPF, Memoirs, Box 47, set 1. Partly in *HST,* pp. 334–335.

Sept. 12, 1946 : PSF, Box 132, 0.

Sept. 17, 1946 : PSF, Box 333, 1946.

Sept. 18, 1946 : PPF, Memoirs, Box 47, set 2. Last paragraph in *HST,* p. 317.

Sept. 20, 1946 : PPF, Memoirs, Box 47, set 1. Partly in *HST,* p. 318, and in Harry S. Truman, *Year of Decisions,* p. 560.

Sept. 26, 1946 : PSF, Box 333, 1946. In *MP,* pp. 7–8.

Oct. 23, 1946 : Papers of Mary Ethel Noland, materials opened Dec. 1978.

Oct. 1946 : PSF, Box 47, Oct. 14, 1946, price controls, radio address (handwritten).

Dec. 11, 1946 : PSF, Box 333, 1946. Partly in *MP,* pp. 128–130, and *HST,* p. 324.

Jan. 1, 1947 : PSF, Box 333, 1947. Mostly in *MP,* pp. 129–130.

Feb. 9, 1946 : PPF, Memoirs, Box 47, set 1.

Feb. 18, 1947 : PSF, Box 85, presidential appointments file, daily sheets, Feb. 17–28, 1947 (handwritten). Part on Marshall in *MP,* p. 150.

Feb. 19, 1947 : PPF, Memoirs, Box 47, set 1.

Mar. 27, 1947 : Papers of Mary Ethel Noland, materials opened Dec. 1978.

Mar. 28, 1947 : PPF, Memoirs, Box 47, set 1. Partly in HST, pp. 345–346.

Mar. 1947 : PSF, Box 322, Ross, Mr. and Mrs. Charles G. (handwritten).

July 9, 1947 : ("Dear Vivian") PSF, Box 332, Truman, Vivian.

July 9, 1947 : ("Gentlemen") PSF, Box 105, trip file, Virginia, Charlottesville (handwritten).

July 25, 1947 : PPF, Memoirs, Box 47, set 1.

Aug. 6, 1947 : Ibid.

Sept. 7, 1947 : Ibid.

Oct. 21, 1947 : Ibid.

Nov. 14, 1947 : Ibid. Mostly in *HST,* p. 356.

Nov. 17, 1947 : PSF, Box 332.

Dec. 25, 1947 : PPF, Memoirs, Box 3, diaries. Mostly in *MP,* pp. 132–133, and *HST,* p. 371.

Feb. 2, 1948 : PPF, Memoirs, Box 3, diaries. With minor changes in *MP,* p. 134.

Feb. 6, 1948 : PSF, Box 311, G.

Feb. 8, 1948 : PPF, Memoirs, Box 3, diaries. Bowdlerized in *MP,* p. 134.

Feb. 12, 1948 : Ibid.
Feb. 14, 1948 : Ibid. Bowdlerized in *MP,* p. 134.
Mar. 6, 1948 : PPF, Memoirs, Box 3.
Mar. 16, 1948 : PSF, Box 321, Roosevelt, Eleanor. Partly in *MP,* pp. 52–53.
Mar. 20, 1948 : PPF, Memoirs, Box 3, diaries. In *HST,* p. 388.
Mar. 21, 1948 : Ibid. Partly in *HST,* p. 389.
Mar. 22, 1948 : PSF, Box 332, Truman, Vivian.
Mar. 30, 1948 : PPF, Memoirs, Box 47, set 1.
Apr. 3, 1948 : PPF, Memoirs, Box 3, diaries.
Apr. 4, 1948 : Ibid. In *MP,* p. 135.
Apr. 8, 1948 : PSF, Box 332, Truman, Vivian.
Apr. 8, 1948 : PPF, Memoirs, Box 47, set 1.
Apr. 17 [?], 1948 : PSF, Box 48, Apr. 17, 1948, American Society of Newspaper Editors (handwritten).
May 6, 1948 : PPF, Memoirs, Box 3, diaries. Partly in *MP,* p. 135.
May 7, 1948 : Ibid. Partly in *MP,* pp. 135–137, and *HST,* p. 407.
May 9, 1948 : Papers of Mary Ethel Noland, materials opened Dec. 1978 (handwritten).
May 12, 1948 : PPF, Memoirs, Box 47, set 1.
May 19, 1948 : Ibid.
May 22, 1948 : PSF, Box 321, Roosevelt, Eleanor.
June 27, 1948 : ("Margie goes") PPF, Memoirs, Box 3, diaries.
June 27, 1948 : ("Dear Earle") PSF, Box 324, Stewart, Mrs. George Earle (handwritten).
June 28, 1948 : PPF, Memoirs, Box 3, diaries. Mostly in *MP,* p. 137.
July 5, 1948 : Ibid.
July 6, 1948 : Ibid.
July 12, 1948 : Ibid. In *HST,* pp. 9–10.
July 13, 1948 : Ibid. In *HST,* p. 10.
July 14, 1948 : Ibid. Third paragraph in *MP,* p. 137, and *HST,* p. 11.
July 15, 1948 : Ibid. In *MP,* pp. 137–140, and *HST,* p. 14.
July 16, 1948 : Ibid. Partly in *MP,* p. 140, and all in *HST,* pp. 14–15.
July 18, 1948 : Ibid.
July 19, 1948 : Ibid. Partly in *MP,* p. 140, and in *HST,* p. 15.
July 31, 1948 : Ibid. Partly in *HST,* p. 18.
Aug. 3, 1948 : Ibid. Partly in *MP,* pp. 140–141, and *HST,* p. 389.
Aug. 18, 1948 : PSF, Box 306, C.
Sept. 11, 1948 : PPF, Memoirs, Box 47, set 1.
Sept. 13, 1948 : PPF, Memoirs, Box 3, diaries. Partly in *MP,* p. 141, and *HST,* p. 35.
Sept. 14, 1948 : Ibid.
Oct. 5, 1948 : PPF, Memoirs, Box 47, set 1. Partly in *HST,* pp. 22, 29.
Nov. 7, 1948 : Ibid. Partly in *HST,* pp. 42–43, 399.
Nov. 14, 1948 : Ibid.
Dec. 13, 1948 : Ibid.
Feb. 12, 1949 : PSF, Box 333, 1949.
May 5, 1949 : PPF, Name File, Box 49, Le.
June 22, 1949 : Papers of Mary Ethel Noland, materials opened Dec. 1948 (handwritten).
June 29, 1949 : PPF, Memoirs, Box 23, draft pp. 4234–4235.
July 8, 1949 : PSF, Box 333, 1949.

July 12, 1949 : PSF, Box 316, M.

Aug. 13, 1949 : Papers of Mary Ethel Noland, materials opened Dec. 1978 (hand-written).

Aug. 20, 1949 : PSF, Box 56, Edwards, India.

Sept. 1, 1949 : Papers of Mary Ethel Noland, materials opened Dec. 1978 (hand-written).

Sept. 8, 1949 : ("Dear Nellie") Papers of Mary Ethel Noland, materials opened Dec. 1978 (manuscript).

Sept. 8, 1949 : ("Dear Sam") PSF, Box 321, R.

Sept. 27, 1949 : ("Dear Mr. Moore") Papers of Mary Ethel Noland, Box 2, HST to the Noland family, 1949. *MP,* pp. 45–46.

Oct. 29, 1949 : ("Dear Nellie") Papers of Mary Ethel Noland, Box 2, HST to the Noland family, 1949 (handwritten).

Oct. 29, 1949 : ("Margaret sings") PSF, Box 278, 1949. All in Charles Robbins and Bradley Smith, *Last of His Kind: An Informal Portrait of Harry S. Truman* (New York, 1979), pp. 124–125.

Nov. 1, 1949 : PSF, Box 278, 1949. Partly in *MP,* p. 143; all in Robbins and Smith, *Last of His Kind,* p. 125.

Jan. 4, 1950 : PSF, Box 333, 1950.

Jan. 15, 1950 : PPF, Memoirs, Box 3, diaries. In *HST,* p. 442.

Feb. 11 [?], 1950 : PSF, Box 128, McCarthy, Joseph.

Feb. 25, 1950 : PSF, Box 59, Smith, Forrest.

Feb. 26, 1950 : PSF, Box 309, Daniels, Jonathan (handwritten).

Mar. 5, 1950 : PSF, Box 333, 1950.

Mar. 11, 1950 : Papers of Mary Ethel Noland, materials opened Dec. 1978 (hand-written).

Mar. 31, 1950 : Ibid.

Apr. 16, 1950 : PSF, Box 333, 1950. In *HST,* pp. 526–527.

June 7, 1950 : PSF, Box 23, pp. 4244–4245.

June 11, 1950 : Ibid., pp. 4246–4248.

June 12, 1950 : PSF, Box 321, Roberts, Roy A. (handwritten).

June 16, 1950 : Papers of Mary Ethel Noland, Box 2, HST to the Noland family, 1950 (handwritten).

June 20, 1950 : PSF, Box 125, L (handwritten).

June 24, 1950 : Papers of Stanley Woodward, Box 1, correspondence with Harry S. Truman, 1950–1953 (handwritten).

June 30, 1950 : PSF, Box 129, MacArthur, Douglas, messages, President Truman (handwritten). Mostly in *HST,* p. 469.

July 7, 1950 : Papers of Mary Ethel Noland, Box 2, HST to the Noland family, 1950 (handwritten).

July 19, 1950 : PSF, Box 312, H.

July 26, 1950 : Papers of Mary Ethel Noland, materials opened Dec. 1978 (hand-written).

Aug. 15, 1950 : PSF, Box 334, longhand notes, undated. The prayer and its accompanying explanation, with the latter suitably amended, appears in the frontispiece to *MP.*

Sept. 7, 1950 : PPF, Memoirs, Box 23, draft pp. 4251–4254.

Sept. 13, 1950 : Papers of Mary Ethel Noland, materials opened Dec. 1978 (hand-written).

Sept. 14, 1950 : PSF, Box 314, J (handwritten). Partly in Robbins and Smith, *Last of His Kind,* p. 118.

Sept. 24, 1950 : Papers of Mary Ethel Noland, materials opened Dec. 1978 (handwritten).

Oct. 13, 1950 : Ibid.

Oct. 21, 1950 : Ibid.

Oct. 25, 1950 : PSF, Box 188, Russia, Stalin.

Nov. 5, 1950 : PSF, Box 333, 1950.

Nov. 17, 1950 : Papers of Mary Ethel Noland, materials opened Dec. 1978 (handwritten).

Nov. 22, 1950 : PSF, Box 316, Mc.

Nov. 25, 1950 : PSF, Box 333, 1950. In *HST,* p. 484.

Nov. 30, 1950 : PSF, Box 333, 1950.

Dec. 2, 1950 : Ibid.

Dec. 5, 1950 : Ibid.

Dec. 7, 1950 : Miscellaneous Historical Documents Relating to Harry S. Truman, Box 13, no. 396.

Dec. 9, 1950 : PSF, Box 333, 1950. Partly in *MP,* pp. 36, 143, and *HST,* pp. 502–503.

Dec. 20, 1950 : PSF, Box 121, Ha–He (handwritten).

Dec. 22, 1950 : PPF, Memoirs, Box 3, diaries.

Dec. 24, 1950 : PPF, Memoirs, Box 3, diaries.

Dec. 27, 1950 : Ibid.

Jan. 10, 1951 : PSF, Box 333, 1951. In *MP,* pp. 143, 147, and partly in *HST,* p. 525.

Mar. 7, 1951 : Ibid.

Apr. 6, 1951 : PSF, Box 278, diary book, 1951. Mostly in *HST,* p. 514.

Apr. 8, 1951 : Ibid.

Apr. 9, 1951 : Ibid. In *HST,* p. 515.

Apr. 10, 1951 : Ibid. In *HST,* p. 515.

June 2, 1951 : Papers of Ralph E. Truman, Box 1, correspondence, 1951 (handwritten).

June 21, 1951 : PSF, Box 333, 1951.

June 25, 1951 : PPF, Memoirs, Box 23, draft pp. 4255–4257.

Aug. 8, 1951 : Papers of Mary Ethel Noland, Box 2, HST to the Noland family, 1951 (handwritten).

Aug. 30, 1951 : PSF, Box 278, diary book, 1951.

Sept. 1, 1951 : PPF, Memoirs, Box 23, draft pp. 4257–4260.

Sept. 2, 1951 : ("The Lord Mayor") PSF, Box 278, diary book, 1951.

Sept. 2, 1951 : ("My dear") PSF, Box 333, 1951.

Sept. 13, 1951 : PSF, Box 118, Douglas, William O.

Oct. 7, 1951 : PSF, Box 333, 1951. In *MP,* p. 47, with Krock's name excised.

Dec. 12, 1951 : Papers of Mary Ethel Noland, materials opened Dec. 1978 (handwritten).

Dec. 18, 1951 : PPF, Secretary's Office File, Box 7, Eisenhower, Dwight D., General (handwritten).

Dec. 26, 1951 : PSF, Box 333, 1951.

Dec. 30, 1951 : PSF, Box 321, Roberts, Roy A. (handwritten).

Jan. 1–2, 1952 : PSF, Box 333, 1952.

Jan. 3, 1952 : Ibid.

Jan. 4, 1952 : Ibid.

Jan. 8, 1952 : Ibid.

Jan. 10, 1952 : ("There has been") PSF, Box 334, longhand notes, undated. Mostly in *MP,* pp. 183–189.

Jan. 10, 1952 : ("Don Dawson") PSF, Box 333, 1952.

Jan. 14, 1952 : Ibid.

Jan. 18, 1952 : Ibid.

Jan. 24, 1952 : PSF, Box 314, K.

Jan. 28, 1952 : ("Dear Dave") PSF, Box 319, Morgan, David H.

Jan. 28, 1952 : ("Dear Grace") PSF, Box 331, Summer, Grace.

Feb. 2, 1952 : Papers of Mary Ethel Noland, materials opened Dec. 1978 (handwritten).

Feb. 9, 1952 : PSF, Box 333, 1952.

Feb. 17, 1952 : Papers of Mary Ethel Noland, materials opened Dec. 1978 (handwritten).

Feb. 20, 1952 : PSF, Box 333, 1952.

Feb. 26, 1952 : Ibid.

[Mar. 2], 1952 : Ibid.

Mar. 3, 1952 : Papers of Mary Ethel Noland, materials opened Dec. 1978 (handwritten).

Mar. 4, 1952 : PSF, Box 333, 1952. Paragraph six, somewhat changed, in Harry S. Truman, *Memoirs: Years of Trial and Hope* (Garden City, N.Y., 1956), p. 492.

Mar. 27, 1952 : Ibid.

Apr. 3, 1952 : Ibid.

Apr. 13, 1952 : Ibid.

Apr. 15, 1952 : Ibid.

May 11, 1952 : Papers of Mary Ethel Noland, Box 2, HST to the Noland family, 1952 (handwritten).

May 15, 1952 : PSF, Box 333, 1952.

May 18, 1952 : Ibid.

June 1, 1952 : Ibid.

June 4, 1952 : Papers of Mary Ethel Noland, Box 2, HST to the Noland family, 1952–1953 (handwritten).

June 8, 1952 : PSF, Box 333, 1952.

June 15, 1952 : Ibid.

July 3, 1952 : PSF, Box 318, Maverick, Maury.

July 6, 1952 : ("Mr. T.") PSF, Box 333, 1952.

July 6, 1952 : ("The Republicans") Ibid.

July 11, 1952 : ("Dear Ethel") Papers of Mary Ethel Noland, materials opened Dec. 1978 (handwritten).

July 24, 1952 : PSF, Box 334, longhand notes, undated (typescript).

July 26, 1952 : PSF, Box 324, Stevenson, Adlai E. (handwritten).

Aug. 16, 1952 : PSF, Box 118, Eisenhower, Dwight D. (folder 1) (handwritten).

Aug. 19, 1952 : PSF, Box 333, 1952.

Aug. 28, 1952 : Ibid.

[Early August 1952] : Ibid.

[Late August 1952] : PSF, Box 334, longhand notes, undated.

Sept. 9, 1952 : PSF, Box 333, 1952.

Sept. 11, 1952 : PSF, Box 314, K (handwritten).

Sept. 23, 1952 : PSF, Box 333, 1952.

Sept. 26, 1952 : Papers of Mary Ethel Noland, materials opened Dec. 1978 (handwritten).

Nov. 15, 1952 : PSF, Box 333, 1952.
Nov. 20, 1952 : Ibid. Mostly in *HST,* pp. 550–551.
Nov. 24, 1952 : Ibid.
Nov. 28, 1952 : Ibid. Partly in *HST,* pp. 553–554.
Dec. 4, 1952 : Ibid.
Dec. 6, 1952 : Ibid.
Dec. 22, 1952 : Ibid.
Jan. 2, 1953 : Papers of Mary Ethel Noland, materials opened Dec. 1978 (hand-
    written).
Jan. 20, 1953 : PSF, Box 278, diary book, 1953.
Jan. 21, 1953 : Ibid.
Mar. 20, 1953 : PSF, Box 334, longhand personal memos, 1953.
[Apr. 1953, undated notes] : PSF, Box 334, longhand notes, undated.
May 20, 1953 : PSF, Box 334, longhand personal memos, 1953.
July 8, 1953 : ("I went walking") Ibid.
July 8, 1953 : ("When you contemplate") PSF, Box 334, longhand notes, undated.
[Sept. 6, 1953] : PPF, Name File, Box 85, Tj–Tz (handwritten).
Oct. 2, 1953 : PPF, Name File, Box 1, Acheson, Dean, correspondence, 1953–1955.
Nov. 29, 1953 : Papers of Vic H. Housholder, Box 1, correspondence between HST
    and Vic Housholder, 1953–1959 (handwritten).
Nov. 30, 1953 : PPF, Name File, Box 85, Tj–Tz (handwritten).
[Nov. 1953] : PPF, Harry Dexter White Case, Box 1, background data on case file
    (handwritten).
[1953?] : PSF, Box 334, longhand notes, undated.
Jan. 9, 1954 : PPF, Name File, Box 85, Tj–Tz (handwritten).
Apr. 24, 1954 : PPF, Trip File, Box 4, Washington–New York (handwritten).
June 2, 1954 : PSF, Box 334, longhand personal memos, 1954.
[July 1954] : Ibid.
Nov. 11, 1954 : Ibid.
[1954?] : PSF, Box 334.
Jan. 7, 1955 : PPF, Name File, Box 5 (handwritten).
Jan. 28, 1955 : PPF, Name File, Box 61, Morse, Wayne, correspondence, 1953–1958.
Feb. 2, 1955 : PSF, Box 334, longhand personal memos, 1955.
Mar. 25, 1955 : PPF, Name File, Box 38, Hennings, Thomas C. (handwritten).
Apr. 6, 1955 : PPF, Name File, Box 16, Churchill, Winston S., correspondence,
    1953–1956 (handwritten).
June 24, 1955 : PPF, Trip File, Box 6, San Francisco (handwritten).
July 1, 1955 : PPF, Name File, Box 25, Doubleday & Company, Inc., correspon-
    dence, 1955.
July 9, 1955 : PPF, Name File, Box 33, Grady, Henry F.
July 24, 1955 : PPF, Name File, Box 85, Tj–Tz (handwritten).
July 31, 1955 : Ibid.
Dec. 10, 1955 : PPF, Name File, Box 50, *Life,* comments, memoirs, quotes, etc.
Jan. 6, 1956 : Ibid.
Feb. 10, 1956 : PPF, Name File, Box 50, *Life,* corrections in memoirs.
Feb. 20, 1956 : PPF, Name File, Box 56, McSween, Donald M.
May [11–15], 1956 : PPF, European Trip, 1956, Box 8, articles on trip, folder 1
    (handwritten).
May 23, 1956 : Papers of Tom L. Evans, Box 5, Truman, Harry S., 1940–1963, folder
    2 (handwritten).

May 27–28–29, 1956 : PPF, European Trip, 1956, Box 8, articles on trip, folder 1 (handwritten).

June 4, 1956 : Ibid.

June 6 [16?], 1956 : Ibid.

June [21?], 1956 : Ibid.

June 24, 1956 : Ibid.

Aug. 19, 1956 : PPF, Name File, Box 80, Stevenson, Honorable Adlai E. (handwritten).

Sept. 11, 1956 : PPF, Name File, Box 35, Hall, Leonard W.

Oct. 18, 1956 : PPF, Name File, Box 56, McNaughton, Frank.

Nov. 28, 1956 : PPF, Secretary's Office File, Box 7, Eisenhower, Dwight D., General (handwritten).

Dec. 6, 1956 : PPF, Name File, Box 18, Clifford, Clark M.

Dec. 11, 1956 : PPF, Secretary's Office File, Box 14, Johnson, Lyndon B., correspondence, 1955–1958.

Dec. 17, 1956 : PPF, Desk File, Box 3, personal handwritten notes.

Jan. 10, 1957 : PPF, Name File, Box 72, Rayburn, Sam, correspondence, 1954–1961.

Jan. 11, 1957 : PPF, Name File, Box 24, Do.

Mar. 15, 1957 : PPF, Name File, Box 1, Acheson, Dean, correspondence, 1956–1957 (handwritten).

Mar. 18, 1957 : PPF, Name File, Box 18, Clifford, Clark M.

Apr. 6, 1957 : PPF, Name File, Box 28, Farley, James A., correspondence, 1953–1958.

Apr. 22, 1957 : PPF, Name File, Box 52, Lloyd, David D., misc.

Oct. 4, 1957 : PPF, Name File, Box 26, *Esquire.*

Oct. 9, 1957 : PPF, Name File, Box 50, *Life* and *Time.*

Dec. 10, 1957 : PPF, Name File, Box 89, Vile, Hy (the statements are handwritten).

Jan. 28, 1958 : PPF, Name File, Box 31, Fulbright, J. William.

Feb. 7, 1958 : PPF, Secretary's Office File, Box 10, Freeman, Orville.

Feb. 11, 1958 : PPF, Name File, Box 52, Lo.

Feb. 15, 1958 : PPF, Secretary's Office File, Box 23, Perlman, Philip B.

Apr. 30, 1958 : PPF, Name File, Box 33, Dr. Wallace H. Graham.

[June 1958] : PPF, Trip File, Box 17, European trip (handwritten).

June 21, 1958 : Papers of Tom L. Evans, Box 5, Truman, Harry S., 1940–1963, folder 2 (handwritten).

July 15, 1958 : ("Hello, Lyndon") PPF, Secretary's Office File, Box 14, Johnson, Lyndon B., correspondence, 1955–1958.

July 15, 1958 : ("Speaker Sam Rayburn") PPF, Name File, Box 72, Rayburn, Sam, correspondence, 1958–1961.

July 15, 1958 : ("How are you, Dean") PPF, Acheson, Dean, correspondence, 1958–1959.

July 19, 1958 : Papers of Clifton and Margaret Truman Daniel, Box 12, Daniel-Truman file, correspondence, President and Mrs. Truman (handwritten).

July 29, 1958 : PPF, Name File, Box 1, Acheson, Dean, correspondence, 1958–1959 (handwritten).

Sept. 6, 1958 : PPF, Desk File, Box 1, Sherman Minton, correspondence, 1958–1962.

Sept. 29, 1958 : PPF, Name File, Box 54, McFaddin, Edward F. (handwritten).

Sept. 30, 1958 : PPF, Name File, Box 34, Gray, Georgia Neese.

Oct. 14, 1958 : PPF, Name File, Box 1, Acheson, Dean, correspondence, 1958–1959.

Oct. 29, 1958 : PPF, Name File, Box 41, Hungary.

Nov. 5, 1958 : PPF, Desk File, Box 3, personal handwritten notes.

Nov. 17, 1958 : PPF, Name File, Box 26, *Esquire.*

[Nov. 23, 1958] : PPF, Desk File, Box 1, general correspondence, 1918–1964.

Dec. 31, 1958 : PPF, Name File, Box 25, Ducournau, J. A.

Jan. 5, 1959 : PPF, Trip File, Box 21, Washington, January 5–11, 1959 (handwritten).

Jan. 8, 1959 : PPF, Desk File, Box 3, personal handwritten notes.

Jan. 16, 1959 : Ibid.

Jan. 21, 1959 : PPF, Desk File, Box 1, general correspondence, 1918–1964 (handwritten).

Feb. 10, 1959 : Ibid.

June 3, 1959 : Papers of Clifton and Margaret Truman Daniel, Box 12, Daniel-Truman file, correspondence, President and Mrs. Truman.

July 3, 1959 : PPF, Desk File, Box 1, general correspondence, 1918–1964 (handwritten).

Aug. 22, 1959 : PPF, Desk File, Box 1, correspondence, Dean Acheson, 1956–1962 (handwritten).

Dec. 8, 1959 : PPF, Secretary's Office File, Box 18, letter held.

Dec. 19, 1959 : PPF, Desk File, Box 1, general correspondence, 1918–1964 (handwritten).

Jan. 20, 1960 : PPF, Name File, Box 24, Dodd, Thomas J.

Jan. 21, 1960 : PPF, Trip File, Box 23, Washington, January 23, 1960 (handwritten)

May 26, 1960 : PPF, Name File, Box 61, Mo.

June 25, 1960 : PPF, Name File, Box 59, Meyer, Mrs. Eugene.

June 30, 1960 : PPF, Secretary's Office File, Box 21, Monroney, Mike.

July 12, 1960 : PPF, Desk File, Box 3, personal handwritten notes.

Aug. 26, 1960 : PPF, Desk File, Box 1, correspondence, Dean Acheson, 1956–1962 (handwritten).

Nov. 17, 1960 : PPF, Name File, Box 53, *Look* magazine; published in *Look,* January 3, 1961.

Nov. 25, 1960 : PPF, Secretary's Office Files, Box 34, W (handwritten).

Apr. 17, 1961 : PPF, Secretary's Office Files, Box 18, Kennedy, John F., personal data (handwritten).

Apr. 21, 1961 : PPF, Name File, Box 61, Monagan, John S.

July 3, 1961 : PPF, Name File, Box 61, Missouri Pacific Lines.

July 7, 1961 : PPF, Desk File, Box 1, correspondence, Dean Acheson, 1956–1962.

Aug. 29, 1961 : PPF, Name File, Box 60, clippings re *Missouri* battleship.

Sept. 25, 1961 : PPF, Name File, Box 1, Acheson, Dean, correspondence, 1960–1963.

Oct. 2, 1961 : PPF, Name File, Box 85, Tj–Tz.

Dec. 26, 1961 : PPF, Secretary's Office File, Box 32, T (handwritten).

Jan. 24, 1962 : PPF, Name File, Box 74, Reuther, Walter.

Feb. 5, 1962 : PPF, Secretary's Office File, Box 24, Post Office, Independence, Mo. (handwritten).

Apr. 11, 1962 : PPF, Name File, Box 84, 35th Division, realignment.

Apr. 23, 1962 : PPF, Name File, Box 53, Lowenthal, Max.

June 28, 1962 : PPF, Secretary's Office File, Box 18, Kennedy, John F., personal data (handwritten).

July 14, 1962 : PPF, Desk File, Box 3, personal handwritten notes.

Aug. 13, 1962 : PPF, Name File, Box 46, Kirwan, Michael J.

Sept. 5, 1962 : PPF, Secretary's Office File, Box 16, K (handwritten).

Sept. 11, 1962 : PPF, Trip File, Box 32, San Francisco (handwritten).

Sept. 12, 1962 : Ibid.

Dec. 8, 1962 : PPF, Desk File, Box 3, personal handwritten notes.

May 14, 1963 : PPF, Name File, Box 1, Acheson, Dean, correspondence, 1960–1963.

Aug. 14, 1963 : Post-Presidential General File, Box 2, Adams (folder 2).

Oct. 15, 1963 : PPF, Name File, Box 55, McKim, Edward D.

June 10, 1964 : PPF, Name File, Box 52, *Look* magazine.

July 22, 1964 : Post-Presidential General File, Box 47, Carr-Carrn.

Nov. 10, 1964 : Papers of Sidney W. Souers, Box 1, correspondence, Harry S. Truman, 1953–1972.

Mar. 19, 1965 : Post-Presidential General File, Box 5, Alsa–Alz.

Jan. 23, 1967 : Papers of Sidney W. Souers, Box 1, correspondence, Harry S. Truman, 1953–1972.

Nov. 28, 1967 : PPF, Name File, Box 47, Korea data.

Nov. 4, 1971 : PPF, Family Correspondence File, Box 2, Martha Ann Truman Swoyer.

INDEX

Names in SMALL CAPITALS *are recipients of letters.*

428

Cleveland (cont'd)
  picture of, 330
  wife of, 205
CLIFFORD, CLARK M., 10–11, 95, 95 *n,* 96
  and miners' strike, 104
  "prima donna," 149
  Letters:
    Talburt cartoon, and Democratic
      convention, 342
    Truman Doctrine, 349–350
Coal industry, 82
Cochran, John J., 231, 376–377
Cockrell, Senator Francis Marion, 164, 228,
  228 *n*
"Coexistence," 384–385
Cold war, 77, 93–94
Colgan, Mary, 116, 116 *n*
Colgan, Myra, 116, 116 *n,* 215, 215 *n,* 220,
  262
Colgan, Rochester and Roma, 254
Colgan, Rochester Campbell, 116 *n*
College students program, 301–302
Commerce Department, 71
Committee for the Investigation of the
  National Defense Program. *See*
  Truman Committee
Communism
  in China, 74, 207
  Russian version of, 44, 56–57, 123
  and world expansion, 105
Communism and Communists in America
  charges against State Department, 74,
    171–172
  HST letter to Gates, 123
  HST on, 44–45
  and Lilienthal, 113
  Nixon charges, 339
  White affair, 299–301
Conant, James B., 60, 60 *n,* 112
Congress, United States, 34, 72, 90, 109–110,
  219, 256 *n,* 314, 341, 379, 388
  Basing Point bill, 183–184
  Brannan Plan and, 155
  Capitol building extension and, 357–358
  and civil rights program, 121
  committee incompetence, 119, 119 *n*
  and demobilization, 81, 100–102
  80th, HST on, 122, 160–161, 389
  91st, HST on, 168, 201
  Eisenhower amendment, 346 *n*
  FEPC bill, 27, 27 *n,* 36–37, 121
  former presidents and membership in,
    393
  Greek-Turkish aid, 105
  HST bipartisan foreign policy, 271
  HST first message to, 17, 19
  Hoover Commission, 27, 27 *n*
  and immigration bill, 258, 258 *n*
  and impeachment process, 22–23
  Internal Revenue scandal and, 221
  Kem rider to European aid, 212, 212 *n*
  and Lilienthal to A.E.C., 111–113
  and MacArthur, 207–208, 213, 213 *n*
  Marines into Lebanon and, 362–366

  Marshall Plan and, 118, 118 *n,* 121,
    125–126, 271
  1946 elections and mineworkers, 103
  1948 special session and Republicans,
    143–144
  1952 and lack of cooperation, 224
  and Potomac fever, 186
  presidential papers and microfilming,
    354–355
  reorganization bills rejected, 156
  special privilege bills, 175–176
  Suez crisis investigation, 344
  and two-thirds rule, 22
  and Tyler, 276
  and universal military service, 71–72,
    132–134
  and White House reconstruction, 243.
  See also House of Representatives;
    Senate; Truman, Harry S., in Senate
Congressional Medals of Honor, 34, 138
  HST on, 101–102, 209, 255
  Marshall and, 118
Congress of Industrial Relations. *See* C.I.O.
CONNALLY, JOHN B., 396
Connally, Senator Tom, 17, 202, 207, 368
  and Capitol building extension, 357–358
  Hitler negotiation statement, 21, 21 *n*
  HST on, 216
  O'Daniel assessment, 60
  and quitting, 247
Connelly, Matthew J., 10, 39, 75, 199, 253,
  288
  as appointments secretary, 60, 67, 157,
    179, 193
  HST evaluation of, 46
  on HST letter to critic of Margaret's
    concert, 4 *n*
  and HST's privacy, 91
Conscientious objectors, 137–138
Conservatives, 68, 68 *n,* 341, 341 *n*
Constitution, U.S., 314, 356 *n,* 359 *n*
  amendments proposed:
    Bricker, 311, 314
    House vote on treaties, 46
    two-thirds rule elimination, 22–23, 46
  authority in Lebanon action, 363
  as basis for civil rights message, 121
  Congressional membership for former
    presidents and speakers, 393–394
  and court interpretation of, 22
  and HST seizure of steel mills, 224
  presidential term limits, 178, 245
Consultant in Washington, definition, 269
Conway, Rose A., 11, 13, 327, 392
  and HST letters, 3, 5–6
  and Ross file and Potsdam diary, 50
Coolidge, Calvin, 64, 177, 242–243, 266, 311
  compared with Eisenhower, 344, 369
  and Congressional leadership, 388
Coolidge, Mrs. Calvin, 38, 205
Cox political machine, 282
"Crackpot cities," 406
Crowley, Leo, 174, 322
Crump, Edward H., 87, 87 *n,* 152